Judaism,
Christianity,
and Islam

JUDAISM, CHRISTIANITY, AND ISLAM

The Classical Texts
and Their Interpretation

VOLUME 2

The Word and the Law and the
People of God

F. E. PETERS

Princeton University Press

Princeton, New Jersey

Published by Princeton University Press, 41 William Street,
Princeton, New Jersey 08540
In the United Kingdom: Princeton University Press, Oxford

Library of Congress Cataloging-in-Publication Data
Peters, F. E. (Francis E.)
Judaism, Christianity, and Islam : the classical texts
and their interpretation / F.E. Peters.
p. cm.
Also published in a single volume.
Includes index.
Contents: v. 1. From covenant to community — v. 2. The word
and the law and the people of God — v. 3. The works
of the spirit.
ISBN 0-691-02044-2 (v. 1 : acid-free paper)
ISBN 0-691-02054-X (v. 2 : acid-free paper)
ISBN 0-691-02055-8 (v. 3 : acid-free paper)
1. Judaism. 2. Christianity. 3. Islam. I. Title.
BL80.2.P455   1990b
291—dc20   90-36670

This book has been composed in Linotron Perpetua type

Princeton University Press books are printed on acid-free
paper, and meet the guidelines for permanence and durability
of the Committee on Production Guidelines for Book
Longevity of the Council on Library Resources

Printed in the United States of America

(Pbk.)   3   5   7   9   10   8   6   4   2

For
Barakat Ahmad
in whose true spirit this work was conceived,
and to whose joyfully recollected memory
it is now gratefully dedicated

Contents

CHAPTER 4

The Law of God

CHAPTER 5

The New Covenants

CHAPTER 6

One God, One Faith, One Community   328

Preface

"Hear, O Israel," the Lord said to His Chosen People near the beginning of their extraordinary relationship. And that is the matter of this book: what His people heard from the Lord and how they understood it. Not merely the original Israelites, but His other peoples, the Christians and Muslims: they too chosen, as they say; they too, as they claim, authentic "sons of Abraham."

What they heard when God spoke to them is not difficult to discover. Jews, Christians, and Muslims alike felt strongly and thought carefully enough about it to preserve the words of God inside the covers of a Book, or rather, three books—the Bible, the New Testament, and the Quran—which they eye somewhat uneasily in each other's hands. So it is in the first instance God's words that have been reproduced here, not in their entirety—the integral texts are readily enough available—but in extracts and, more importantly, in a manner that will make it somewhat simpler to comprehend the other element of what is undertaken in this work: How did the Jews, Christians, and Muslims understand what they had heard?

The words of God to Abraham and later to Moses on Sinai, they had all heard. The Bible is Scripture for all three religious communities, and indeed it is the basis of each's claim to be God's own people. But each group understood those words differently, whether as a basis of belief or as a directive to action. And even in each group's own, more particular and privileged communication with or from God—the Jews' Mishna, for example, or the letters of Paul, or the traditions from the Prophet Muhammad—there is little enough agreement within the community itself on what exactly God meant or what precisely was the good to be done or the evil to be avoided.

What I have attempted is to lay out the kinds of issues these three intimately related groups chiefly thought about, the questions that most interested them, and particularly such matters as might encourage comparison among the three; I have then selected standard or well-known or important texts to illustrate those matters. Jews, Christians, and Muslims all thought about the Law of God, for example, and how God ought to be worshiped, about authority and the authorities, about angels and heaven and hell; each group attempted on occasion to state what it believed and to make its members somehow conform to it; and most consequential of all perhaps, the three religious communities shared an invincible conviction that God's revelation to them was not confined to that revered and well-guarded Book we call Scripture.

This is obviously not a history of Judaism, Christianity, and Islam, and even less of the three communities of believers. The historically minded will doubtless be puzzled, and perhaps dismayed, at the sometimes odd juxtaposition of authorities or events. I have no remedy for either the puzzlement or the dismay except to refer them to histories of the faiths or the communities, of which there is certainly no lack. Here the objective is to keep the three communities of believers in one line of sight and to focus on each through a single topic that interested them all. Thus, after the first four chapters, which follow a rough time line, the presentation moves to a topical arrangement that violates the chronological order at almost every turn but has the advantage, I hope, of hearing each group out on subjects of parallel or mutual or polemical concern.

It is, in any event, the same way the sources themselves deal with the matter. Though Scripture is often cast in the form of history, not many of those who came after viewed the sacred books through the eyes of the historian. There is the Jew Josephus, yes, and the Christian Eusebius, and Muhammad's biographer Ibn Ishaq. But for the rest, the authors represented in these pages are chiefly lawyers, theologians, priests, and visionaries—Jewish, Christian, and Muslim believers who were disinterested in the past as past, since for them the past was, like the Torah in the Talmud and like the Bible in both the Gospels and the Quran, eternally present. In reading the third-century rabbis, for example, one cannot really tell that there was no longer a Temple in Jerusalem and that no priests had made sacrifice there for more than a century, much less when that catastrophic destruction took place or what merely human acts contributed to it.

Nor were those same authorities much interested in the present as present. We catch contemporary reflections, of course, but their primary concern was not to bring us up to date on the present state of the People of God, on how well or poorly the Law of God was being observed. Our authors tell us, for example, that there were rules governing the conduct of Christians and Jews living under Islam; but they do not tell us, as other kinds of sources do, which regulations were actually in force and for whom, or which were simply on the books. Since the "books" in question are likely to have been holy books or equally holy traditions, to be on them or in them was what really mattered and not how many "commoners of the land" were actually fornicating, killing their neighbors, or violating the Sabbath. We have ways of discovering, or guessing about, the latter, but not from our lawyers and divines, who had more important things to concern them.

In reproducing rather than retelling Scripture, I have allowed God speak for Himself, and I have extended the courtesy to the Jews, Christians, and Muslims as well. And those children of a voluble God have spoken, sometimes clearly and eloquently, at times obscurely, perhaps because they did not understand or perhaps because they chose not to say; sometimes gently and sometimes rudely, especially when they are speaking of each other. I have kept my own explanations to a minimum on the simple principle that all these "Peoples of the Book" are capable of and should be permitted to speak for themselves. I have supplied some factual data, provided contexts where such seemed required, and attempted some explanatory transitions across what is a somewhat discontinuous terrain. Much is missing, to be sure: saints are often more interesting than their writings and religious art more striking than tracts on iconoclasm. God's own preference for history over theology is well known.

I have made here almost no judgments about authenticity: these are the received texts, scriptural and otherwise, of each community. And I have tried, despite strong professional and personal inclinations to the contrary, not to seduce the reader into the enormous historical and textual problems that almost every one of these texts—and often every line and every single word of them—has raised over the centuries among believers and nonbelievers alike. Thus there are no traces here of the revelations of Julius Wellhausen or Ignaz Goldziher, no echoes of the prophetic voices of Rudolf Bultmann or Joseph Schacht, of Jacob Neusner or Patricia Crone, no sign of "P" or "E" or "J" or the even more celebrated "Q". And finally, I have attempted to reduce technical vocabulary, particularly of the transliterated variety, to an absolute minimum: lovers of *halakha* and *hadith* will have to be served elsewhere.

This work was originally composed as a companion for my *Children of Abraham: Judaism, Christianity, Islam*. It is in a sense the flesh to the latter's bone, and, in the ineluctable manner of flesh, has put on quite a bit of weight in the process. Nor is the order exactly the same as in that earlier work. Here the matter is divided into three parts: From Covenant to

Community; The Word and the Law and the People of God; The Works
of the Spirit. But even though the arrangement is different, the same
general topics are covered. More important, the time parameters of the
earlier work are this one's as well: we begin here literally at the beginning,
but break off while each religious complex is still in its "classical" or,
perhaps less provocatively, its "scholastic" period. To put it another way,
this collection ends before the great movements of modernism and re-
form touched—at different moments and in differing degrees—Judaism,
Christianity, and Islam and rendered them different. Not everyone will be
happy with such a peremptory leave-taking, particularly those who prefer
the reformed to the traditional versions of these communities. No matter.
Given the limitations of the guide, it cannot be otherwise.

The only abbreviations requiring explanation are: B.C.E. = Before
the Common Era, and C.E. = the Common Era. The M prefix before a
title means Mishna; BT = Babylonian Talmud and JT = Jerusalem or
Palestinian Talmud.

The texts used for this work have all been published in one place or
another, often in many places since, as I have said, my objective throughout is to place before the reader the "classical texts" of the three religious
communities. They are not only published; most of them are very well
known to the members of the community whose heritage they are. Thus
they have also been translated out of their original Hebrew and Aramaic,
Greek and Latin, Arabic and Persian into a variety of other languages,
including English. The question is not where to find the texts but which
to choose and whose version to prefer.

Of the translations used in compiling this dossier, some are mine and
some, as noted in the Acknowledgments, are from other hands. Where
I have used others' versions, I have generally modified them only to the
extent of standardizing names—the English word "God" has replaced the
translators' untranslated "Allah" throughout, for example—and of re-
ducing all dates to those of the Common Era.

Stockport, New York

Acknowledgments

Translations of the Hebrew Bible are derived from *A New Translation of the Holy Scriptures according to the Massoretic Text*, second edition, Philadelphia: Jewish Publication Society of America, 1982.

Translations of the biblical apocrypha are derived from *The Apocryphal Old Testament*, edited by H.D.F. Sparks, Oxford: Clarendon Press, 1984.

Translations of the deutero-canonical books and the New Testament are derived from *The New English Bible with the Apocrypha*, corrected impression of the second edition, New York: Oxford University Press, 1972. Translations of the New Testament apocrypha are derived from Edgar Hennecke and Wilhelm Schneemelcher (eds.), *New Testament Apocrypha*, 2 vols., translated by R. McLean Wilson et al., Philadelphia: Westminster Press, 1963–1965.

Translations of the Quran are derived from Ahmed Ali, *Al-Qur'an*, Princeton: Princeton University Press, 1988.

A Brief Chronology

B.C.E. is an abbreviation of "Before the Common Era" and C.E. of the "Common Era." The Common Era is that of the Gregorian calendar, where time is measured before or after what was thought to be the birth year of Jesus: in Latin, *Anno Domini*, the "Year of the Lord," abbreviated A.D. In fact, Jesus' date of birth is now placed in or about 4 B.C.E.

Muslims also use a "before" and "after" system. In their case the watershed date is that of the *Hijrah* or Emigration of Muhammad from Mecca to Medina in 622 C.E., called in the West A.H., or *Anno Hegirae*.

Jewish time reckoning is only "after," that is, from the Creation of the World, normally understood to be about 4000 years B.C.E.

B.C.E.

ca. 1700	God's Covenant with Abraham
ca. 1200	The exodus from Egypt; the giving of the Torah to Moses on Mount Sinai
ca. 1000	David, king of the Israelites, captures Jerusalem and makes it his capital
ca. 970	Solomon builds the First Temple in Jerusalem
621	Josiah centralizes all Jewish worship in the Temple in Jerusalem
587	Babylonians under Nebuchadnezzar carry Israelites into exile in Babylon; the destruction of Solomon's Temple
538	Exiles return to Judea; Ezra; Nehemiah; rebuilding of Jerusalem Temple
332	Alexander the Great in the Near East; Greek dynasties rule Palestine
ca. 280	Translation of Bible in Greek: the "Septuagint"
200	The Seleucid dynasty of Syria replaces the Ptolemies as rulers of Palestine
175–164	Antiochus IV Epiphanes; profanation of the Temple
164	Maccabean revolt; Jewish independence
164–37	The Hasmonean dynasty rules Palestine

37–4	Herod the Great, king of Judea
ca. 25–45 C.E.	Philo in Alexandria
20	Herod begins restoration of the Temple
ca. 4	Birth of Jesus in Bethlehem

C.E.

6	Romans take over direct rule of Judea
26–36	Pontius Pilate, Roman prefect of Judea
ca. 30	Execution of Jesus in Jerusalem
the 50s	Letters of Paul
ca. 60–70	Composition of Mark, earliest of the Gospels
ca. 62	Death of James in Jerusalem and Peter and Paul in Rome
66	Jewish insurrection in Palestine; flight of Yohanan ben Zakkai to Jabneh (Jamnia) and of Jewish Christians to the Transjordan
70	Romans under Titus destroy Herod's Temple
ca. 80–100	Remaining three canonical Gospels written
ca. 100	Death of the Jewish historian Josephus
135	Second Jewish revolt in Palestine; Jerusalem leveled and Jews forbidden to live there
ca. 200	Widespread persecutions of Christians in the Roman Empire; redaction of the Mishna by Judah "the Prince"
ca. 250	Antony, the first hermit, withdraws to the desert of Egypt
303	Last violent persecution of Christians by Diocletian
313	Constantine, the first Christian emperor, suspends persecution of Christians
318	Pachomius founds the first monastery, or community of ascetics, in Egypt
325	First ecumenical council of the Christian Church at Nicea
330	Constantine and his mother Helena begin the conversion of Jerusalem into a Christian holy city
340	First Christian monasteries founded in the West
381	Decree establishing Christianity as the official religion of the Roman Empire
399	Death of the Christian mystic Evagrius of Pontus
410	Visigoths sack Rome
425	Office of Nasi, or Patriarch, abolished in the Roman Empire
430	Death of Augustine, Latin theologian of Hippo in North Africa
451	Ecumenical council of Chalcedon
ca. 500	Completion of the *gemaras* at Tiberias and (ca. 600) in Iraq: thus the final versions of the "Jerusalem" and "Babylonian" Talmuds
ca. 535	Benedict founds his monastery at Monte Cassino
ca. 570	Birth of Muhammad at Mecca

1134–1204	Moses Maimonides, Jewish theologian and lawyer
1187	Muslims under Saladin retake Jerusalem
1198	Death of the Muslim philosopher Ibn Rushd (Averroes)
1225–1274	Thomas Aquinas; the height of medieval Christian theology in the West
ca. 1300	Compilation of the *Zohar*, the primary work of Kabbala
1323	Pope Boniface VIII publishes the bull *Unam Sanctam*
1377	Ibn Khaldun's *Prolegomenon to History*
1453	Constantinople falls to the Turks
1492	Christian reconquest of Spain completed; Jewish migrations to Islamic lands in North Africa and the Near East
1488–1575	Joseph Caro, author of *Shulhan Aruch*
1517	Luther posts his controversial theses; beginning of the Protestant Reformation

Introduction

Judaism, Christianity, and Islam—the three religious communities sprung from the promise to Abraham, or rather, from competition for it—all rest their claims where that promise is recorded, in the Scripture, the Word of God. And yet all three have a complex interscriptural relationship. The Jews have what seems to be the simplest position: the Bible—"our Bible," the Jew would claim, with all the evidence unmistakably on his side—is the sum and substance of God's written revelation. Early on there may have been some question of what precisely that Bible comprised and in what precisely consisted the role of the human "author" in the process. Those issues settled, however, the question, though assuredly not the Book itself, could be closed.

The Christians at first could have no other view but that. They too were Jews, and so the Bible—and that alone—was their Scripture. It was certainly treated as such in the texts that later came to form the New Testament. But Jesus was also the Christ, the Anointed One, and the Son of God, and both he and his redemptive work constituted the fulfillment of the promised New Covenant. That is a theological judgment, but there is a literary consequence not far behind it: the works that "revealed" him, the "Good News of Jesus Christ" and its connected literature, were likewise revelation, and so, it was concluded, Scripture in their own, Christian right.

The nonconverted Jews, the vast majority, would have none of that, of course. If the Christians wandered into their thoughts about Scripture, it was in the context of what these new sectarians had done and were doing with the authentic Scripture, the Bible, and what the Jewish community should do about it. They could retranslate that Scripture, and they could revise some of their interpretations of Messianic passages; but by and large both the Christian double-Scripture theory and their claims more generally could be ignored. The Christians for their part obviously could not afford to ignore the Bible, not because of its clear denomination of the Jews as the Chosen People—that consideration might indeed have counseled them to do precisely that—but because the original body of the followers of Jesus were exclusively Jews. Christians' sense of their own identity—and their legitimacy, when that identity came to be questioned—rested on their conviction that they were the "true Israel," the remnant promised by Scripture that would inherit the Promise. Furthermore, that fulfillment had been accomplished through the coming of the long-awaited Messiah in the person of Jesus of Nazareth. So the Christians had perforce to extend their embrace—half-hearted on the part of some—to what they began to call the "Old Testament."

At first glance the Muslim position on Scripture would seem to be as simple as the Jewish one: the Quran is the sum of the Divine Revelation. Indeed, theirs is perhaps a simpler position than the Jewish one, since there is no real problem of a Quranic canon in Islam and no question at all of authorship: God through His angel Gabriel dictated the Quran—every single word of it—to Muhammad. When we look more closely, however, we discover that the Quran itself acknowledges other and earlier revelations: the "Tawrah" to the Jews through Moses and the "Injil" to the Christians through Jesus. These are undoubtedly authentic revelations, as authentic as the Quran in their way, and the faults that produced the need for the third and final revelation called the Quran lay not in those other books or in their revealer-messengers but in the communities that used them, the "Peoples of the Book," as the Muslims called them.

That interpretation does not, however, constitute the Quran a "New-New Testament" vis-à-vis the other two. On the Muslim view, the Quran resumes and repeats the earlier revelations; the Muslim is thus freed, as the Christian is not, of the obligation of making his case out of the other books, or even of consulting them. Some Muslims did indeed consult them, as our texts will show, but chiefly for polemical purposes: to convict the Jews and Christians of falsifying their own Scriptures, or, chiefly in response to the Christian approach to the Messiah, to find foreshadowings of the Prophet of Islam in those earlier books.

That Scripture was a kind of battleground both within and among the three religious communities should occasion no surprise. The words of God are by their very nature not only the source of every prayer and a guide for all worship and conduct; they provide as well the matter of every brief and the court of last and authoritative appeal. And they are expressed not as we might imagine that God would pronounce, with unmistakable and irrefutable clarity, but in the manner of human discourse—here seemingly clearly, here allusively or ambiguously, or even with apparent self-contradiction. These judgments, shared by Jewish,

Christian, and Muslim interpreters alike, are all tentative. These are, after all, the words of God; one must proceed slowly to judgment.

But judgment there was in all those houses, and a great flood of interpretation: pious and polemical exegesis; exegesis by the number, by color, by letter of the alphabet; exegesis philosophical and philological, pedestrian and poetical, imaginative and impenetrable; exegesis to find the Messiah and not to find him; exegesis to uncover the name of God and to conceal it; and, of course, acres of exegesis to demonstrate that *we*, and we alone, are in fact the true Children of Abraham.

The limits of exegesis are no less than the limits of human ingenuity. But for all its impressive variety and virtuosity, human intelligence is not always convincing as to the truth of Scripture. Far more persuasive was another ally brought into the lists: tradition, or rather, *the* Tradition, since we are not speaking here simply of longstanding or customary ways of thinking or behaving. In the three communities *tradition* has a precise technical meaning: it is the "unwritten Scripture," the body of teaching issued from the same divine source as the Scripture and passed down orally through known channels from generation to generation for the instruction or edification of the believers and, of course, as an authoritative guide for understanding the Scripture, whose companion piece it is.

Scripture and tradition are thus the joint parents not only of exegesis but also of doctrine. Out of them—Scripture as matrix, tradition as the eliciting and shaping agent—comes a great deal of the complex religious culture that we call simply Judaism or Christianity or Islam. In Christianity, where it claimed the authority of the Apostles, tradition underwrote the growth of Christian dogma, which was considered as nothing more than rendering explicit—"defining," as it was said—understandings that went back to Jesus himself and had been passed on through an unbroken Apostolic succession. In Judaism and Islam, however, tradition—the "tradition of the Fathers" in the first, the "custom of the Prophet" in the second—had as its primary task the support of the structure of religious law, from its most general principles to its most detailed prescriptions and prohibitions. Tradition could be, and was, used to modify and even abrogate scriptural precepts, to shrink or extend the legal purview of the Book itself.

Though Christianity appears far more concerned with orthodoxy than orthopraxy, the Christian community as a whole faced a difficult legal problem: What was its position as heir to a Covenant whose warp and woof was a legal system of great detail and complexity, the Torah given to Moses on Sinai? Was there a Covenant without the Law? The beginning of an answer to that troublesome question appears in the Gospels themselves, in a nuanced response of Paul, but the issue was by no means closed—not so long, at least, as there was a highly prescriptive "Old Testament" to confront the now waxing and now waning legal interests of the "New Testament." The Christians eventually disengaged themselves, Covenant still intact, from Torah law. Paul's insight on the spiritual obsolescence of the Jewish Law was maintained, but the connection was not entirely repudiated: from circumcision to the dietary laws, the Christians could have their Pentateuch and allegorize it too.

The question of who or what was a Jew received particular attention after the disruption of the Exile and the wholesale scattering of the Jewish community into colonies all across the Mediterranean and West Asian world. There were, as it turned out, many ways to be Jewish, even the Jesus way, and many ways of looking upon the community. The Jesus way was not long in being rejected, however. The reciprocal rejection of Jew and Christian may have closed the matter for the Jew, but it opened the question in a new and uncharted form for the Christian. Who was a Christian and what was the Christian community were troubling issues from the late first century onward. Tests and definitions of faith were devised and applied, most of them strikingly different from what a contemporary Jew might have judged an appropriate measure. Orthodoxy and orthopraxy are both solutions to a search for normative doctrine. What the Jews had once debated among themselves and then, fleetingly, with the new Christians became in the end a trialog, one held, wondrously, under the auspices of the newest claimants to the heritage of Abraham.

Judaism, and later Islam, had to settle for doctrine; Christianity had within its power the creation of dogma—authoritative teaching *defined* as such by a competent body. Judaism and Christianity were both sacerdotal societies; their chief form of worship was sacrifice, and that primary act was performed by a professional subcommunity of priests: a hereditary caste in Judaism, a designated class in Christianity. But whatever it was in the beginning, the teaching function in Judaism developed laterally into another professional class, the post-Exilic scribes, later the rabbis. Among the Christians it developed upward to a higher level of the priesthood, the episcopate. Whereas the later Muslims savants known as the *ulama* were almost identical functional copies of the rabbis, the Christian bishop owed nothing to either of those types. He taught not from expertise but from authority; and when in synod, he could define—raise teaching from doctrine to dogma.

The new Muslim claimants to "the religion of Abraham," and so the heirs to his Covenant, had no need to interpret either Torah or Gospel, to exorcize or allegorize the Old Law; Islam proceeded directly to an enunciation of the Law of God out of the manifest and exclusive evidence of the Quran and the custom of the Prophet. Nor did it have to engage in that legal enterprise, as the later Jews and earlier Christians did, under the sovereignty and the laws of others. The Muslims' political independence was a right won together with their religious autonomy. For Islam the Law of God was also the law of the state: community and polity were identical from the outset, and so the work of studying, understanding, and refining God's will could proceed under the calm and protective shelter of Islamic sovereignty.

The Word and the Law and the People of God

1. The Words of God: Revelation and Scripture

At diverse times and places and through different agents, as the Scripture itself puts it, God manifested Himself to men. There were epiphanies among those manifestations, startling visions of the Godhead, encounters direct, like that between Moses and Yahweh on Sinai or the three disciples shown Jesus radiantly transfigured on Mount Tabor. But what set off the prophet from the visionary was that those few trusted prophets were given a message for His community, His chosen people. These verbal communications, often of great length, were eventually committed to writing and so constituted a book, or better, the Book, since none could rival God's own words. In this sense all of Scripture has God as its author. The recipients of these revelations nevertheless attempted to puzzle out the relationship of the human prophetic agent to the Book of the Word of God that bore his name on its leaves.

1. Who Wrote the Bible?

We begin apodictically with the rabbis' assured review of the authors of the various books that constituted the Jewish Bible.

Moses wrote his own book [the Torah], the section on Balaam and the Book of Job. Joshua wrote his own book and the last eight verses of the Torah [on the death of Moses]. Samuel wrote his own book and the books of Judges and Ruth. David wrote the Psalms, using compositions of ten sages: Adam, Melchizedek, Abraham, Moses, Heman, Idithun, Asaph, and the three sons of Core. Jeremiah wrote his own book and the book of Kings and Lamentations. Ezekiel and his group wrote Isaiah, Proverbs and the Song of Songs. The men of the Great Synagogue wrote Ezekiel, the Twelve (Minor Prophets), Daniel and Esther; and Ezra wrote his book and the Chronicles up to his own time. (BT.Baba Batra 14b–15a)

2. The Divine Voice on Sinai

The Talmud's account is terse and academic, as befits the academics who composed it. But the Bible itself suggests in this scene between Moses and the Israelites that the problem of authorship was not quite so simple.

The day you stood before the Lord your God at Horeb, when the Lord said to me, "Gather the people to Me that I may let them hear My words, in order that they may learn to revere Me as long as they live on earth, and may so teach their children." You came forward and stood at the foot of the mountain. The mountain was ablaze with flames to the very skies, dark with densest clouds. The Lord spoke to you out of the fire; you heard the sound of words but perceived no shape—nothing but a voice. He declared to you the Covenant which He commanded you to observe, the Ten Commandments; and He inscribed them on two tablets of stone. At the same time the Lord commanded me to impart to you laws and rules for you to observe in the land which you are about to cross into and occupy. (Deuteronomy 4:10–14)

Moses was the Jewish prophet par excellence, and however later generations chose to explain the mode of communication between God and His prophets, Moses or any other, the passage of Deuteronomy represents something else: the direct speech of God to all the people, a public not a prophetic revelation of the divine will. Did God then actually speak? "Perish the thought," Philo says. "God is not a man."

The ten words or oracles [that is, the Ten Commandments], in reality laws or ordinances, were revealed by the Father of All when the nation, men and women alike, were assembled together. Did He utter them Himself in the guise of a voice? Perish the thought: may it never enter our mind, for God is not a man in need of mouth, tongue and windpipe. It seems to me rather that God on that occasion performed a truly holy miracle, by commanding an invisible sound to be created in the air more marvelous than all the instruments and fitted with perfect harmonies, not inanimate, nor yet composed of body and soul like a living creature, but a rational soul full of lucidity and clarity, which, shaping the air and heightening its tension and transforming it into a flaming fire, sounded forth, like breath through a trumpet, an articulate voice so great that those farthest away seemed to hear it with the same distinctness as those nearby. . . . The power of God, breathing on the newly made voice, stirred it up and caused it to blaze forth, and spreading it on every side, rendered its end more luminous than its beginning by inspiring in the soul of each another kind of hearing far superior to that through the ears. For that sense, being in a way sluggish, remains inert until struck by air and put into motion, but the hearing of the mind inspired by God reaches out to make the first advance to meet the spoken words with the swiftest speed. (Philo, *The Ten Commandments* 32–35) [PHILO 1981: 156]

A somewhat less philosophical explanation, indeed no explanation at all, is offered by the rabbi who is made the spokesman for traditional Judaism in Judah Halevi's The Khazar King, *an imaginary dialogue written ca. 1130–1140 C.E. The charge has just been made that the account in Deuteronomy, with its talk of tablets and a voice, smacks of the "personification" that Philo so laboriously attempted to avoid. Halevi's rabbi responds.*

Heaven forbid that I should assume what is against sense and reason. The first of the Ten Commandments enjoins the belief in divine providence. The second command contains the prohibition of the worship of other gods, or the association of any being with Him, the prohibition to represent Him in statues, forms or images, or any personification of Him. How should we not deem Him above personification, since we do so with many of His creations, e.g., the human soul, which represents man's true essence. . . . We must not, however, endeavor to reject the conclusions to be drawn from revelation. We say, then, that we do not know how the intention became corporealized and the speech evolved which struck our ear (on Sinai), nor what new thing God created from nothing, nor what existing thing He employed. He does not lack the power. We say that He created the two tablets and engraved a text on them, in the same way that He created the heavens and the stars by His will alone. God desired it and they became concrete as He wished it, engraved with the text of the Ten Words. We also say that He divided the Red Sea and formed it into two walls, which He caused to stand to the right and the left of the people (on their way out of Egypt), for whom He made easy wide roads and smooth ground for them to walk on without fear and trouble. This rendering, constructing and arranging are attributed to God, who required no tool or intermediary, as would be necessary for human toil. As the water stood at His command, shaped itself at His will, so the air which touched the prophet's ear assumed the form of sounds, which conveyed the matters to be communicated by God to the prophet and the people. . . .

I do not maintain that this is exactly how things occurred; the problem is no doubt too deep for me to fathom. But the result was that everyone who was present at the time became convinced that the matter proceeded from God direct. It is to be compared to the first act of creation. The belief in the Law connected with those scenes (on Sinai) is as firmly established in the mind as the belief in the creation of the world, and that He created it in the same manner in which He—as is known—created the two tablets, the manna, other things. Thus disappear from the soul of the believer the doubts of the philosophers and the materialists. (Judah Halevi, *The Khazar King*) [HALEVI 1905: 62–63]

3. Prophetic Inspiration

At many points in his works Philo attempts to explain how the inspiration of the prophets, of whom Moses is the archetype, operates. Here he uses, as is frequent in ancient philosophy, the method of analogy. The sun as the analog of human reason was already a commonplace in the Platonic tradition from which Philo was drawing, but it was well suited to the particular text under discussion.

Admirably does Moses describe (in the Torah) the inspired Abraham, when he says "about sunset there fell on him an ecstasy" (Gen. 15:12; the Hebrew has: "a deep sleep"). "Sun" is his figurative name for our mind. For what the reasoning faculty is in us, the sun is in the world, since both of them are light-bringers, one sending forth to the whole world that which our senses perceive, the other shedding mental rays upon ourselves through the medium of apprehension. So while the radiance of the mind is still all around us, when it pours as it were a noonday beam into the whole soul, we are self-contained, not possessed. But when it comes to its setting, naturally ecstasy and divine possession and madness fall upon us. For when the light of God shines, the human light sets; when the divine light sets, the human dawns and rises. This is what regularly befalls the fellowship of prophets. The mind is evicted at the arrival of the divine Spirit, but when that departs the mind returns to its tenancy. Mortal and immortal may not share the same home. And therefore the setting of reason and the darkness which surround it produce ecstasy and inspired frenzy. To connect what is coming with what is here written Moses says, "it was said to Abraham" (Gen. 15:13). For indeed the prophet, even when he seems to be speaking, really holds his peace, and his organs of speech, mouth and tongue, as wholly in the employ of Another, to show forth what He wills. Unseen by us, that Other beats on the chords with the skill of a master-hand and makes them instruments of sweet music, laden with every harmony. (Philo, *Who Is the Heir?* 263–266) [PHILO 1945: 74–75]

Philo returns to this notion that the prophet is simply the instrument of God and invokes the same image.

No pronouncement of a prophet is ever his own; he is an interpreter prompted by Another in all his utterances, when, knowing not what he does, he is filled with inspiration, as the (human) reason withdraws and surrenders the citadel of the soul to a new visitor and tenant, the Divine Spirit, which plays upon the vocal organism and raises sounds from it, which clearly express its prophetic message. (Philo, *On the Special Laws* 4.49) [PHILO 1945: 75]

As we shall see, later generation of philosophers, Jewish and Muslim, will prefer other explanations of the phenomenon of prophecy, based on a different, more Aristotelian understanding of how the mind works. We turn now to the result of that prophetic inspiration, the Torah.

4. Moses Writes the Torah

Moses our teacher wrote the book of Genesis together with the whole Torah from the mouth of the Holy One, blessed be He. It is likely that he wrote it on Mount Sinai for there it was said to him, "Come up to Me unto the mount, and be there; and I will give you the tablets of stone and the Torah and the commandments which I have written, to teach them" (Exod. 24:12). The "tablets of stone" include the tablets and the writing that are the Ten Commandments. The "commandment" includes the number of all the commandments, positive and negative. If so, the expression "and the Torah" includes the stories from the beginning of Genesis (and is called Torah-teaching) because it teaches people the ways of faith. Upon descending from the mount, he [Moses] wrote the Torah from the beginning of Genesis to the end of the account of the Tabernacle. He wrote the conclusion of the Torah at the end of the fortieth year of wandering in the desert when he said, "Take this book of the Law and put it in the side of the Ark of the Covenant of the Eternal your Lord" (Deut. 31:26).

This view accords with the opinion of the Talmudic sage who says that the Torah was written in sections (BT.Gittin 60a). However, according to the sage who says that the Torah was given in its entirety, everything was written in the fortieth year when he [Moses] was commanded, "Now write this song for you and teach it to the Children of Israel; put it in their mouths" (Deut. 31:19), and, as he was further instructed,

"Take this book of the Law and put it in the side of the Ark of the Covenant of the Eternal your Lord."

In either case it would have been proper for him to write at the beginning of the book of Genesis: "And God spoke to Moses all these words, saying . . ." The reason it was written anonymously [that is, without that phrase] is that Moses our teacher did not write the Torah in the first person like the prophets who did mention themselves. For example, it is often said of Ezekiel, "And the word of the Eternal came to me saying, 'Son of man . . .' " (Ezek. 3:16–17), and it is said of Jeremiah, "And the word of the Eternal came to me" (Jer. 1:4). Moses our teacher, however, wrote this history of all former generations and his own genealogy, history and experiences in the third person. Therefore he says, "And the Lord spoke to Moses, saying to him" (Exod. 6:2), as if he were speaking about another person. And because this is so, Moses is not mentioned in the Torah until his birth, and even at that time he is mentioned as if someone else was speaking about him. . . .

The reason for the Torah being written in this form [that is, in the third person] is that it preceded the creation of the world, and, needless to say, it preceded the birth of Moses our teacher. It has been transmitted to us by tradition that it [the Torah] was written with letters of black fire upon a background of white fire (JT.Shekalim 13b). Thus Moses was like a scribe who copies from an ancient book, and therefore he wrote anonymously.

However, it is true and clear that the entire Torah—from the beginning of Genesis to "in the sight of all Israel" [that is, the last words in Deut. 34:12]—reached the ear of Moses from the mouth of the Holy One, blessed be He, just as it is said elsewhere, "He pronounced all these words to me with His mouth, and I wrote them down in ink in the book" (Jer. 36:16). The Lord informed Moses first of the manner of creation of heaven and earth and all their hosts, that is, the creation of all things, high and low. Likewise of everything that had been said by prophecy concerning the esoterics of the Divine Chariot (in the vision of Ezekiel) and the process of creation and what has been transmitted about them to the Sages. And also with the account of the four forces of the lower world: the force of minerals, vegetation in the earth, living motion and the rational soul. With regard to all these matters—their creation, their essence, their powers and functions, and the disintegration of those of them that are destroyed—Moses our teacher was apprised, and all of it was written in the Torah, explicitly or by implication. (Nachmanides, *Commentary on Genesis*) [NACHMANIDES 1971: 7–9]

5. Are the Prophets Torah?

The Law was revealed to Moses and to the people by God at Sinai and written down by Moses at the divine command. Thus Moses' five books enjoy a guaranteed authenticity and authority. What then of the second great division of the Bible, the "Prophets"? Are they too "Torah"?

Rabbi Isaac said: The Prophets drew from Sinai the inspiration for all their future utterances, for God spoke "with him who stands here with us this day" (Deut. 29:15), that is, with those who were already created, "and also with those who are not here with us this day"; these latter are the souls which are destined to be created (in the future). So too it does not say "the burden of the Lord to Malachi" (Mal. 1:1), but "by the hand of Malachi," to show that the prophecy was already in his hand at Mount Sinai. So too in Isaiah 48:16 it says, "From the hour when the Torah was given, there am I," that is, "From the hour when the Torah was given, I received this prophecy." This applies not to the Prophets alone, but to all the sages who are destined to arise in after days, for the Decalog is described in Deuteronomy 5:22 as "One great voice," and this was divided first into seven, and then into seventy tongues for all mankind. (*Tanhuma* 11:124a–124b)

Asaph said: "Give ear, O my people, to my Law" (Ps. 78:1), and Solomon said, "Forsake not my Law" (Prov. 4:2). Israel said to Asaph, "Is there another law, that you speak of *my* Law? We have already received the Law on Sinai." He said to them: "There are sinners in Israel who say that the Prophets and the Holy Writings are not Torah and so we will not obey them" (Dan. 9:10). But the Prophets and the Holy Writings are indeed Torah. Hence it says, "Give ear, O my people, to my Law." (*Tanhuma* 10a)

6. The Pre-Mosaic Prophets and Their Works

By the second and third Christian century there were circulating in both Christian and Jewish circles a great many pseudepigraphs—or, somewhat less politely, forgeries—some of them attributed to latter-day scribes like Baruch or Ezra and others purporting to be the works of patriarchal figures like Enoch or a cooperative composition like the "Testament of the Twelve Patriarchs." The Christian bishop Augustine (d. 430 C.E.) takes up the question of their antiquity and their inclusion in the canon. In the course of the discussion he is led to reflect on more general questions of history and revelation, of the canon and the apocrypha.

If I may recall far more ancient times, our patriarch Noah was certainly living even before the great deluge, and I might unreservedly call him a prophet inasmuch as the ark he made, in which he escaped with his family, was itself a prophecy of our times. What of Enoch, the seventh from Adam? Does not the canonical letter of the Apostle Jude declare (Jude 14) that he prophesied? But the writings of these men could not be held to be authoritative either among the Jews or us on account of their too great antiquity, which made it seem needful to regard them with suspicion, lest false things should be set forth instead of true. For some writings which are said to be theirs are quoted by those who, according to their own humor, loosely believe what they please. But the purity of the canon has not admitted these writings, not because the authority of these men who pleased God is rejected, but because the writings are not believed to be theirs.

Nor ought it to appear strange if writings for which so great antiquity is claimed are held in suspicion, seeing that in the very history of the kings of Judah and Israel containing their deeds, which we believe to belong to the canonical Scripture, very many things are mentioned which are not explained there, but are said to be found in other books which the prophets wrote, the very names of these prophets being sometimes given, and yet they are not received in the canon which the people of God received. Now I confess that the reason for this is hidden from me; only I think that even those men, to whom certainly the Holy Spirit revealed those things which ought to be held as of religious authority, might write some things as men of historical diligence and other things as prophets by divine inspiration; and these things were so distinct that it was judged that the former should be ascribed to themselves and the latter to God speaking through them; and so the one pertained to the abundance of knowledge, the other to the authority of religion.

In that authority the canon is guarded. So that, if any writings outside of it are now brought forward under the name of the ancient prophets, they cannot serve as even an aid to knowledge because it is uncertain whether they are genuine; and on this account they are not trusted, especially those of them in which some things are found that are even contrary to the truth of the canonical books, so that it is quite apparent that they do not belong to them. (Augustine, *City of God* 18.38)

[AUGUSTINE 1948: 2:445]

7. David and the Psalms

The Christians, like the Jews before them and the Muslims after, generally attributed the Psalms to David. But that there was discussion on the issue of their authorship and what form it took is revealed by these remarks of Augustine.

In the progress of the city of God through the ages, David first reigned in the earthly Jerusalem as a shadow of that which was to come. Now David was a man skilled in songs, who dearly loved musical harmony, not as a vulgar delight but with a believing disposition, and by it served his God, who is the true God, by the mystical representation of a great thing. For the rational and well-ordered concord of diverse sounds in harmonious variety suggests the compact unity of the well-ordered city. Thus all his prophecy is in psalms, of which one hundred and fifty are contained in what we call the *Book of Psalms*, of which some will have it that those only were composed by David which are inscribed with his name. But there are also some who think none of them was composed by him except those which are marked "Of David," while those which have in the title "For David" have been composed by others who assumed his person. Which opinion is refuted by the voice of the Savior himself in the Gospel, when he says (Matt. 22:44) that David himself by the Spirit said Christ was his Lord; for the 110th Psalm begins thus, "The Lord said to my Lord, you shall sit at My right hand when I make your enemies the footstool under your feet." And truly that very psalm, like many more, has in the title not "Of David" but "For David."

Those seem to me to hold the more credible opinion who ascribe to David the authorship of all these hundred and fifty psalms, and think that he prefixed to some of them the names even of other men who prefigured something pertinent to the matter, but chose to have no man's name in the titles of the rest, just as God inspired him in the management of this variety, which, although dark, is not meaningless. Neither ought it move one not to believe this that the names of some prophets who lived long after the times of King David are read in the inscriptions of certain psalms in that book, and that the things said there seem to be spoken of as it were by them. Nor was the prophetic Spirit unable to reveal to King David, when he prophesied, even these names of future prophets, so that he might prophetically sing something which should suit their persons; just as it was revealed more than three hundred years before the event to a certain prophet, who predicted his future deeds along with his name, that

King Josiah should arise and reign (1 Kings. 13:2; cf. 2 Kings. 23:15–17). (Augustine, *City of God* 17.14) [AUGUSTINE 1948: 2:392]

8. Writing Down the Prophecies of Jeremiah

The Scriptures themselves give an occasional hint about the writing down of revelations, at least as far as the prophets are concerned, as in this text from Jeremiah.

In the fourth year of Jehoiakim son of Josiah of Judah [that is, 605 B.C.E.], this word came to Jeremiah from the Lord: Get a scroll and write upon it all the words that I have spoken to you—concerning Israel and Judah and all the nations—from the time I first spoke to you in the days of Josiah to this day. Perhaps when the house of Judah hear all the disasters I intend to bring upon them, they will turn back from their wicked ways, and I will pardon their iniquity and their sin. So Jeremiah called Baruch, son of Neriah, and Baruch wrote down in the scroll at Jeremiah's dictation all the words which the Lord had spoken to him. Jeremiah instructed Baruch, "I am in hiding; I cannot go to the House of the Lord. You go and read aloud the words of the Lord from the scroll which you wrote at my dictation, to the people in the House of the Lord on a fast day; thus you will be reading them to all the Judeans who come in from the towns. . . ." Baruch son of Neriah did just as the prophet Jeremiah had instructed him—to read the words of the Lord from the scroll in the House of the Lord. (Jeremiah 36:1–8)

As the message of the scroll circulates, Jeremiah and Baruch are warned to go into hiding. The scroll, meanwhile, is locked in one of the rooms of the palace, and its presence is reported to the king.

The king sent Jehudi to get the scroll, and he fetched it from the chamber of the scribe Elishama. Jehudi read it to the king and to all the officials who were in attendance on the king. Since it was the ninth month, the king was sitting in the winter house with a fire burning in the brazier before him. And every time Jehudi read three or four columns, [the king] would cut it up with a scribe's knife and throw it into the fire in the brazier, until the entire scroll was consumed by the fire in the brazier. (Jeremiah 36:21–23)

9. The Cessation of Prophecy in Israel
after the Exile

By the second century B.C.E. *the Jews had come to realize that the voice of prophecy, at least as that was understood in the days before the Exile, had ceased in Israel. For the philosopher Maimonides (d. 1204), who regarded prophecy as a natural, albeit rare, human function, the cause of the silence was not so much the stilling of God's voice as the troubled times, the "sadness and langor" that affected the entire society.*

You know that every bodily faculty sometimes grows tired, is weakened, and is troubled, and at other times is in a healthy state. Accordingly, you will find that the prophecy of the prophets ceases when they are sad or angry, or in a mood similar to one of those two. You know their saying that "prophecy does not descend (during a mood of) sadness or languor" (BT.Shabbath 30b), that prophetic revelation did not come to Jacob our father during the time of his mourning because of the fact that his imaginative faculty was preoccupied with the loss of Joseph; and that the prophetic revelation did not come to Moses, peace be upon him, after the disastrous incident of the spies and until the whole generation of the desert perished, in the way that revelation used to come before, because—seeing the enormity of their crime—he suffered greatly from this matter. . . . Similarly you will find that several prophets prophesied during a certain time and that afterwards prophecy was taken away from them and could not be permanent because of an accident that had supervened. This is indubitably the essential and proximate cause of the fact that prophesy was taken away during the time of the Exile. For what languor or sadness can befall a man in any state that would be stronger than that due to his being a thrall slave in bondage to the ignorant who commit great sins and in whom the privation of true reason is united to the perfection of the lusts of beasts? "And there shall be no might in your hand" (Deut. 28:32). This was with what they had been threatened. And this is what is meant by the saying: "They shall run to and fro to seek the word of the Lord and shall not find it" (Amos 8:12). And it also says: "Her kings and princes are among the nations, the Law is no more; yes, her prophets find no visions from the Lord" (Lam. 2:9). This is true and the cause thereof is clear. For the instrument has ceased to function. This also will be the cause of prophecy being restored to us in its habitual form, as has been promised in the days of the Messiah, may he be revealed soon. (Maimonides, *Guide of the Perplexed* 2.37) [MAIMONIDES 1963: 372–373]

10. The Septuagint

The Hebrew Bible, which was already being interpreted in Aramaic in Palestine at the time of Ezra and Nehemiah, received a full and formal translation into Greek, almost certainly in Egypt and under the impulse of the large colony of Greek-speaking Jews there. Just when this took place is uncertain, though our chief source on the event, the Letter of Aristeas, *claims that it occurred at the time of the king Ptolemy Philadelphus (283–245 B.C.E.). The manner in which it was done was of some importance, particularly to the Christians, who adopted it as their official transcript of the Bible.*

He [Ptolemy Philadelphus] gave orders to (his minister) Demetrius to draw up a memorandum on the writing down of all the books of the Jews. For all the business of state was carried out by decrees and with the utmost accuracy by those Egyptian kings; nothing was done in a careless or haphazard manner. I have inserted here copies of the memorandum and the letters. . . . The following is a copy of the memorandum. The Memorandum of Demetrius to the Great King: "Since you have ordered me, my Lord, O King, to collect the the books required to complete your library (at Alexandria) and to repair those which are defective, I have accordingly taken great pains to fulfill your wishes, and I now have the following proposal to lay before you. The books of the law of the Jews, together with some few others, are missing from the library. They are written in Hebrew characters and language and have been carelessly in-terpreted [or translated], and I am informed by their experts that they do not represent the original text, since they have never been protected by royal care. What is now required is that they be corrected for your library since the law which they contain, being of divine origin, is full of wisdom and free of all blemish. As a consequence (of this faulty text) literary men and poets and the mass of historical writers have refrained from referring to these books, even those who have lived and are living in accordance with them, because their conception of life is so sacred and religious, as Hecateus of Abdera says. By your leave, my Lord, a letter shall be written to the High Priest in Jerusalem requesting that he send six elders from each of the tribes—men who have lived the noblest life and are most expert in their law—that we may discover the points on which the ma-jority of them are in agreement, and thus, after we have an accurate translation, we can install it in a conspicuous place in a manner that befits both the work and your purpose. May continual prosperity be yours!" (*Letter of Aristeas* 28–32)

It did so please the king. A request and gifts were sent to the High Priest in Jerusalem, Eliezer, who responded by dispatching seventy-two elders, "good men and true," together with a copy of Scripture. They arrive safely, are feted, and the work begins.

Demetrius took the men, and going along the sea wall, which is seven stadia in length, to the island (off the coast at Alexandria), he crossed the bridge and went to the northern districts of Pharos Island. There he assembled them in a beautiful and secluded house which had been built on the shore. He then invited them to carry out the work of translation, and everything they needed for the work was placed at their disposal. So they set to work, comparing their several versions and bringing them into agreement, and whatever they agreed upon was suitably copied out under the direction of Demetrius. . . . Every day they met and worked in a delightfully quiet and sunny place. And so it happened that the work of translation was finished in seventy-two days, just as if it had been planned that way.

When the work was finished, Demetrius assembled all the Jews in the place where the translation had been made and had it read through to all in the presence of the translators, who met with great enthusiasm from the people because of the great benefits which they had conferred upon them. They also warmly praised Demetrius and urged him to have the entire Law transcribed, copied and presented to their leaders. After the books had been read through, the priests and the elders among the translators and the Jewish community and the leaders of the people announced that since the translation was so outstanding and accurate it should properly remain as it was and no alteration be made in it. And when the whole company expressed their agreement, they bade them pronounce, in accordance with their custom, a curse upon anyone who should make any alteration either by adding anything or changing in any way whatever any of the words that had been written or by making any excisions. This was a very wise precaution to ensure that the Book [literally, the Bible, *he Biblos*, the earliest recorded example of this usage] might be preserved unchanged for all future time. (Ibid. 301–311)

Although the Letter *of Aristeas explicitly states that the translation was done at the initiative of the Egyptian king, the same text insists that the version was the product of a consensual effort on the part of the translators and received the cooperation of the High Priest and the enthusiastic and unanimous approval of the Jewish people of Alexandria. Philo, an Alexandrian Jew living at least a century after the* Letter, *tells much the same story about the Greek translation, with even greater emphasis on the miraculous and doubtless divinely inspired unanimity that prevailed among the translators.*

Facing Alexandria lies the island of Pharos (and) ... because they considered this to be the most suitable place in the district where they might find peace and tranquillity and where the soul could commune with the Laws with none to disturb its privacy, they [that is, the translators] took up their residence there. They took the Sacred Books, lifted them up toward heaven in their hands, and asked God that they might not fail in their purpose. And He heard their prayers, with the result that the greater part, or even the whole, of the human race might be profited and led to a better life by continuing to observe such wise and truly admirable ordinances.

Sitting here in seclusion, with none present save the elements of nature, earth, water, air, heaven—the creation of which was to be the first theme of the sacred revelation, for the Laws begin with the story of the world's creation—they became as it were possessed, and under inspiration, wrote, not each scribe something different, but the word for word identical thing, as though it had been dictated to each by an invisible prompter. Yet who is not aware that every language, and Greek especially, is rich in terms, and that the same thought can be expressed in many ways by changing single words or whole phrases and cutting the expression to the occasion? This was not the case, we are told, with this Law of ours, but the Greek words used corresponded literally with the Chaldean [that is, the Hebrew], and were exactly appropriate to the things they signified. (Philo, *The Life of Moses* 2.45–65)

11. The Septuagint as a Supplementary Revelation

By the fifth century C.E. this Greek version, called the Septuagint, the one used by both Philo and Paul, had won undisputed pride of place in the Christian Church. As Philo had already noted and as Augustine here reaffirms even more strongly, it shared something of the quality of a revelation in its own right.

While there were other interpreters who translated these sacred oracles out of the Hebrew tongue into Greek, as Aquila, Symmachus and Theodotion, and also that translation which, as its author is unknown, is quoted as the fifth edition, yet the Church has received this Septuagint translation just as if it were the only one; and it has been used by the Greek Christian people, most of whom are not aware that there is any other. From this translation there has also been made one in the Latin tongue, which the Latin churches use. Our times, however, have enjoyed the advantage of the presbyter Jerome (d. 419 C.E.), a man most learned and skilled in all three languages, who translated these same Scriptures into the Latin speech, not from the Greek but from the Hebrew.

Augustine was aware that by this time the Jews had long since disavowed the Septuagint; but he also knew the stories we have just reviewed concerning the translation of the latter. For him those stories—and the fact that by then the Christian tradition was irrevocably committed to the Septuagint—were sufficient guarantee of its authenticity and accuracy.

But although the Jews acknowledge this very learned labor of his to be faithful, while they contend that the Septuagint translators have erred in many places, still the churches of Christ judge that no one should be preferred to the authority of so many men, chosen for this very great work by Eleazer, who was then High Priest. For even if there had not appeared in them one spirit, without doubt divine, and the seventy learned men had, after the manner of men, compared together the words of their translation, that what pleased them all might stand, no single translator ought to be preferred to them; but since so great a sign of divinity has appeared in them, certainly, if any other translator of their Scriptures from the Hebrew into any other tongue is faithful, in that case he agrees with those seventy translators, and if he is found not to agree with them, then we ought to believe that it is they who possess the prophetic gift. For the same spirit who was in the prophets when they spoke these things was in the seventy men when they translated them, so assuredly they could also say something else, just as if the prophet himself had said both, because it would be the same spirit who said both; and could say the same thing differently, so that, although the words were not the same, yet the same meaning should shine forth to those of good understanding; and could omit or add something, so that even by this it might be shown that there was in that work not human bondage, which the translator owed to the words, but rather divine power, which filled and ruled the mind of the translator.

Some, however, have thought that the Greek copies of the Septuagint version ought to be emended from the Hebrew copies; yet they did not dare to take away what the Hebrew lacked and the Septuagint had, but only added what was found in the Hebrew copies and was lacking in the Septuagint, and noted them by placing at the beginning of the verses certain stars which they call asterisks. And those things which the Hebrew copies have not and the Septuagint has, they have in like manner marked at the beginning of the verses with horizontal spit-shaped marks like those by which we denote ounces. . . .

If, then, as it behooves us, we behold nothing else in these Scriptures than what the spirit of God has spoken through men, if anything is in the Hebrew copies and not in the version of the Seventy, the spirit of God did not choose to say it through them, but only through the prophets. But whatever is in the Septuagint and not in the Hebrew copies, the same spirit chose to say through the latter, thus showing that both were prophets. (Augustine, *City of God* 18.43)   [AUGUSTINE 1948: 2:450–451]

12. The Scriptures and Piety
(ca. 132 B.C.E.)

Among the many books of Jewish piety in general circulation in the two centuries before the Christian era was one titled "The Wisdom of Jesus ben Sira," in Latin called "Ecclesiasticus." It was written in Hebrew sometime about 180 B.C.E. and then translated into Greek by the author's grandson for the benefit of the Egyptian community of Jews, many of whom no longer understood Hebrew. The work begins with the translator's own remarks, in which occurs the earliest reference to all three of the classical divisions of the Bible: the Law, the Prophets, and the Writings.

A legacy of great value has come to us through the Law, the Prophets and the writers who followed in their steps, and for this Israel's traditions of discipline and wisdom deserve recognition. It is the duty of those who study Scripture not only to become expert themselves, but also to use their scholarship for the benefit of the outside world through both the spoken and the written word. So my grandfather Jesus (ben Sira), who had industriously applied himself to the study of the Law, the Prophets and the other writings of our ancestors, and had gained a considerable proficiency in them, was moved to compile a book of his own of themes of discipline and wisdom, so that, with futher help, scholars might make greater progress in their studies by living as the Law directs.

You are asked then to read with sympathetic attention and make allowances if, in spite of all the devoted work I have put into the translation, some of the expressions appear inadequate. For it is impossible for a translator to find precise equivalents for the original Hebrew in another language. Not only with this book, but with the Law, the Prophets and the rest of the writings, it makes no small difference to read them in the original.

When I came to Egypt and settled there in the thirty-eighth year of the reign of King Euergetes [that is, 132 B.C.E.,] I found great scope for education; and I thought it very necessary to spend some energy and labor on the translation of this book. Ever since then I have been applying my skill night and day to complete it and to publish it for the use of those who have made their home in a foreign land, and wish to become scholars by training themselves to live according to the Law. (Wisdom of Jesus ben Sira, Preface)

13. Josephus on the Biblical Canon
(ca. 85 C.E.)

The tract called Against Apion *was written by Josephus, the Pharisee who deserted the cause of the Zealot nationalists in their war against Rome in 66–70 C.E. It is an apologia intended, like most of his other works, not merely to redress certain grievances but to explain Judaism to a Gentile world. Thus it includes a description of the sacred books of the Jews.*

Since among us (Jews) it is not permitted to everyone to write the records, and there is no discrepancy in what is written; and since, on the contrary, the prophets alone had this privilege, obtaining their knowledge of the most remote and ancient history through the inspiration which they owed to God, and committing to writing a clear account of the events of their own time just as they occurred, it naturally and even necessarily follows that we do not possess myriads of inconsistent books in conflict with each other. Our books, those that are justly accredited, are but twenty-two and contain the record of all time.

Of these, five are the Books of Moses [that is, the Torah], comprising the laws and the traditional history from the birth of man down to the death of the lawgiver. This period falls only a little short of three thousand years. From the death of Moses until Artaxerxes who succeeded Xerxes as king of Persia, the prophets subsequent to Moses wrote the history of the events of their own times in thirteen books [that is, the Prophets]. The remaining books [that is, the Writings] contain hymns to God and precepts for the conduct of human life.

From Artaxerxes to our own time the complete history has (also) been written, but it has not been deemed worthy of equal credit with the earlier books because of the failure of the exact succession of the prophets. (Josephus, *Against Apion* 1.7–8)

14. Canon and Sanctity

The men who made the actual decisions regarding what was Scripture and what was not were not generous in explaining the grounds for their choices. We must be content with passing remarks, like this one in the Talmud.

That man must be remembered for a blessing, namely Hananiah ben Hezekiah; but for him, the Book of Ezekiel would have been withdrawn (from the canon), for its words contradict the words of the Torah. What did he do? Three hundred measures of oil were brought up to him and he sat in an upper room and expounded it. (BT.Hagigah 13a)

The effect of Hananiah's laborious exegesis presumably reconciled the discrepancies between Ezekiel, Exodus, and Leviticus and permitted it to be included in the scriptural canon.

The rise of the Pharisees, with their emphasis on the extension of ritual purity, placed the question of the sanctity of Scripture in a new context. As a sacred, and hence a taboo object, "all scrolls (of Scripture) render the hands unclean, except the scroll that is used in the Temple court" (M.Kelim 15:6). There were objections to this proscription (see Chapter 3 below), but the Mishna passes directly to the determination of what precisely constituted Scripture—and so could "render the hands unclean"—and what was not. First, there was the physical question.

The blank spaces in a scroll (of the Scriptures) that are above and below (the text), and that are at the beginning and the end, render the hands unclean. Rabbi Judah says: The blank space at the end does not render the hands unclean until the roller is attached to it.

If the writing in a scroll was erased yet there still remained eighty-five letters, as many as there are in the paragraph (beginning) "And it came to pass when the Ark set forward . . . " (Num. 10:35ff.), it still renders the hands unclean. A (single) written sheet (in a Scripture scroll) in which are written eighty-five letters . . . renders the hands unclean. (M.Yadaim 3:4–5)

The same Mishnaic tractate Yadaim then passes directly to the larger question of which books constitute Scripture and which do not, still from the point of view of the transmission of ritual impurity. The controversy has to do with two works in the third division of the Bible, after Torah and the Prophets, called "the Writings."

All the Holy Scriptures render the hands unclean. The Song of Songs and Ecclesiastes render the hands unclean. Rabbi Judah says: The Song of Songs renders the hands unclean, but there is disagreement about Ecclesiastes. Rabbi Yosi says: Ecclesiastes does not render the hands unclean, and there is disagreement about the Song of Songs. Rabbi Simeon says: Ecclesiastes is one of the things about which the School of Shammai adopted the more lenient and the School of Hillel the more stringent ruling. Rabbi Simeon ben Azzai said: I have heard a tradition from the seventy-two elders [that is, of the Great Sanhedrin] on the day when they made Rabbi Eliezer head of the assembly that the Song of Songs and Ecclesiastes both render the hands unclean. Rabbi Akiba said: God forbid! No man in Israel ever disputed about the Song of Songs, that it does not render the hands unclean, for all the ages are not worth the day on which the Song of Songs was given to Israel. For all the Writings are holy, but the Song of Songs is the Holy of Holies. And if there was anything in dispute, the dispute was about Ecclesiastes alone. (M.Yadaim 3:5)

The discussion in Yadaim later returns to the question of translation, whether the few Aramaic passages in Scripture, like Ezra 4:8–7:18 and Daniel 2:4–6:28, enjoy the same sanctity as those in Hebrew. They do, as it turns out, but subsequent translations of the Bible do not share that same holiness.

The (Aramaic) version that is in Ezra and Daniel renders the hands unclean. If this (Aramaic) version is written [that is, translated] into Hebrew, or the Hebrew (passages in Scripture) done in an (Aramaic) version, or in Hebrew script, it does not render the hands unclean. (M.Yadaim 4:5)

15. On the Status of the Christians' So-called Scriptures

Further on in the tractate Yadaim, the later rabbinic tradition reflects upon the earlier Pharisaic one. The point of departure is, as we have just seen, a discussion of the degree of sanctity inherent in the portions of the books of Ezra and Daniel originally written in Aramaic and then translated into Hebrew. The Pharisees maintained that these books were in fact canonical and so shared in the same holiness and the same characteristic of "rendering the hands unclean" as the original Hebrew parts of Scripture. There were those who objected—not, however, on the question of the Aramaic sections of Scripture but on the very idea of Scripture rendering the hands unclean.

The Sadducees say, We cry out against you, O you Pharisees, for you say, "The Holy Scriptures render the hands unclean," but the writings of Hamiram do not render the hands unclean.

"Hamiram" is textually uncertain. It might refer to the "Minim" or heretics; on one view, such references are to the Jewish-Christians. The same text continues:

Rabban Yohanan ben Zakkai said, Have we nothing against the Pharisees save this, for behold, they say, "The bones of an ass are clean and the bones of Yohanan the High Priest are unclean." . . . They [that is, the Pharisees] answered him, "Our love for them is the measure of their uncleanness—that no man should make spoons of the bones of his father or his mother. So it is with the Holy Scripture: our love of them is the measure of their uncleanness; thus since the writings of Hamiram are held in no account, they do not render the hands unclean." (M.Yadaim 4:5–6)

If "Hamiram" is here only an uncertain reference to the Christians, the issue of whether Christian writings in any sense constituted Scripture is more fully and explicitly discussed in the Tosefta. The case in point is a fire that occurs on the Sabbath, and the question is what books may be rescued from the blaze under such circumstances.

All sacred books may be saved from burning (on the Sabbath) whether they are read on the Sabbath or not. Regardless of the language in which they are written, if they become unfit for use they must be hidden away. Why are certain of the biblical books [like the "Writings"] not read? So that they may not nullify the House of Study. The case of a scroll may be saved with the scroll, and the container of the phylacteries together with them, even though there is money in them. Where should they be taken for safety? To an alley which is not a thoroughfare. Ben Bathyra says: even to an alley which is a thoroughfare. (M.Shabbat 16:1)

Thus authentic Scripture may be saved. What else?

We do not save from a fire (on the Sabbath) the Gospels and the books of the Minim. Rather, they are burned in their place, they and their Tetragrammata [that is, occurrences of the sacred name of God that might appear in them]. Rabbi Yosi the Galilean says: During the week one should cut out their Tetragrammata and hide them away and burn the remainder. Rabbi Tarfon said: May I bury my sons! If (these books) should come into my hand, I would burn them along with their Tetragrammata. For even if a pursuer were running after me, I would sooner enter a house [or temple] of idolatry than enter their [that is, the Minim's] houses. For the idolaters do not know Him and deny Him, but these know Him and deny Him. . . . Said Rabbi Ishmael: If for the sake of peace between husband and wife the Ever-Present One has commanded that a book written in holiness be erased by means of water, how much more so should the books of the Minim which bring enmity between Israel and their Father Who is in heaven be erased, they and their Tetragrammata. . . . Just as we do not save them from a fire, so we do not save them from a cave-in, or from water or from anything which would destroy them. (Tosefta Shabbat 13:5)

16. Ezra Rewrites the Scriptures

Among the noncanonical Jewish books circulating under the name of Ezra in the first centuries of the Christian Era is that known as "The Second Book of Esdras"— Esdras is the Greek form of the name Ezra. The book was written in the main by a Palestinian Jew sometime about 100 C.E., and it contains an account of Ezra's work on the Holy Scriptures after the return from the Babylonian Exile. It is Ezra who speaks here.

"May I speak in your presence, Lord? I am about to depart, by your command, after giving warning to those of my people who are now alive. But who will give warning to those born hereafter? The world is shrouded in darkness, and its inhabitants are without light. For your Law was destroyed in the fire [that is, the Babylonian destruction of Jerusalem], and so no one can know about the deeds you have done or intend to do. If I have won your favor, fill me with your holy spirit, so that I may write down the whole story of the world from the very beginning, everything that is contained in your Law; then men will have the chance to find the right path and, if they choose, gain life in the last days."

"Go," He replied, "call the people together, and tell them not to look for you for forty days. Have a large number of writing tablets ready, and take with you Seraiah and Dibri, Shelemiah, Ethan and Asiel, five men all trained to write quickly. Then return here and I will light a lamp of understanding in your mind, which will not go out until you have finished all you are to write. When your work is complete, some of it you must make public; the rest you must give to wise men to keep secret. Tomorrow at this time you shall begin to write."

I went as I was ordered and summoned all the people and said, "Israel, listen to what I say. . . . From this moment no one must talk to me or look for me for the next forty days." I took with me the five men I had been told, and we went away to the field, and there we stayed. On the next day I heard a voice calling me, which said: "Ezra, open your mouth and drink what I give you." So I opened my mouth, and was handed a cup of what seemed like water, except that its color was the color of fire. I took it and drank, and as soon as I had done so my mind began to pour forth a flood of understanding, and wisdom grew greater and greater within me, for I retained my memory unimpaired. I opened my mouth to speak, and I continued to speak unceasingly. The Most High gave understanding to the five men, who took turns in writing down what was said, using characters which they had not known before. They remained at work through the forty days, writing all day, and taking food only at night. But as for me, I spoke all through the day; even at night I was not silent. In the forty days ninety-four books were written. At the end of the forty days the Most High spoke to me. "Make public the (twenty-four) books you wrote first [that is, the twenty-four books of the canonical Hebrew Bible]," He said, "to be read by good and bad alike. But the last seventy books [that is, the apocrypha and pseudepigrapha] are to be kept back and given to none but the wise among your people. They contain a stream of understanding, a fountain of wisdom, a flood of knowledge." And I did so. (2 Esdras 14:19–48)

17. A Christian Insertion in a Jewish Work

Not long after the composition of that Jewish work called 2 Esdras—that is, sometime in the second century C.E.—a prologue (Chapters 1–2) of unmistakable and not very subtly disguised Christian sentiments was added to it by another anonymous hand. Once again it is Ezra who purportedly speaks.

I, Ezra, received on Mount Horeb a commission from the Lord to go to Israel; but when I came they scorned me and rejected God's commandment. Therefore I say to you Gentiles, you who hear and understand: "Look forward to the coming of your shepherd, and he will give you everlasting rest; for he who is to come at the end of the world is close at hand. Be ready to receive the rewards of the kingdom; for light perpetual will shine upon you for ever and ever. Flee from the shadow of the world and receive the joy and splendor that await you. I bear witness openly to my Savior. It is he whom the Lord has appointed; receive him and be joyful, giving thanks to the One who has summoned you to the heavenly realms. Rise, stand up, and see the whole company of those who bear the Lord's mark and sit at His table. They have moved out of the shadow of this world and have received shining robes from the Lord. Receive, O Sion, your full number, and close the roll of those arrayed in white who have faithfully kept the Law of the Lord. The number of Your sons whom You so long desired is now complete. Pray that the Lord's kingdom may come, so that your people, whom He summoned when the world began, may be set apart as His own.

I, Ezra, saw on Mount Sion a crowd too large to count, all singing hymns in praise of the Lord. In the middle stood a very tall young man, taller than all the rest, who was setting a crown on the head of each one of them; he stood out above them all. I was enthralled at the sight and asked the angel, "Sir, who are these?" He replied, "These are those who have laid aside their mortal dress and put on the immortal, those who acknowledged the name of God. Now they are being given crowns and palms." And I asked again, "Who is the young man setting crowns on their heads and giving them palms?" and the angel replied, "He is the Son of God, whom they acknowledged in this mortal life." I began to praise those who had stood so valiantly for the Lord's name. Then the angel said to me, "Go and tell my people all the great and wonderful acts of the Lord God that you have seen." (2 Esdras 2:33–48)

18. Early Testimony on the Gospels

The author to Theophilus: many authors have undertaken to draw up an account of the events that have happened among us, following the traditions handed down to us by the original eyewitnesses and servants of the Gospel. And so I in my turn, your Excellency, as one who has gone over the whole course of these events in detail, have decided to write a connected narrative for you, so as to give you authentic knowledge about the matters of which you have been informed. (Luke 1:1–4)

So begins the Gospel according to Luke. The style is formal, even learned, but the author had no sense that he was writing "Scripture"—as indeed he was not. When an early Christian said "Scripture," he was invariably referring to the Bible. But the Gospels, as the testimony to Jesus' Messianic claims and as an authentic account of his redemptive work, also had a substantial claim on the Christians' attention. Part of that attention was devoted to the question of who wrote those four books.

Five books of Papias [ca. 130 C.E.] are extant, bearing the title *Expositions of the Oracles of the Lord.* Ireneus relates that this is his only work, and adds, "Papias, the hearer of John and the companion of Polycarp, a man of an earlier generation testifies to these things in his fourth book. His work is in five volumes." Now Papias himself in the introduction to his writings makes no claim to be a hearer and eyewitness of the holy Apostles, but to have received the contents of the faith from those who were known to them. He tells us of this in his own words: "I shall not hesitate to set down for you, along with my interpretations, all things which I learned from the elders with care and recorded with care, being well assured of their truth. . . ."

"Now [John] the Elder used to say this also (Papias continues): Mark became the interpreter of Peter and wrote down accurately, but not in order, as much as he remembered of the sayings and doings of Christ. For he was not a hearer or a follower of the Lord, but afterwards, as I said, of Peter, who adapted his teachings to the needs of the moment and did not make an ordered exposition of the sayings of the Lord. And so Mark made no mistake when he thus wrote down some things as he remembered them; for he made it his special care to omit nothing of what he heard and to make no false statements therein." This is what Papias relates concerning Mark.

Now concerning Matthew, it is stated; "So Matthew recorded the oracles in the Hebrew tongue, and each interpreted them to the best of his ability." Papias also makes use of the testimonies of the first letter of John and of the letter of Peter. (Eusebius, *Church History* 3.39)

[According to Ireneus, bishop of Lyons at the end of the second century] Matthew published his Gospel among the Hebrews in their own tongue, when Peter and Paul were preaching the Gospel in Rome and founding the church there. After their departure, Mark, the disciple and interpreter of Peter, himself handed down to us in writing the substance of Peter's preaching. Luke, the follower of Paul, set down in a book the Gospel preached by his teacher. Then John, the disciple of the Lord, who also leaned on his breast, himself produced his Gospel, while he was living in Ephesus in Asia. (Ibid. 5.8)

19. The New Testament Canon

As the Christians came to understand that these writings too constituted a Scripture for the New Covenant, they were faced with the same questions of authenticity and canon that confronted the Jews. A consensus on four Gospels was probably reached early on, but some questions remained, as emerges from the text called the "Muratorian Canon." It was written down in Latin in the eighth century but probably goes back to a Greek original from the end of the second century, that is, to the time of Ireneus.

. . . The third book of the Gospel is the one according to Luke. Luke, the physician, when, after the Ascension of Christ, Paul had taken him to himself as a companion on his travels, wrote in his own name what he had been told, although he had not himself seen the Lord in the flesh. He put down the events as far as he could learn them, and he began his account with the birth of John (the Baptist).

The fourth Gospel is the one by John, one of the disciples. . . . When his fellow disciples and bishops urged him (to write such a work), he said, "Fast with me for three days beginning today, and then let us tell the others whatever may be revealed to each of us." On the same night it was revealed to Andrew, one of the Apostles, that it was John who should narrate all things in his own name as they (all) recalled them. . . .

The Acts of all the Apostles are included in one book. Luke addressed them to the most excellent Theophilus, because some of them occurred when he was present; and he makes this clear by leaving out the sufferings of Peter and the journey of Paul after the latter left Rome for Spain.

As for the Letters of Paul . . . he wrote to no more than seven churches, in this order: the first to the Corinthians, the second to the Ephesians, the third to the Philippians, the fourth to the Colossians, the fifth to the Galatians, the sixth to the Thessalonians, the seventh to the Romans. . . . In addition to these he wrote one (letter) to Philemon, one to Titus, and two to Timothy. They were written in personal affection, but they have been sanctified by being held in regard by the Catholic Church for the regulation of Church discipline. There is extant also a letter to the Laodiceans, and another to the Alexandrians, forged under Paul's name to further the heresy of Marcion. And there are many others which cannot be received into the Catholic Church since it is not fitting for vinegar to be mixed with honey.

The Letter of Jude and the two bearing the name of John are accepted in the Catholic Church; also (the book called) "Wisdom" and written by the friends of Solomon in his honor. We also receive the Apocalypse of John and (one letter) of Peter; [there is a second] which some of us refuse to have read in church. The "Shepherd" is a work written very recently in our own day by Hermas, in the city of Rome, when his brother, Bishop Pius, held the Chair of the Church of Rome. For this reason it too should be read, but not publicly in church to the people, either among the Prophetic books, since their number is complete, or among the Apostles. (Muratorian Canon)

20. There Can Be Only Four Gospels

A good deal of the early discussion on the Christian canon of Scripture was historical in its orientation and method, as we shall see. But the Christian fathers were no less fond of a priori reasoning than contemporary rabbis, and so they were more than willing to demonstrate that there could be no more than four Gospels.

But it is not possible that the Gospels can be either more or fewer in number than they are. For since there are four zones of the world in which we live, and four principal winds, while the Church has been scattered throughout the world, and the pillar and ground of the Church is the Gospel and the spirit of life; it is fitting that she should have four pillars, breathing incorruption on every side, and vivifying men afresh. From this fact it is evident that the Word, the Artificer of all, He that sitteth upon the Cherubim and holds together all things, when he was manifested to men, gave us the Gospel under four forms but bound together by one Spirit. . . . For the Cherubim too were four-faced, and their faces were images of the dispensation of the Son of God. For it [the Scripture: Rev. 4:7] says, "the first living creature was like a lion," symbolizing His effectual working, His supremacy and royal power [Mark]; "the second was like a calf," signifying His sacrificial and sacerdotal order [Luke]; but "the third had the face of a man," an evident description of His advent as a human being [Matthew]; "the fourth was like a flying eagle," pointing out the gift of the Spirit hovering with His wings over the Church [John]. (Ireneus, *Against the Heresies* 3.11:11)

21. The Historicity of the Gospels

Ireneus' arguments are obviously allegorical; but early in the tradition the Christians also developed arguments that spoke to the Gospels in more historical terms, perhaps, as the following selection suggests, because they were constrained to. Here Origen takes on a pagan polemicist named Celsus.

Unless the Evangelists were devoted to the truth, but were, as Celsus maintains, writing fictions, they would never have made mention of the denial of Peter or the scandal of Jesus' disciples. For even if these things had happened, who could have proved that they happened thus? On the contrary, it was appropriate to pass over such events in silence if the authors had as their intention to teach the readers of the Gospels to despise death, since it was a question of the profession of Christianity that was at stake. (Origen, *Against Celsus* 2.15)

Other arguments for the authenticity of the Gospels were adduced, like these from the Western Christian Arnobius (d. 337 C.E.), and likely too against a pagan polemicist.

You do not believe in these deeds [that is, the miracles of Jesus]? But those who saw them and witnessed them with their own eyes believed them and passed them on as credible to us of a later generation. And who were those men you ask? People of all sorts, incredulous humankind, who, if they had not seen the events out in the open and brighter than the light itself, would never have given their assent to such incredible events. We are not to say, are we, that the men of that time were so vain, lying, stupid and bestial that they imagined they had seen what they had not and which had never occurred, supported it with false testimonies and child-like assertions; and when it was possible to live in peace and harmony, they assumed these gratuitous grounds for hostility and preferred a mal-odorous reputation?

But, you say, the Gospels were written by unlettered and crude men and so it is no easy matter to credit them. But is this not all the more reason to think that they are not cooked up with lies, since they were the products of simple minds incapable of subtle embellishments? (Arnobius, *Against the Heathen* 1.58; 2.5)

And once again in the East:

And if these miracles of Christ were lies which his disciples had conspired to invent, it would indeed be an admirable piece of work, how so many people could have preserved their unanimity on these fictions until they died, and that no one of them was ever moved by the fear of what happened to those who died before him to quit the company and contradict the others by betraying what they had agreed upon among themselves. (Eusebius, *Evangelical Preparation* 3.5)

Often the Evangelists are detected in disagreements. But certainly that is a powerful argument for their veracity. If they had agreed among themselves on every detail, on times and places and words, no one of them would have been believed by their enemies but it would have been thought that these writings had been composed by a human consensus, and that this kind of consensus does not arise from the simple truth. Indeed, that very discrepancy in small details dispels suspicion from them and clearly vindicates the trustworthiness of the writers. (John Chrysos-tom, *Homilies on Matthew* 1.?)

22. Did Paul Write the "Letter to the Hebrews"?

How sophisticated some of the critical reasoning could become is evident in Origen's reflections on the stylistic criterium for authenticity as applied to the New Testament Letter to the Hebrews. The reporter is Eusebius.

Furthermore he [Origen; d. ca. 255 C.E.] discusses the *Letter to the Hebrews* in the homily he wrote on it. "That the character of the diction

of the letter entitled 'To the Hebrews' has not the Apostle (Paul's) rude-
ness in speech, who confessed himself 'rude in speech' (1 Cor. 11:6), that
is, in style, but that the letter is better Greek in the framing of its diction,
will be admitted by everyone who is able to discern differences of style.
But again, on the other hand, that the thoughts of the letter are admirable, and not inferior to the acknowledged writings of the Apostle, to this
also everyone will consent as true who has given attention to reading the
Apostle."

Further on he [Origen] adds the following remarks: "But as for
myself, if I were to state my own opinion, I should say that the thoughts
are the Apostle's, but that the style and composition belong to one who
called to mind the Apostle's teachings and, as it were, made short notes
on what his master said. If any church, therefore, holds this letter as
Paul's, let it be commended for this also. For not without reason have
men of old time handed it down as Paul's. But who wrote the letter, in
truth God knows. Yet the account which has reached us [is twofold],
some saying that Clement, who was bishop of the Romans, wrote the
letter; others that it was Luke, who also wrote the Gospel and the Acts."
(Eusebius, *Church History* 6.25)

23. The New Testament Canon
in the Fourth Century

Eusebius continues, now speaking in his own voice of his own times.

Now that we have reached this point, it is reasonable to sum up the
writings of the New Testament already mentioned. Well, then, we must
set in the first place the quartet of the Gospels, which are followed by the
book of the Acts of the Apostles. After this we must reckon the letters of
Paul; following this we must pronounce genuine the extant first letter of
John, and likewise the letter of Peter. After this we must place, if it really
seems right, the Apocalypse of John. . . . These then belong to the acknowledged writings.

But of those which are disputed, but are nevertheless familiar to
most people, there is extant the letter of James, as it is called, and that of
Jude; and the second letter of Peter; and the second and third of John, so
named, whether they belong to the evangelist or perhaps to some other
of the same name as he.

Among the spurious writings there are to be placed also the book of
the Acts of Paul, and the Shepherd, as it is called, and the Apocalypse of

Peter; and in addition to these, the extant letter of Barnabas, and the Teachings of the Apostles, as it is called; and moreover, as I said, the Apocalypse of John, if it seems right. This last, as I said, is rejected by some, but others give it a place among the acknowledged writings. And among those some have reckoned also the Gospel of the Hebrews, a work which is especially acceptable to such Hebrews as have received the Christ. (Eusebius, *Church History* 3.25)

24. Orthodox and Heretical Apocrypha

Eusebius continues on the subject of writings rejected from the canon, the so-called apocrypha and pseudepigrapha.

Now all of these (spurious and questionable works) would be among the disputed writings; but nevertheless we have been compelled to make a catalogue of these also, distinguishing those writings which the tradition of the Church has deemed true and genuine and acknowledged from the others outside their number, which, though they are not canonical but even disputed, yet are recognized by most churchmen. [And this we have done] in order that we might be able to know both these same writings and also those which the heretics put forward in the name of the Apostles, whether as containing Gospels of Peter and Thomas and Matthias, or even of some others besides these, or as containing the Acts of Andrew and John and other Apostles. None of these has been deemed worthy of any kind of mention in a treatise by a single member of successive generations of churchmen; and the character and style also is far removed from the apostolic manner, and the thought and intent of their contents is so absolutely out of harmony with true orthodoxy as to establish the fact that they are certainly the forgeries of heretics. For this reason they ought not to be placed among the spurious writings, but refused as altogether monstrous and impious. (Eusebius, *Church History* 3.25)

25. Editing the Christian Scriptures

Though the practice was condemned by the Great Church, some Christians felt free to make their own choice of what was or was not Scripture, while others edited the canonical texts themselves.

Those who are called Ebionites . . . use only the Gospel according to Matthew; they reject the Apostle Paul, calling him an apostate from the Law. The prophetic writings (of the Bible) they strive to expound with special exactness, and persevere in customs according to the Law, and in the Jewish mode of life, even to the extent of worshiping Jerusalem, as if it were the abode of God. (Ireneus, *Against the Heresies* 1.26:2)

If the Ebionites, who were likely the spiritual descendants of the original Jewish Christians, were chiefly concerned with establishing Jesus' claim to be the Jewish Messiah while they continued to observe, in despite of Paul's teaching, the full body of the Jewish law, another group wished to remove all ties with the Jewish past and with the so-called "Old Testament," which enshrined and glorified the malevolent Jewish deity called Yahweh.

Marcion [ca. 160 C.E.] . . . mutilated the Gospel according to Luke, removing all narratives of the Lord's birth, and also removing much of the teaching of the discourses of the Lord where he is most manifestly described as acknowledging the maker of the universe as his Father. Thus he persuaded his disciples that he himself was more trustworthy than the Apostles, who handed down the Gospel; though he gave them not a Gospel but a fragment of a Gospel. He mutilated the Letters of the Apostle Paul in the same manner, removing whatever is manifestly spoken by the Apostle concerning the God who made the world, where he says that He is the Father of our Lord Jesus Christ, and setting aside all the Apostle's teachings drawn from the prophetic writings (of the Bible) which predict the coming of the Lord. (Ireneus, *Against the Heresies* 1.27:2–3)

26. The Latin "Vulgate" Translation of Scripture

Early in the career of Christianity there had been Latin versions of the New Testament for the use of the Christians of Europe and North Africa. But the translation that eventually became "official" was that called the "Vulgate," done by the scholar and monk Jerome (d. 420 C.E.), who spent much of his life in Palestine. Jerome finished translating the New Testament about 386 and then turned to the Old Testament, for which he used the Hebrew text, and finished that in 404. The following passage is from the preface to his translation of the Gospels, addressed to Pope Damasus in Rome.

You urge me to revise the old Latin version and, as it were, to sit in judgment on the copies of Scripture that are now scattered throughout the whole world; and, since they differ one from the other, you ask me to make a judgment about their agreement with the Greek original. The labor is one of love, but at the same time both dangerous and presumptuous; for, in judging others, I must be content to be judged by all; and how

dare I to change the language of the world in its hoary old age, and carry
it back to the early days of its infancy? When a man, whether he be
learned or unlearned, takes this book in his hands and sees that the text
differs from the one familiar to him, will he not break out immediately
into violent language, and call me a forger and a profane person for having
the audacity to add anything to the ancient books, or to make any changes
or corrections in them?

There are, however, two consoling reflections which enable me to
bear the odium—in the first place the command comes from you, who
are the supreme bishop; and, secondly, even on the testimony of those
who revile us, readings at variance with the early copies cannot be right.
For if we are to put our faith in the (earlier) Latin texts, it is for our
opponents to tell us which; for there are almost as many versions of texts
as there are copies. If, on the other hand, we are to gather the truth from
a comparison of many, why not go back to the original Greek and correct
the mistakes introduced by inaccurate translators and the blundering
emendations made by confident but ignorant critics, and, further, all the
things that have been inserted or changed by copyists more asleep than
awake?

This brief preface deals only with the four Gospels—which are to be
accepted in the following order, Matthew, Mark, Luke, John—as they
have been revised through a comparison of the Greek manuscripts, and
only the early ones. But to avoid any great divergences from the Latin
(version) which we are accustomed to read, I have used my pen with
some restraint; and while I have corrected only such passages as have
seemed to convey a different meaning, I have allowed the rest to remain
as they are. (Jerome, *Preface to the Gospels*)

27. Jewish and Christian Tampering with Scripture: A Muslim Critique

*The Quran insists (3:81; 7:157; 61:6) that both the Jewish and the Christian
Scriptures refer to the Prophet of Islam, much in the way, perhaps, that the coming
of Jesus had been announced in the Old Testament. A search of those Scriptures
failed to reveal any clear reference to Muhammad, however, which left to Muslim
apologetes the task of vindicating the Quran and demonstrating that the Jews and
Christians had tampered with the texts of the Books of God. One of the first to
attempt such a demonstration in a systematic fashion was the Muslim theologian
Juwayni (d. 1085 C.E.) in his work entitled* The Noble Healing.

Certain clear passages in the Quran, whose information cannot be doubted, show that the texts of the Torah and the Gospel make mention of the Prince of Apostles, that the prayers of God were upon him. It is this motive that has induced Muslim scholars to declare that the texts were altered. The Jews and Christians in fact deny this announcement of the Prophet, and summon to their aid arguments which are like "a mirage in the desert. The thirsty man supposes it is water, but when he comes up to it, he finds that it is nothing" (Quran 24:39). . . .

What astonishes me is that the Jews and the Christians have conceded the fact of the alteration and at the same time regard as senseless someone who speaks of it as a possibility. They defend the impossibility of such a thing after agreeing that it did in fact take place. Listen to this ignorance. According to them, the affirmation of the fact of alteration is conditional to its possibility; but the conditions of such a possibility involve editing copies of the Torah and the Gospel dispersed all over the face of the earth, and of being assured of the willingness of each individual of the two religions, scholars, ascetics, the devout and the pious as well as the sinner, and of their agreement on one single opinion and one common expression, despite the wide differences of opinion. . . .

My position, then, with the aid of God, is that most of the errors that occur in the sciences arise from the fact that arguments are accepted without examination and without reason's making a careful examination of their premises. We shall mention the defects in this argument (of the Jews and Christians) and show wherein the carelessness of their authors lies.

Juwayni first takes the circumstances that show the possibility of altering the Torah.

The Torah which is presently in the hands of the Jews is that which was written by Ezra the scribe after the troubles that Nabuchadnezzar imposed upon them. This latter wrought carnage among the groups of religious Jews, sparing only isolated groups, whose small number allows us to disregard them. He gave over their wealth as booty to his troopers and soldiers and he destroyed their books. Ignorant of the norms of their religious law, he [here, it seems, Antiochus IV] had decided in favor of the corrupt state of the practices of this law: he put up an idol in their place of worship and made public announcement by a herald warning against even a mention of the law. Things remained in this state until an entire generation had passed away. Then those who were in exile found some leaves of the Torah; they took refuge in caves and made pretenses in order to be able to read them in secret.

This (present Torah copy) Ezra wrote 545 years before the mission of the Messiah, upon whom be peace, and when there was not a single Christian upon the earth. It was at this moment that the alteration of the text was possible since it was not a question of re-editing copies of the Torah scattered all over the world, as has been said, nor of counting on the willingness of individuals from different factions, nor were copies of the Torah in the hands of both Jews and Christians. In fact, they only came into Christian hands after they had been altered.

So there was only one doer of this deed, either Ezra himself or, if one puts it after Ezra, whoever it was who recopied Ezra's copy. More, an alteration on his part was possible from the fact that he was eager to see his power extended and by the fact that he was not credited with that kind of impeccability which would have prevented his commission of either light or serious faults. . . . It has been said that the love of power is the last thing to be made to leave the heads of the righteous, and power had considerable importance for the Israelites. And anyone who knows well the chronicles of world history and has followed their extraordinary developments finds there that men greater than Ezra have been moved by the love of power to act senselessly, rejecting the bonds of reason and of religion.

The Jews and the Christians can be convicted each out of the other's mouth on the fact of alteration.

The reason why the Jews and Christians unanimously agree that the text was in fact altered is that the copies that each group has are clearly contradictory. . . . The motive for the difference is, according to the Christians, that the Torah testifies that the Messiah, on whom be peace, would be sent at the time he was, and the copies of the Torah in their hands support the truth of what they say. They maintain, then, that the Jews have changed their copies of the Torah to prevent the recognition of the mission of the Messiah, on whom be peace. The Jews for their part say that the Christians have changed their copies and that the Messiah, on whom be peace, will not come until the end of the seventh period, and their copies support the truth of what they say. Thus both parties agree that the text has been in fact changed, and each group puts a rope around the neck of the other.

For our part, we shall now mention the contradictions between the two versions: In the Jews' Torah, Adam, when he was 130 years old, begot Seth, and in the Christians', he was 230 years old when he begot Seth.

Juwayni then goes step by step through the age of the Patriarchs and shows the differences in the chronology of the Jewish and Christian versions of the Torah. He concludes:

These are the very expressions of the Torah, and you see how extraordinary and hateful is this divergence between the two religious groups. And they differ not on the kind of point where opinions vary according to the different points of views of scholars and there arise variations according to how much is assumed. Rather, each group maintains that its text came down to Moses, peace be upon him, and that is the very essence of the tampering.

Finally, there is the matter of the Samaritans' Torah. Its text differs from that in the hands of the two other religious groups, and on the basis of that fact alone one could make a very convincing argument for the fact that the texts were altered.

Juwayni next takes up the Gospels.

There is first of all the enormous error the Christians made in not carefully preserving what they had to transmit, and no reasonable man can hope to correct that. The reason why they fell into this error is that they were careless in a matter that required urgent attention, in times propitious to the alteration and loss of texts, and in the matter of an oral transmission.

Matthew says clearly in his Gospel that he composed it nine years after the Ascension of the Messiah, on whom be peace; as for John, he says explicitly that he assembled his text thirty or more years after the Ascension; likewise Mark, twelve years after the Ascension; and Luke, twenty-two, or according to others twenty years after the Ascension. That is the point made manifestly in the Gospels, and thence arises the error against which there is no defense; more, even if someone attempts to dissemble through the imagination, he cannot achieve what he sets out to do.

Juwayni's first point of attack on the Gospels is the contradictions between and the errors in Matthew and Luke's versions of the genealogy of Jesus. Then he takes up the varying versions of Peter's denial of Jesus, the prediction and the fact after the latter's arrest. He concludes on the matter of this second case:

But the event that took place was unique, as were the moment, the place and the circumstances of the act. But generally when the circumstances in two accounts are identical and yet the accounts differ, one is forced to conclude that one of the two is false. You see then the integrity in the transmission of these Gospels; and how ironic that they pretend that the Evangelists were immune to error and that they transmitted their Gospels from the time of the Messiah, on whom be peace, as one would who personally heard these narratives, preserving what he heard, and carefully keeping the order of the narrative and the very words. According to my opinion, they allowed a great deal of time to pass before composing the Gospels, and both forgetfulness and carelessness got the better of them.

There are other examples of differences among the Gospels. Juwayni concludes with this one.

It is likewise extraordinary that Matthew had mentioned in his Gospel that when the Messiah was crucified and had rendered up his spirit, "the Temple was riven from top to bottom in two pieces, the earth quaked, the stones were shattered, tombs opened, and the bodies of the saints were resuscitated and left their tombs" (Matt. 27:51–53). Those are his own words in his Gospel, and yet no other Evangelist mentions it. But if the facts which he narrated, and which are of such an extraordinary strangeness, took place as he described them, they would be great miracles which one would have great reason to report and which everyone near and far would have recognized. Even people who were incapable of carefully preserving the events of the life of the Messiah, upon whom be peace, or of retaining the accounts, would have loved to have told of such facts and to have immersed themselves in stories on this theme. . . .

All of which shows that Matthew lied or that the three other Evangelists have shown their carelessness by forgetting to mention these extraordinary facts. And they are well charged with negligence since they did not habitually forget. But it would be even stranger that they pretended not to have knowledge of the facts; in effect if such extraordinary miracles actually took place, everybody in the province, near or far, would have known, yes, and in other provinces as well. (Juwayni, *The Noble Healing*) [JUWAYNI 1968: 40–83]

28. A Muslim History of Prophecy

Juwayni can move easily and knowingly across the text and matter of the Bible and the Gospels. It is, in fact, a familiar terrain to the Muslim since it was described in the Quran itself.

We sent down the Torah which contains guidance and light, in accordance with which the prophets who were obedient to God gave instruction to the Jews, as did the rabbis and the priests, for they were the

custodians and witnesses of God's writ. . . . Later in the train (of prophets), We sent Jesus son of Mary, confirming the Torah which had been
sent down before him, and gave him the Gospel containing guidance and
light for those who preserve themselves from evil and follow the straight
path. . . . And to you We have revealed the Book containing the truth,
confirming the earlier revelations, and preserving them. (Quran 5:44–48)

*The Quran, then, is a Book like those other books, and its bearer, Muhammad, a
messenger in the tradition of Moses and Jesus—but, for all that, merely a messenger. God's word rests far above his merely mortal powers.*

When Our clear messages are recited to them, those who do not
hope to meet Us say: "Bring a different Quran, or make amendments in
this one." Say: "It is not for me to change it of my will. I follow only what
was revealed to me. If I disobey my Lord, I fear the punishment of an
awful Day." (Quran 10:15)

Muhammad is only a messenger, and many a messenger has gone
before him. So what if he dies or is killed! Will you turn back and go away
in haste? He who turns back and goes away in haste will do no harm to
God. (Quran 5:144)

*These notions became commonplaces in the Islamic tradition, as is evident in this
version of sacred history, the details supplied and the lacunae filled in, by the literary
virtuoso Jahiz (d. 886 C.E.).*

When the situation becomes dangerous because the ancient traditions no longer inspire men's complete confidence, God sets a term at the
end of each period of time, a sign to renew the strength of the traditions
and renew the teaching of the Messengers when it grows faint. In this
manner Noah renewed the traditions dating from the period between
Adam and himself by giving true testimony and producing effective signs,
so as to safeguard the traditions from corruption and protect them from
damage. The (Prophetic) traditions and proofs of earlier generations had
not been entirely obliterated or destroyed, but when they were about to
be, God sent His signs so that His proofs might not disappear from the
earth. That is why the end-time of a period is called "the enfeeblement."
There is, however, an unmistakable difference between bending and
breaking. Then God sent Abraham at the end of the second period,
namely that between the time of Noah and himself; this was the longest
"enfeeblement" the world had yet experienced, for Noah remained
among his people, expounding and reasoning and explaining, for 950
years, and the first of His signs was also the greatest, namely the Flood,

in which God drowned all the people of the earth except Noah and his followers. . . .

Then the Prophets followed one after the other in the period between Abraham and Jesus. Because their proofs followed one upon the other, their signs clear, their acts numerous, and their deeds well known, because all of that took deep root in people's hearts and souls and the whole world spoke of it, their teachings were neither overturned nor diminished nor corrupted during the entire period from Jesus to the Prophet (Muhammad). But when they were on the point of becoming weakened, enfeebled and spent, God sent Muhammad, who renewed the teachings of Adam, Noah, Moses, Aaron, Jesus and John (the Baptist), and gave further detail to them; for Muhammad is righteous, and his witness is true, declaring that the Hour was at hand and that he was the seal of the Prophets. We knew then that his proofs would endure until the term set for it by God. (Jahiz, *The Proofs of Prophecy* 133–134)

Almost any educated Muslim could write such a summary. Witness this example from the Muslim theologian al-Nasafi (d. 1114 C.E.), who is careful to draw the distinction between private or personal written revelations—what he calls the "Scrolls"— from the "Books"—the four revealed codes of Law.

It must be recognized that all the books (of Scripture) which God has sent down (by revelation) to the Prophets and Apostles are the uncreated word of God. Of these there were one hundred Scrolls and four Books. (Of the Scrolls) God sent fifty to Seth the son of Adam, on whom be peace. Thirty were sent to Idris [that is, Enoch], on whom be peace; ten to Abraham, on whom be peace; and ten to Moses, on whom be peace, before the Torah was sent down to him. It was called "The Book of Naming" and was revealed before the drowning of the Pharaoh; then God sent down the Torah after the drowning of the Pharaoh. Later God sent down the Psalter to David, upon whom be peace, and then He sent down the Gospel to Jesus, on whom be peace, who was the last of the Prophets among the Children of Israel. Then God, may He be praised and exalted, sent down the Quran to Muhammad, upon whom be God's blessing and peace, who is the last of the Messengers. Anyone who disavows a (single) verse in any of these Scriptures is in unbelief.

Should anyone say, "I believe in all the Messengers," and then disavow one of the Messengers about whom there is no (scriptural) text, saying, "this one does not belong among them," he would not be in a state of unbelief, but he would be in heresy. This holds so long as he does not enter another religion, but if he enters another religion he is an apostate and may be killed. . . . Be it known, moreover, that the Prophets, upon whom be peace, are 124,000, and the Apostles among them are 313, according to the tradition transmitted from Abu Dharr, with whom may God be pleased, going back to a statement of the Apostle of God, upon whom be God's blessing and peace. In some of the Prophetic traditions the (number of the) Prophets is given as a thousand thousand, or two hundred thousand and more, but the correct thing in this matter is for you to say, "I believe in God and in all the Prophets and Apostles, and in all that has come from God by way of revelation according as God willed." By thus doing you will not affirm someone to be a Prophet who was not, nor will you affirm someone not to be a Prophet who was. (Nasafi, *Sea of Discourse on Theology*) [JEFFERY 1962: 447–448]

29. The Divine Origin of the Quran

The messenger of the Quran may have been a mere mortal, but there was no doubt about the origin of the message he carried to men.

And this (Quran) is a revelation from the Lord of all the worlds,
Which the trusted spirit descended with
To your heart that you may be a warner
In clear Arabic.
(Quran 26:192–195)

As the Quran instructs us, this quality of "trustworthiness" is shared by the heavenly Spirit—identified by the Islamic tradition as Gabriel—with God's chosen Apostle.

This is indeed the word of an honored Messenger,
Full of power, well-established with the Lord and Master of the Throne,
Obeyed and worthy of trust.
Your companion is not mad.
He had surely seen Him on the clear horizon.
And he is chary of making public what is unknown.
(Quran 81:19–24)

It is He who sent His Messenger with guidance and the true faith in order to make it superior to all other religions, though the idolaters may not like it. (Quran 9:33)

The message, the Quran also announces to the world, is not intended only for pagans.

O People of the Book, Our Apostle has come to you announcing many things of the Scripture that you have suppressed, passing over some others. To you has come light and a clear Book from God, through which God will lead those who follow His pleasure to the path of peace, and guide them out of the darkness into light by His will, and to the path that is straight. (Quran 5:15–16)

O you People of the Book, Our Apostle has come to you when Apostles had ceased to come long ago, lest you said: "There did not come to us any messenger of good news or warnings." So now there has reached you a bearer of good tidings and of warnings; for God has the power over all things. (Quran 5:19)

This is the Book free of doubt and involution,
a guidance for those who preserve themselves from evil
and follow the straight path,
who believe in the Unknown, and fulfill their devotional obligations,
and spend in charity of what We have given them;
who believe in what has been revealed to you
and what was revealed to those before you,
and are certain of the Hereafter.
They have found the guidance of their Lord and will be successful.
(Quran 2:1–5)

Thus does God Himself characterize the Book He has sent down to Muhammad, His servant, this very Book in which He is Himself speaking. How and under what circumstances that sending down took place are less easily accessible, though there are clues in that same Book.

It is not given to man that God should speak to Him, except by suggestion or indirectly, or send a messenger to convey by His command whatsoever He please. He is all-high and all-wise.
And so We have revealed to you (Muhammad) the Spirit of Our command. You did not know what the Scripture was before, or faith, and We made it a light by which We show the way to those of Our creatures as We please. (Quran 42:51–52)

And this Quran is not such as could be composed by anyone but God. It confirms what has been revealed before, and is an exposition of what has been decreed for mankind, without any doubt, by the Lord of the worlds.
Do they say (of the Prophet): "He has composed it?" Say to them: "Bring a sura like this, and call anyone apart from God you can to help you, if what you say is true." (Quran 10:37–38)

Do they say (of the Prophet): "He has forged (the Quran)?" Say: "Then bring ten suras like it, and call upon anyone except God to help you, if what you say is true."

If they do not answer you, then know it has been revealed with the knowledge of God, and that there is no god but He. (Quran 11:13–14)

These were not the only objections raised by Muhammad's contemporaries. They demanded signs.

We have given examples of every kind of men in this Quran in various ways, and even then most men disdain every thing but disbelief. They say: "We will not believe you until you make a spring of water gush forth from the earth for us; or until you acquire an orchard of date palm trees and grapes, and produce rivers flowing through it, or let chunks of sky fall over us, as you assert." (Quran 17:89–92)

Behind such a request seems to be a more profound doubt: that Muhammad is but a man and thus ill qualified to be a heavenly messenger.

Nothing prevented men from believing when guidance came to them, but they said: "Has God sent (only) a man as a messenger?" Say: "If angels had peopled the earth and walked about in peace and quiet, We would surely have sent to them an angel as a messenger." (Quran 17: 94–95)

To which compare:

And they say: What sort of prophet is this who eats food and walks in the marketplaces? Why was no angel sent to him to act as an admonisher with him? (Quran 25:7)

Those who do not hope to meet Us say: "Why are no angels sent down to us, or why do we not see our Lord?" (Quran 25:21)

30. Muhammad's Ascension into Heaven

There was a way, Muhammad was told by the Quraysh—whether in mockery or sincerity we cannot tell—by which their fellow Meccan could demonstrate his supernatural vocation.

And they say: "We will certainly not believe you until you . . . ascend to the skies, though we shall not believe in your having ascended till you bring down a Book for us which we can read." Say to them: "Glory be to my Lord! I am only a man and a messenger." (Quran 17:95)

Thus Muhammad's opponents at Mecca, the doubting and not entirely unsophisticated Quraysh, demanded two signs validating his claim to prophecy: that he should ascend into heaven and that he should return to them with a book that was intelligible to them. The response lay in the Quran itself. Sura 17:1 contains an enigmatic reference to a miraculous journey whereby Muhammad was carried by God at night from Mecca to another place, eventually identified as Jerusalem. But according to tradition, the voyage did not end there. The source is Ibn Ishaq's Life of the Prophet.

One whom I have no reason to doubt told me on the authority of Abu Saʿid al-Khudri: I heard the Messenger say, "After the completion of my business in Jerusalem (on the occasion of the Night Journey) a ladder was brought to me finer than any I have ever seen. It was that to which the dying man looks when death approaches. My companion mounted it with me until we came to one of the gates of heaven called the Gate of the Watchers. An angel called Ismail was in charge of it, and under his command were twelve thousand angels, each of them having (another) twelve thousand angels under his command." As he told the story the Messenger used to say, "and none knows the armies of God but He" (Quran 74:31). "When Gabriel brought me in, Ismail asked who I was, and when he was told that I was Muhammad, he asked if I had been given a mission, and on being assured I had, he wished me well."

"Then I was taken up to the second heaven and there were the two maternal cousins, Jesus son of Mary and John son of Zakariah. Then to the third heaven and there was a man whose face was as the moon at full. This was my brother Joseph son of Jacob. Then to the fourth heaven and there was a man called Idris, 'and We have exalted him to a lofty place' (Quran 19:56–57). Then to the fifth heaven and there was a man with white hair and a long beard; never before have I seen a more handsome man than he. This was the beloved among his people, Aaron son of Imran. Then to the sixth heaven and there was a dark man with a hooked nose like the Shanuʾa. This was Moses son of Imran. Then to the seventh heaven and there was a man sitting on a throne at the gate of the immortal mansion. Every day seventy thousand angels went in, not to come back until the Resurrection Day. Never have I seen a man more like myself. This was my father Abraham." (Life 268–270) [IBN ISHAQ 1955: 184–186]

31. The Night of Destiny

Was this heavenly ascension the occasion when Muhammad received the Book? The text just cited does not seem to suggest it. But on the evidence of the Quran—and of the Bible and the Jewish tradition—Moses certainly received his Book on one single occasion. The Quranic evidence is not so certain for Jesus, but in his case too *the Book appears to have been delivered once and for all. Muhammad's circumstances were patently different: both the Quran and the biographical traditions about the Prophet show the Quran being delivered chapter by chapter, and even occasionally verse by verse. That must have prompted remarks, since the Quran averts to this quality that sets Muhammad apart from the other bearers of revelation.*

We have divided the Quran into parts that you might recite it to men slowly, with deliberation. That is why We sent it down by degrees. (Quran 17:106)

The Muslim tradition certainly discussed the problem, chiefly in the context of the month of Ramadan, a holy month the Quran itself closely associates with the act of revelation.

Ramadan is the month in which the Quran was revealed as guidance to man and clear proof of the guidance, and a criterion (of falsehood and truth). (Quran 2:185)

The Muslim commentator Zamakhshari (d. 1134 C.E.) supplies additional details on this epochal event.

"In which the Quran was revealed": . . . The meaning of these words is: in which it *began* to be revealed. This occurred during the Night of Destiny. Some say that the Quran may have been sent down as a whole to the lowest heaven (on this night), and then later section by section to the earth. Others say that the meaning is "(the month of Ramadan) on account of which the Quran was revealed." . . . The following is transmitted from the Prophet: the sheets (of writing) of Abraham come down on the first night of Ramadan; the Torah was sent down on the sixth night into the month; the Gospel, the thirteenth; and the Quran, after a lapse of twenty-four (nights into Ramadan). (Zamakhshari, *The Unveiler of the Realities, ad loc.*)

The Quran returns to the same event in another verse, and once again the commentator fills out the narrative.

The perspicuous Book is a witness that We sent it down on a night of blessing—so that We could warn—on which all affairs are sorted out and divided as commands from Us. (Quran 44:2–5)

Most traditions say that the "night of blessing" is the same as the Night of Destiny [that is, the twenty-fourth of Ramadan], for God's word says: "Behold, We sent it [that is, the Quran] on the Night of Destiny" (Quran 97:1). Moreover, His words "on this night every wise bidding is determined" correspond with His words "In it the angels and the spirit descend, by the leave of their Lord, upon every command" (Quran 97:4). Finally, this also corresponds with his words "The month of Ramadan wherein the Quran was sent down" (Quran 2:185). According to most of the Prophetic traditions, the Night of Destiny falls during the month of Ramadan.

If one were to ask what is the significance of the sending down of the Quran on this night, I would respond: It is said that God first sent it down in its entirety from the seventh heaven to the lowest heaven. Then He commanded excellent writers to transcribe it on the Night of Destiny. Gabriel subsequently revealed it piece by piece to the Messenger of God. (Zamakhshari, *The Unveiler, ad loc.*)

32. The Heavenly Book

Islam shares with Judaism belief in a heavenly prototype of Scripture, here called in the Quran's own words "the Mother of the Book," or so the lines were understood by the Muslim commentators.

I call to witness the clear Book, that we made it an Arabic Quran that you may perhaps understand. It is inscribed in the Mother of the Book with Us, sublime, dispenser of (all) laws. (Quran 43:2–4)

Zamakhshari explains.

"Perhaps": This word expresses a wish, because there is a connection between this term and expressions of hoping. So we can say it means: We have created the Book in Arabic and not in any other language because We intended that the Arabs should understand it and not be able to say: "If only the verses of the Book had been sent forth clearly!"

The original text (of the Book) is the tablet corresponding to the words of God: ". . . it is a glorious Quran, in a well-preserved tablet" (Quran 85:21ff.). This writing is designated the "Mother of the Book" because it represents the original in which the individual books are preserved. They are derived from it by copying. (Zamakhshari, *The Unveiler of the Realities, ad loc.*)

Zamakhshari was here simply summarizing what the Quran itself asserts: that the Book of revelation is one and is preserved in Heaven. It contains all God's decrees and sums up all wisdom.

He has the keys of the Unknown. No one but He has knowledge; He knows what is on the land and in the sea. Not a leaf falls without His knowledge, nor a grain in the darkest recesses of the earth, nor any thing green or seared that is not noted in the clear Book. (Quran 6:59)

. . . There is not the weight of an atom on the earth and in the heavens that is hidden from your Lord, nor is there anything smaller or greater than this but is recorded in the clear Book. (Quran 10:61)

Do you not know that God knows whatever is in the heavens and the earth? This surely is in the Book; this is how God works inevitably. (Quran 22:70)

There is no calamity that befalls the earth or yourselves but that it was in the Book before We created them. This is how God works inevitably. (Quran 57:22)

It is this same Book whose exemplars were given to the earlier peoples of God's choice—to Moses for the Jews (Quran 28:43, 32:23, etc.) and to Jesus for the Christians (Quran 3:43, 19:31)—and whose validity the Quran now validates and confirms.

And this is a revelation from the Lord of all the worlds,
With which the trusted Spirit descended
Upon your heart, that you may be a warner
In clear Arabic.
This was indicated in Books of earlier people.
Was it not a proof for them that the learned men of Israel knew it? (Quran 26:191–197)

What We have revealed to you in the Book is the truth, and proves what was sent before it to be true. (Quran 35:31)

All the more reason why those "People of the Book" should accept this new exemplar being revealed through the Apostle Muhammad.

Say to them: "O People of the Book, what reason have you for disliking us other than that we believe in God and what was sent down before us?" (Quran 5:59)

33. The Quran: Created or Uncreated?

It was the view that the Quran was in its primal form a book in heaven and thence was sent down to Muhammad, first whole and then in discrete revelations, that embroiled the Muslims' Scripture in an internal theological controversy that has little direct echo in either Judaism or Christianity. If the Quran is the "speech" of God, His Word, then it is necessarily one of His attributes, a subject that provoked lively interest among early Muslim theologians, who were just beginning to explore the connection between essence and accidents as those Greek-defined notions were applied to God. Whether that interest antedated the debate or the debate provoked

*the interest in a conceptual system that helped the parties to argue or defend their
positions is difficult to say. But by the middle of the eighth century the issue had
been broached. Indeed, it had gained such notoriety that in the 830s it became the
benchmark of one of the few officially promulgated definitions of orthodoxy—and
so of heresy—in Islam: the Caliph al-Ma'mun (813–833 C.E.) required Muslims
to swear that the Quran was the created speech of God and threatened the recusants
with imprisonment.*

*One who chose not to swear on that occasion was the jurist Ahmad ibn Hanbal
(d. 855 C.E.), whose "profession of faith" includes the following article on the
Quran.*

The Quran is the Word of God and it is not created. It is not wrong
to say, "It is not created," for God's Word is not separate from Him, and
there is nothing of Him that is created. Beware of discussing this with
those who speak about this subject and talk of the "creation of sounds"
and such matters, and those who go midway and say "I don't know
whether the Quran is created or uncreated, but it is God's Word." Such
a one is guilty of a religious innovation, as is the one who says "It is
created," for it is God's Word and that is not created. (Ahmad ibn Hanbal, *Creed*) [WILLIAMS 1971: 29]

*In despite of Ma'mun and the theologians who may have had the Caliphal ear at
the time, it was the position of Ibn Hanbal—that the Quran is uncreated and
eternal—that became the normative one in Islam. But whereas Ibn Hanbal simply
asserts it in the document just cited, later theologians were willing to argue the case
at length and in detail. This, for example, is how the theological argument is
integrated into the received accounts of the revelation of the Quran by al-Nasafi (d.
1114 C.E.) in his* Sea of Discourse on Theology.

The Quran is God's speaking, which is one of His attributes. Now
God in all of His attributes is One, and with all His attributes is eternal
and not contingent, (so His speaking is) without letters and without
sounds, not broken up into syllables or paragraphs. It is not He nor is it
other than He. He caused Gabriel to hear it as sound and letters, for He
created sound and letters and caused him to hear it by that sound and
those letters. Gabriel, upon whom be peace, memorized it, stored it (in
his mind) and then transmitted it to the Prophet, upon whom be God's
blessing and peace, by bringing down a revelation and a message, which
is not the same as bringing down a corporeal object and a form. He
recited it to the Prophet, upon whom be God's blessing and peace, the
Prophet memorized it, storing it up (in his mind), and then recited it to
his Companions, who memorized it and recited it to the Followers, the

Followers handed it on to the upright, and so on until it reached us. It is (now) recited by tongues, memorized by hearts and written in codices, though it is not contained by the codices. It may be neither added to nor taken from; just as God is mentioned by tongues, recognized by hearts, worshiped in places, yet He is not confined to existence in those places nor in those hearts. It is as He said, "Those who follow the Messenger, the unlettered Messenger, whom they find mentioned in the Torah and the Gospel which they have" (Quran 7:157), for they found (in those Books) only his picture, his description, not his person. Similarly, Paradise and Hell are mentioned, but they are not actually present among us. All this is according to the school of the truly orthodox. (Nasafi, *Sea of Discourse*) [JEFFERY 1962: 398]

34. "Bring a Sura Like It"

We have already seen the Quran's own response to accusations that it represents nothing more than the invention of Muhammad. Go, God challenges the doubters, and produce another Book like it.

This Quran is not such as could be composed by anyone but God. It confirms what has been revealed before, and is an exposition of what has been decreed for mankind, without any doubt, by the Lord of the worlds.

Do they say (of the Prophet): "He has composed it?" Say to them: "Bring a sura like it, and call anyone apart from God you can to help you, if what you say is true." (Quran 10:37–38)

The Quran, then, was not only of heavenly origin; it was, as a direct consequence of that origin, inimitable by mere man, Muhammad or any other, and so the challenge issued in this sura went unanswered. That fact remained the chief probative miracle of Islam, the "sign" that Muhammad resolutely refused to produce but that God produced for him and so verified His religion and His Prophet. The essayist al-Jahiz (d. 868 C.E.) reflects on this.

Muhammad had one unique sign, which affects the mind much in the same manner that (Moses') parting of the seas affected the eyes, namely, when he said to the Quraysh in particular and the Arabs in general—and they included many poets and orators, and eloquent, shrewd, wise, tolerant, sagacious, experienced and farsighted men—"If you can equal me with but a single sura, my claims will be false and you will be entitled to call me a liar." Now it is impossible that among people like the Arabs, with their great numbers, the variety of their tastes, their language, their overflowing eloquence, and their remarkable capacity for elegant language, which has enabled them to describe . . . everything that crawls or runs, and in short everything that the eye can see and the mind picture, who possess every kind of poetic form . . . the same people who were the first to show hatred toward him and make war, suffering losses themselves and killing some of his supporters, that among these people, I say, who were the fiercest in hatred, the most vengeful, the most sensitive to favor and slight, the most hostile to the Prophet, the quickest to condemn weakness and extol strength, no orator or poet should have dared take up the challenge.

Knowing everything we do, it is inconceivable that words should not have been their weapon of choice . . . and yet that the Prophet's opponents should have unanimously refrained from using them, at a time when they were sacrificing their possessions and their lives, and that they should not all have said, or that at least one of them should have said: Why do you kill yourselves, sacrifice your possessions and forsake your homes, when the steps to be taken against him are simple and the way of dealing with him easy: let one of your poets or orators compose a speech similar to his, equal in length to the shortest sura he has challenged you to imitate, or the meanest verse he has invited you to copy? (Jahiz, *Proofs of Prophecy* 143–144)

35. The Earliest Sura

Medieval Muslim and modern Western scholars have long attempted to arrange the suras or chapters of the Quran in some kind of chronological order, chiefly in an effort to integrate them into the biographical data on the life of the Prophet. As this quest proceeded, there were various candidates for the earliest of the revelations, among them Sura 74.

> O you, enfolded in your mantle,
> Arise and warn!
> Glorify your Lord,
> Purify your inner self,
> And banish all trepidation.
> (Quran 74:1–5)

When we turn to the medieval Muslim commentators, we find a variety of opinions on which might have been the earliest sura.

Some say that this [that is, 74:1–5] was the first sura to be sent down. Jabir ibn Abdullah related (the following) from the Messenger of

God: "I was on Mount Hira (near Mecca) when someone called out to me, 'Muhammad, you are the Messenger of God.' I looked to the right and to the left but saw nothing. Then I looked up above me and there I saw something." —In the report according to (his wife) Aisha he says, "I glanced up above me and there I saw someone sitting on a throne between heaven and earth," meaning it was the Angel Gabriel who had called out to him— "I was frightened," the tradition continues, "and returned to Khadija (Muhammad's first wife) and called out: 'Dress me in a mantle, dress me in a mantle!' Then Gabriel came and said 'O you, enfolded in your mantle. . . .' "

From al-Zuhri it is related, on the other hand, that the first sura to come down was "Recite in the name of the Lord" down to the words of God "what he has not known" (Sura 96:1–5). (After the revelation of this sura) the Messenger of God became sad (because the revelations had ceased) and he began to climb to the tops of the mountains. Then Gabriel came to him and said, "You are the Prophet of God." And then Muhammad returned to Khadija and called out: "Dress me in a mantle and pour cold water over me!" Thereupon there came down the sura (which begins) "O you, enfolded in your mantle. . . ."

Still others say that the Prophet heard certain things from the (members of the tribe of) the Quraysh which displeased him, and that this caused him to grieve. Afterwards he was wrapped in his robe reflecting on what grieved him, as is customy with grieving people. Then he was commanded (through the present sura) to warn his countrymen continuously (of the punishment of God), even when they insulted him and caused him injury. (Zamakhshari, *The Unveiler of the Realities, ad loc.*)

36. The Heart of the Quran: The "Throne Verse"

God's throne in heaven plays an important role in both Jewish and Muslim piety, as we shall see in Chapter 2 below. In Islam the explicit mention of God's heavenly seat in the Quran set in train a series of speculations on both the throne and the verses in which it appeared.

God! There is no god but He, the living, the eternal, self-subsisting, ever sustaining. Neither does somnolence affect Him nor sleep. To Him belongs all that is in the heavens and the earth, and who can intercede with Him except by His leave? Known to Him is all that is present before men and what is hidden and that which is to come upon them, and not

no

even a little of His knowledge can they grasp except what He wills. His Throne extends over the heavens and the earth, and He tires not protecting them: He alone is high and supreme. (Quran 2:255)

Qurtubi (d. 1273) relates ... on the authority of Muhammad ibn al-Hanifiyya: "When the Throne Verse was revealed, every idol and king in the world fell prostrate and the crowns of kings fell off their heads. Satans fled, colliding with one another in confusion until they came to Iblis [their chief]. . . . He sent them to find out what had happened, and when they came to Medina they were told that the Throne Verse had been sent down. . . ."

Tabarsi (d. 1153) relates on the authority of Abdullah ibn Umar that the Prophet said: "Whoever recites the Throne Verse after a prescribed prayer, the Lord of Majesty Himself shall receive his soul at death. He would be as if he had fought with the Prophet of God until he was martyred." . . . Ali also said: "I heard the Messenger of God say, 'O Ali, the chief of humankind is Adam, the chief of the Arabs is Muhammad, nor is there pride in this. The chief of the Persians is Salman [an early Persian convert to Islam], the chief of the Byzantines is Suhayb [Christian convert among the Companions of the Prophet] and the chief of Abyssinia is Bilal [another convert and Islam's first muezzin]. The chief of the mountains is Mount Sinai, and the chief of the trees is the lote tree. The chief months are the sacred months and the chief day is Friday. The chief of all speech is the Quran, the chief of the Quran is the (second) sura, "The Cow," and the chief of "The Cow" is the Throne Verse. O Ali, it consists of fifty words and every word contains fifty blessings.' "

[AYOUB 1984: 247-248]

37. The "Satanic Verses"

If speculation on the Quran's mention of the throne of God is essentially the work of piety, other verses in the Book raised enormously complex exegetical and legal questions. The verses in question, the so-called "Satanic verses," occur in Sura 22 and are addressed to Muhammad.

We have sent no messenger or apostle before you with whose recitations Satan did not tamper. Yet God abrogates what Satan interpolates; then He confirms His revelations, for God is all-knowing, all-wise. This is in order to make the interpolations of Satan a test for those whose hearts are diseased and hardened. (Quran 22:52-53)

In connection with this itself quite extraordinary verse, the Muslim exegetical tradition has preserved a rather startling piece of information, namely, that some of the verses of the Quran originally read quite differently.

The occasion of the revelation of the present verse (22:52) is the following: As the members of the tribe of the Messenger of God turned away from him and took their stand in opposition to him, and as his relatives also opposed him and refused to be guided by what he brought to them, then, as a result of extreme exasperation over their estrangement, and of the eager desire and longing that they be converted to Islam, the Messenger of God hoped that nothing would be revealed to him that would make them shy away. . . . Now this wish persisted until the sura called "The Star" (Sura 53) came down. At that time he (still) found himself with that hope in his heart regarding the members of his tribe. Then he began to recite (53: 19–23):

> "Have you considered al-Lat and al-Uzza
> And Manat, the third, the other?
> Are there sons for you and daughters for Him?
> This is certainly an unjust apportioning.

"These are only names which you and your fathers have invented. No authority was sent down by God for them. They only follow conjecture and will-fulfillment, even though guidance had come already from their Lord."

When, however, he came to God's words "And Manat, the third, the other," Satan substituted something else conformable to the wish that the Messenger of God had been harboring, that is, he whispered something to him which would enable the Messenger to fulfill his wish. In an inadvertent and misleading manner his tongue hurried on ahead of him, so that he said: "These (goddesses) are the exalted cranes. Their intercession (with God) is to be hoped for. . . ." Yet the Messenger of God was not clear at this point until the protection (of God) reached him and he became attentive again.

Some say that Gabriel drew his attention to what had happened, or that Satan himself spoke these words and brought them to the people's hearing. As soon as the Messenger of God prostrated himself in prayer at the end of the sura, all who were present did it with him and felt pleased (that they had had their way). That the opportunity for doing this would be given to Satan constituted a temptation and it was God's test through which the hypocrites should increase in grievance and injury, but the believers should increase in enlightenment and assurance. (Zamakhshari, *The Unveiler of the Realities, ad loc.*)

38. The Revelation and Its Copy

The intrusion of these spurious verses into the Quran, followed by their removal, is mirrored in reverse by the question whether our copies of the Quran—its written exemplars—contain all the material revealed by God to His Prophet. The text itself gives us no reason to think that such is not the case, but the Muslim tradition preserves another recollection. As we shall see shortly, the Shi'ite Muslims have charged that the received text was indeed tampered with for sectarian reasons; but there are other, more fundamental cases of omissions that are more anomalous. The best-known example is that of a verse that prescribed stoning as a penalty for adultery and that was, on unimpeachable testimony, "memorized and recited" as part of the Quran in Muhammad's own lifetime. Yet it occurs nowhere in the text of the Book (see Chapter 5 below). If the "stoning verse" is the most celebrated example of genuine revelation not incorporated into the "copy" of the Quran, it is not the only one, as these canonically accepted traditions suggest.

Ubayy reports: "The Messenger of God said to me, 'God has commanded me to instruct you in the reciting of the Quran.' He then recited 'Did not those who rejected the Prophet among the People of the Book and the associators. . . .' The verse continued, 'Did the offspring of Adam possess a wadi of property,' or 'Were the offspring of Adam to ask for a wadi of property and he received it, he would ask for a second, and if he received that, he would demand a third wadi. Only dust will fill the maw of the offspring of Adam, but God relents to him who repents. The very faith in God's eyes is the original belief, not Judaism or Christianity. Who does good, it will never be denied him.' " (Suyuti, *Perfection in the Quranic Sciences*) [Cited by BURTON 1977: 82–83]

Ibn Abbas said, "Did the offspring of Adam possess two wadis of wealth, he would desire a third. Only dust will fill the maw of the offspring of Adam, but God relents to him who repents." Umar asked, "What is this?" Ibn Abbas replied that Ubayy had instructed him to recite this (as part of the Quran). Umar took Ibn Abbas to confront Ubayy. Umar said, "We don't say that." Ubayy insisted that the Prophet had so instructed him. Umar then asked him, "Shall I write it into the copy in that case?" Ubayy said, "Yes." This was before the copying of the Uthman codices (without the verses in question) and on which the practice now rests. (Burhan al-Din al-Baji, *Responsa*) [Cited by BURTON 1977: 83]

39. Uthman's Recension of the Quran

The assembled and ordered text of the Quran as we now possess it was the result of a cooperative work begun soon after the death of the Prophet. It was brought to completion by Uthman, an early companion of the Prophet and the third Caliph of the Muslim community (644–656 C.E.).

Zayd ibn Thabit said: Abu Bakr (Caliph, 632–634 C.E.) sent for me at the time of the battle of al-Yamama, and Umar ibn al-Khattab (Caliph, 634–644 C.E.) was with him. Abu Bakr said: Umar has come to me and said:

"Death raged at the battle of al-Yamama and took many of the reciters of the Quran. I fear lest death in battle overtake the reciters of the Quran in the provinces and a large part of the Quran be lost. I think you should give orders to collect the Quran."

"What," I asked Umar, "will you do something which the Prophet of God himself did not do?"

"By God," replied Umar, "it would be a good deed."

Umar did not cease to urge me until God opened my heart to this and I thought as Umar did.

Zayd continued: Abu Bakr said to me: "You are a young man, intelligent, and we see no fault in you, and you have already written down the revelation for the Prophet of God, may God bless and save him. Therefore go and seek the Quran and assemble it."

By God, if he had ordered me to move a mountain it would not have been harder for me than his order to collect the Quran. "What," I asked, "will you do something which the Prophet of God himself, may God bless and save him, did not do?"

"By God," replied Abu Bakr, "it would be a good deed."

And he did not cease to urge me until God opened my heart to this as He had opened the hearts of Abu Bakr and Umar.

Then I sought out and collected the parts of the Quran, whether written on palm leaves or flat stones or in the hearts of men. Thus I found the end of the "Sura of Repentance" (Quran 9:129–130), which I had been unable to find anywhere else, with Abu'l-Khuzayma al-Ansari. These were the verses "There came to you a Prophet from amongst yourselves. It grieves me that you sin . . ." to the end.

The leaves were with Abu Bakr until his death, then with Umar for as long as he lived, and then with Hafsa, the daughter of Umar.

Anas ibn Malik said: Hudhayfa ibn al-Yaman went with Uthman

when he was preparing the army of Syria to conquer Armenian and Azerbayjan, together with the army of Iraq. Hudhayfa was shocked by the differences in their reading of the Quran, and said to Uthman, "O Commander of the Faithful, catch this community before they differ about their book as do the Jews and the Christians."

Uthman sent to Hafsa to say, "Send us the leaves. We shall copy them in codices and return them to you."

Hafsa sent them to Uthman, who ordered Zayd ibn Thabit, Abdullah ibn al-Zubayr, Sa'id ibn al-As and Abd al-Rahman ibn al-Harith ibn Hisham to copy them into codices. Uthman said to the three of them who were of the tribe of the Quraysh, "If you differ from Zayd ibn Thabit on anything in the Quran, write it according to the language of the Quraysh, for it is in their language that the Quran was revealed."

They did this, and when they had copied the leaves into codices, Uthman returned the leaves to Hafsa. He sent copies of the codex which they made in all directions and gave orders to burn every leaf and codex which differed from it. (Bukhari, *Sahih* 3.392–394) [LEWIS 1974: 2:1–2]

40. Who Put Together the Suras?

One striking feature of the Quran as we possess it is the fact that only one sura, Sura 9, also called "Repentance" or "Immunity," does not open with the formula "In the Name of God, the Compassionate, the Merciful." The following Prophetic tradition explains the anomaly and sheds some light as well on how the suras might have been put together.

Ibn Abbas said he asked Uthman what had induced him to deal with (Sura 8 called) "The Spoils," which is one of the medium-sized suras, and with (Sura 9 called) "Immunity," which is one with a hundred verses, joining them without writing the line containing "In the Name of God, the Compassionate, the Merciful," and putting it among the seven long suras (at the beginning of the Quran). When he asked again what had induced him to do that, Uthman replied: "Over a period suras with numerous verses would come down to the Messenger of God, and when something came down to him he would call one of those who wrote and tell him to put those verses in the sura in which such-and-such was mentioned, and when a (single) verse came down he would tell them to put it in the sura in which such-and-such is mentioned. Now 'The Spoils' was one of the first to come down in Medina, and 'Immunity' was among the last of the Quran to come down, and the subject matter of one resembled that of the other, so because the Messenger of God was taken (by death) without having explained to us whether it ('Immunity') belonged to it ('The Spoils'), I joined them without writing the line containing 'In the Name of God, the Compassionate, the Merciful," and put it among the long suras." Ahmad ibn Hanbal, Tirmidhi and Abu Dawud transmitted this tradition. (Baghawi, *Mishkat al-Masabih* 8.3)

41. The Seven "Readings" of the Quran

The Quran, with its vowels unmarked in the manner of Semitic writing and transcribed in a still somewhat defective script—the Quran is the earliest Arabic literary text committed to writing—was open to different manners of reading and pronunciation. The Hebrew Bible had gone through similar uncertainties until its own textual standardization. Here we stand at the beginning of the same process as it affected the Quran.

Umar ibn al-Khattab said: I heard Hisham ibn Hakim ibn Hizam reciting the sura (called) "The Criterion" [that is, Sura 25] in a manner different from my way of reciting it, and it was the Messenger of God who taught me how to recite it. I nearly spoke sharply to him, but I delayed until he had finished, and then catching his cloak by the neck, I brought him to God's Messenger and said: "Messenger of God, I heard this man reciting 'The Criterion' in a manner different from that in which you taught me to recite it." He told me to let the man go and bade him to recite. When he recited it in the manner in which I had (earlier) heard him recite it, God's Messenger said, "Thus it was sent down." He then told me to recite it, and when I had done so he said, "Thus it was sent down. The Quran was sent down in seven modes of reading, so recite according to what comes most easily."

Ibn Abbas reported God's Messenger as saying, "Gabriel taught me to recite in one mode, and when I replied to him and kept asking him to give me more, he did so till he reached seven modes." Ibn Shihab said he had heard that these seven modes were essentially one, not differing about what is permitted and what is prohibited. (Baghawi, *Mishkat al-Masabih* 8.3.1)

These Prophetic traditions represent the beginning of one aspect of the textual study of the Quran in Islam, that devoted to a proper "reading." Ibn Khaldun (d. 1406 C.E.), who stands at the end of the process, describes how it evolved.

The Quran is the word of God that was revealed to His Prophet and that is written down between the two covers of copies of the Quran. Its

transmission has been continuous in Islam. However, the men around
Muhammad transmitted it on the authority of the Messenger of God in
different ways. These differences affect certain of the words in it and the
manner in which the letters were pronounced. They were handed down
and became famous. Eventually, seven specific ways of reading the Quran
became established. Transmission of these Quranic readings with their
particular pronunciation was also continuous. They came to be ascribed
to certain men from among a large number of persons who had become
famous as their transmitters. The Seven Quran Readings became the basis
for reading the Quran. Later on other readings were occasionally added
to the seven. However, they are not considered by the authorities on
Quran reading to be as reliably transmitted (as the Seven).

The (Seven) Quran Readings are well known from books which deal
with them. Certain people have contested the continuity of their transmission. In their opinion they are ways of indicating the pronunciation,
and pronunciation is something which cannot definitely be fixed. This,
however, they thought not to reflect upon the continuity of the transmission of the Quran (itself). The majority do not admit their view. The
majority asserts the continuity of the transmission of the Seven Readings.
Others asserted the continuity of all Seven, save for certain fine points of
pronunciation. . . . Quran readers continued to circulate and transmit
these readings, until the knowledge of them was fixed in writing and
treated systematically. (Ibn Khaldun, *Muqaddima* 6.10)
[IBN KHALDUN 1967: 2:439–440]

The discipline of Quran readings is often extended to include also
the discipline of Quran orthography, which deals with usage of the letters
in copies of the Quran and with the orthography of the Quran. The
Quran uses many letters that are used differently than is usual in writing. . . . When the divergences in the usage and norm of writing made
their appearance, it became necessary to deal with them comprehen-
sively. Therefore, they too were written down when scholars fixed the
sciences in writing. (Ibid. 6.10) [IBN KHALDUN 1967: 2:442]

42. Textual Corruptions?
The Shi'ite View

God had helped you during the Battle of Badr at a time when you
were helpless. So act in compliance with the laws of God; you may well
be grateful. (Quran 3:123)

Some Muslim scholars had difficulty with this particular verse in the transmitted Quran.

"When you were helpless . . . ": al-Qummi and al-Ayyashi say according to (the Imam) Ja'far al-Sadiq: They were not helpless, for the Messenger of God was among them. (Actually the following) came down: "when you were weak. . . ." Al-Ayyashi reports according to Ja'far al-Sadiq that Abu Basir recited the verse in this manner in al-Sadiq's presence. Ja'far said that God had not revealed the verse in that form, but what had come down was "when you were few. . . ." In a Prophetic tradition it is said that God never cast down His Messenger and so what had been revealed was "when you were few. . . ." In several reliable reports it is said that they numbered three hundred and thirteen. (Kashi, *The Pure in the Interpretation of the Quran, ad loc.*)

This kind of textual criticism may have had no other object than to express a reservation on what was considered an unlikely thing for God to have said of His own Prophet. But in other instances the criticism is more direct and more pointed, namely that the text of God's Book had been tampered with in order to advance one sectarian view at the expense of another. The latter was most often the Shi'ites or "Party of Ali," who thought that spiritual leadership in the community had been reserved for Muhammad's cousin Ali ibn Abi Talib and his descendants. The silence of the Quran on this claim inevitably brought forth Shi'ite charges of tampering.

. . . And the oppressors will now come to know through what reversals they will be overthrown! (Quran 26:227)

Al-Qummi says: God mentioned their enemies and those who did wrong against them. He has said (in 26:227), "Those who have done wrong against the law of the family of Muhammad will (one day) know what kind of turning upside down they will experience." This is the way the verse was actually revealed. (Kashi, *The Pure, ad loc.*)

And this is the way the same Muhammad Murtada al-Kashi, a Shi'ite commentator (d. ca. 1505 C.E.), interpreted another critical Quranic passage.

O Messenger, announce what has reached you from your Lord, for if you do not, you will not have delivered His message. God will preserve you from men; for God does not guide those who do not believe. (Quran 5:67)

"Announce what has reached you": that is, concerning Ali. According to the tradition of the authorities on doctrine, this verse was actually revealed in this (extended) form [that is, including "concerning Ali"].

"For if you do not . . . ": If you discontinue the delivery of what has been sent down to you concerning Ali's guardianship (over the believers), and you keep this secret, then it is as if you delivered none of the message of the Lord concerning that which requires reconciliation. Some also read: "His message concerning the confession of the unity of God. . . ."

"God does not guide those who do not believe": In the *Collection* (of al-Tabarsi) it is said on the authority of Ibn Abbas and Jabir ibn Abdullah that God commanded His Prophet to place Ali before men and to (publicly) inform them of his guardianship (over them). The Prophet, however, was afraid that they would say, "He is protecting his cousin," and that a group of his companions might find this distressing. The present verse came down regarding this. On the following day, the Prophet took Ali gently by the hand and said: "Whose protector I am, their protector (also) is Ali." Then he recited the verse in question. (Kashi, *The Pure, ad loc.*)

43. The Proofs of Prophecy

Among the voluminous works of the essayist al-Jahiz (d. 886 C.E.) is one entitled The Proofs of Prophecy. In it he took up the question of why the earliest generations of Muslims did not, like the Christians, make a systematic collection of the various and many proofs of Muhammad's prophetic calling.

Let us return to the question of the signs and tokens of the Prophet, and the arguments in favor of his proofs and testimonies. I say this: If our ancestors, who compiled written editions of the Quran, which up to that point had been scattered in men's memories, and united the people behind the reading of Zayd ibn Thabit, while formerly other readings were in free circulation, and established a text free from all additions and omissions, if those early Muslims had likewise collected the signs of the Prophet, his arguments, proofs, and miracles, the various manifestations of his wondrous life, both at home and abroad, and even on the occasion when he preached to a great multitude, to a crowd so large that its testimony cannot be questioned except by ignorant fools or the bigoted opponents (of Islam), if they had done so, today no one could challenge the truth of these things, neither the godless dualist, nor the stubborn materialist, not even the licentious fop, the naive moron, or callow stripling. This tradition of the Prophet would then have been as well known among the common people as among the elite, and all our notables would see the truth (of their religion) as clearly as they see the falsity (of the beliefs) of Christians and Zoroastrians. . . .

The first Muslims were led (to commit this omission) by their confidence in the manifest nature (of the acts of the Prophet); but we ourselves have come to this state because dunces, youths, madmen and libertines lack the proper care and show themselves totally unconcerned, callow and neglectful; also because, before acquiring even the elements of dialectical theology, they filled their heads with more subtleties than their strength can manage or their minds contain. (Jahiz, *The Proofs of Prophecy* 119)

44. Muhammad, the Seal of the Prophets

Christianity rested its claim upon a Messiah who was sent not so much to teach the Kingdom of God as to proclaim it in his own person. For the Christian, Jesus did not belong in the company of the prophets but represented a unique figure in God's plan, the Son of God promised from the beginning and whose redemptive death required no sequel. With Islam we are back on biblical ground, however. Muhammad is one of a line of prophets stretching back to Adam and reaching forward through Abraham and Moses, David and Solomon, until it reached Jesus. And, according to the Quran, although Muhammad had predecessors, he would have no successor.

Muhammad is not the father of any man among you, but a messenger of God and the seal of the Prophets. God has knowledge of every thing. (Quran 33:40)

The commentators took the verse as self-evident.

"But (he is) a messenger of God": Every messenger is the father of his religious community insofar as they are obliged to respect and honor him, and he is obliged to care for them and give them advice. . . .

"And the seal of the Prophets": . . . If one asks how Muhammad (as the seal of the Prophets) can be the last Prophet when Jesus will come down at the end of time [that is, to announce the Day of Judgment and suffer death], then I reply that Muhammad's being the last of the prophets means that no one else will (afterwards) be active as a prophet; Jesus was active as a prophet before Muhammad. And when Jesus comes down he will do this because he devotes himself to the law of Muhammad and performs his prayer according to Muhammad's direction of prayer [that is, facing Mecca], as if he were a member of this community. (Zamakhshari, *The Unveiler of the Realities, ad loc.*)

Another already cited verse opens the perspective somewhat.

We have sent no messenger or apostle before you with whose recitations Satan did not tamper. (Quran 22:52)

The second half of the verse requires its own exegesis, as we have already seen in connection with the "Satanic verses." Our concern here is with the opening phrase, which speaks to an important distinction.

"We have sent no messenger or prophet . . . ": This is a clear proof that there is a difference between a "Messenger" (*rasul*) and a "Prophet" (*nabi*). It is related from the Prophet that once when he was asked about the Prophets, he replied: "There are one hundred and twenty-four thousand." And when he was then asked how many Messengers there were among those, he answered, "The great host of three hundred and thirteen." The distinction between the two is that a Messenger is one of the Prophets to whom the Book is sent down, together with a miracle confirming it. A Prophet, on the other hand, who is not an Apostle, is one to whom no book has been sent down, but who was commanded only to restrain people on the basis of the earlier revealed Law. (Zamakhshari, *The Unveiler, ad loc.*)

45. Muhammad among the Prophets

The question mooted by Zamakhshari is in part exegetical—the occurrence in the Quran of two distinct terms, "Messenger" and "Prophet"—but arises as well from the need to separate and distinguish Muhammad from the other prophets, biblical and nonbiblical, mentioned in the Quran. Zamakhshari's criterion, that the Messenger is the recipient of a public revelation, which separates Muhammad from Jeremiah or Isaiah, for example, and brackets him with Moses and Jesus, was not the only distinction possible. In the passage of Suyuti (d. 1505 C.E.) that follows, the comparison is straightforward, detailed, and obviously popular. The context is said to be a meeting between Muhammad, accompanied by Umar, and the Jews of Medina. When Umar praises Muhammad, the Jews retort that he must be talking about Moses. Umar turns to Muhammad and asks, "Alas for my soul, was Moses better than you?"

Then the Messenger of God, may God bless him and grant him peace, said: "Moses is my brother, but I am better than he, and I was given something more excellent than he was." The Jews said: "This is what we wanted!" "What is that?" he asked. They said: "Adam was better than you; Noah was better than you; Moses was better than you; Jesus was better than you; Solomon was better than you." He said: "That is false. I am better than all these and superior to them." "You are?" they asked. "I am," he said. They said, "Then bring a proof of that from the Torah."

Muhammad agrees but must invoke the assistance of one of his Jewish converts, Abdullah ibn Salam, to check the Torah, presumably because he could read Hebrew, while Muhammad was, as the Muslim tradition maintained, "unlettered." The discussion reported by Suyuti continues.

"Now why," Muhammad asked, "is Adam better than I?" "Because," they answered, "God created him with His own hand and breathed into him of His spirit." "Adam," he then replied, "is my father, but I have been given something better than anything he has, namely, that every day a herald calls five times from the East to the West: 'I bear witness that there is no god but the God and I bear witness that Muhammad is the Messenger of God.' No one has ever said that Adam was the Messenger of God. Moreover, on the Day of Resurrection the Banner of Praise will be in my hand and not in that of Adam." "You speak but the truth," they replied, "that is so written in the Torah." "That," he said, "is one."

Said the Jews: "Moses is better than you." "And why?" he inquired. "Because," they said, "God spoke to him four thousand four hundred and forty words, but never did He speak a thing to you." "But I," he responded, "was given something superior to that." "And what was that?" they asked. Said he: "Glory be to Him who took His servant by night (Quran 17:1), for He bore me up on Gabriel's wing until He brought me to the seventh heaven, and I passed beyond the Sidra tree of the Boundary at the Garden of Resort (Quran 53:14–15) till I caught hold of a leg of the Throne, and from above the Throne came a voice: 'O Muhammad, I am God. Beside me there is no other god.' Then with all my heart I saw my Lord. This is more excellent than that (given to Moses)." "You speak but the truth," they replied, "that is so written in the Torah." "That," he said, "makes two."

Noah is then similarly disposed of. "Well," said Muhammad, "that is three."

They said: "Abraham is better than you . . . God Most High took him as a friend." He answered, "Abraham was indeed the friend of God, but I am His beloved. Do you know why my name is Muhammad? It is because He derived it from His name. He is Al-Hamid, the Praiseworthy, and my name is Muhammad, the Praised, while my community are the Hamidun, those who give praise." "You speak but truly," they replied, "this is greater than that." "That is four."

"But Jesus," they said, "is better than you . . . because he mounted up to the pinnacle of the Temple in Jerusalem, where the satans came to bear him away, but God gave command to Gabriel who with his right wing smote them in their faces and cast them into the fire." "Nevertheless," he said, "I was given something better than that. I returned from fighting with the polytheists on the day of Badr exceedingly hungry, when there met me a Jewish woman with a basket on her head. In the basket there was a roasted kid, and in her sleeve some sugar. She said: 'Praise be to God who has kept you safe. I made a vow to God that if you returned safely from this warlike expedition I would not fail to sacrifice this kid for you to eat.' Then she set it down and I put my hand to it, which caused the kid to speak, standing upright on its four feet, and saying, 'Eat not of me, for I am poisoned.' " "You speak but true," they said. "That is five, but there remains one more, for we claim that Solomon was better than you."

"Why?" he asked. "Because," they said, "God subjected to him satans, jinn, men and winds, and taught him the language of the birds and insects." "Yet," he replied, "I have been given something superior to that. God subjected to me Buraq (the miraculous beast that bore Muhammad on the Night Journey), who is more precious than all the world. He is one of the riding-beasts of Paradise. . . . Between his eyes is written 'There is no god but the God. Muhammad is the Messenger of God.' " "You speak truly," they said, "we bear witness that there is no god but the God and that you are His servant and Messenger." (Suyuti, *Glittering Things*)
[JEFFERY 1962: 334–336]

Finally, in the course of his Night Journey and Ascension to Heaven, Muhammad was given sight of his fellow prophets, whose physical appearance is relayed, on his authority, in his standard biography.

Al-Zuhri alleged as from Sa'id al-Musayyab that the Messenger described to his companions Abraham, Moses and Jesus as he saw them that night, saying: "I have never seen a man more like myself than Abraham. Moses was a ruddy-faced man, tall, thinly fleshed, curly haired with a hooked nose as if he were of the Shanu'a. Jesus son of Mary was a reddish man of medium height with lank hair and with many freckles on his face as though he had just come from a bath. One would suppose that his head was dripping with water, though there was no water on it. The man most like him among you is Urwa ibn Mas'ud al-Thaqafi." (*Life* 266)
[IBN ISHAQ 1955: 183–184]

46. The Prophet-King of the Virtuous City

Muslim contact with Greek philosophical thought introduced other, more rigorous ways of thinking about the question of prophecy, whether of the modalities of the transmission or of the characteristics of the prophet. The first of the Muslim thinkers to integrate Greek political and cognitive theories into a religious system like Islam's, which hinged upon a prophetic revelation, was al-Farabi (d. ca. 950 C.E.). Philo of Alexandria had already done some of the work in the first century by putting Moses and the philosophers side by side as parallel phenomena. Farabi was perhaps the first to resume the discussion in Islam, but now within the framework of Plato's political theories and with considerable help from Hellenic theories of cognition. These enabled Farabi to explain how the process of prophetic revelation occurred.

Since what is intended by man's existence is that he attain supreme happiness, he—in order to achieve it—needs to know what happiness is, make it his end, and hold it before his eyes. Then, after that, he needs to know the things he ought to do in order to attain happiness, and then do the actions. In view of what has been said about the differences of natural dispositions of individual men, not everyone is disposed to know happiness on his own, or the things he ought to do, but needs a teacher and a guide for this purpose.

That teacher and guide is the prophet or, to put it within Farabi's own Plato-derived categories, the ideal ruler of the equally idealized polity called by Farabi "the virtuous city." How that prophet-king receives his own illumination is the next subject taken up by the Muslim philosopher.

The supreme ruler without qualification is he who does not need anyone to rule him in anything whatever, but has actually acquired the sciences and every kind of knowledge, and has no need of a man to guide him in anything. He is able to comprehend well each one of the particular things he ought to do. He is able to guide well all others to everything in which he instructs them, to employ all those who do any of the acts for which they are equipped, and to determine, define and direct these acts toward happiness. This is found only in the one who possesses great and superior natural dispositions, when his soul is in union with the (separate and higher) Active Intellect. He can only attain this (union with the Active Intellect) by first acquiring the passive intellect and the intellect called the acquired; for, as was stated in *On the Soul*, union with the Active Intellect results from possessing the acquired intellect. This man is the true prince according to the ancients; he is the one of whom it ought to be said that he receives revelation. For man receives revelation only when he attains this rank, that is, when there is no longer an intermediary between him and the Active Intellect; for the passive intellect is like matter and substratum to the acquired intellect, and the latter is like matter and substratum to the Active Intellect. It is then that the power that enables man to understand how to define things and actions and how to direct them toward happiness, emanates from the (separate and higher) Active Intellect to the (human) passive intellect. This emanation that proceeds from the Active Intellect to the passive through the mediation of the acquired intellect is revelation. Now because the Active Intellect emanates from the being of the First Cause [that is, God], it can for this reason be said that it is the First Cause that brings about revelation to this man through the mediation of the Active Intellect. The rule of this man is the supreme rule; all other human rulerships are inferior to it and derived from it. Such is his rank. (Farabi, *The Political Regime* 47–50)

[LERNER & MAHDI 1972: 35–37]

47. The Prophet as Lawgiver

This emanation of the intelligible truths from the higher, angelic Active Intellect into the highly developed intellect of an individual man becomes the accepted mode of prophecy among the philosophers. The prophet is, then, a philosopher in his understanding of those truths and becomes a prophet only by turning toward society and converting those truths, or at least some of them, into an idiom comprehensible to the masses who cannot philosophize and so need guidance on their path to happiness and salvation. So it is set forth by one of Farabi's successors in the Islamic philosophical tradition, the physician, statesman, and polymath Ibn Sina (d. 1038 C.E.), or Avicenna as he came to be called in the West. In this passage from his Book of Deliverance *it is first established that man is a social animal and will of necessity associate with other men and transact business. These transactions require a code of law, which in turn calls for a lawgiver, someone "in the position to speak to men and constrain them to accept the code; he must therefore be a man." Avicenna continues.*

Now it is not feasible that men should be left to their own opinions in this matter so that they will differ each from the other, every man considering as justice that which favors him, and as injustice that which works against his advantage. The survival and complete self-realization of the human race requires the existence of such a lawgiver. . . .

It follows therefore that there should exist a prophet, and that he should be a man; it also follows that he should have some distinguishing feature which does not belong to other men, so that his fellows may recognize him as possessing something which is not theirs, and so that he may stand out apart from them. This distinguishing feature is the power to work miracles.

Such a man, if and when he exists, must prescribe laws for mankind governing all their affairs, in accordance with God's ordinance and authority, God inspiring him and sending down the Holy Spirit upon him. The fundamental principle upon which his [that is, the prophet's] code rests will be to teach them that they have One Creator, Almighty and Omniscient, whose commandments must of right be obeyed; that the Command must belong to Him who possesses the power to create and that He has prepared for those who obey Him a future life of bliss but wretchedness for such as disobey Him. So the masses will receive the prescriptions, sent down upon his tongue from God and the Angels, with heedful obedience. (Avicenna, *Book of Deliverance*) [AVICENNA 1951: 42–44]

48. Avicenna on the Prophethood of Muhammad

There is little in Avicenna's description of the lawgiver to suggest that Muhammad had either a unique role among the prophets or that the possibility of prophetic revelation ended with him. But in one of his works, On the Proof of the Prophecies, *Avicenna appears to take up the case of the prophethood of Muhammad, for reasons he explains as the outset.*

You have asked—may God set you aright—that I sum up for you in a treatise the substance of what I said to you with a view to eliminate your misgivings about accepting prophecy. You are confirmed in these misgivings because the claims of the advocates of prophecy are either logically possible assertions that are treated as necessary without the benefit of (rigorous) demonstrative argument or even of (secondary) dialectical proof, or else impossible assertions on the order of fairy tales, such that the very attempt on the part of their advocate to expound them deserves derision.

Avicenna then gives his own succinct explanation of what prophetic revelation is and how it occurs.

Revelation is the emanation and the angel is the received emanating power that descends on the prophets as if it were an emanation continuous with the Universal Intellect. It is rendered particular, not essentially, but accidentally, because of the particularity of the recipient. Thus the angels have been given different names because (they are associated with) different notions; nevertheless, they form a single totality, which is particularized, not essentially, but accidentally, by the particularity of the recipient. The message, therefore, is that part of the emanation termed "revelation" which has been received and couched in whatever mode of expression is deemed best for furthering man's good in both the eternal and the corruptible worlds as regards knowledge and political governance, respectively. The messenger is the one who conveys what he acquires of the emanation termed "revelation," again in whatever mode of expression is deemed best for achieving through his opinions the good of the sensory world by political governance and of the intellectual world by knowledge.

There immediately follows this curiously reticent conclusion.

This, then, is the summary of the discourse concerning the affirmation of prophecy, the showing of its essence, and the statements made about revelation, the angel and the thing revealed. As for the validity of the prophethood of our prophet, of Muhammad, may God's prayers and peace be upon him, it becomes evident to the reasonable man once he compares him with the other prophets, peace be on them. We shall refrain from elaboration here. (Avicenna, *On the Proof of Prophecies* 120–124) [LERNER & MAHDI 1972: 113–115]

49. Maimonides on Prophecy

Farabi's thinking on prophecy and prophethood is particularly evident in the philosophical works of Maimonides (d. 1204 C.E.). As has been remarked, Islam, like Judaism, mediated its revelation through prophets, and so the Jewish thinker found as much to meditate upon in Hellenic thought on the subject of inspiration as the Muslims had before him.

The opinions of people concerning prophecy are like their opinions concerning the eternity of the world or its creation in time. I mean by this that just as the people to whose mind the existence of the deity is firmly established, have, as we have set forth, three opinions concerning the eternity of the world or its creation in time, so there are three opinions concerning prophecy. . . .

The first opinion—that of the multitude of those among the pagans who considered prophecy as true and also believed by some of the common people professing our Law—is that God, may He be exalted, chooses whom He wishes among men, turns him into a prophet, and sends him with a mission. According to them it makes no difference whether this individual is a man of knowledge or ignorant, aged or young.

However, they also posit as a condition his having a certain goodness and sound morality. For up to now people have not gone so far as to say that God sometimes turns a wicked man into a prophet unless He has first, according to this opinion, turned him into a good man.

The second opinion is that of the philosophers. It affirms that prophecy is a certain perfection in the nature of man. This perfection is not achieved in any individual from among men except after a training that makes that which exists in the potentiality of the species pass into actuality. . . . According to this opinion, it is not possible that an ignoramus should turn into a prophet; nor can a man not be a prophet on a certain evening and be a prophet on the following morning, as though he had made some discovery. Things are rather as follows: When, in the case of a superior individual who is perfect with respect to his rational and moral qualities, his imaginative faculty is in its most perfect state and when he has been prepared in the way that you will hear, he will necessarily become a prophet, inasmuch as this is a perfection that belongs to us by nature. According to this opinion, it is not possible that an individual should be fit for prophecy and prepared for it and not become a prophet, no more than it is possible that an individual having a healthy temperament should be nourished with excellent food without sound blood and similar things being generated from that food.

The third opinion is the opinion of our Law and the foundation of our doctrine. It is identical with the philosophic opinion except for one thing. For we believe that it may happen that one who is fit for prophecy and prepared for it should not become a prophet, namely on account of the divine will. To my mind this is like all the miracles and takes the same course as they. For it is a natural thing that everyone who according to his natural disposition is fit for prophecy and who has been trained in his education and study should become a prophet. But he who is prevented from it is like him who has been prevented, like Jereboam (1 Kings 13:4), from moving his hand or, like the King of Aram's army going out to seek Elisha (2 Kings 6:18), from seeing. As for its being fundamental with us that the prophet must possess preparation and perfection in the moral and rational qualities, it is indubitably the opinion expressed in their dictum: "Prophecy only rests upon a wise, strong, and rich man" (BT. Shabbath 92a). . . . As for the fact that someone who prepares is sometimes prevented from becoming a prophet, you may know from the history of Baruch, son of Neriah. For he followed Jeremiah, who taught, trained and prepared him. And he set himself the goal of becoming a prophet, but was prevented, as he says: "I am weary with my groaning and find no rest" (Jer. 45:3). Thereupon he was told through Jeremiah: "Thus shall you say to him: Thus says the Lord etc. . . . And do you seek great things for yourself? Seek them not" (Jer. 45:2, 5). It is possible to say that this is a clear statement that prophecy was too great a thing for Baruch. Similarly, it may be said, as we shall explain, that in the passage, "Yes, her prophets find no vision from the Lord" (Lam. 2:9), this was the case because they were in exile.

We shall find many texts, some of them scriptural and some of them dicta of the Sages, all of which maintain this fundamental principle that God turns whomever He wills, whenever He wills it, into a prophet, but only someone perfect and superior to the utmost degree. But with regard to one of the ignorant among the common people, this—I mean, that he should turn into a prophet—is not possible according to us except as it is possible that He should turn an ass or a frog into a prophet. It is our fundamental principle that there must be training and perfection, where-upon the possibility arises to which the power of the deity becomes attached. (Maimonides, *Guide of the Perplexed* 2.32) [MAIMONIDES 1963: 360–362]

50. Moses Unique among the Prophets

If what Maimonides says is true of all prophets, he is willing to make the case—the same that Avicenna was apparently reluctant to make regarding Muhammad—that Moses stands apart from all those who went before him or came after him. And the first argument for this, Maimonides insists with a sidelong glance at Islam, is that "to every prophet except Moses our Master prophetic revelation comes through an angel." Then there is Scripture itself.

To my mind the term "prophet" used with reference to Moses and to the others is amphibolous. The same applies, in my opinion, to his miracles and to the miracles of others, for his miracles do not belong to the class of the miracles of other prophets. The proof taken from the Law as to his prophecy being different from that of all who came before him is constituted by His saying: "And I appeared to Abraham, etc., but by My name, the Lord, I made not known to them" (Exod. 6:3). Thus it informs us that his (Moses') apprehension was not like the Patriarchs', but greater—nor, all the more, like that of others who came before. As for the difference between his prophecy and that of all those who came after, it is stated by way of communicating information in the dictum: "And there has not arisen a prophet since in Israel like Moses, whom the Lord knew face to face" (Deut. 34:10). Thus it has been made clear that his apprehension is different from that of all men who came after him in

Israel, which is "a kingdom of priests and a holy nation" (Exod. 19:6) and "in whose midst is the Lord" (Num. 16:3), and, all the more, from the apprehension of those who came in other religious communities.

It is not merely the quality of Moses' apprehension of the divine presence that sets him apart; there is also the evidence of the signs and miracles worked through him.

As for the difference between his miracles in general and those of every prophet in general, it should be said that all the miracles worked by the prophets or for them were made known to very few people only. Thus, for example, the signs of Elijah and Elisha. . . . The same holds good for the signs of all the prophets except Moses our Master. For this reason Scripture makes it clear, likewise by way of information with reference to him, that no prophet will ever arise who will work signs both before those who are favorably and those who are unfavorably disposed toward him, as was done by Moses. (Maimonides, *Guide of the Perplexed* 2.35) [MAIMONIDES 1963: 367–368]

51. Muhammad on Moses and the Torah

Muhammad, as might be expected, had a quite different view of the matter, as appears in this report attributed to him in the Muslim tradition.

Jabir told how Umar ibn al-Khattab brought God's Messenger a copy of the Torah saying, "Messenger of God, this is a copy of the Torah." When he received no reply he began to read from it to the obvious displeasure of the Messenger of God, so Abu Bakr said, "Confound you, do you not see how the Messenger of God is looking?" So Umar looked at the face of God's Messenger and said, "I seek refuge in God from the anger of God and His Messenger. We are satisfied with God as Lord, with Islam as religion and with Muhammad as Prophet." Then God's Messenger said, "By Him in whose hand my soul rests, were Moses to appear to you and you were to follow him and abandon me, you would err from the right path. Were Moses alive and and came in touch with my Prophetic mission, he would follow me." (Baghawi, *Mishkat al-Masabih* 1.6.3)

52. On the Inspiration of the Quran

European Christian opinion on Islam, its Prophet, and its Sacred Book was generally brutal and ignorant. In some cases there was little excuse for the ignorance since there were not a few Christians who had been and would continue to go to the

Middle East on pilgrimage, and so had been exposed to Islam at first hand. And of those there were even some few who learned Arabic and had studied both Islam and its Scripture. One of those latter was Ricoldo di Monte Croce, a Dominican monk who lived for an extended period in the East from 1288 onwards and who had not only visited Jerusalem but had studied in Baghdad. He had some appreciation of his subject, surely, but he was also an heir to the experience of the Crusades, whose atrocities had coarsened perceptions on both sides. More, Ricoldo was unabashedly a missionary, striving for the conversion of the infidel and awaiting, if need be, his own martyrdom at their hands. His Itinerary *was written in 1294 C.E.*

The Saracens can be easily convicted of error and refuted by the Holy Books and the authority of Sacred Scripture, by the books of the philosophers and the way of reason, and even more easily by the Alcoran itself which manifests its own abominable falsity to anyone who reads it. They can also be easily confounded by the scandalous life of their own prophet Muhammad, who led a life consumed by indulgence, adultery and rapine down to his last breath. . . . The Saracens themselves say that Muhammad, a single man, could not produce the Alcoran without God's help, with its many references to the Old and New Testaments. In fact, there are many more things there *against* the Old and New Testaments. And finally, it is known as an absolute certainty in many parts of the East that Muhammad had three teachers, namely two Jews, one of them Salon [Salman] the Persian and the name of the other Abdullah, which means "servant of God," son of Sela. These two became Saracens and taught him a great deal about the Old Testament and the Talmud. The third was a monk and his name was Bahheyin [Bahira], a Jacobite, who narrated to him much from the New Testament and certain information from a book about the infancy of the Savior and about the Seven Sleepers, and Muhammad wrote down those things in the Alcoran. But his chief teacher was, I think, the devil. (Ricoldo di Monte Croce, *Itinerarium*)

[LAURENT 1873: 137–141]

2. On Understanding Scripture

1. "In the Beginning":
The Great Exegesis

We have already seen some of the approaches taken toward understanding the Bible. A great deal of attention was given to the cultic and legal matters that loom so large in both the Torah and the Jewish life that flowed from it. But the Book begins with neither cult nor law but with what first the Jews and later the Christians and Muslims recognized as the beginning of God's discourse on His own creation. With the opening verse of Genesis we are standing, quite literally, at the beginning of the universe.

We do not know how these words were understood by the first generation of believers to have heard them, though surely even they struggled for some understanding. For examples of preserved interpretations we must move far later into the tradition, in this instance to a work called the "Book of Jubilees," the work of an anonymous Jewish author of the second century B.C.E. The approach is straightforward, in many instances a summary retelling of Genesis, though with some interesting additions—the angels, for example.

On the first day He created the tall heavens and the earth and the waters and all the spirits who served Him: the angels of the presence, the angels of sanctification, the angels of the spirit of fire, the angels of the spirits of the winds, of the clouds, of darkness, of snow, hail and hoarfrost, the angels of the voices of thunder and lightning, the angels of the spirits of cold and heat, of winter, spring, autumn and summer, and of all the spirits of His creatures in Heaven and on the earth. He created the abysses and darkness, twilight and night, and light, dawn, and day, and He prepared them in the knowledge of His heart. Thereupon we saw His works and praised them.

When the account reaches the fourth day of creation, some of the author's cultic interests appear.

And on the fourth day He created the sun and the moon and the stars, and placed them in the firmament of heaven to give light on earth, to rule over day and night, to separate light from darkness. And God appointed the sun to be a great sign on the earth for days and for sabbaths and for months, for feasts, years, sabbaths of years, for jubilees, and every season of the year. (Jubilees 2:1, 8)

The Law was first given to Moses on Sinai many centuries after the events described in the opening of Genesis. That, however, was the "given" version of the Law; there was another, heavenly Torah that long antedated the Sinai revelation, as Jubilees reveals in speaking of Adam.

After Adam had completed forty days in the land where he was created, he was brought into the Garden of Eden to till and keep it. His wife was brought in on the eightieth day.

Genesis 2:15–25 makes no mention of those intervals, but there is a point to mentioning them here. The author, it appears, has his eyes fixed more closely on Leviticus 12:1–4 than on the text of the second chapter of Genesis.

For that reason the commandment is written on the heavenly tablets in regard to the mother: "She who bears a male shall remain in her uncleanness seven days and thirty-three days in the blood of purification. She shall not touch any hallowed things, nor enter into the sanctuary until the days for the male or female child are accomplished." This is law and testimony written down for Israel. (Jubilees 3:10)

The task of explicating Genesis began before Jubilees and continues to the present day through many different channels and from a great many different perspectives. Typical of what might fairly be called a "consensual" approach is the work called Midrash Rabbah, or the "Great Exegesis." Although that part of it which deals with Genesis—the Midrash Genesis Rabbah—is dated as it stands to the fifth Christian century, it is likely a composite of various opinions of Palestinian rabbis of the two or three preceding centuries. The texture is obviously much richer and more anecdotal, but it does not differ greatly from what one reads in Jubilees: it is a "legalizing," nonsectarian approach to the opening of the Bible.

"In the beginning God created": Six things preceded the creation of the world; some of them were actually created, while the creation of others was already contemplated. The Torah and the Throne of God were created (before the creation of the world). The Torah, for it is written, "The Lord made me as the beginning of His way, prior to His works of old" (Prov. 8:22). The Throne of God, as it is written, "Your throne is established of old . . ." (Ps. 93:2). The creation of the Patriarchs was contemplated, for it is written, "I saw your fathers as the first-ripe in the fig tree at her first season" (Hos. 9:10). (The creation of) Israel was contemplated, as it is written, "Remember Your congregation, which You have gotten aforetime" (Ps. 74:2). (The creation of) the Temple was contemplated, for it is written, "Your throne of glory, on high from the beginning, the place of our sanctuary" (Jer. 17:12). The name of the Messiah was contemplated, for it is written, "His name exists before the sun" (Ps. 72:17). Rabbi Ahabah ben Zeʿira said: Repentance too, as it is written, "Before the mountains were brought forth, etc." (Ps. 90:2), and from that very moment, "You turn man to contrition, and say: Repent, you children of men" (ibid. 90:3). I still do not know which was first, whether the Torah preceded the Throne of Glory or the Throne of Glory preceded the Torah. Rabbi Abba ben Kahana said: The Torah preceded the Throne of Glory, for it says, "The Lord made me as the beginning of His way, before His works of old," that is, before that of which it is written, "Your throne is established of old."

Rabbi Huna, reporting Rabbi Jeremiah in the name of Rabbi Samuel ben Rabbi Isaac, said: The intention to create Israel preceded everything else. This may be illustrated thus: A king was married to a certain lady, and had no son of her. On one occasion the king was found going through the marketplace and giving orders: "Take this ink, inkwell and pen for my son," at which people remarked: "He has no son; what does he want with ink and pen? Strange indeed!" Subsequently they concluded: "The king is an astrologer and has actually foreseen that he is destined to beget a son!" Thus, had not the Holy One, blessed be He, foreseen that after twenty-six generations [that is, from Adam to Moses] Israel would receive the Torah, He would not have written therein, "Command the Children of Israel."

Rabbi Banayah said: The world and the fullness thereof was created only for the sake of the Torah: "The Lord for the sake of wisdom founded the earth" (Prov. 3:19). Rabbi Berekiah said: For the sake of Moses: "And he chose The Beginning [that is, creation] for himself, for there a portion of a ruler was reserved" (Deut. 33:21).

Rabbi Huna said in Rabbi Mattenah's name: The world was created for the sake of three things: the dough offering, tithes and firstfruits, as it is said, "In the beginning God created." Now "beginning" refers to the dough offering, for it is written, "Of the beginning of your dough" (Num. 15:20); again "beginning" refers to tithes, for it is written, "The beginnings of your grain" (Deut. 18:4); and finally, "beginning alludes to firstfruits, for it is written, "The beginning (or firstfruits) of your land, etc." (Exod. 23:19). (*Genesis Rabbah* 1.4–7) [MIDRASH RABBAH 1977: 1:6–7]

2. The Kabbala on Torah, Body and Soul

There is more to explaining the Torah than taking it phrase by phrase and extracting moral or legal lessons from them. Some Greeks believed their myths had an "undersense." In certain Jewish circles it was not so much a question of an "undersense" as an entire "under Torah." So, at any rate, it is expressed in one of the primary documents of what the Jews came to call the "Kabbala." Kabbala—variously Qabbalah and Cabala in the vagaries of English transcription—is quite simply "the tradition," something handed down. What was handed down was somewhat less simple, however: it is a large body of esoteric learning, theosophy of both the alphabetic and the numerical variety—in short, the mysteries of God and His creation.

"Kabbala" is a generic term, but one of the primary works of which it is constituted is the Zohar, or "Book of Splendor," a tract purporting to be the esoteric reflections on the Torah of the second-century C.E. rabbi Simeon ben Yohai, but more likely the editorial work of the Spanish scholar Moses of Leon (d. 1305) operating on older and very heterogeneous material. And it is here that we learn of the body and soul of the Torah.

Rabbi Simeon said: Woe to the man who says that Torah intends to set forth mere stories and common tales. If that were so, then we would ourselves be able at once to put together a torah out of such common tales, and indeed a far more worthy one. And if it is the intention of the Torah to disclose everyday matters, then the rulers of this world have far better books; let us find them and make a torah of them.

We suddenly find ourselves back in the world of Jubilees, with its heavenly tablets of the Law.

All the words of Torah are sublime and lofty mysteries. See how the upper world and the lower world are in perfect balance—Israel below corresponds to the angels above. . . . When the angels descend into the world below they clothe themselves in a manner appropriate to this world, for if they did not do so, they would not be able to remain in this world, nor could the world endure them. And if it is so with the angels, how much more so must it be with the Torah, which created the angels and all the worlds, and through which all the worlds are maintained. When the Torah came down into this world, it clothed itself with the garments of this world, otherwise the world could not have endured it.

So the stories of the Torah are only the Torah's outer clothing. That man is lost who mistakenly thinks that that clothing is the Torah itself, and that there is nothing more to it. He shall have no portion in the world to come. That is why David said: "Open my eyes so that I may see wondrous things of Your Torah" (Ps. 119:18), that is to say, that I may see what is underneath the Torah's outer garment.

You see how a man's clothing is visible to all, and only the fool, when he sees someone clothed in fine raiment, looks no further: he considers the clothing as if it were the body, and then the body as if it were the soul. In like manner the Torah has a body, namely, the commandments of the Torah which are called "the bodies of the Torah." This body is clothed in garments composed of earthly tales. Foolish people look only at those garments, these tales of the Torah. They go no further, nor do they look at what is beneath the outer clothing. But those who are wiser look not at the clothes but at the body beneath them. And the genuine Sages, the servants of the Most High King, those who stood at Mount Sinai, look only at the soul of the Torah, which is the most elemental principle of all, the True Torah, and in the world to come they are destined to look at the soul of the soul of the Torah. (*Book of Splendor* 3.152a)

3. The "Work of Creation"

We have an opportunity to "look at the soul of the soul of the Torah" through the lens of the Zohar *itself.*

Before the Holy One, blessed be He, had created any image, or fashioned any form, He was alone without any likeness or form. Whoever seeks to apprehend Him as He was, prior to creation, when He existed without image, is forbidden to represent Him with any kind of form or image, whether it be with the letter H or Y, or even with the Holy Name, or with a single letter or sign of any kind. Thus, "You saw no kind of image" (Deut. 4:15) means: you did not see anything which possesses image or form.

But after He had fashioned the image of the Chariot of Supernal Man, He descended into it and was known through the image of YHWH [that is, Yahweh], so that men might apprehend him through His attributes, through each of them severally, and He was called El, Elohim, Shaddai, Zeva'ot, and YHWH, so that men might apprehend Him through His attributes. . . . For if His radiance had not been shed over all creation, how could men have apprehended Him, or how could the verse be true, "The whole earth is full of His glory" (Isa. 6:3)?

Woe to the man who would equate God with any single attribute, even with one that is truly His own. . . . It is like the sea. The waters of the sea in themselves cannot be grasped and give no form, but when they are poured into a vessel—the earth—they receive form. . . . In like manner the Cause of causes formed ten Primordial Numbers. He called Crown the source. In it there is no end of the flow of His radiance, and on this account He called Himself The Infinite. He possesses neither shape nor form, nor does any vessel exist there to contain Him or any means of knowing Him. It is to this that the saying refers, "Do not investigate things too hard for you, or inquire into what is hidden from you" (BT.Hagigah 13a).

The cautionary note cited from the Talmud was neither the beginning nor the end of the matter. The earlier Mishna is somewhat more specific.

The Work of Creation should not be expounded in the presence of two (persons), nor [the Work of] the Chariot in the presence of one, unless he is a sage and already has an independent understanding of the matter. (M.Hagiga 2:1)

The Mishna is obviously not concerned with the unexceptional exposition of Genesis of the type we have already seen from the "Great Exegesis." What is at stake here is what is being called the "Work of Creation," that is, the type of esoteric reading of Genesis already cited from the Book of Splendor. This kind of theosophic cosmogony must have had a long history, but its classic Jewish formulation is to be found in the Book of Creation, composed in Palestine sometime between the third and sixth century C.E. God created the world, the brief tract explains, by three principles: by limit, by letter, and by number.

There are ten Primordial Numbers and twenty-two Basic Letters.

. . .

The ten Primordial Numbers are:
One: the Spirit of the Living God.
Two: Air from the Spirit [the same word in Hebrew]. He engraved and carved out of the Air the twenty-two basic letters: three mother letters, seven double and twelve simple letters; and each of them has the same Spirit.
Three: Water from the Air. He engraved and carved out of the Water chaos and disorder, mud and mire. He made them into a kind of

seedbed; He raised them as a kind of wall; He wove them into a kind of roof. He poured snow of them and they became earth. . . .

Four: Fire from Water. He engraved and carved out of the Fire the Throne of Glory, the Offanim, the Seraphim, the Holy Creatures and the angels who minister. . . . He chose three of the simple letters, Y, H and W, and made them into His great name [that is, Yahweh]. With them He sealed six extremities. . . . (*Book of Creation* 1–15)

The six extremities are height, depth, east, west, south, and north, and they are the remaining six Primordial Numbers. Thus, in this system the Primordial Numbers 1–10 appear to be the primary emanations of God, with the Spirit of God emerging from 1, then the basic elements Air, Water, and Fire from 2–4. Out of the Air God then "engraves" the twenty-two letters of the Hebrew alphabet, from which come in turn everything from the constellations of the Zodiac to the organs of the human body. Out of Water come the primordial chaos and the physical universe. Finally, out of Fire arrives the spiritual universe, including that Throne-Chariot which became the point of departure for so much of Jewish mysticism. And what is the origin of all this esoteric learning apparently unknown to the Bible? The Book of Creation *concludes:*

When our father Abraham had come, inspected, investigated and understood, and had successfully engraved, combined, carved and computed, then the Lord of all was revealed to him. He set Abraham in His bosom, kissed him on the head, called him His own beloved, and He designated him His son. He made a covenant with him and with his descendants forever, "And Abraham believed in the Lord and He accounted it to him as righteousness" (Gen. 15:6).

This is the Book of the Letters of Abraham our father which is known as "The Laws of Creation." Whoever looks into it, there is no limit to his wisdom. (*Book of Creation* 61, 64)

4. Ramban on Genesis

The thoughts of the rabbis represented in the "Great Exegesis" and of those anonymous sages who stand behind the Kabbala appear to be irreconcilable worlds apart. That they were not—that both the esoteric and the legal-homiletic understanding of Scripture dwelled together at the heart of the Jewish tradition—can be seen in this selection from the great Provençal scholar Nachmanides (d. ca. 1270 C.E.), the universally revered and undoubtedly orthodox "Ramban."

"In the beginning God created": Rashi wrote: "This verse cries aloud for elucidation, as our Rabbis have explained it: 'For the sake of

Torah, which is called "The Beginning," as when it is said, "The Eternal One made me as the beginning of His way"; and for sake of Israel, who is also called "The Beginning," as when it is said, "Israel is the Eternal's hallowed portion, the beginning of His increase." ' "

This exegesis of our Rabbis is very hidden and secret for there are many things the rabbis found that are called "beginnings" and concerning which they give homiletic explanations, and those wanting in faith total up the number (of such things). For example, they [that is, the Rabbis] have said: "For the merit acquired by (fulfilling the commandments associated with) three things has the world been created: for the merit of the dough offering, for the merit of the tithes and for the merit of the firstfruits." "Beginning" surely signifies the dough offering, as it is said, "The beginning of your dough." "Beginning" certainly signifies the tithes, as it is said, "the beginning of your grain." "Beginning" surely signifies the firstfruits, as it is said, "the beginning (or firstfruits) of your land. . . .' "

Their intent in the above texts is as follows: the word "beginning" alludes to the creation of the world by Ten Primordial Numbers, and hints in particular to the Primordial Number called Wisdom, in which is the foundation of everything, even as it says "the Eternal has founded the earth by wisdom" (Prov. 3:19). This is the dough offering, and it is holy; it has no precise measure [that is, no fixed amount is prescribed by the Law], thus indicating the little understanding created beings have of it. Now just as a man counts ten measures—this alludes to the Ten Primordial Numbers—and sets aside one measure of the ten as a tithe, so do the wise men contemplate the tenth Primordial and speak about it. The dough offering, which is the single commandment pertaining to the dough, alludes to this. Now Israel, which is called "The Beginning" as mentioned above, is "the congregation of Israel," which is compared in the Song of Songs to a bride and whom Scripture in turn calls "daughter," "sister," and "mother." The Rabbis have already expressed this in a homiletic interpretation of the verse, "Upon the crown wherewith his mother has crowned him" (Song of Sol. 3:11), and in other places. Similarly, the verse concerning Moses, "and He chose The Beginning for himself," which they [that is, the Rabbis] interpret to mean that Moses our teacher contemplated the Deity through a lucid mirror, and he saw that which is called "The Beginning" for himself, and therefore he merited the Torah. Thus all the above interpretations have one meaning. Now it is impossible to discuss this explanation at length in writing, and even an allusion is dangerous since people might have thoughts concerning it which are

untrue. But I have mentioned this (brief explanation cited above) in order
to close the mouths of those wanting in faith and of little wisdom, who
scoff at the Rabbis. (Nachmanides, *Commentary on Genesis*)
[NACHMANIDES 1971: 20–22]

*What Nachmanides intends here is obviously more than simply elucidating the text.
He has, of course, to take account of the man who was by then already the major
interpreter of the Bible, the French scholar Rashi (d. 1105 C.E.) cited in the text.
More will be heard of Rashi throughout Nachmanides' commentary, but in this
passage the attempt is to reconcile, and defend, his more homiletically minded
predecessors with what he obviously considers the more fundamental esoteric reading
of Genesis.*

5. A Muslim Creation Story

*Just as in Jewish homiletic exegesis God created certain idealized forms of being
before turning to the making of material things, so too in Islam certain events
preceded the creation of the world. The following account is drawn from a genre that
was a rich source of such haggadic narratives in Islam, the "Stories of the Prophets."
This one is by the eleventh-century author al-Kisaʾi. Unlike either* Midrash Rabbah *or Nachmanides, the narrative makes no pretense of being a* commentary *upon
the Bible but simply an explanation of an event. One of its intentions is obviously
to harmonize the Quranic remarks about creation with the general tenor of the
Genesis account, though the actual text of this latter has faded almost invisibly into
the background of the Muslim narrative.*

Saʿid ibn Abbas, with whom may God be pleased: The first thing
that God created was the Preserved Tablet on which is preserved (a
record) of all that has been and all that will be till the Day of Resurrection
(cf. Quran 85:22). No one knows what is on it save God Most High. It is
of white pearl, and God created for it from another jewel a Pen whose
length is a five hundred year's journey, whose point is split, and from
which light flows as ink flows from the pens of this world. Then a call
came to the Pen, "Write," whereat the Pen from the terror of the sum-
moning trembled and shook so that there was a quavering in its "Glory
be to God" like the rumbling of thunder, then it entered on the Tablet
all that God bade it enter of all that is to be till the Day of Resurrection.
So the Tablet was filled up and the Pen ran dry, and he who is to be
fortunate was made fortunate, and he who is to be unfortunate was made
unfortunate.

Next is created a white pearl "the size of the heavens and the earth," which is transformed into water, reflecting Quran 21:30: "And from water We have produced every living thing." The account then continues, with echoes of Ezekiel 1 and 10 and Isaiah 61:1 (= Matt. 5:34–35).

Then God created the Throne out of a green jewel whose size and whose light no one can describe, and it was put on the billowing waves of the water. Wahb ibn Munabbih [another early Muslim authority] said that none of the former Scriptures failed to mention the Throne and the footstool, for God created them from two mighty jewels. Ka'b al-Ahbar said that the Throne has seventy thousand tongues with which it glorifies God in a variety of languages. It was upon the water, as He says: "Now His throne was upon the water" (Quran 11:7). Ibn Abbas said that every architect builds the foundation first and later sees to the roof, but God created the roof first since He created the Throne (atop the seven heavens) before He created the heavens and the earth. He said that then God created the wind, giving it wings the size and number of which no one save God knows, and He commanded it to bear up the water on which the Throne was, and it did so. So the Throne was upon the water and the water was upon the wind.

The narrative turns to the Throne, with obvious echoes of Ezekiel 1:8–11 and Revelation 4:4, though of which precisely it is impossible to say.

Then, said he [that is, Ibn Abbas], God created the Throne-bearers who at present are four, but when the Day of Resurrection comes God will aid them with four others, as the Most High has said: "And above them eight on that day will bear the Throne of your Lord" (Quran 69:17). They are of such a size as to be beyond description, and each of them has four forms, one in the form of a human, which makes intercession for the sustenance of men, another in the form of a bull, which makes intercession for the sustenance of domestic animals, another in the form of a lion, which makes intercession for the sustenance of wild beasts, and one in the form of an eagle, which makes intercession for the sustenance of the winged creatures.

Ibn Abbas, with whom may God be pleased, said that the footstool is of a jewel other than the jewel from which God created the Throne. Wahb said that there are angels associated with the Throne, some kneeling on their knees, some standing on their feet, bearing the Throne on their necks, but sometimes they get weary and then the Throne is borne up solely by the might of God. (He taught that) the footstool is from the light of the Throne, but others say that the footstool is God's knowledge and that the Throne is God's knowledge with regard to His creation, but this is false in the light of what Abu Dharr al-Ghifari has related of how he asked the Messenger of God, upon whom be God's blessing and peace, which was the most excellent verse in the Quran, and he answered, "the Throne Verse" [2:255; see Chapter 1 above]. Then he said, "The seven heavens would be in the footstool like a bracelet in the desert wastes, and the Throne is as much superior to the footstool as the footstool to a bracelet." (Kisa'i, *Stories of the Prophets*) [JEFFREY 1962: 161–163]

6. The Divine Purpose in Creation

All these explanations of Creation, Jewish and Muslim alike, have as their objective the integration of other, nonscriptural but authoritative traditions into the account in Genesis. There was, however, another way to proceed, by attempting to rational-ize the essentially mythic story in Genesis, to give it cause and purpose and rational shape. Among the first of the "People of the Book" to attempt this was a Hellenized Jew of Alexandria, Philo (ca. 25 C.E.), who had gone to school not only in the Law and Scripture but at the feet of Greek and Roman philosophers.

On the fourth day (of Creation), the earth being now finished, God ordered the heaven in varied beauty. Not that he put the heaven in a lower rank than the earth, giving precedence to the inferior creation [that is, the earth] and accounting the higher and the more divine [that is, the heaven] worthy only of the second place; but to make clear beyond all doubt the mighty sway of His sovereign power. For being aware before-hand of the ways of thinking that would mark the men of future ages, how they would be intent on what looked probable and plausible, with much in it that could be supported by argument, but would not aim at the sheer truth; and how they would trust phenomena rather than God, admiring sophistry rather than wisdom; and how they would observe in time to come the circuits of sun and moon, on which depend summer and winter and the changes of spring and autumn, and would suppose that the regular movements of the heavenly bodies are the causes of all things that year by year come forth and are produced out of the earth; so that there might be none who owing either to shameless audacity or to overwhelm-ing ignorance should venture to ascribe the first place to any created thing, "let them," He said, "go back in thought to the original creation of the universe, when, before the sun or the moon existed, the earth bore plants of all sorts and fruits of all sorts; and having contemplated this, let them form in their minds the expectation that hereafter too shall it bear these at the Father's bidding, whensoever it may please Him." For he has no need of His heavenly offspring [that is, the heavenly bodies] on which he bestowed powers but not independence. . . . This is the reason why the earth put forth plants and bore herbs before the heaven was finished. (Philo, *The Creation of the World* 45–46) [PHILO 1945: 52–53]

7. Jacob's Pillow and Jacob's Ladder and Jacob's Thigh

Philo reasons about Scripture in a straightforward and even dogmatic fashion, with all the ease and elegance of someone well schooled in a self-assured tradition. The rabbinic method is quite different, as we may easily note, though no less assured. We have already seen something of the range of their Scriptural interpretation on Creation in the collective work known as the "Great Exegesis." Here are the same authorities on three objects associated with the story of Jacob in Genesis 28 and 33. The first has to do with the pillow of stones he placed under his head (Gen. 28:11), and is complicated by the textual question of whether there was one or more than one stone, a crux the following explanations indirectly attempt to solve.

Rabbi Judah said: He [Jacob] took twelve stones, saying: "The Holy One, blessed be he, has decreed that twelve tribes should spring forth. Now neither Abraham nor Isaac has produced them. If these cleave to one another, then I know that I will produce the twelve tribes." When therefore the twelve stones united, he knew that he was to produce the twelve tribes. Rabbi Nehemiah said: He took three stones, saying: "The Holy One, blessed be He, united His name with Abraham; with Isaac too He united His name. If these three stones become joined, then I am assured that God's name will be united with me too." And when they did so join, he knew that God would unite His name with him. The Rabbis say: (He took) the least number that (the plural) "stones" can connote, to wit, two, saying, "From Abraham there came forth Ishmael and the children of Keturah; from Isaac there came forth Esau. As for me, if these two stones join, I will be reassured that nothing worthless will come forth from me." (*Genesis Rabbah* 68:11) [MIDRASH RABBAH 1977: 1:623]

In the next passage, having to do with Jacob's dream of a ladder with angels ascending and descending (Gen. 28:12), the manner is allegorical, of the foreshadowing type later much favored by the Christians, and based on a correspondence of details.

Ben Kappara said: No dream is without its interpretation. "And behold a ladder" symbolizes the stairway (leading to the top of the altar in the Temple); "set up on the earth" is the altar, as it says, "An altar of earth you shall make for Me" (Exod. 20:21); "and the top of it reached to heaven" (refers to) the sacrifices, the odor of which reached to heaven; "and behold the angels of God" (refers to) the High Priests; "ascending and descending on it" (refers to) ascending and descending the stairway; "and behold, the Lord stood beside him" (reflects) "I saw the Lord standing beside the altar" (Amos 9:1).

The Rabbis connected it to Sinai. "And he dreamt" and "behold a ladder" symbolizes Sinai; "set up on the earth," as it says "And they stood on the lower part of the mount" (Exod. 19:17); "and the top of it reached to heaven" (compare) "And the mountain burned with fire to the heart of heaven" (Deut. 4:11). "And behold the angels of God" alludes to Moses and Aaron. "Ascending": "And Moses went up to God" (Exod. 19:3); "and descending": "And Moses went down from the mount" (Exod. 19:14). "And behold the Lord stood beside him": "And the Lord came down upon Mount Sinai" (Exod. 19:20). (*Genesis Rabbah* 68:12)
[MIDRASH RABBAH 1977: 1:625]

The last example arises from what must have appeared to the rabbis like an open invitation to commentary, the legal aside that concludes the narrative passage in Genesis 32:22–32: "This is why the Israelites to this day do not eat the sinew of the nerve that runs in the hollow of the thigh; for the man had struck Jacob on that nerve in the hollow of his thigh." The later lawyers were not, in any event, discouraged from believing that the last word had not been said on the matter. The earlier cited passage from the "Great Exegesis" was searching for symbolism in Jacob's ladder; here the quest is legal.

Rabbi Hanina said: Why is it called "the sinew of the nerve" (*gid ha-nashed*)? Because it slipped (*nashah*) from its place. Rabbi Huna said: The branches of the nerve sinew are permitted (to be eaten), but Israel are holy and (so) treat it as forbidden (as well). Rabbi Judah said: He [the angel] touched only one of them and (so) only one of them was forbidden. Rabbi Yosi said: He touched only one of them, but both of them became forbidden. One Mishnaic authority teaches: It is reasonable to suppose that it was the right one, which is Rabbi Judah's view; while another authority teaches: It is reasonable to suppose that it was the left one, which is Rabbi Yosi's view. The opinion that it was the right one (is based on the verse): "And he touched the hollow of his thigh" (ibid. 26), while the opinion that it was the left one is based on the verse "because he

touched the hollow of Jacob's thigh." (*Genesis Rabbah* 78:6)
[MIDRASH RABBAH 1977: 1:719]

8. The Method of the Midrashim

The Midrash Rabbah is but one example of Jewish homiletic commentary, with its edifying motives and occasional flights of interpretation as imaginative as those cited from the Muslim al-Kisaʾi. The genre was long a scriptural commonplace by Nachmanides' day. But it was obviously not to everyone's taste. A fastidiously described critique of the Midrashim and their spirited defense by one of Judaism's principal intellectuals—one whose own interests were as little congruent with these of the Rabbis as were those of Nachmanides—may be observed in the writing of the Spanish philosopher and legal scholar Moses Maimonides (d. 1204 C.E.). The biblical text in question is from Leviticus.

Mark, on the fifteenth day of the seventh month, when you have gathered in the yield of your land, you shall observe the festival of the Lord [that is, of Tabernacles or Sukkoth] (to last) seven days: a complete rest on the first day and a complete rest on the eighth day. On the first day you shall take the product of *hadar* trees [traditionally understood as the citron], branches of palm trees, boughs of leafy trees and willows of the brook, and you shall rejoice before the Lord your God seven days. (Leviticus 23:39–40)

The branches bound together constituted what was called in Hebrew a lulab. *In the Mishna treatise called Sukkah the Rabbis of the first and second century C.E. had explored the legal questions that might arise in connection with it.*

Earlier the *lulab* was carried seven days in the Temple, but in the provinces one day only. After the Temple was destroyed, Rabbi Yohanan ben Zakkai ordained that in the provinces it should be carried seven days in memory of the Temple. . . .

If the first festival day of the feast (of Sukkoth) falls on a Sabbath, all the people bring their *lulabs* to the synagogue (on the day before). The next day they come early and each man identifies his own *lulab* and carries it; for the Sages have said: None can fulfill his obligations on the first festival day of the feast with someone else's *lulab*. But on the other days of the feast a man may fulfill his obligation with someone else's *lulab*. (M.Sukkah 3:12–13)

The homiletic commentaries on Scripture used the same starting point of the verses in Leviticus on the fronds bound into the lulab, *but they proceeded in a very different direction.*

"... The fruit of citrus trees, palm fronds and leafy branches and willows from the riverside...." "The fruit of the citrus tree": these are the Israelites. As the citron has taste and smell, some among the Israelites have both Torah and good works. "Palm fronds": these are the Israelites. As the date has taste but not smell, so are there Israelites who have Torah but not good works. "Leafy branches": these are Israelites. As the myrtle has smell but no taste, so there are Israelites who have good works but no Torah. "Willows from the riverside": these are Israelites. As the willow has neither taste nor smell, so there are Israelites who have neither Torah nor good works. What is God to do with them? God says, "Bind all together in one bundle, and one will atone for the other." (*Leviticus Rabbah* 30:12)

It is apropos of this same passage in the "Great Exegesis" on Leviticus that Moses Maimonides, the Spanish philosopher and scholar of the Law, gives us his reflections on the homiletic approach to Scripture.

As for the four species (of fronds) that constitute a *lulab*, the Sages, may their memory be blessed, have set forth some reason for this in the manner of the Midrashim whose manner is well known to all those who understand their discourses. For these Midrashim have, in their opinion, the status of poetical conceits; they are not meant to bring out the meaning of the text in question. Accordingly, with regard to the Midrashim, people are divided into two classes: A class that imagines that the Sages have said these things in order to explain the meaning of the text in question, and a class that holds the Midrashim in slight esteem and holds them up to ridicule, since it is clear and manifest that this is not the meaning of the (biblical) text in question.

The first class strives and fights with a view to proving, as they deem, the correctness of the Midrashim and to defending them, and they think that this is the true meaning of the biblical text and that the Midrashim have the same status as the traditional legal decisions. But neither of the two groups understands that the Midrashim have the character of poetical conceits whose meaning is not obscure for someone endowed with understanding. At that time this method was generally known and used by everybody, just as the poets used poetical expressions. Thus the Sages, may their memory be blessed, say: "Bar Kappara teaches (concerning the verse) 'With your equipment (*azenekha*) you will have a spike ...' (Deut. 23:13) [the verse continues: "and when you squat outside (the camp), you shall scrape a hole with it and then turn and cover your excrement"]: do not read *azenekha*, 'your equipment' but *aznekha*, 'your ear.' This teaches us that whenever a man hears a reprehensible thing, he should put a finger into his ear." Would that I knew whether, in the opinion of these ignoramuses, this Tannaite [that is, Bar Kappara] really believed this to be the interpretation of this text, that such was the purpose of this commandment that *yathed*, "spike," means a finger, and that *azenekha*, "your equipment," refers to the two ears. I do not think that anyone of sound intellect will be of this opinion.

This is (actually) a most witty poetical conceit by which Bar Kappara instills a noble moral quality, which is in accordance with the fact that just as it is forbidden to tell them, so it is forbidden to listen to obscene things; and he props it up through a reference to a (biblical) text, as is done in poetical compositions. Similarly, all the passages in the Midrashim enjoining "Do not read thus," but thus, have this (same) meaning. (Maimonides, *Guide of the Perplexed* 3.45) [MAIMONIDES 1963: 572–573]

9. Legal Exegesis

The "Great Exegesis," or Midrash Rabbah, *is an example of the homiletic or "edifying" interpretation of Scripture. Another equally common approach, indeed a necessary one since so much of the Torah is given over to legal matters, is to extract the full legal content and meaning from those prescriptions. In some cases the approach is quite straightforward, as here in Philo's meditation on the allegorical content of the fifth commandment of the Decalog.*

The fifth commandment, which has to do with honoring parents, contains in an allegory many necessary precepts, for old and young, for rulers and ruled, for benefactors and beneficiaries, for slaves and masters. "Parents" here stands for all those in a position of authority: elders, rulers, benefactors and masters, while "children" stands for all those in an inferior station: the young, subject, beneficiaries, slaves. Hence the commandment implies many other injunctions: the young should reverence the old, the old supervise the young; subjects should obey their rulers and rulers consider their subjects' interests; beneficiaries should aim at repaying favor for favor, benefactors not look for a return as if they were moneylenders; servants should exhibit an obedience which expresses love toward the master, masters show themselves gentle and meek and so redress the inequality of status between themselves and their slaves. (Philo, *On the Decalog* 165–166)

Philo is a well-defined and well-known figure from Alexandria at the beginning of the Christian era. But, as was the case with the homiletic exegesis, here too we often have to deal with collective works, where the legal aphorisms of various rabbis, sometimes credited and sometimes not, are arranged, more often by association than by logic, verse by verse through the books of the Torah. The following is an extract from just such a compilation made on Exodus and called Mekilta. *The verse commented upon is Exodus 20:2: "I am the Lord thy God."*

And it was for the following reason that the nations of the world were asked to accept the Torah, in order that they should have no excuse for saying: "Had we been asked, we would have accepted it." For behold, some of them were asked and they refused to accept it, for it is said: "And he said 'The Lord came from Sinai etc.'" (Deut. 33:2). He appeared to the children of Esau, the wicked, and said to them, "Will you accept the Torah?" They said to him, "What is written in it?" He said to them, "You shall not murder." They then said to him, "The very heritage that our father (Esau) left to us was: 'And by the sword you shall live'" (Gen. 27:40). He then appeared to the children of Amon and Moab. He said to them, "Will you accept the Torah?" They said to him, "What is written in it?" He said to them, "You shall not commit adultery." They, however, said to him they were all of them children of adulterers, as it is said, "Thus were both the daughters of Lot with child by their father" (Gen. 19:36). Then he appeared to the children of Ishmael. He said to them, "Will you accept the Torah?" They said to him, "What is written in it?" He said to them, "You shall not steal." They then said to him, "The very blessing that was pronounced upon our father (Ishmael) was: 'And he shall be as a wild ass of a man; his hand shall be upon everything'" (Gen. 40:15). . . . And when He came to the Israelites and "at His right hand was a fiery law for them" (Deut. 33:2), they all opened their mouths and said, "All that the Lord has spoken will we do and obey" (Exod. 24:7). And thus it says, "He stood and measured the earth; He beheld and drove asunder the nations" (Hab. 3:6).

This story of the "offering of the Torah," drawn anonymously from some nonscriptural source and presented without any further justification than that it had happened, is followed by a more formal, attributed argument, which is in turn reinforced by a parable.

Rabbi Simeon ben Eleazer says, "If the sons of Noah could not endure the seven commandments enjoined upon them, how much less could they have endured all the commandments of the Torah! To give a parable. A king had appointed two administrators. One was appointed over the supply of straw and the other over the treasure of silver and gold. The one appointed over the straw supply was held in suspicion. But he used to complain about the fact that they had not appointed him over the treasure of silver and gold. The people then said to him, "Scoundrel! If you were under suspicion in connection with the straw supply, how could they trust you with the treasure of silver and gold?" Behold, it is a matter of reasoning by the method of inference from minor to major. If the sons of Noah could not endure the seven commandments enjoined on them, how much less could they have endured all the commandments of the Torah?

Why was the Torah (given on Mount Sinai and) not given in the Land of Israel? In order that the nations of the world should not have the excuse for saying, "Because it was given in Israel's land, therefore we have not accepted it." Another reason: To avoid causing dissension among the tribes. Else one (tribe) might have said, "In my territory the Torah was given." And another might have said, "In my territory the Torah was given." Therefore the Torah was given in the desert, publicly and openly, in a place belonging to no one. To three things the Torah is likened: to the desert, to fire and to water. This is to tell you that, just as these three things are free to all who come into the world, so also are the words of the Torah free to all who come into the world. (*Mekilta* Bahodesh 5)

10. The Seven Rules of Interpretation

At the end of the parable adduced by Simeon ben Eliezer and cited above, there occurs the brief editorial comment: "it is a matter of reasoning by the method of inference from minor to major." The reference is somewhat offhand, as to something already well known, as indeed it was. Sometime early in the Christian era an attempt had been made to conceptualize what had doubtless long been going on among the rabbis in expounding the legal texts of Scripture. The result was the "Seven Rules of Hillel," a summary of the chief ways of either deriving or harmonizing legal prescriptions from Scripture. It is attributed to Rabbi Hillel the Elder, a somewhat older contemporary of Jesus. The following is how the rules stand in their technically shortened expression in the treatise called The Fathers According to Rabbi Nathan.

Seven rules of interpretation Hillel the Elder expounded before the Bene Bathyra, to wit: (1) a fortiori; (2) analogy; (3) deduction from one verse; (4) deduction from two verses; (5) (inference) from the general and the particular and from the particular and the general; (6) similarity elsewhere; (7) deduction from context. These are the seven rules which Hillel expounded (in his dispute) before the Bene Bathyra. (*The Fathers According to Rabbi Nathan* 37) [ABOTH RABBI NATHAN 1955: 154]

Which means to say: (1) What applies in the lesser case will certainly apply in the greater case; (2) where the same expression is used in two different verses, the same legal considerations will apply; (3) where the same expression is found in a number of verses, legal considerations applicable in one will be applicable in all; (4) a general principle can be deduced from a "family" of at least two texts and be applied more generally; (5) a general principal is limited by a particular instance or a particular instance is raised to the level of a general principle; (6) a problem in one text may be resolved by reference to another, even without the verbal similarities of (2) and (3) above; and (7) a meaning is established by its context.

11. The Conflict of Legal and Homiletic Exegesis

It is readily apparent from the remarks of Maimonides cited above that at least some Jews had problems with the traditional ways of understanding Scripture, particularly with the method known as "haggadic" or "homiletic" exegesis. Although the rationalizing Maimonides was willing to make a defense of sorts of this latter reading of Scripture, it was surely not with a great deal of enthusiasm. The case is only somewhat better made by someone who was far more traditional, the "Rabbi" who is the chief speaker in The King of the Khazars *and the mouthpiece for its author, Judah Halevi. The passage begins with the Rabbi offering an extremely flattering characterization of the Mishna, the written edition of comment upon the Jewish oral law prepared by Rabbi Judah the Prince ca. 200 C.E.*

They [its redactors] treated the Mishna with the same care as the Torah, arranging it in sections, chapters and paragraphs. Its traditions are so reliable that no suspicion of invention could be upheld. Besides this the Mishna contains a large amount of pure Hebrew which is not borrowed from the Bible. It is greatly distinguished by terseness of language, beauty of style, excellence of composition, and the comprehensive employment of homonyms, applied in a lucid way and leaving neither doubt nor obscurity. This is so striking that everyone who looks at it with genuine scrutiny must be aware that mortal man is incapable of composing such a work without divine assistance. Only he who is hostile to it, who does not know it, and never endeavored to read and study it, hearing some general and allegorical utterances of the Sages, deems them senseless and defective.

But the well-informed king of the Khazars, who gives his name to this dialogue of Halevi, raises certain criticisms with his interlocutor.

The Khazar King: Indeed, several details of their sayings [that is, of the Mishna authorities] appear to me inferior to their general principles. They employ verses of the Torah, for example, in a manner without regard to common sense. And one can only say that the application of such verses, now for legal deductions and another time for homiletic purposes, does not tally with their real meaning. Their homiletic stories and tales are often contrary to reason.

The Rabbi: Did you notice how strictly and minutely comments on the Mishna and the Baraitha are given (in the Talmud)? They [that is, the Rabbis represented there] speak with a thoroughness and a lucidity which do equal justice to both the words and the meaning of them.

The Khazar King: I am well aware of the perfection they brought to the art of dialectics, but the argument still stands.

The Rabbi: May we assume that he who proceeds with so much thoroughness should not know as much of the content of a verse as we do?

The Khazar King: This is most unlikely. Two things are possible. Either we are ignorant of their method of interpreting the Torah, or the interpreters of the Rabbinic law are not identical with the exegetes of the Holy Scripture. The latter point of view is absurd. But it is seldom that we see them [that is, the Rabbis] give a verse a rational and literal interpretation (in their exegetical works), but on the other hand, (in the Mishna and Talmud) we never find them interpreting a legal ruling except on the lines of strict logic.

The Rabbi: Let us rather assume two other possibilities. Either they employ secret methods of interpretation which we are unable to discern but which were handed down to them together with the (known) method of the "Thirteen Rules of Interpretation," or else they use biblical verses as a kind of fulcrum of interpretation in a method called "Asmakhta" and make them a sort of hallmark of tradition. An instance is provided by the following verse: "And the Lord God commanded man, saying, Of every tree of the garden you may freely eat" (Gen. 2:16). It forms the basis of the "seven Noachide laws" in the following manner:

"Commanded . . ." refers to jurisdiction.

"The Lord . . ." refers to the prohibition of blasphemy.

"God . . ." refers to the prohibition of idolatry.

"Man . . ." refers to the prohibition of murder.

"Saying . . ." refers to the prohibition of incest.

"Of every tree of the garden . . . ," the prohibition of rape.

"You may freely eat . . . ," a prohibition of flesh from a living animal."

There is a wide difference between these injunctions and the verse (with which they are associated). The people, however, accepted these seven laws as a tradition, connecting them with the verse as an aid to memory.

It is also possible that they applied both methods of interpreting verses, or others which are now lost to us, and considering the well-known wisdom, zeal, and number of the Sages which excludes a common plan, it is our duty to follow them. If we feel any doubt, it is not due to their words, but to our own intelligence. This also applies to Torah and its contents: we must ascribe the defective understanding of it to ourselves. As for the homiletic interpretations, many serve as a basis and introduction for explanations and legal injunctions. . . . Verses of this kind serve as a fulcrum and introduction, rendering a subject eloquent, apposite and showing that it is based on truth. To the same category belong (rabbis') tales of visions of spirits, a matter which is not strange in such pious men. Some of the visions they saw were the consequences of their lofty thoughts and pure minds, others were real apparitions, as was the case with those seen by the prophets. . . .

Other rabbinic sayings are parables employed to express mysterious teachings which are not to be made public. For they are of no use to the masses, and were only handed over to a few select persons for research and investigation, if a proper person—one in an era, or in several—could be found. Other sayings appear senseless on the face of them, but that they have their meaning becomes apparent after but a little reflection. (Judah Halevi, *The Khazar King* 3.67–72) [HALEVI 1905: 191–196]

12. The Scripture Interprets Itself

The description of the construction of the Temple in the Book of Kings (1 Kings 6–7) passes directly from the account of the building to another passage quite different in tone and tenor from the preceding narrative. It is a meditation of Solomon himself and is presented in the form of an interior dialogue on the propriety of God's possessing a house. Almost certainly this text reflects the sensibility of a later, post-Exilic age that had lost the Temple and for whom the transcendent God of Israel dwelled nowhere if not in the universal heaven. It is, in effect, Scripture reflecting upon itself.

(And Solomon continued:) "But will God really dwell on earth? Even the heavens to their uttermost reaches cannot contain You, how much less this House that I have built! Yet turn, O Lord my God, to the prayer and supplication of Your servant, and hear the cry of prayer which Your servant offers before You on this day. May Your eyes be open day and night toward this House, toward the place of which You have said 'My name shall abide there'; may You hear the prayers which Your servant will offer toward this place. And when you hear the supplications which Your servant and Your people Israel offer toward this place, give heed in Your heavenly abode—give heed and pardon."

. . . (Solomon continues:) "When they sin against You—for there is no man who does not sin—and You are angry with them and deliver them to the enemy, and their captors carry them off to an enemy land, near or far; and then they take it to heart in the land to which they have been carried off, and they repent and make supplication to You in the land of their captors, saying, 'We have sinned, we have acted perversely, we have acted wickedly,' and they turn back to You with all their heart and soul, in the land of the enemies who have carried them off, and pray to You in the direction of their land which You gave to their fathers, of the city which You have chosen, and of the House which I have built in Your name—oh, give heed in Your heavenly abode to their prayer and supplication and uphold their cause." (1 Kings 8:27–49)

That Temple destroyed by the Babylonians in 587 B.C.E. was once again rebuilt in the same century, but the notion that God could not be confined to one place persisted. It was encouraged by the prophets; but the transcendence of God, His remoteness in time and place and being from the world of men, received its strongest encouragement from Jewish contact with post-Alexander Hellenism, with its own strongly increasing sense of a spiritual God. That contact is most strongly reflected, as we have already seen, in the works of Philo, a practicing Jew from the deeply Hellenized milieu of Alexandria. This is Philo on the true Temple of God.

The highest and true Temple of God is, we must believe, the whole universe, having for its sanctuary the holiest part of all existence, namely heaven, for its votive offerings the stars, for its priests the angels, who are the servitors of His powers, unbodied souls, not mixtures of rational and irrational natures as ours are, but with the irrational eliminated, completely mind, pure intelligences, in the likeness of the Monad. The other Temple is made by hand; for it was fitting not to inhibit the impulses of men who pay their tribute to piety and wish by means of sacrifices to express their thanks for the good things that befell them or to ask for pardon and forgiveness for errors committed. But he (Moses) provided that there should not be temples built either in many places or many in the same place, judging that since God is one, there should also be only one Temple. (Philo, *The Special Laws* 1.66–67) [PHILO 1981: 279]

This technique of Scripture interpreting itself is a commonplace one. Deuteronomy is in a sense an interpretation of Exodus and Leviticus; Chronicles, of Kings; and the

Exilic prophets, of the whole biblical past. Jewish religious sensibilities changed during and after the Exile, as we have seen, and with them the understanding of the Bible. Here, for example, is how the noncanonical "Wisdom of Solomon" understood the biblical histories of Adam, Cain, Noah, and Abraham.

Wisdom it was who kept guard over the first father of the human race, when he alone had not yet been made; she saved him after his fall, and gave him the strength to master all things. It was because a wicked man forsook her in his anger that he murdered his brother in a fit of rage and so destroyed himself. Through his fault the earth was covered with a deluge, and again wisdom came to the rescue, and taught the one good man how to pilot his plain wooden hulk. It was she, who when heathen nations leagued in wickedness were thrown into confusion, picked out one good man and kept him blameless in the sight of God, giving him strength to resist his pity for his child. (Wisdom 10:1–5)

And of the Exodus from Egypt:

It was she [Divine Wisdom] who rescued a god-fearing people, a blameless race, from a nation of oppressors; she inspired a servant of the Lord, and with his signs and wonders he defied formidable kings. She rewarded the labors of god-fearing men, she guided them on a marvelous journey and became a covering for them by day and a blaze of stars by night. She brought them over the Red Sea and guided them through its deep waters; but their enemies she engulfed, and cast them up again out of the fathomless deep. . . . Wisdom, working through a holy prophet, brought them success in all they did. They made their way across an unpeopled desert and pitched camp in untrodden wastes; they resisted every enemy, and beat off hostile assaults. When they were thirsty they called upon you, and water to slake their thirst was given them out of the hard stone of a rocky cliff. (Wisdom 10:15–11:4)

Or the famous passage in Ecclesiasticus (The Wisdom of Jesus ben Sira) that begins:

Let us now sing the praises of famous men,
the heroes of our nation's history,
through whom the Lord established His renown,
and revealed His glory in each succeeding age.
Some held sway over kingdoms
and made themselves a name by their exploits.
Others were sage counselors,
who spoke out with prophetic power.
Some led the people by their counsels

or by their knowledge of the nation's law;
out of the fund of their wisdom they gave instruction.
Some were composers of music or writers of poetry.
Others were endowed with wealth and strength,
living peacefully in their homes.
All these won fame in their own generation
and were the pride of their times.
Some there were who have left a name behind them
to be commemorated in story.
There are others who are unremembered;
they are dead, and it is as though they never existed,
as though they had never been born
or left children to succeed them.
Not so our forefathers; they were men of loyalty,
whose good deeds have never been forgotten.
Their prosperity is handed on to their descendants,
and their inheritance to future generations.
Thanks to them their children are within the covenants,
the whole race of their descendants.
Their line will endure for all time,
and their fame will never be blotted out.
Nations will recount their wisdom,
and God's people will sing their praises.
(Ecclesiasticus 44:1–15)

There follows (44:16–50:24) a rapid survey of the heroes of Israel from Enoch to the contemporary High Priest, Simon son of Onias. Their chief deeds are mentioned in summary and their praises sung, all for the benefit of a reader who already knows their stories.

The Quran gives a similar review in Sura 21, appropriately called "The Prophets," and here too the listener must be presumed to have heard the stories before.

We gave Moses and Aaron the Criterion (of right and wrong), and a light and a reminder for those who take heed for themselves, who are fearful of their Lord inwardly and dread the Hour. And this is a blessed reminder that We have sent down. Will you deny it?

We had earlier given Abraham true direction, for We knew him well. When he said to his father and his people, "What are these idols to which you cling so passionately?" they replied: "We found our fathers worshiping them." He said: "You and your fathers are in clear error."

They said: "Are you speaking in earnest or only jesting?" He said: "In fact it was your Lord, the Lord of the heavens and the earth, who created them; and I bear witness to this. I swear by God I will do something to your idols when you have turned your back and gone." So he smashed them to pieces. . . .

They wished to entrap him, but We made them greater losers. So We delivered him and Lot, and brought them to the land We had blessed for all the people. And We bestowed on him Isaac, and Jacob as an additional gift, and made them righteous. And We made them leaders to guide the people by Our command; and We inspired them to perform good deeds and perform worship and pay the alms tithe; and they obeyed Us.

To Lot We gave wisdom and knowledge, and saved him from a people who acted villainously and were certainly wicked and disobedient. Thus We admitted him to Our grace. He is surely one of the righteous.

And Noah, when he called to Us before this. We heard him and saved him and those with him from great distress; and We helped him against the people who rejected Our signs as lies. They were a wicked people indeed, so We drowned them one and all.

And David and Solomon, when they pronounced judgment about the field which was eaten up at night by sheep belonging to certain people. We were witnesses to their judgment. We made Solomon understand the case, and bestowed on each wisdom and knowledge. We subdued the hills and the birds to sing his praise along with David. We taught him the art of making coats of mail to shield you from each other's violence. We made tempestuous winds obedient to protect Solomon which blew swiftly to sail at his bidding to the land We had blessed. We are cognizant of every thing. And many of the devils, some dived (for pearls) for him and did other work, and We kept watch over them.

And Job, when he called to his Lord: "I am afflicted with distress, and You are the most compassionate of all." So We heard his cry and relieved him of the misery he was in. We restored his family to him, and along with them gave him others similar to them as a grace from Us and a reminder for those who are obedient.

And mention Ishmael and Idris and Dhu al-Kifl. They were men of fortitude, and they were admitted to Our grace. Verily they were among the doers of good.

And mention the Man of the Fish [that is, Jonah], when he went away in anger and imagined We will not test him. Then he called out in the darkness: "There is no God but You. All glory to You! Surely I was a sinner." We heard his cry and saved him from anguish. That is how We deliver those who believe.

And Zachariah, when he called to his Lord: "Do not leave me alone and childless, for You are the best of givers." So We heard him and gave him John, and cured his wife (of barrenness). These were men who vied in good deeds with one another, and prayed to Us with love and awe, and were meek before Us.

And she who preserved her chastity [that is, Mary, the mother of Jesus], into whom We breathed a life from Us, and made her and her son a token for mankind.

Behold, this, your community is one community and I am your Lord, so worship Me. (Quran 21:48–92)

Finally, there is this instruction from Nehemiah, glossed by the Babylonian Talmud.

They read in the scroll of the Teaching [that is, Torah] of the Lord, translating [or, distinctly] it, giving the sense; so they understood the reading. (Nehemiah 8:8)

"They read in the scroll of the Teaching": this means the written text; "distinctly": this is the Targum; "giving the sense": this has reference to the division into verses; "so they understood the reading": this means the diacritical signs, and some rabbis say that this is the Masora. (BT.Nedarim 37b)

13. "There Are Seven Paths in the Knowledge of the Torah"

The entire range of Scriptural interpretation, from the literal to the most mystical, is laid out by Abraham Abulafia (d. 1292 C.E.), an intellectual follower of Maimonides but a convinced esotericist and student of Kabbala.

There are seven paths in the knowledge of the Torah.

The first path consists in understanding the simple meaning of the Torah text, for a biblical text may not be detached from its simple meaning. This is the way best suited for the multitude of people, men, women and children. Since some people are learned and some altogether unfamiliar with anything except the letters . . . it is appropriate that the uneducated except for the knowledge of the letters be taught some traditions so that they may possess religion in its conventional form. . . .

The second path includes those who study various commentaries, but what they have in common is that they revolve around the simple meaning and pursue it from all angles as in the expositions of the Mishna and the Talmud which expound the surface meaning of the Torah. This is illustrated by the interpretation of the phrase "circumcision of the heart." The Torah ordains that it be circumcised, as it is written (Deut. 10:16), "And you shall circumcise the foreskin of your heart." This command-ment cannot be observed literally. It must, therefore, have an explana-tion. This is to be understood in the light of the verse (Deut. 30:6), "And the Lord your God will circumcise your heart," with the accompanying verse (30:2), "And you shall return to the Lord your God." The term "heart" must, therefore, be taken here as alluding to a return to God.

But this allegorical reading of the text, Abulafia carefully explains, should not replace the literal meaning, as the Christians did with precisely this set of texts.

But the circumcision of the child on the eighth day cannot be un-derstood in the same way, for it cannot be applied to penitence. . . .

The third path embraces the study of the biblical text from the perspective of *midrash* and homiletic exegesis, and the derivatives from these types of study. This is illustrated by the inquiry as to why there is no mention that "God saw that it was good" (only) after the second day of creation, and the answer that it was because the organization of the waters was not completed on the second day. There are other such expo-sitions. This path is called "searching/expounding" (*derash*) to indicate that here there is room to search and probe and also that this subject may be expounded in public. . . .

For Abulafia, as for most students of Scripture, whether Jews, Christians, or Mus-lims, not all types of explanations are suitable for all believers—"the multitude," as Abulafia calls them. Certain approaches to God's word should be reserved for "the select few."

The fourth path embraces parables and riddles. In this path begins the divergence between the select few and the multitude. The multitude will understand things according to the three paths mentioned earlier. Some will follow the simple text and some will seek explanations for them and some will understand them according to the "searching/ex-pounding" method. But the select few will realize that these are parables and they will search after their meaning, and here they will encounter double-meaning terms, as that subject has been explained in (Maimo-nides') *Guide of the Perplexed.*

Abulafia lived in an age when the connection of both Christianity and Islam to Judaism was patent to most sophisticated Jews, particularly to those living in Spain. The connection does not, however, diminish Israel's claim to uniqueness, which

Abulafia locates in its possession of the esoteric teaching known generally as Kab-
bala, or "the Tradition." It was not a notion shared by many of "the multitude,"
who would more likely subscribe to the view that it was the Unwritten Law that was
the characteristic mark of Israel, as will be explained in Chapter 3 below. Abulafia
continues.

The fifth path includes only the secrets of the Torah. The four paths
mentioned earlier are shared by people of all nations, their masses in the
first three and their wise men in the fourth. The fifth path begins the
levels of secrets possessed by the Jews alone. In this we are differentiated
from the world's general populace as well as its wise men, but also from
the Jewish sages, the rabbis, whose views revolve around the circle of the
latter three of the paths mentioned above.

I cite as an illustration of this (fifth) path the secret meanings disclosed to us by the fact that the (Hebrew) letter "B" with which the
Torah begins is large, and the large letters of the alphabet appear in all
twenty-four books of the Bible . . . or by the inverted form of the base in
the two (forms of) the (Hebrew) letter "N" enclosing the chapter de-
scribing the movement of the Holy Ark (Num. 10:35). . . . There are
many similar mysteries handed down by tradition . . . and nothing of the
truths of those mysteries has been disclosed to any people except ours.

Abulafia shows himself well aware that he is expressing an attitude with which some
Jews, "those who follow the way of the nations"—the Gentile-minded, as he calls
them—would take exception.

One who follows the way of the nations may mock, thinking that
these letters were written that way without any reason and thus they
misrepresent the tradition, and they are guilty of grave error. But those
who have mastered the truths of these paths recognized their distinction
and these mysteries have been made clear to them, for they are holy. This
path is the beginning of the general wisdom of combining letters. This
path is appropriate only for those who fear God and meditate His name.

On the sixth path Abulafia passes from simple esotericism to mysticism, or better, an
esotericism directed not toward understanding alone but toward a direct apprehen-
sion of God.

The sixth path is very deep and who can attain it? . . . It is fitting for
those who withdraw from the world in their desire to draw close to God
to the point that they themselves shall experience His active presence in
themselves. These are the people who seek to resemble in their activity
the actions of the Active Intellect [that is, a higher intelligence, of an
angel, the Holy Spirit or of God Himself]. This path embraces the secret

of the "seventy languages" which, by the rules of *gematria* [that is, the system of substituting their numerical equivalents for the letters of a word], is equivalent to the "combination of letters" [that is, they both have a numerical equivalent of 1214]. This involves the return of the letters to their original essence in memory and in thought, analogous to the ten noncorporeal primordial numbers which involve a holy mystery, and all things holy have at least ten constituents.

These are, of course, the same ten primordials already seen in the esoterical account of Genesis called "The Book of Creation," a staple of all Kabbalistic cosmogonies. Abulafia proceeds to illustrate the holiness of ten.

Thus Moses ascended no higher than the ten heavenly realms, and the *Shekina*, the divine presence, descended no more than the ten heavens, and the world was created by ten divine commands, and the Torah was given by Ten Commandments, and there are many cases involving ten which illustrate this. Under the rubric of this path is also involved (the exegetical methods of) *gematria*, *notarikon* [that is, the reading of letters in a word as abbreviations of other words], and the interchange of letters, and then new interchanges to be repeated up to ten times. This halts only because of the weakness of human intelligence, for there is no limit to this process of permutation.

The seventh path is a special path and it includes all the others and it is the Holy of Holies and it is fitting for prophets only. This is the circle that revolves around all things. In attaining it one comprehends the message that descends from the Active Intellect to the power of speech.

Abulafia then gives a brief résumé of the theory of prophecy, which derives, as he says, from Maimonides and which, we may add, Maimonides took up from his Muslim predecessors, themselves the heirs to the theory of Aristotle and his Greek commentators on the existence of a higher and separated intellect. Once united, however temporarily, with this so-called Active Intellect, the human faculty is capable of higher planes of activity, among them prophecy. Abulafia concludes on a cautionary note.

It is improper to describe the manner by which this path, the Holy of Holies, proceeds, by writing about it in a book. It is impossible to disclose this to anyone, not even the main points, unless in his yearning he has learnt as a preliminary, in a direct communication from a teacher, the forty-two and the seventy-two names of God. I have therefore included here in my description, which is the essence of brevity, all that is needed to be said on the subject. (Abulafia, *The Seven Paths of the Torah*)

[BOKSER 1981: 102–104]

14. The Anthropomorphisms in Scripture

What may have first turned believers away from the literal to an "other" under-standing of Scripture was the fact that the plain sense made no sense, or that the plain sense was simply unacceptable. One large category of such "unacceptable" meanings of Scripture, if not for the original recipients of the revelation then assuredly for a later generation of believers with a more spiritually refined view of God, was anthropomorphism, the portrayal of God in grossly material or corporeal or even human terms. The Greeks had early on questioned themselves about their own poets' presentation of the gods in that manner, and they were uneasy with the answers well before the Jews discovered the problem in their own Scripture. The Bible is filled with such anthropomorphisms; and although the Septuagint translators had already softened a number of expressions referring to God's members and very humanlike actions and reactions in their Greek version of the Hebrew, the earliest systematic treatment of the problem is found in Philo.

After all the rest, as has been said, Moses tells us that man was created after the image of God and after His likeness (Gen. 1:26). This is quite well put, for nothing earthborn resembles God more than man. Let no one, however, represent that likeness through the characteristics of the body; for neither is God in human form, nor is the human body Godlike. The word "image" is here used with regard to the mind, the sovereign of the soul; for it is after the pattern of that unique and univer-sal Mind as an archetype that the mind in each individual was formed. It is in a way a god to him who carried it impressed in his mind; for the relationship the great Ruler bears to the world as a whole is precisely that which the human mind holds within man. It is invisible, while itself seeing all things, and though it apprehends the substances of others, its own substance is unknown. (Philo, *The Creation of the World* 69)
[PHILO 1981: 137]

"I will blot out from the face of the earth man whom I made, from man to beast, from reptiles to the winged fowl of heaven, because I was angered that I made him" (Gen. 6:7). Again, some on hearing these words assume that the Existent feels wrath and anger, whereas He is not suscep-tible to any emotion at all. For anxiety is peculiar to human weakness, but neither the irrational emotions nor the parts and limbs of the body are at all appropriate to God.

Nonetheless, such expressions are used by the Lawgiver (Moses) just so far as they furnish an elementary lesson, for the admonition of those who could not otherwise be brought to their senses. For among the laws that consist of commands and prohibitions, laws, that is, in the strict sense of the word, two ultimate summary statements are set forth concerning the First Cause, one that "God is not like a man" (Num. 23:19); the other that He is as a man. But though the former is guaranteed by absolutely secure criteria of truth, the latter is introduced for the instruction of the many. Wherefore it is also said of Him, "like a man He shall discipline His son" (Deut. 8:5). Thus it is for discipline and admonition, not because God's nature is such, that this is said of Him. Among men some are lovers of the soul, some of the body. The companions of the soul, who are able to associate with intelligible and incorporeal natures, do not compare the Existent to any form of created thing. They have excluded Him from every quality, for one of the things that pertains to His blessedness and supreme felicity is that His existence is apprehended as simple, without any distinguishing characteristic; and thus they have allowed a representation of Him only in respect of existence, not endowing Him with any form. But those who have concluded a treaty and a truce with the body are unable to doff the garment of flesh and see a nature uniquely simple and self-sufficient in itself, without admixture or composition. They therefore conceive of the Universal Cause precisely as they do of themselves, not taking into account that while a being that comes into existence through the union of several faculties needs several parts to serve the needs of each, God being uncreated and bringing all the others into being had no need of anything belonging to things generated.

For what are we to think? If He makes use of bodily organs, He has feet to to go forward. But wither will He go, since He fills everything? To whom will He go, when none is His equal. And to what purpose? For it cannot be out of concern for His health, as it is with us. Hands too He must have, both to receive and to give, yet He receives nothing from anyone, for aside from His lack of need, all possessions are His, and He gives by employing as His minister of His gifts the Logos [or Word] through whom He created the world. Nor does He have any needs of eyes. . . . What need is there to speak of the the organs of nourishment? If He has them, He takes nourishment, and after filling up, He rests; and after resting He has another need, and what follows on this I will not even discuss. These are the mythical inventions of the impious who theoretically represent the deity as of human form and as effectively having human emotions.

Why then does Moses speak of feet and hands, of entrances and exits, with regard to the Uncreated, or of His arming to ward off His enemies? For he represents Him as bearing a sword and using shafts and winds and devastating fire—roaring hurricane and thunderbolt the Prophets call them, using different expressions, and say they are the weapons of the Primal Cause. Why again does He speak of His jealousy, His wrath, His transports of anger and similar emotions, which he details and describes in human terms?

To those who make such inquiries he answers thus: "Sirs, who seeks to frame the best laws must have one goal, to profit all those who come in contact with them. Those who have been favored with good natural endowments and a training irreproachable in every respect, and thus find their later course through a highway broad and straight, have truth as their traveling companion; and being initiated by her into the authentic mysteries of the Existent, they do not assign to Him any of the traits of created being. . . . But those who are of a dull and obtuse nature, who have been ill served in their early training, incapable as they are of sharp vision, are in need of monitoring physicians who will devise the proper treatment of their present condition. . . . Let all such learn the lies that will benefit them, if they are incapable of becoming wise through truth. Thus the most esteemed physicians do not dare tell the truth to those dangerously ill in body, since they know that they will thereby become more disheartened and their sickness will not be cured, whereas through the consolation of the opposite approach they will bear their present condition more lightly and the illness will abate. . . .

Now since the lawgiver has become a supreme physician for the morbid states and maladies of the soul, he set himself one task and goal, to excise the diseases of the mind, roots and all, so that nothing remains to bear the germ of incurable disease. In this way he hoped to be able to extirpate them by representing the Primal Cause as employing threats, showing displeasure and implacable anger, and also using weaponry for his assaults on the unrighteous. For only thus can the fool be chided. Accordingly, it seems to me that with the two aforementioned principles, "God is as a man," and "God is not as a man," he has woven together two others closely akin and consistent with them, fear and love. For I know that all the exhortations to piety in the Law refer either to love or fear of the Existent. To those, then, who acknowledge no human part or emotion concerning the Existent, and honor Him for His own sake alone, love is the most appropriate, but fear is most suitable to the others. (Philo, *That God Is Immutable* 51–69)

[PHILO 1981: 139–141]

15. An Allegorical Interpretation of the Promised Land

Philo's exegesis of Scripture, an enterprise that constitutes the bulk of his published work, is profoundly allegorical, seeking out the "deeper" or "spiritual" meaning that lay beneath the literal understanding of the words. Here, for example is his interpretation of the text in Genesis that reads, "On that day He made a covenant with Abraham, saying, To your seed I will give this land from the river of Egypt to the great river Euphrates" (Gen. 15:18).

The literal meaning is that it describes the boundaries of the region between the two rivers, that of Egypt and the Euphrates, for anciently the land and the river were homonymously called "Egypt." . . . But as for the deeper meaning, it indicates felicity, which is the culmination of three goods: the spiritual, the bodily, and those which are external. This (teaching) was praised by some of the philosophers who came afterward, such as Aristotle and the Peripatetics, Moreover, this is said to have (also) been the legislation of Pythagoras. For Egypt is the symbol of the bodily and external goods, while the Euphrates is the symbol of the spiritual, for through them veritable and true joy comes into being, having as its source wisdom and every virtue. And the boundaries rightly take their beginning from Egypt and they end at the Euphrates. For in the end it is difficult to attain those things that pertain to the soul; but first one must proceed through the bodily and external goods, health and keenness of sense and beauty and strength, which are wont to flourish and grow and be attained in youth. And similarly those things that pertain to profitable business and piloting and agriculture and trade. All such things are proper to youth, especially those things that have been rightly mentioned. (Philo, *Questions and Their Solutions on Genesis* 3.16) [PHILO 1981: 228–229]

16. The Pleasures of Paradise

Jews and Christians after Philo struggled with this question of anthropomorphism in Scripture, but none quite so long or so hard as the Muslims. It is not that the Quran is more anthropomorphic than those other revelations; rather, the Muslim was, from his view of the origin and nature of the Book, somewhat less easy with allegorizing God's words for whatever reason. And yet it was done. The Quran, for example, has a great deal to say about the afterlife, and assurances to the pagans of Mecca of the physical reality of both Paradise and Gehenna are part of the earliest revelations in the Quran. Here we may note the words of Sura 76, which dates from the early Meccan period of Muhammad's career.

Was there not a time in the life of man when he was not even a thing? Verily We created man from a sperm yoked (to the ovum) to bring out his real substance, then gave him hearing and sight. We surely showed him the way that he may be either grateful or deny. We have prepared for unbelievers chains and collars and a blazing fire.

Surely the devotees will drink cups flavored with palm blossoms from a spring of which the votaries of God will drink and make it flow in abundance. Those who fulfill their vows and fear the Day whose evil shall be diffused far and wide, and feed the needy for the love of Him, and the orphans and the captives, saying: "We feed you for the sake of God, desiring neither recompense nor thanks. We fear the the dismal day calamitous from our Lord."

So God will protect them from the evil of that day, and grant them happiness and joy, and reward them for their perseverance with Paradise and silken robes where they will recline on couches feeling neither heat of the sun nor intense cold. The shade will bend over them, and low will hang clusters of grapes. Passed round will be silver flagons and goblets made of glass, and crystal clear bottles of silver, of which they will determine the measure themselves. There they will drink a cup flavored with ginger from a spring by the name of Salsabil. And boys of everlasting youth will go about attending them. Looking at them you would think they were pearls dispersed.

When you look around you will see delights and a great dominion. On their bodies will be garments of the finest silk and brocade, and they will be adorned with bracelets of silver; and their Lord will give them the purest draught to drink. (Quran 76:1–21)

The Muslim commentators approach these and other Quranic descriptions of Paradise in a number of different ways. Here, for example, is a cosmology, a laying out of the celestial geography of Paradise in the context of its creation; into its fabulous details have been integrated some of the themes of Islamic theodicy. Often in the three religions this cosmology comes in the form of a vision, but here the details have been supplied in a rather straightforward manner, presumably on the authority of the Prophet, and relayed through his contemporary Ibn Abbas.

Ibn Abbas, may God be pleased with him, said that then [that is, after the creation of the heavens] God created Paradise, which consists of eight gardens. . . . The eight gardens have gates of gold, jewel-encrusted and inscribed. On the first gate is written: "There is no god but the God and Muhammad is the Messenger of God." On the second is written: "The Gate of those who pray the five (liturgical daily) prayers, observing perfectly the ablutions and the prostrations." On the third is written: "The Gate of those who justify themselves by the purity of their souls." On the fourth gate is written: "The Gate of those who encourage the doing of what is approved and discourage the doing of what is disapproved." On the fifth gate is written: "The Gate of him who holds himself back from lusts." On the sixth gate is written: "The Gate of those who perform the Greater and Lesser Pilgrimage." On the seventh gate is written: "The Gate of those who go out on Holy War." On the eighth gate is written: "The Gate of those who desire," that is, those who avert their eyes (from unseemly things) and perform good works such as showing due affection to parents and being mindful of one's kin. By these gates will enter those whose works have been of the kind written on them. (Kisaʾi, *Stories of the Prophets*) [JEFFERY 1962: 172–173]

It is not always easy, or perhaps even useful, to connect a certain exegetical approach with a specific literary genre. The last passage cited above, which has a distinct homiletic flavor, occurs in a collection of narratives, the Stories of the Prophets. *The following sections of the homiletic* Arousing the Heedless *by Abuʾl-Layth al-Samarqandi (d. 983 C.E.) easily combine a Quranically based moral exhortation—the individual Prophetic tradition has already glossed the Quran, and Samarqandi braids a catena of these texts to make his own point—with an undisguised interest in the fabulous elements of Paradise.*

It is related of Ibn Abbas, may God be pleased with him, that he used to say: In Paradise are dark-eyed maidens of the type called "toys," who have been created out of four things, from musk, ambergris, camphor and saffron, stirred into a dough with water of life. All the celestial maidens love them dearly. Were one of them to spit into the ocean its waters would become sweet. On the throat of each of them is written: "He who would desire to have the like of me, let him do the works of obedience to my Lord." Mujahid said that the ground of Paradise is of silver, its dusk of musk, the trunks of its trees are of silver, their branches of pearl and emerald, their leaves and fruits hang low so that he who would eat standing can reach them, and likewise he who would eat sitting or even lying can reach them. Then he recited: "Its fruit clusters hang low" (Quran 86:14), that is, its fruits are near so that both he who is standing and he who is sitting can reach them. Abu Hurayra, may God be pleased with him, said: By Him who sent down the Book to Muhammad, upon whom be God's blessing and peace, the dwellers in Paradise increase in beauty and handsomeness as in this world the inhabitants increase in decrepitude. (Samarqandi, *Arousing the Heedless*) [JEFFERY 1962: 240–241]

There are problems with such anthropomorphisms. They are raised, not unnaturally, by a Christian polemicist.

The sage Abu'l-Fadl al-Haddadi has related to us . . . from Zayd ibn Arqam, who said: There came a man of the People of the Book to the Prophet, upon whom be God's blessing and peace, and said: "O Abu'l-Qasim [that is, Muhammad], do you pretend that the inhabitants of the Garden (really) eat and drink?" "Surely," he replied, "by Him in whose hand is my soul, every one of them will be given the capacity of a hundred men in eating and drinking and having intercourse." The man said: "But someone who eats or drinks has a need of relieving himself, whereas Paradise is too fine a place for there to be in it anything so malodorous." Muhammad replied: "A man's need to relieve himself will be satisfied by perspiring, which will be as sweet-smelling as musk." (Samarqandi, *Arousing the Heedless*) [JEFFERY 1962: 243]

In the following passage the physical delights of Paradise begin to recede into the background, and the exegetical focus turns to the vision of God in the afterlife.

In another tradition it is related that God, may He be exalted, will say to His angels, "Feed my saints," whereupon various kinds of food will be brought, in every bite of which they will find pleasure different from that they found in any other. When they have had their fill of eating, God, may He be exalted, will say, "Give My servants drink," whereupon drinks will be brought, in which they will find a pleasure different from that which they found in any other. When they have finished, God, may He be exalted, will say to them: "I am your Lord. I have made My promise to you come true. Now ask of Me and I will give it to you." They will reply: "O our Lord, we ask that You should be well pleased with us." This they will say two or three times, whereupon He will say: "I am well pleased with you, but today I have an increase (for you). I shall favor you with a token of regard greater than all that." Then the Veil will be removed and they will look upon Him for such a period as God wills. Then they will fall on their faces in a prostration, remaining prostrated for such a time as God pleases, whereat He will say to them: "Raise your heads. This is no place for worshiping." At that they will quite forget all the other enjoyment they have been having, for to see their Lord is the most precious of all their joys. (Samarqandi, *Arousing the Heedless*) [JEFFERY 1962: 242–243]

Samarqandi knows very well that this vision presents a problem, and so he intervenes to offer a correction and his own interpretation.

The lawyer [that is, the author, Abu'l-Layth al-Samarqandi], may
God have mercy on him, says: When he [presumably Muhammad, the
source of the anonymously transmitted tradition] speaks about the Veil
being lifted, he means the veil which is over them [that is, over the
glorified souls] which prevents them from seeing Him. As for his statement that they will look upon Him, some say (it means) that they will
look on a token such as they had not previously seen. Most of the learned,
however, say that it is to be taken according to its literal meaning, and
that they will actually see Him, though we know not how, save that it will
not be in an anthropomorphic manner, just as here on earth they knew
Him, but not in an anthropomorphic manner. (Samarqandi, *Arousing the
Heedless*) [JEFFERY 1962: 242–243]

17. Exegesis by the Number

*We have already seen that the sixth of Abulafia's "seven paths of knowledge of the
Torah" included a technique known as gematria. The ancients gave each letter of
the alphabet a numerical value, and these numerical equivalents of letters provided,
of course, an attractive and universally accepted way of penetrating into a sacred
text, as both Philo and the Christian Fathers understood and practiced long before
the medieval Jewish Kabbalists. The first example is from a Christian author probably but recently converted from Judaism.*

You will say, "But surely this people [the Jews] received circumcision as the seal of their Covenant?" Why, every Syrian and every Arab is
physically circumcised, and so are the idol priesthoods; but does that
make them members of the Jews' covenant? Even the very Egyptians
practice circumcision.

Dear children of love, here is a full explanation of it all. Circumcision
was given to us in the first place by Abraham; but he, when he circumcised himself, did so in spiritual prevision of Jesus. He got his instruction
from three letters of the alphabet, for the Scripture tells us that "out of
his own household Abraham circumcised eighteen and three hundred"
(Gen. 14:14, 17:23). How does his spiritual intuition come into this?
Well, notice how it specifies the eighteen first, and then, separated from
this, the three hundred. Now in writing eighteen, the ten is expressed by
the letter "I" and the eight by "E"; and there, you see, you have IE(sus).
And then, since grace was to come by a Cross, of which "T" is the shape,
it adds "and three hundred." Thus it indicates "Jesus" with two of the
letters and "the Cross" with the third. All this is perfectly well known to

Him who has graciously planted the seeds of His teaching in our hearts;
and a better interpretation than this I have never given to anybody. I am
persuaded, though, that you have every right to know it. (*Letter of Barnabas*
[ca. 130 C.E.] 9) [STANIFORTH 1968: 205–206]

*Other, better educated Christians and Jews could do much better than this. Au-
gustine, for example, explicates the number six.*

The ratio of the single to the double arises, no doubt, from the
ternary number, since one added to two makes three. But the whole
which these make reaches to the senary number, for one and two and
three make six. And this number on that account is called perfect because
it is completed in its own parts, for it has these three: one-sixth, one-third
and one-half; nor is there any other part found in it. . . . The sixth part
of it, then, is one; the third part, two, and the half, three. But one and two
and three complete the same six.

Holy Scripture commends to us the perfection of this number, especially in this, that God finished His works in six days, and on the sixth day
man was made in the image of God. And the Son of God came and was
made the Son of man, that he might re-create us after the image of God,
in the sixth age of the human race. For that is now the present age,
whether a thousand years apiece was assigned to each age, or whether we
trace our memorable and remarkable epochs or turning points of time in
the divine Scriptures, so that the first age is to be found from Adam until
Noah, and the second thence onwards to Abraham, and then next, according to the division of Matthew the Evangelist, from Abraham to
David, from David to the carrying away to Babylon, and from then to the
labor of the Virgin, which three ages joined to those other two make five.
Accordingly, the birth of the Lord began the sixth, which is now going
onwards until the hidden end of time.

We recognize also in this senary number a kind of figure of time, in
that threefold mode of division by which we compute one portion before
the Law, another under the Law, and a third under grace. In which last
time we have received the sacrament of renewal, that we may be renewed
also in the end of time, in every part, by the resurrection of the flesh, and
so may be made whole of our entire infirmity, not only of soul but also
of body. And thence that woman who was made whole and upright by
the Lord after she had been bowed by infirmity through the binding of
Satan (Luke 13:10–17) is understood to be a type of the Church. . . . And
this woman had her infirmity for eighteen years, which is thrice six. . . .
Nearly too in the same place in the Gospel (Luke 13:6–9) is that fig tree

which was convicted also by the third year of its miserable barrenness. But intercession was made for it, that it might be left alone for that year, that if it bore fruit, well; if otherwise, it should be cut down. For both three years belong to the same threefold division, and the months of three years make a square of six, which is six times six. . . .

And not without reason is the number six understood to be put for a year in the building up of the body of the Lord, as a figure of which he said he would raise up in three days the Temple destroyed by the Jews. For they said, "Forty and six years was this Temple in building" (John 2:20). And six times forty-six makes two hundred and seventy-six. And this number of days completes nine months and six days, which are reckoned, as it were, ten months for the pregnancy of women; not because all come to term on the sixth day after the ninth month, but because the perfection itself of the body of the Lord is found to have been brought in so many days to the birth, as the authority of the Church maintains upon the tradition of the elders. For he is believed to have been conceived on the twenty-fifth of March, upon which day he also suffered; so the womb of the Virgin, in which he was conceived, where no one of mortals was begotten, corresponds to the new grave in which he was buried, "wherein was never man laid" (John 19:41–42), neither before nor since. But he was born, according to tradition, on December twenty-fifth. If, then, you reckon from that day to this you find two hundred and seventy-six days, which is forty-six times six. (Augustine, *City of God* 4.4–5) [AUGUSTINE 1948: 2:735–736]

Or Philo himself on seven:

So august is the dignity inherent by nature in the number seven that it has a unique relation distinguishing it from all other numbers with the first ten: for of these some beget without being begotten; some are begotten but do not beget; some do both of these, both beget and are begotten: seven alone is not found in any of those categories. We must establish this assertion by giving proof of it. Well then, one begets all the subsequent numbers, while it is begotten by none whatever; eight is begotten twice four, but begets no number within the decade; four again holds the place of both, of parent and offspring, for it begets eight by being doubled and is begotten by twice two.

It is the nature of seven alone, as I have said, neither to beget nor to be begotten. For this reason other philosophers liken this number to the motherless virgin Nike, who is said to have appeared out of the head of Zeus, while the Pythagoreans liken it to the principle of all things, for that which neither begets nor is begotten remains changeless; for creation takes place in change, since there is change both in that which begets and in that which is begotten, in the one that it may beget and in the other that it may be begotten. There is only one thing that neither causes change nor experiences it, the original Ruler and Sovereign. Of Him seven may be fitly said to be the symbol. Evidence of what I say is supplied by (the Pythagorean philosopher) Philolaus in these words: "There is," he says, "a supreme Ruler of all things, God, ever One, abiding, without change, Himself (alone) like to Himself, different from all others." (Philo, *On the Creation of the World* 99)

18. The Literal and the Allegorical in the Bible

There were, for all the willingness to indulge in allegorical exegesis in order to avoid the pitfalls of anthropomorphism, grave dangers in pushing that type of interpretation too far, particularly as regards the external observance of the Law, as Philo himself is quick to insist.

There are some who, taking the laws in their literal sense as symbols of intelligible realities, are overprecise in their investigation of the symbol, while frivolously neglecting the letter. Such people, I, for my part, should blame for their cool indifference, for they ought to have cultivated both a more precise investigation of things invisible and an unexceptional stewardship of things visible. As it is, as if living alone by themselves in a wilderness, or as if they had become disembodied souls, knowing neither city nor village nor household nor any company of humans at all, transcending what is approved by the many, they track the absolute truth in its naked self. And yet these men are taught by Sacred Scripture to be concerned with public opinion, and to abolish no part of the customs ordained by inspired men, greater than those of our own day.

For all that the Seventh Day teaches us the power of the Unoriginate and the non-action of created beings, let us by no means annul the laws laid down for its observance, kindling the fire, tilling the earth, carrying burdens, instituting indictments, sitting in judgment, demanding the return of deposits, recovering loans, or doing all else that is permitted on days which are not holy. And though it is true that the holy day is a symbol of spiritual joy and thankfulness to God, let us not bid adieu to the annual seasonal assemblies. And though it is true that circumcision indicates the cutting out of pleasure and all passions and the removal of godless conceit under which the mind supposed itself capable of engendering through its own powers, let us not abrogate the law laid down for circumcising. For we shall be neglecting the Temple service and a thousand other things if we are to pay regard only to that which is revealed by the inner meaning. We ought rather to look on the external observance as resembling the body and the inner meaning as resembling the soul. Just as we then provide for the body, inasmuch as it is the abode of the soul, so we must attend to the letter of the laws. For if we keep these, we shall obtain an understanding of those things of which they are symbols, and in addition we shall escape the censure and the accusations of the multitude. (Philo, *The Migration of Abraham* 89–93) [PHILO 1981: 81–82]

19. Giving a Little Grace to the Scholars

Almost all Jews would assent to the sentiments just cited from Philo, but the majority would likewise agree that, no matter how great the danger, it was impossible or inadvisable to adhere to a literal interpretation in all instances. One who warned of the dangers and at the same time permitted himself and others considerable allegorical space in the body of Scripture was Nachmanides (d. ca. 1270 C.E.). He was by no means a literalist; indeed, he was the first major Jewish commentator on the Torah to regard Genesis through the prism of the Kabbala, that storehouse of Jewish, Hellenic, and Islamic esotericism that was gaining increased attention in Jewish circles. The reader of Nachmanides' commentary could not say, however, that he had not been warned.

Now our Sages have already said (B.Rosh Hashanah 21b): "Fifty gates of understanding were created in the world and all were transmitted to Moses with one exception, as it was said, 'You have made him a little lower than the angels' (Ps. 8:6)." . . . Everything that was transmitted to Moses our teacher through the forty-nine gates of understanding was written in the Torah explicitly or by implication in words, in the numerical value of the letters or in the form of the letters, that is, whether written normally or with some change of form such as bent or crooked letters and other deviations, or in the tips of the letters and their crownlets, as the Sages have said (B.Menachoth 29b): "When Moses ascended to heaven he found the Holy One, blessed be He, attaching crownlets to certain letters of the Torah. He [Moses] said to Him: 'What are these for?' The Lord said to him: 'One man is destined to interpret mountains of Law on their basis.' 'Whence do you know this?' He answered him: 'This is a law given to Moses on Mount Sinai.' " For these hints cannot be understood except from mouth to mouth from Moses, who received it on Sinai.

Based on this tradition, the Sages have said in the Great Commentary on the Song of Songs concerning King Hezekiah (when he was visited by a delegation from the king of Babylon): "He showed them the Book of Crownlets." This book is known and is available to everyone. In it is explained how many crowned *alephs* there are in the Torah, how many *beths*, and the frequency of the rest of the letters and the number of crownlets on each one. The praise which the Sages bestowed on this book and the disclosure of Heze-kiah's secret to the delegation were not for the crownlets themselves but rather for a knowledge of their essence and their meanings, which consist of many exceedingly profound secrets.

There in the Great Commentary on the Song of Songs (1:28), the Sages have also said: "It is written: 'And He declared to you His covenant,' which means, He declared to you the Book of Genesis, which relates the beginning of His creation, 'which He commanded you to perform, even the ten words' (Deut. 4:13), meaning the ten commandments, ten for Scripture and ten for Talmud. For from what source did Elihu the son of Barachel the Buzite come and reveal to Israel the secrets of the behemoth (Job 40:15) and the leviathan (Job 40:25)? And from what source did Ezekiel come and reveal to them the mysteries of the Divine Chariot (Ezek. 1)? It is this which Scripture says, 'The king has brought me into his chambers,' " meaning that everything can be learned from the Torah.

Solomon is, of course, the prime example of the human who drank deeply of secret knowledge and lore. After quoting a number of examples of Solomon's Torah-derived but somewhat more than human wisdom, Nachmanides returns to the main question of his commentary.

And now know and see what I shall answer to those who question me concerning my writing a commentary on the Torah. I shall conduct myself in accordance with the custom of the early scholars to bring peace to the mind of the students, tired of the exile and afflictions, who read in the Seder [that is, Torah selections assigned for reading on Sabbaths and festivals] on the Sabbaths and the festivals, and attract them with the plain meanings of Scripture, and with some things that are pleasant to the listeners and give "grace."

The Hebrew word for "grace" is actually an abbreviation for "hidden wisdom," that is, of the Kabbala.

. . . [T]o the scholars . . .

Now behold I bring into a faithful covenant and give proper counsel to all who look into this book not to reason or to entertain any thought concerning any of the mystic hints which I write regarding the hidden matters of the Torah, for I do hereby firmly make known to him that my words will not be comprehended or known at all by any reasoning or contemplation, except from the mouth of a wise Kabbalist speaking into the ear of an understanding recipient. Reasoning about them is foolish; any unrelated thought brings much damage and withholds the benefit. "Let him not trust in vanity, deceiving himself" (Job 15:31), for these reasonings will bring him nothing but evil, as if they spoke falsely against the Lord, which cannot be forgotten. . . . Rather let such see in our commentaries novel interpretations of the plain meanings of Scripture and Midrashim, and let them take moral instruction from the mouths of our holy Rabbis: "Into that which is beyond you, do not seek; into that which is more powerful than you, do not inquire; about that which is concealed from you, do not desire to know; about that which is hidden from you, do not ask. Contemplate that which is permitted to you, and engage not yourself in hidden things." (Nachmanides, *Commentary on Genesis*) [NACHMANIDES 1971: 10–16]

20. Dull Masses and Minds Tied Down to Sensibles

Almost from its appearance in the Jewish tradition, the practice of allegorical exegesis was accompanied by warnings that it was not appropriate for every believer, that it should be reserved for the mature and the learned. This advice appears sagacious enough, but it led, not too far down the path, to a profound distinction between "pure truth"—the domain of the philosopher, on the one hand—and the crude and materialistic expressions by which the prophet, who certainly knew far better, was constrained to address the masses in Scripture. What follows is one expression of such a view, in this case from the Muslim philosopher Ibn Sina, or, as the West called him, Avicenna (d. 1038 C.E.).

As for religious law, one general principle is to be admitted, to wit, that religions and religious laws promulgated through a prophet aim at addressing the masses as a whole. Now it is obvious that the deeper truths concerning the real Unity (of God), to wit, that there is one Creator, who is exalted above quantity, quality, place, time, position and change, which lead to the belief that God is one without anyone to share His species, nor is He made of parts, quantitative or conceptual, that neither is He transcendent nor immanent, nor can He be pointed to as being anywhere—it is obvious that these deeper truths cannot be communicated to the multitude. For if this had been communicated in its true form to the bedouin Arabs or the crude Hebrews, they would have refused straightway to believe and would have unanimously proclaimed that the belief to which they had been invited was a belief in an absolute nonentity.

This is why the whole account of the Unity (of God) in religion is (expressed) in anthropomorphisms. The Quran does not contain even a hint to (the deeper truth about) this important problem, nor a detailed account concerning even the obvious matters needed about the doctrine of Unity, for a part of the account is apparently anthropomorphic, while the other part contains absolute transcendence [that is, the total unlikeness of God to His creation], but in general terms, without specification or detail. The anthropomorphic phrases are innumerable, but they [that is, the orthodox interpreters of the Quran] do not accept them as such. If this is the position concerning the Unity (of God), what of the less important matters of belief?

Some people may say: "The Arabic language allows wide use and metaphor; anthropomorphisms like the hand and the face (of God), His coming down in the canopies of clouds, His coming, going, laughter, shame, anger are all correct (linguistically); only the way of their use and their context show whether they have been employed metaphysically or literally." . . . Let us grant that all these (expressions) are metaphors. Where, then, we ask, are the texts which give a clear indication of pure Unity to which doubtlessly the essence of this righteous faith—whose greatness is acclaimed by the wise men of the entire world—invites? . . .

Upon my life, if God the Exalted did charge a prophet that he should communicate the reality about these (theological) matters to the masses with dull natures and with minds tied down to pure sensibles, and then constrained him to pursue relentlessly and successfully the task of bringing faith and salvation to those same masses, and then, to crown all, He charged him to undertake the purifying training of all the souls so they may be able to understand these truths, then He has certainly laid upon him a duty incapable of fulfillment by any man—unless the ordinary man receives a special gift from God, a supernal power or a divine inspiration, in which case the instrumentality of the prophet will be superfluous.

But let us even grant that the Arabian revelation is metaphor and allegory according to the usage of the Arabic language. What will they say about the Hebrew revelation—a monument of utter anthropomorphism from beginning to end? One cannot say that that book is tampered with through and through, for how can this be with a book disseminated through innumerable people living in distant lands, with so different ambitions—like Jews and Christians with all their mutual antagonisms?

All this shows that religions are intended to address the masses in terms intelligible to them, seeking to bring home to them what transcends their intelligence by means of metaphor and symbol. Otherwise, religions would be of no use whatever. (Ibn Sina, *Treatise on Sacrifice*) [RAHMAN 1958: 42–44]

21. Abraham and Sarah as Matter and Form

Philo may have understood how to separate, and at the same time to reverence, both the literal and the allegorical sense of Scripture. But the attractions of the latter at the expense of the plain meaning of God's word continued to be felt in the Jewish community, and an increased familiarity with secular learning, most of it Greek in origin and much of it transmitted to the Jews through Muslim scholars like Ibn Sina, did nothing to lessen the danger. In 1305 C.E. Solomon ben Adret, a leading figure in the struggle between philosophy and the traditional learning, issued the following warning from Barcelona to his fellow Jews in Provence.

It is now some time since our attention was drawn by people from the land of Provence, the chosen remnant, who were jealous for the faith of Moses and the Jews, to the fact that there are men who falsify the Law, and that he is regarded as wise who sits down to demolish the walls and who destroys the words of the Law. They hew out for themselves cisterns, broken cisterns, and they impute to the words of the Law and the words of the sages meanings which are not right. Concerning the two Laws [that is, the written and the oral Torah] they utter in the synagogues and the houses of study words by which none can live. Regardless of the glory of all Israel, they break down all the fences of the Law, and against our holy fathers they put forth their tongue, a thing which even the worshipers of idols have not done. For they say that Abraham and Sarah represent matter and form, and that the twelve tribes of Israel are the twelve constellations. . . . The blasphemers of God further say that the holy vessels which were sanctified, the Urim and the Thummim [cf. Exod. 28:15–21], are the instrument known as the astrolabe, which men make for themselves. . . .

A man who does such things reduces the entire Bible to useless allegories; indeed they trifle with and pervert all the commandments in order to make the yoke of their burden lighter to themselves. Their reports terrify us, and all who arrive here tell us new things. "Truth has stumbled in the street" (Isa. 59:14), for some of them say that all that was written from the section of Genesis as far as the giving of the Law is nothing more than allegory. . . . They show that they have no faith in the plain meaning of the commandments.

The chief reason for all this is that they are infatuated with alien sciences, "of Sidon and Moab" (Judg. 10:9), and pay homage to the Greek books. . . . The children that are consecrated to heaven from their mothers' womb are drawn away from the breasts and are taught the books and the language of the Chaldeans, instead of rising early to study the Jewish faith in the houses of their teachers. Now a boy born upon the knees of natural science, who sees Aristotle's sevenfold proofs concerning it, really believes in it, and denies the Chief Cause. If we refute him, he becomes all the more impious. They read the Law with their lips, but their heart is not sound inwardly, and they pervert it in seven ways. . . . They are ashamed when they speak and they lecture; they speak with their mouths but make hints with the finger that it is impossible to change nature, and they thereby declare to all that they do not believe in the creation of the universe, or in any of the miracles recorded in the Torah. (Solomon ben Adret, *Letter to Provence*)

22. The Past Foreshadows the Future

Tell me now, you who are so anxious to be under law, will you not listen to what the Law says? It is written there that Abraham had two sons, one by his slave and the other by his free-born wife. The slave woman's son was born in the course of nature, the free woman's through God's promise. This is an allegory. The two women stand for two covenants. The one bearing children into slavery is the covenant that comes from Mount Sinai: that is Hagar. Sinai is a mountain in Arabia and it represents the Jerusalem of today, for she and her children are in slavery. But the heavenly Jerusalem is the free woman; she is our mother. For Scripture says: "Rejoice, O barren woman who never bore child; break into a shout of joy, you who never knew a mother's pangs; for the deserted wife shall have more children than she who lives with the husband." (Paul, *To the Galatians* 4:21–27)

This is a capital text for the entire Christian understanding of Scripture, that is, the Jewish Bible, which in the earliest Christian times constituted the only Holy Book. With great ease and confidence Paul asserts, "The two women stand for two covenants" and so teaches all succeeding generations of Christians how they are to read and understand their Jewish past—not simply as a repository of prophecy concerning the Messiah, which Jesus fulfilled in his own life, as the Gospels themselves, and in particular Matthew, already insisted, but as a testimony to a deeper reality. The prophecies of the Bible not only predict the New Dispensation of Jesus, but the very events of biblical history reflect those that are to come: they foreshadow them. A classic statement of the theory can be found in Augustine (d. 430 C.E.), cast in the same categories of an earthly and a heavenly Jerusalem invoked by Paul.

Wherefore just as that divine oracle to Abraham, Isaac and Jacob, and all the other prophetic signs and sayings which are given in the earlier sacred writings, so also prophecies from this time of the kings pertain partly to the nation of Abraham's flesh, and partly to that seed of his in which all nations are blessed as fellow heirs of Christ by the New Testament, to the possessing of eternal life and the kingdom of the heavens. Therefore they pertain partly to the bond maid who births to bondage, that is, the earthly Jerusalem, which is in bondage with her children; but partly to the free city of God, that is, the true Jerusalem eternal in the heavens, whose children are all those who live according to God in the earth. But there are (also) some things among them which are understood to pertain to both, to the bond maid properly and to the free woman figuratively. . . .

And this kind of prophecy, as it were compacted and commingled of both the others in the ancient canonical books, containing historical narratives, is of very great significance and greatly exercises the wits of those who search Holy Scripture. For example, what we read of historically as predicted and fulfilled in the seed of Abraham according to the flesh [that is, the Jews], we must also inquire the allegorical meaning of, as it is to be fulfilled in the seed of Abraham according to faith [that is, in the Church]. And so much is this the case that some have thought that there is nothing in these books either foretold and effected, or effected though not foretold, that does not insinuate something else which is to be referred by figurative signification to the city of God on high, and to her children who are pilgrims in this life.

But if this be so, then the utterances of the prophets, or rather the whole of those Scriptures that are reckoned under the title of the Old Testament, will be not of three but of two different kinds. For there will be nothing there which pertains to the terrestrial Jerusalem only, if whatever is there said and fulfilled, or concerns her, signifies something which also refers by allegorical prefiguration to the celestial Jerusalem. . . .

But just as I think that they err greatly who are of the opinion that none of the records of affairs in that kind of writing means anything more than that they happened, so I think those very daring who contend that the whole gist of their contents lies in their allegorical significations. Therefore I have maintained that they are threefold, not twofold. Yet, in holding this opinion, I do not blame those who may be able to draw out of everything there a spiritual meaning, only saving, first of all, the historical truth. (Augustine, *City of God* 12.3) [AUGUSTINE 1948: 2:368–369]

We can observe Augustine the exegete at work and the various types of exegesis in the following passage on the description of Paradise in chapters 2 and 3 of the Book of Genesis. His first concern, though not his chief one, is to save the historical truth.

Some allegorize all that concerns Paradise itself, where the first men, the parents of the human race are, according to the truth of Holy Scripture, recorded to have been. And they understand all its trees and fruit-bearing plants as virtues and habits of life, as if they had no existence in the external world but were only spoken of or related for the sake of spiritual meaning. As if there were no terrestrial Paradise! As if there never existed those two women, Sarah and Hagar, nor the two sons who were born to Abraham, the one of the bond woman, the other of the free, because the Apostle (Paul) says that in them the two covenants were prefigured. . . . No one, then, denies that Paradise may signify the life of the blessed; its four rivers, the four virtues; its trees, all useful knowledge; its fruits, the customs of the godly; its tree of life, wisdom itself, the mother of all good; and the tree of the knowledge of good and evil, the experience of a broken commandment. (Augustine, *City of God* 13.21) [AUGUSTINE 1948: 2:229]

23. Moralizing Exegesis

Augustine's examples of a moralizing exegesis of this passage of Genesis are neither randomly chosen nor invented by him. They come from Philo, the Hellenized Jew who lived and wrote in Alexandria in the first years of the Christian era. Almost all of his works are in the form of an extended philosophical commentary on the Torah, and the one called On the Allegory of the Laws deals with the same second and third chapters of Genesis.

And God caused to come forth from the earth every tree, providing delight to the sight and food for nourishment, and in the middle of the garden the tree of life and the tree of the knowledge of good and evil (Gen. 2:9).

Moses then points out what trees of virtue God plants in the soul. These are the various individual virtues, and the acts that correspond to them, total moral victory, and what philosophers call the common duties. These are the plants of the garden. He characterizes these plants to show that what is good is also most delightful amd pleasurable. While some of the arts and sciences are theoretical but not practical, such as geometry and astronomy, and others are practical but not theoretical, like the arts of the carpenter and the coppersmith and all the arts that are called mechanical, virtue is both theoretical and practical; for it obviously involves theory, since philosophy, the road that leads to it, includes theory through its three parts of logic, ethics and physics; but it also involves conduct, for virtue is the art of the whole of life, and life includes all kinds of conduct.

And while virtue embraces both theory and practice, it is also of surpassing excellence in other respects; for indeed the theory of virtue is perfect in beauty, and the practice and exercise of it is a prize to be striven after. Thus Moses says that it is both "beautiful to look upon"—an expression indicating its theoretical side—and "good to eat," words which point to its excellence in use and practice.

Now the tree of life is virtue in the broadest sense, which some call simply "goodness." From it the particular virtues derive their existence. This is also why it is located in the middle of the garden, where it occupies the central, all-encompassing position, so that it might be attended in royal fashion by bodyguards on either side. But some say that it is the heart that is called the tree of life, since it is both the cause of life and it has been given the central place in the body, as it naturally would, being, in their view, the ruling principle. But these people should remember that they are holding an opinion more appropriate to the physician than to the philosopher, while we, as we have said, maintain that virtue in its most generic aspect is called the tree of life. . . .

A river goes forth from Eden to water the garden, thence it is separated into four sources: the name of the first is Pheison; this is what encircles all the land of Havila, where the gold is, and the gold of that land is good; and where there is the ruby and the emerald. And the name of the second is Geon; this encompasses all the land of Ethiopia. And the third river is Tigris; this is the one that runs in front of Assyria. And the fourth river is Euphrates (Gen. 2:10–14).

By these rivers Moses intends to indicate the particular virtues. These are four in number: prudence, self-mastery, courage and justice. The large source, of which the other four are derivatives, is virtue in its general sense, which we have already called goodness. The four derivative rivers are the same number of virtues. The genus virtue first arises from

Eden, that is, the wisdom of God, which is full of joy and brightness and exultation, glorying and priding itself only in God its Father; but the specific virtues, which are four in number, are derived from the generic virtue, which like a river waters the perfect achievements of each of them with an abundant flow of noble actions. (Philo, *On the Allegory of the Laws* 1.56–64)

24. Augustine on the Christian Interpretation of Scripture

Augustine, then, is aware of this rather straightforward Jewish reproduction of Stoic ethical theory. Although he accepts its validity, he has his own, more specifically Christian, and so "more profitable" way of reading the same passage in Genesis.

These things can also and more profitably be understood of the Church, so that they become prophetic foreshadowings of things to come. Thus Paradise is the Church, as it is called in the Song of Songs (Song of Sol. 4:13); the four rivers of Paradise are the four Gospels; the fruit trees, the saints and the fruit of their works; the tree of life is the Holy of Holies, Christ; the tree of the knowledge of good and evil, the will's free choice. For if man despises the will of God, he can only destroy himself; and so he learns the difference between consecrating himself to the common good and reveling in his own. . . . These and other similar allegorical interpretations may be suitably put upon Paradise without giving offense to anyone, while yet we believe the strict truths of history, confirmed by its circumstantial narrative of facts. (Augustine, *City of God* 13.21) [AUGUSTINE 1948: 2:229–230]

25. Origen on the Triple Sense of Scripture

Newly converted Gentile Christians schooled in the methods of Greek literary exegesis became increasingly adept at extracting a variety of understandings from Scripture. One of the first to do so was Origen (d. ca. 254 C.E.), a graduate of the university of Alexandria, who was a pioneer Christian theologian and the foremost Christian biblical scholar of his time.

The cause of false opinions and of impious or ignorant assertions about God appears to be nothing else than that the Scriptures are not understood according to their spiritual meaning but are interpreted according to the mere letter. And therefore to those who believe that the Sacred Books are not the composition of men, but were composed by the inspiration of the Holy Spirit, according to the will of the Father of all things through Jesus Christ, and that they have come down to us, we must point out the modes of interpretation which appear correct to us, who cling to the standard of the heavenly Church according to the succession of the Apostles of Jesus Christ.

Now that there are certain mystical economies made known in the Holy Scriptures, all, even the most simple of those who adhere to the word, have believed; but what these are, the candid and modest confess they do not know. If, then, one were to be perplexed by the incest of Lot with his daughters, and about the two wives of Abraham, and the two sisters married to Jacob, they can return no answer but this, that they are mysteries not understood by us. . . .

The way, then, as it seems to me, in which we ought to deal with the Scriptures and extract from them their meaning is the following, which has been ascertained from the sayings (of the Scriptures) themselves. By Solomon in the Proverbs we find some rule as this enjoined respecting the the teaching of the divine Writings, "and portray them in a threefold manner, in counsel and knowledge, to answer words of truth to those who propose them to you" (Prov. 22:20). One ought, then, to portray the ideas of Holy Scripture in a threefold manner upon his soul in order that the simple man may be edified by the "flesh," as it were, of Scripture, for so we name the obvious sense; while he who has ascended a certain way may be edified by the "soul," as it were. The perfect man, and he who resembles those spoken of by the Apostle (Paul) when he says, "We speak wisdom to those who are perfect, but not the wisdom of the world . . ." (1 Cor. 2:6–7), may receive edification from the spiritual law which is the shadow of things to come. *For as a man consists of body and soul and spirit, so in the same way does the Scripture consist, which has been arranged by God for the salvation of men.* (Origen, *On First Principles* 4.9–11)

Granted that there are three senses of Scripture that correspond to the division of the human person into body, soul, and spirit, how does one know when to depart from the literal or "corporeal" sense of Scripture and interpret it in a spiritual fashion? God himself, Origen responds, has provided the signals.

Since, if the usefulness of the legislation and the sequence and beauty of the history (found in Scripture) were universally evident, we should not believe that anything else could be understood in the Scriptures save what was obvious, the Word of God has arranged that certain stumbling blocks, and offenses and impossibilities should be introduced into the midst of the law and the history, so that we may not, though being drawn away in all directions by the merely attractive nature of the language, either fall away from the true doctrines, as learning nothing worthy of God, or, by not departing from the letter, come to the knowledge of nothing more divine. And this too we must know: that since the principal aim is to announce the "spiritual" connection in these things that are done and that ought to be done, where the Word found that things done according to the history could be adapted to these mystic senses, He made use of them, concealing from the multitude the deeper meaning. . . . And at other times impossibilities are recorded for the sake of the more skillful and inquisitive, in order that they may give themselves over to the task of investigating what is written and so attain a becoming conviction of the manner in which a meaning worthy of God must be sought out in such subjects. (Ibid. 4.15)

26. "Giving a Greek Twist to Foreign Tales"

The effect of Origen on his Christian contemporaries may be gauged by this homage by Gregory, called "the Wonderworker," to the man who converted and instructed him.

He [Origen] himself interpreted and clarified whatever was obscure and enigmatic (in Scripture), as in fact are many utterances of the sacred voices, whether because God is accustomed to speak in that fashion to men so that the divine word may not enter bare and unveiled into some unworthy soul, as most are; or perhaps because time and antiquity have caused the oracles of God, which are by nature most clear and simple, to appear indistinct and dark to us. . . . But Origen made them clear and brought them into the light. This gift was his alone of all men whom I have known personally. (Gregory Thaumaturgus, *Io Origen*)

Origen was as well known in pagan intellectual circles as he was in the newly emerging Christian ones. But his methods of Scriptural exegesis did not receive such high marks among the Hellenists, who in the third century were beginning to understand something of the appeal, and the threat, of Christianity. Origen may have attended classes at Alexandria with Plotinus, the chief Platonist of late antiquity, and this is the reaction of one of Plotinus' students, Porphyry (ca. 275 C.E.), to the Christian intellectual and what he represented.

"Enigmas" is the pretentious name given by the Christians to the perfectly plain statements of Moses, thus glorifying them as oracles filled with hidden mysteries and beguiling the critical faculty by their extravagant nonsense. . . . This absurd nonsense should be put to the account of a man I met when I was still quite young, who enjoyed a great reputation and, thanks to the works he left behind him, still enjoys it. I mean Origen, whose fame among teachers of these theories is widespread. He was a pupil of Ammonius (in Alexandria), the most distinguished philosopher of our time. He acquired a great deal of theoretical knowledge with the help of his master, but when it came to choosing the right way of life, he went in the opposite direction. For Ammonius was (born) a Christian and was raised as a Christian by his parents, but when he began to think philosophically he promptly changed to a law-abiding way of life; Origen, on the other hand, a Greek schooled in Greek thought, plunged headlong into un-Greek recklessness. When he was filled with that, he sold himself and his dialectical skills. He lived like a Christian in his defiance of the law, but in his metaphysical and theological ideas he played the Greek, giving a Greek twist to foreign tales. He constantly connected himelf with Plato, and was at home among the writings of Numenius and Cronius, Apollophanes, Longinus, and Moderatus, Nicomachus, and the more eminent disciples of Pythagoras. He also used the books of Chaeremon the Stoic and Cornutus, which taught him the allegorical method of interpreting the Greek mysteries, a method he applied to the Jewish Scriptures. (Porphyry, *Against the Christians*)

27. A Christian Meditation on the Psalms

The Christians elicited those "prophetic foreshadowing of things to come" from all the books of the Bible, but some of the chief and most popular texts were to be found in the Psalms. One of the most commonly cited and commented upon of David's "prophecies" concerning the Messiah who was to issue from his line was Psalm 110.

> The Lord said to my lord,
> "Sit at My right hand
> while I make your enemies your footstool."
> The Lord will stretch forth from Sion your mighty scepter;
>   hold sway over your enemies!
> Your people come forward willingly on your day of battle.
> In majestic holiness, from the womb,
>   from the dawn, yours was the dew of youth.
> The Lord has sworn and will not relent.
>   "You are a priest forever,
>   after the manner of Melchizedek."
> The Lord is at your right hand.

He crushes kings in the day of His anger.
He works judgment upon the nations,
    heaping up bodies,
    crushing heads far and wide.
He drinks from the stream on his way;
    therefore he holds his head high.

For the Jews of the era of its composition this poem or hymn likely had a liturgical function connected with the coronation of an Israelite king. For Augustine, as for most Christians since the days of the Apostles—and for Jesus himself, as the Gospel (Matt. 22:44) would have it—Psalm 110 was a prophecy pure and simple, and as such could be referred immediately to Christ the Messianic priest-king, as it was by Peter in a sermon reported in the Acts of the Apostles.

Men of Israel, listen to me. I speak of Jesus of Nazareth, a man singled out by God and made known to you through miracles, portents and signs, which God worked among you through him, as you well know. When he had been given up to you, by the deliberate plan and choice of God, you used heathen men to crucify and kill him. But God raised him up to life again, setting him free from the pangs of death, because it could not be that death should keep him in its grip. For David says of him:

"I foresaw that the presence of the Lord would be with me always,
For He is my right hand so that I may not be shaken;
Therefore my heart was glad and my tongue spoke my joy;
Moreover my flesh shall dwell in hope,
For You will not abandon my soul to death,
Nor let Your loyal servant suffer corruption.
You have shown me the ways of life,
You will fill me with gladness by Your presence."
(Ps. 16:8–11)

Let me tell you plainly, my friends [Peter continues], that the Patriarch David died and was buried and his tomb is here [that is, in Jerusalem] to this very day. It is clear therefore that he spoke (in those lines) as a prophet, who knew that God had sworn to him that one of his own direct descendants would sit on his throne; and when he said that he was not abandoned to death and his flesh never suffered corruption, he spoke with foreknowledge of the Resurrection of the Messiah.

The Jesus we speak of has been raised by God, as we can all bear witness. Exalted thus with God's right hand, he received the Holy Spirit from the Father, as was promised, and all that we now see and hear flows from him. For it was not David who went up to heaven: his own words are "The Lord said to my Lord, 'Sit at my right hand while I make your enemies your footstool.' " Let all Israel then accept as certain that God has made this Jesus, whom you crucified, both Lord and Messiah. (Acts of the Apostles 2:22–36)

By the time of Augustine the emphasis had shifted from this psalm's prediction of the Messiahship of Jesus to a foreshadowing of his priesthood and the invocation of Melchizedek.

Just as that psalm (Ps. 45) also where Christ is most openly proclaimed as Priest, so even here (in Psalm 110) as King. "The Lord said to my Lord, you shall sit at My right hand when I make your enemies your footstool under your feet." That Christ sits at the right hand of the Father is believed, not seen; that his enemies also are put under his feet does not yet appear; it is being done, it will appear at last; yes, this is now believed; afterward it shall be seen. But what follows, "When the Lord from Sion hands you your scepter, march forth through the ranks of your enemies," is so clear that to deny it would imply not merely unbelief and mistake, but downright impudence. And even the enemies must certainly confess that from Sion has been sent the law of Christ which we call the Gospel, and acknowledge it as the symbol of his power. But that he rules in the midst of his enemies, these same enemies among whom he rules bear witness, gnashing their teeth and being consumed, and having power to do nothing against him.

Then what he says a little later, "The Lord has sworn and will not change His purpose," by which words He intimates that what He adds is immutable, "You are a priest forever in the succession of Melchizedek," who is permitted to doubt of whom these things are said, seeing that now there is nowhere a priesthood and sacrifice after the succession of Aaron, and everywhere men offer under Christ as the Priest, which Melchizedek showed when he blessed Abraham?

Therefore to these manifest things are to be referred, when rightly understood, those things in the same psalm that are set down a little more obscurely, and we have already made known in our popular sermons how these things are to be rightly understood. So also in that where Christ utters through prophecy the humiliation of his Passion, saying, "They have pierced my hands and my feet; they have numbered all my bones; yes, they looked and stared at me" (Ps. 22:16–17). By which words he certainly meant his body stretched out on the Cross, with the hands and feet pierced and perforated by the striking through of the nails, and that he had in that way made himself a spectacle to those who looked and stared. And he [David] adds, "They parted my garments among them, and over my clothing they cast lots" (Ps. 22:8–9). How this prophecy has been fulfilled the Gospel history narrates.

Then, indeed, the other things also which are said there less openly are rightly understood when they agree with those which shine forth with so great clarity, especially because those things also which we do not believe as past but survey as present, are beheld by the whole world, being now exhibited just as they were read of in this very psalm predicted so long before. (Augustine, *City of God* 17.17) [AUGUSTINE 1948: 2:395–396]

28. Explaining Away the Torah

The early Christian was faced with the problem of what to do with that other, sometimes embarrassing Word of God that had been given to the Jews. In many instances the Bible could be read typologically, as we have just seen the Psalms were, but the detailed and concrete provisions of the Law required a more varied treatment. The Letter of Barnabas, *possibly written by an Alexandrian Jewish convert to Christianity sometime about 130 C.E., represents one very early Christian attempt to come to terms with the Torah. The first passage shows how the verses on the scapegoat in Leviticus 16:5ff., quoted in the author's usual freewheeling style, are to be read as a foreshadowing of Christ.*

Notice the directions: "Take a couple of goats, unblemished and well matched; bring them for an offering, and let the priest take one of them for a burnt offering." And what are they to do with the other? "The other," He declares, "is accursed." —Now see how plainly the type of Jesus appears— "Spit on it, all of you; thrust your goads into it, wreathe its head with scarlet wool, and so let it be driven into the desert." This is done and the goat keeper leads the animal into the desert, where he takes the wool off and leaves it there, on a bush we call a bramble, the same plant whose berries we usually eat when we come across it in the countryside; nothing has such tasty fruit as a bramble. Now what does that signify? Notice that the first goat is for the altar and the other is accursed, and that it is the accursed one that wears the wreath. That is because they shall see him on That Day clad to the ankles in his red woolen robe and will say, "Is this not he whom we once crucified, and mocked, and pierced and spat upon? Yes, this is the man who told us that he was the Son of God." But how will he resemble the goat? The point of there being two similar goats, both of them fair and alike, is that when they see him coming on the Day, they are going to be struck with terror

at the manifest parallel between him and the goat. In this ordinance, then, you see typified the future sufferings of Jesus. (*Letter of Barnabas* 7)
[STANIFORTH 1968: 203]

The same author's treatment of the dietary laws is not typological but allegorical.

And now for that saying of Moses, "You are not to eat of swine; nor yet of eagle, hawk or crow; nor of any fish that has not got scales." In this there are three distinct moral precepts which he had received and understood. For God says in Deuteronomy, "I will make a covenant with this people that will embody my rules for holiness" (Deut. 4:1); so, you see, the divine command is in no sense a literal ban on eating, and Moses was speaking spiritually. The meaning of his allusion to swine is this: what he is really saying is "you are not to consort with the class of people who are like swine, inasmuch as they forget all about the Lord while they are living in affluence, but remember him when they are in want, just as a swine, so long as it is eating, ignores its master, but starts to squeal the moment it feels hungry, and then falls silent again when it is given food."

If the method is to work, the author must possess in this instance—the list of prohibited foods in Leviticus is a long one—a considerable knowledge of animal physiology and behavior.

Among other things, He [Moses] also says, "You are not to eat of the hare" (Lev. 11:6), by which he means that you are not to debauch young boys, or become like those who do; because the hare grows a fresh orifice in its backside every year and has as many of these holes as the years of its life. And "you are not to eat the hyena" [this prohibition does not occur in the Bible] signifies that you are to be no lecher or libertine, or copy their ways, since that creature changes its sex annually and is a male at one time and a female at another. The weasel too he speaks of with abhorrence, and not without good reason; his implication being that you are not to imitate those who, we are told, are filthy enough to use their mouths for the practice of vice, nor to frequent the abandoned women who do the same, since it is through its mouth that this animal is impregnated. (*Letter of Barnabas* 10) [STANIFORTH 1968: 206–207]

By his allegorical method the author of the Letter of Barnabas *has freed the Christian from the literal observance of the Law while maintaining the validity of the Mosaic revelation. His moralizing treatment here of Leviticus 11 had a long history in the Christian tradition.*

29. The Fleshly and the Spiritual Understanding
of the Mosaic Law

Augustine, following Paul's lead, had little difficulty in reading the New Testament out of the Old. But as we have already seen in the case of the Letter of Barnabas, the Jewish Bible posed more particular exegetical problems for the Christian. The Christians early on confronted the possibilities of either rejecting the Bible outright, as Marcion and others suggested, and so completely dissociating themselves from the Jews, or else of accepting the Torah as authoritative and thus binding upon themselves. The first choice was rendered unlikely by the Gospels' own method of arguing the case for the Messiahship of Jesus out of the fulfillment of biblical prophecies, a practice continued by Paul and most of the Christian tradition. The second choice, to remain Torah-observant Jews while accepting the Messiahship of Jesus, recommended itself to many of the early Christians, who were themselves born Jews. It was aborted first by the decision to admit Gentiles into the Christian community and then by Paul's theological accommodation to that fact. Thus the Bible, the Christians' "Old Testament," had to remain authoritative as God's revelation, as could be demonstrated in its typological sense, but it was no longer binding in at least some of its prescriptions.

Augustine touched upon the problem in more than one of his writings. In the City of God, he takes it up in theological rather than legal terms.

In the words "Remember the Law of Moses my servant, which I commanded to him in Horeb for all Israel" (Mal. 4:4), the prophet (Malachi) opportunely mentions precepts and statutes, after declaring the important distinction hereafter to be made between those who observe and those who despise the Law. He intends also that they learn to interpret the Law spiritually, and find Christ in it, by whose judgment that separation between good and bad is to be made. For it is not without reason that the Lord himself said to the Jews, "Had you believed Moses, you would have believed, for he wrote of me" (John 4:46). For by receiving the Law carnally without perceiving that its earthly promises were figures of things spiritual, they fell into such murmurings as audaciously to say (to Malachi), "It is in vain to serve God; and what profit is it that we have kept His ordinance, and that we have walked suppliantly before the face of the Lord Almighty? And now we call aliens happy . . . " (Mal. 3:14). (Augustine, *City of God* 20.27) [AUGUSTINE 1948: 2:556]

Many other Christian exegetes—Jerome for one—wrestled with the legal aspects of the problem of the Christian and the Mosaic Law both before and after Augustine. By the time Thomas Aquinas came to write his Summa Theologica *(1265–1272*

C.E.) the main outlines of a solution were firmly in place. The method of proceeding is the scholastic one developed in the medieval universities.

Question 102, article 2: Whether the Ceremonial Precepts (of the Old Law) Have a Literal Cause or Merely a Figurative Cause?

First Objection: It would seem that the ceremonial precepts have not a literal but merely a figurative cause. For among the ceremonial precepts, the chief were circumcision and the sacrifice of the Passover lamb. But neither of these had any but a figurative cause because each was given as a sign. For it is written: "You shall circumcise the skin of your foreskin, that it may be for a sign of the covenant between Me and you" (Gen. 17:11); and of the celebration of Passover it is written: "It shall be a sign in your hand and as a memorial before your eyes" (Exod. 13:9). Therefore much more did the other ceremonial precepts have none but a figurative reason.

Second Objection: Further, an effect is proportioned to its cause. But all the ceremonial precepts are figurative, as stated above. Therefore they have only a figurative cause.

Third Objection: Further, if it is a matter of indifference whether a certain thing, considered in itself, be done in a particular way or not, it seems that it has not a literal cause. Now there are certain points in the ceremonial precepts which appear to be a matter of indifference, as to whether they are done in one way or in another: for instance, the number of animals to be offered, and other such particular circumstances. Therefore there is no literal cause for the precepts of the Old Law.

On the contrary: Just as the ceremonial precepts foreshadowed Christ, so did the stories of the Old Testament; for it is written that "all (these things) happened to them in figure" (1 Cor. 10:11). Now in the stories of the Old Testament, besides the mystical or the figurative, there is the literal sense. Therefore the ceremonial precepts had also literal, besides their figurative causes.

I answer: As was stated above, the reason for whatever conduces to an end must be taken from that end. Now the end of the ceremonial precepts (of the Mosaic Law) was twofold, for they were ordained to the divine worship for that particular time as well as to the foreshadowing of Christ. . . . Accordingly, the reasons for the ceremonial precepts of the Old Law can be taken in two ways. First, in respect of the worship of God that was to be observed for that particular time; and these reasons are literal, whether they refer to the shunning of idolatry, or recall certain divine benefits, or remind men of the divine excellence, or point out the disposition of mind which was then required in those who worshiped God. Secondly, their reasons can be gathered from the point of view of their being ordained to foreshadow Christ; and thus their reasons are figurative and mystical, whether they refer to Christ himself and the Church, which pertains to the allegorical sense, or to the morals of the Christian people, which pertains to the moral sense, or to the state of future glory, inasmuch as we are brought thereto by Christ, which pertains to the anagogical sense.

Reply to First Objection: Just as the use of metaphorical expressions in Scripture belongs to the literal sense, because the words are employed in order to convey that particular meaning, so also the meaning of these legal ceremonies (like circumcision and Passover) which commemorated certain divine benefits because of which they were instituted, and of other similar ones which belonged to that time, does not go beyond the order or literal causes. Consequently, when we assert that the cause of the celebration of Passover was its signification of the delivery from Egypt or that circumcision was a sign of God's covenant with Abraham, we assign them a literal cause.

Reply to Second Objection: This argument would avail if the ceremonial precepts had been given merely as figures of things to come and not for the purpose of worshiping God then and there.

Reply to Third Objection: As we stated when speaking of human laws, there is a reason for them in the universal, but not in regard to the particular conditions, which depend on the judgment of those who frame them. So too many particular determinations in the ceremonies of the Old Law have no literal cause but only a figurative one; whereas, considered universally, they have a literal cause. (Aquinas, *Summa Theologica* I/2, ques. 102, art. 2) [AQUINAS 1915. 2.062 004]

30. Jesus on Parables and Their Meaning

In common with the rabbis of his own and later times, Jesus often taught in parables. On more than one occasion he also provided a private exegesis of their meaning for the benefit of his disciples.

The same day Jesus went out and sat by the lakeside, where so many people gathered around him that he had to get into a boat. He sat there and all the people stood on the shore. He spoke to them in parables, at some length.

He said: "A sower went out to sow. And as he sowed, some seed fell along the footpath, and the birds came and ate it up. Some seed fell on rocky ground, where it had little soil, and it sprouted quickly because it had no depth of earth; but when the sun rose the young grain was scorched, and as it had no root it withered away. Some seed fell among thistles; and the thistles shot up and choked the wheat. And some of the seed fell into good soil, where it bore fruit, yielding a hundredfold or, it might be, sixtyfold or thirtyfold. If you have ears, then hear."

The disciples went up to him and asked, "Why do you speak to them in parables?" He replied, "It has been granted to you to know the secrets of the kingdom of Heaven, but to those others it has not been granted. For the man who has will be given more, till he has enough and to spare; and the man who has not will forfeit even what he has. That is why I speak to them in parables; for they look without seeing and listen without hearing or understanding. There is a prophecy of Isaiah that is being fulfilled for them: 'You may hear and hear, but you will never understand; you may look and look, but you will never see. For this people's mind has become gross; their ears are dulled, and their eyes are closed. Otherwise their eyes might see, their ears hear and their mind understand, and then they might turn again and I would heal them.' But happy are your eyes because they see, and your ears because they hear! Many prophets and saints, I tell you, desired to see what you now see; to hear what you now hear, but never heard it."

These are strong words and appear to echo Philo's almost contemporary sentiments on the problem of popular misconceptions about Scripture. Then Jesus gives his rather straightforward moral exegesis of the parable to his disciples, and it becomes clear that he was referring to spiritual, not intellectual, ignorance.

You, then, may hear the parable of the sower. When a man hears the word that tells of the Kingdom but fails to understand it, the evil one comes and carries off what has been sown in his heart. There you have the seed sown along the footpath. The seed sown on rocky ground stands for the man who, on hearing the word, accepts it at once with joy; but as it strikes no root in him he has no staying power, and when there is trouble or persecution on account of the word he falls away at once. The seed thrown among thistles represents the man who hears the word, but worldly cares and the false glamour of wealth choke it, and it proves barren. But the seed that fell into good soil is the man who hears the word and understands it, who accordingly bears fruit, and yields a hundredfold or, it may be, sixtyfold or thirtyfold. (Matthew 13:1–23)

31. A Parable of Muhammad

Interestingly, a similar parable, with attached exegesis, is attributed to Muhammad in one of the traditions circulating under his name.

Abu Musa reported that the Messenger of God said: "The guidance and knowledge with which God has commissioned me is like abundant rain which fell on some ground. Part of it was good, and absorbing the water, it brought forth abundant herbage and pasture; and there were some hollows in it which retained the water by which God gave benefit to men, who drank, gave drink and sowed seed. But some of it fell on another portion which consisted only of bare patches which could not retain the water or produce herbage. That [that is, the hollows] is like the one who becomes versed in religion and receives benefit from the message entrusted to me by God, so he knows for himself and teaches others; and (the bare patches) are like the one who who does not show regard for that and does not accept God's guidance with which I have been commissioned. (Baghawi, *Mishkat al-Masabih* 1.6.1)

32. How the Apostles Taught

To return to the Christian tradition, by the time we arrive at the opening decades of the second century, when Origen was writing his summa of Christian teaching called On First Principles, *the question of understanding Christian teachings had been broadened to include the question of intellectual ignorance, or rather its converse, intellectual training. Origen had received just such a training at Alexandria, and it is here factored into the Apostolic tradition.*

Just as there are many among the Greeks and barbarians alike who promise us the truth, and yet we gave up seeking for it from all who claimed it for false opinions after we had come to believe that Christ was the son of God and had become convinced that we must learn the truth from him; in the same way, when we find many who think they hold the doctrine of Christ, some of them differing in their beliefs from the Christians of earlier times, and yet the teaching of the Church, handed down in unbroken succession from the Apostles, is still preserved and continues to exist in the churches up to the present day, we maintain that that only is to be believed as the truth which in no way conflicts with the tradition of the Church and the Apostles.

But the following facts should be understood. The holy Apostles, when preaching the faith of Christ, took certain doctrines, those namely which they believed to be the necessary ones, and delivered them in the plainest terms to all believers, even to such as appeared to be somewhat dull in the investigation of divine knowledge. The grounds of their statements they left to be investigated by such as should merit the higher gifts of the Spirit, and in particular by such as should afterwards receive through the Holy Spirit Himself the graces of language, wisdom and knowledge. There were other doctrines, however, about which the Apostles simply said that things were so, keeping silence as to how or why; their intention undoubtedly being to supply the more diligent of those who came after them, such as should prove to be lovers of wisdom [that is, "philosophers" in the most literal sense], with an exercise on which to display the fruit of their ability. The men I refer to are those who train themselves to become worthy and capable of receiving wisdom. (Origen, *On First Principles* 2–3)

Origen then proceeds to give a summary of basic Christian beliefs, including the divine inspiration of Scriptures, both Old and New Testament. As he puts it, "there was not one Spirit in the men of old and another in those who were inspired at the coming of Christ." That consideration leads in turn to another.

Then there is the doctrine that the Scriptures were composed through the Spirit of God and that they have not only the meaning that is obvious but also another which is hidden from the majority of readers. For the contents of Scripture are the outward forms of certain mysteries and the images of divine things. On this point the entire Church is unanimous, that while the whole Law is spiritual, the inspired meaning is not recognized by all, but only by those who are gifted with the grace of the Holy Spirit in the word of wisdom and knowledge. (Ibid. 8)

33. The Christian Is Instructed on How To Read Scripture

The entire rich body of Scripture contained far more complex matter than rabbinic parables, however. As we have already seen, the Church's new intellectuals, with their professional training in rhetoric, hastened to assist the Christian to a better understanding of the word of God. Augustine devoted an entire treatise to Christian instruction, an instruction that inevitably included guidance on the reading and comprehension of Scripture.

The entire treatment of the Scriptures is based upon two factors: the method of discovering what we are to understand and the method of teaching what has been understood. . . . All teaching is concerned with either things or signs, but things are learned by means of signs. I have defined a thing in the accurate sense of the word as that which is not used to signify anything, for example, wood, stone, animal or others of this kind. But I do not include the tree which we read Moses cast into bitter waters to take away their bitterness (Exod. 15:25), nor the stone which Jacob placed under his head (Gen. 28:11), nor that ram which Abraham sacrificed in place of his son (Gen. 22:13). These are indeed things, but they are also symbols of other things. There are other signs whose whole usefulness consists in signifying. Words belong to this class, for no one uses words except to signify something. From this is understood what I designate as signs, namely those things which are employed to signify something. Therefore, every sign is also a thing—for whatever is not a thing is absolutely nothing—but not every thing is also a sign. So in this division of things and signs, when I speak of things, I shall do so in such a way that, although some of them can be used to signify, they will not disturb the division according to which I am treating first of things and then of signs. (Augustine, *On Christian Instruction* 1.1–2) [AUGUSTINE 1947: 27–29]

The instruction on things and their use in accordance with Scripture constitutes Augustine's teaching of Christian morality. Then, as promised, he takes up the question of signs.

Things which have been written fail to be understood for two reasons; they are hidden by either unknown or ambiguous signs. These signs are either literal or figurative. They are literal when they are employed to signify those things for which they were instituted. When we say *bos* we mean ox, because all men call it by this name in the Latin language, just as we do. Signs are figurative when the very things which we signify by the literal term are applied to some other meaning; for example, we say *bos* and recognize by that word an ox to which we usually give that name; but again, under the figure of the ox, we recognize a teacher of the Gospel. This is intimated by Holy Scripture, according to the interpretation of the Apostle Paul, in the text: "You shall not muzzle the ox that treads out the grain" (Deut. 25:4; cf. 1 Cor. 9:9). (Augustine, *On Christian Instruction* 2.10) [AUGUSTINE 1947: 72]

Jews and Muslims devoted a great deal of attention to establishing a correct text of Scripture. The Christian had an additional problem in that he was coming to God's word via translation—in the case of the Old Testament, through a Greek translation, which was in turn translated into Latin. Even in the case of the New Testa-

ment, most of Augustine's flock would be reading it not in the Greek in which it was written but in a Latin translation.

Obviously, an unknown word or an unknown expression causes the reader to be perplexed. If these come from foreign languages, we must ask about them from men who use those languages, or learn the languages, if we have the time and the ability, or study a comparison of the various translators. . . . The multitude of translators is a very important aid, when they have been considered and debated upon by a comparison of texts. However, avoid all that is positively false. For in correcting texts, the ingenuity of those who desire to know the Sacred Scriptures should be exercised principally in such a way that uncorrected passages, at least those coming from a single source of translation, yield to those that have been rectified.

In emending any Latin translations, we must consult the Greek texts; of these the reputation of the seventy translators [that is, the Septuagint] is most distinguished with regard to the Old Testament. These translators are now considered by the more learned churches to have translated under such sublime inspiration of the Holy Spirit that from so many men there was only one version. . . . Therefore, even if we should discover something in the Hebrew original other than they have interpreted it, it is my opinion that we should yield to the divine direction. This guidance was accomplished through them so that the books which the Jewish nation refused to transmit to other nations, either because of reverence or jealousy, were revealed so far ahead of time, with the aid of the authority of King Ptolemy, to those nations who would believe through our Lord. . . .

However, in reference to figurative expressions, if by chance the reader is caused perplexity by any unknown signs, he must decipher them partly through a knowledge of language, partly through a knowledge of things. The pool of Siloam, where the Lord ordered the man whose eyes he had smeared with clay made of spittle to wash his face (John 9:7), is applicable in some degree as an analogy and unquestionably alludes to some mystery. Nevertheless if the Evangelist had not explained that name from an unknown language, such an essential implication would be hidden from us. So also, many Hebrew names which have not been interpreted by the authors of those books unquestionably have no small power to help toward explaining the obscurities of Scriptures, if someone is able to translate them. Some men, expert in that language, have rendered a truly valuable service to succeeding ages by having interpreted all these words apart from Scripture. . . . Because these have been revealed and translated, many figurative passages in the Scriptures are interpreted. (Ibid. 2.14–16) [AUGUSTINE 1947: 79–82]

For a proper understanding of Scripture, Augustine continues, one must possess a knowledge of many things, including the properties of animals, vegetables, and minerals, of numbers, music, and history, of men, their arts, sciences, and institutions. Thus armed, and forearmed as well against the errors of the pagans who perfected these sciences, the student may then approach what is the main task of the exegete: to understand the ambiguities of Scripture.

When literal words cause Scripture to be ambiguous, our first concern must be to see that we have not punctuated them incorrectly or mispronounced them. Then, when a careful scrutiny reveals that it is doubtful how it should be punctuated or pronounced, we must consult the rule of faith which we have learned from the clearer passages of Scriptures and from the authority of the Church. . . . If both meanings, or even all of them, if there should be several, sound obscure after recourse has been had to faith, we must consult the context of both the preceding and the following passage to ascertain which of several meanings indicated it would consent to and permit to be incorporated in itself.

But when the ambiguity can be explained neither through a principle of faith nor through the context itself, there is nothing to prevent our punctuating the sentence according to any interpretation that is made known to us. . . . The same principles which I proposed for uncertain punctuations must also be followed for undetermined pronunciations. For these also, unless the excess negligence of the reader prevents it, are corrected either by the rules of faith or by the preceding or the succeeding context. (Ibid. 3.1–3) [AUGUSTINE 1947: 117 120]

The obscurities of figurative words, which I must discuss next, require extraordinary attention and persistence. First of all, we must be careful not to take a figurative expression literally. What the Apostle (Paul) said has reference to this: "The letter kills but the spirit gives life" (2 Cor. 3:6). When a figurative expression is understood as if it were literal, it is understood carnally. And nothing is more appropriately named the death of the soul than that which causes the quality of the soul which makes it superior to the beasts—that is, intelligence—to be subjected to the flesh by a close conformity to the literal sense. A man who conforms to the literal meaning considers figurative words as if they were literal and does not transfer what is signified by a literal word to its other sense. If he hears about the Sabbath for example, he thinks only of one day of the seven which are repeated in continuous sequence. When he hears of sacrifice, his thoughts do not rise above the usual sacrifices of the victims of flocks and the fruits of the earth. It is a wretched slavery of soul, indeed, to be satisfied with signs instead of realities, and not to be able to elevate the eye of the mind above the sensible realities to drink in eternal light.

Nevertheless, this slavery of the Jewish people was far different from the usual one of other nations, since the Jews were subjected to temporal things, but in such a way that the One God was honored in all these things. And although they observed the symbols of spiritual things instead of the things themselves, unaware of what they represented, they yet considered it a settled fact that by such servitude they were pleasing the One God of all, whom they did not see. The Apostle (Paul) wrote that this subjection was like that of little children under a tutor (Gal. 3:24ff.). And so those who adhered stubbornly to such symbols could not tolerate the Lord's disdain for those things when the time of their revelation had come. For that reason their leaders stirred up malicious accusations that he healed on the Sabbath, and the people, bound to those signs as if to realities, did not believe that he, who was unwilling to give heed to the signs as they were observed by the Jews, either was God or had come from God. (Ibid. 3.5–6) [AUGUSTINE 1947: 124–125]

To this precept, in accord with which we are careful not to consider a figurative or transferred form of speech as if it was literal, we must add another: That we are not to attempt to interpret a literal expression as if it were figurative. Therefore I must first point out the method of making sure whether a passage is literal or figurative. *In general that method is to understand as figurative anything in Scripture which cannot in a literal sense be attributed either to an upright character or to a pure faith.* Uprightness of character pertains to the love of God and our neighbor; purity of faith, to the knowledge of God and our neighbor. Further, everyone's hope is in his own conscience, so far as he knows that he is advancing in the love and knowledge of God and his neighbor. (Ibid. 3.10) [AUGUSTINE 1947: 129]

Whatever harshness and apparent cruelty in deed and word we read of in Holy Scripture as used by God on His saints is efficacious in destroying the power of lust. If it speaks plainly we must not refer it to another significance as if it were a figurative expression. . . . The things which seem almost wicked to the unenlightened, whether they are only words or whether they are even deeds, either of God or of men whose sanctity is commended to us, these are entirely figurative. . . . (However) what is

frequently sinful in other persons is a symbol of some sublime truth in the person of God or a prophet. Certainly union with an adulteress is one thing in the case of corrupt morals, but it is another in the case of the prophesying of the prophet Hosea (Hos. 1:2). It is shameful to strip the body at banquets of the drunken and the lascivious, but it is not for that reason to be naked in the baths. Consequently, we must prudently take into account what is proper for places, circumstances and persons, so that we may not indiscreetly convict them of sin. (Ibid. 3.12)
[AUGUSTINE 1947: 132–133]

If a passage is didactic, either condemning vice, or crime, or prescribing utility or kindness, it is not figurative. But if it appears to prescribe vice or crime, or to condemn utility or kindness, it is figurative. The Lord said, "Unless you eat the flesh of the Son of Man and drink his blood, you shall not have life in you" (John 6:54). This seems to prescribe a crime or vice; therefore it is a figure of speech directing that we are to participate in the Lord's passion and treasure up in grateful and salutory remembrance the fact that his flesh was crucified and wounded for us. Scripture says, "If your enemy is hungry, give him food; if he is thirsty, give him drink" (Prov. 25:21–22). This undoubtedly prescribes a kindness, but the part that follows, "for in doing so you will heap coals of fire upon his head," you might suppose was commanding a crime of malevolence. So do not doubt that it is a figurative expression. Although it can have a twofold interpretation, by the one intending harm and by the other good, charity should call you away from the former to kindness, so that you may understand that the coals of fire are the burning lamentations of repentance by which that man's pride is healed and he grieves that he has been the enemy of the man who relieves his misery. (Ibid. 3.16) [AUGUSTINE 1947: 136]

Augustine returns to the question of distinguishing where the literal and where the figurative reading is to be applied to Scriptural texts.

We must discover first of all whether the expression we are trying to understand is literal or figurative. When we have made certain that it is figurative, it is easy, by employing the rules concerning (such) things . . . to reflect upon it in all its aspects until we reach the idea of truth, particularly when practice, invigorated by the observance of piety is added to it. . . .

When the expression is seen to be figurative, the words of which it is composed will be discovered to be derived either from similar things or from those related by some affinity. But since things appear similar to

each other in many ways, we should not imagine that there is any precept
that we must believe that because a thing has a certain analogical meaning
in one place, it always has this meaning. For example, the Lord represented leaven in a comdemnatory fashion when he said, "Beware the
leaven of the Pharisees" (Matt. 16:10), and as an object of praise when he
said, "The kingdom of heaven is like a woman who hid leaven in three
measures of flour, until all of it was leavened" (Matt. 13:33).

The rule of this diversity, therefore, has two forms. Anything that is
a sign of one thing and then another is such that it signifies either things
that are contrary or else things that are only different. They indicate
contraries, for instance, when the same thing is expressed by way of
analogy at one time in a good sense and at another in a bad sense, like the
leaven mentioned above. . . . Yet there are some passages where there is
uncertainty with respect to the meaning in which they ought to be understood; for example, "In the hand of the Lord there is a cup of strong wine
full of mixture" (Ps. 75:8). It is doubtful whether this signifies the wrath
of God, but not to the extreme penalty, that is, to "the dregs"; or
whether it signifies the grace of the Scriptures passing from the Jews to
the Gentiles, because (it continues) "he has poured out from this to that,"
although certain practices continue among the Jews which they understand carnally, because "the dregs thereof are not emptied." (Ibid. 3.24–
25) [AUGUSTINE 1947: 143–145]

A man who thoroughly examines the Holy Scriptures in an endeavor to find the purpose of the author, through whom the Holy Spirit
brought the Scriptures into being, whether he attains his goal or whether
he elicits from the words another meaning which is not opposed to the
true faith, he is free from blame if he has proof from some other passage
of the Holy Scriptures. In fact, the author perhaps saw that very meaning
too in the same words which we are anxious to interpret. And certainly,
the Spirit of God who produced these words through him also foresaw
that this very meaning would occur to the reader or the listener; further,
he took care that it should occur to him because it is also based on truth.
For what could God have provided more generously and more abun-
dantly in the Holy Scriptures than that the same words might be understood in several ways, which other supporting testimonies no less divine
endorse?

When, however, a meaning is elicited that is such that its uncertainty cannot be explained by the unerring testimonies of the Holy Scriptures (themselves), it remains for us to explain it by the proof of reason,

even if the man whose words we are seeking to understand was perhaps unaware of that meaning. This is a dangerous practice, however. It is much safer to walk by means of the Holy Scripture. When we are trying to search out those passages that are obscured by figurative words, we may either start out from a passage which is not subject to dispute, or, if it is disputed, we may settle the question by employing the testimonies that have been discovered elsewhere in the same Scripture. (Ibid. 3.27–28) [AUGUSTINE 1947: 147–148]

34. The Catholic Interpretation of Scripture

Augustine was attempting to give practical instruction. Vincent of Lerins, in his Commonitorium *(434 C.E.) had another concern: that Scripture be read and understood according to the mind of the Church Catholic.*

It always was, and it is today, the usual practice of Catholics to test the true faith by two methods: first, by the authority of the divine Canon (of Scripture), and then by the tradition of the Catholic Church. Not that the Canon is insufficient in itself in each case. But because most false interpreters of the Divine Word make use of their own arbitrary judgment and thus fall into various opinions and errors, the understanding of Holy Scripture must conform to the single rule of Catholic teaching, and this especially in regard to those questions upon which the foundations of all Catholic dogma are laid. (Vincent of Lerins, *Commonitorium* 29)

35. How the Muslim Reads the Quran

Instruction on how to read the Quran began with the Prophet himself, or so this tradition circulated under his name would have it.

Abu Hurayra reported God's messenger as saying: "The Quran came down showing five aspects: what is permissible, what is prohibited, what is firmly fixed, what is obscure, and parables. So treat what is permissible as permissible and what is prohibited as prohibited, act upon what is firmly fixed, believe in what is obscure, and take a lesson from the parables." (Baghawi, *Mishkat al-Masabih* 1.6.2)

If that advice seems somewhat schematic for a genuine Prophetic utterance, the highly systematic and scholastic view of the sciences connected with reading and understanding the Quran that the Spanish social philosopher and historian Ibn Khaldun inserted in his Prolegomenon to History *in 1377 C.E. is less cause for surprise.*

It should be known that the Quran was revealed in the language of the Arabs and according to their rhetorical methods. All the Arabs understood it and knew the meaning of the individual words and composite statements. It was revealed in chapters [that is, suras] and verses in order to explain the Oneness of God and the religious duties appropriate to the various occasions.

Some passages . . . are early and are followed by other, later passages that abrogate the earlier ones. The Prophet used to explain these things, as it is said, "So that you may explain to the people what was revealed to them" (Quran 14:46). He used to explain the unclear statements (in the Quran) and to distinguish the abrogating statements from those abrogated by them, and to inform the men around him of this sense. Thus the men around him became acquainted with the subject. They knew why individual verses were revealed and the situation that had required them, and this directly on Muhammad's authority. Thus the verse of the Quran "When God's help comes and the victory" (110:1) refers to the announcement of the Prophet's death, and similar things.

These explanations were transmitted on the authority of the men around Muhammad [that is, the "Companions of the Prophet"; see Chapter 3 below] and were circulated by the men of the second generation (after him). They continued to be transmitted among the early Muslims, until knowledge became organized in scholarly disciplines and systematic scholarly works began to be written. At that time most of these explanations were committed to writing. The traditional information concerning them, which had come down from the men around Muhammad and the men of the second generation, was transmitted farther. That material reached al-Tabari [d. 923], al-Waqidi [d. 823] and al-Thaʿalibi [d. 1035] and other Quran interpreters. They committed to writing as much of the traditional information as God wanted them to do.

The linguistic sciences then became technical discussions of the lexicographical meaning of words, the rules governing vowel endings, and style in the use of word combinations. Systematic works were written on these subjects. Formerly these subjects had been habitual with the Arabs, and so no recourse to oral and written transmission had been necessary with respect to them. Now, that was forgotten, and these subjects were learned from books by philologists. They were needed for the interpretation of the Quran, because the Quran is in Arabic and follows the stylistic technique of the Arabs. Quran interpretation thus came to be handled in two ways.

One kind of Quran interpretation is traditional. It is based on information received from the early Muslims. It consists of knowledge of the abrogating verses and of the verses that are abrogated by them, of the reasons why a verse was revealed, and the purposes of individual verses. All this can be known only through the traditions based on the authority of the men around Muhammad and the men of the second generation. The early scholars had already made complete compilations on the subject. . . .

The other kind of Quran interpretation has recourse to linguistic knowledge, such as lexicography and the stylistic form used for conveying meaning through the appropriate means and methods. This kind of Quran interpretation rarely appears separately from the first kind. The first kind is the one that is wanted essentially. The second made its appearance only after language and the philological sciences had become crafts. However, it has become preponderant, as far as certain Quran commentaries are concerned. (Ibn Khaldun, *Muqaddima* 6.10)

[IBN KHALDUN 1967: 2:443–446]

36. Where Did the Muslim Commentators Get Their Information?

Abdullah ibn Amr reported that God's Messenger said: "Pass on information from me, even if it is only a verse of the Quran; and relate traditions from the Banu Isra'il, for there is no restriction." . . . Bukhari transmitted this tradition. (Baghawi, *Mishkat al-Masabih* 2.1.1)

Ibn Khaldun concurred that such a transmission from Jewish sources had occurred, particularly when it came to fleshing out some of the narrative material in the Quran, and he had the social theory to enable him to explain it.

The early scholars' works (on the Quran) and the information they transmit contain side by side important and unimportant matters, accepted and rejected statements. The reason is the Arabs had no books or scholarship. The desert attitude and illiteracy prevailed among them. When they wanted to know certain things that human beings are usually curious to know, such as the reasons for existing things, the beginning of creation, and the secrets of existence, they consulted the earlier People of the Book and got their information from them. The People of the Book were the Jews who had the Torah and the Christians who followed the religion (of the Jews). Now the People of the Torah who lived among the

Arabs at that time were themselves Bedouins. They knew only as much about these matters as is known to ordinary People of the Book. The majority of those Jews were Himyarites [that is, South Arabians] who had adopted Judaism. When they became Muslims, they retained the information they possessed, such as information about the beginning of creation and information of the type of forecasts and predictions. That information had no connection with the (Jewish or Christian) religious laws they were preserving as theirs. Such men were Ka'b al-Ahbar, Wahb ibn Munabbih, Abdullah ibn Salam, and similar people.

The Quran commentaries were filled with material of such tendencies transmitted on their authority; it is information that entirely depends on them. It has no relation to (religious) laws, such that one might claim for it the soundness that would make it necessary to act (in accordance with it). The Quran interpreters were not very rigorous in this respect. They filled the Quran commentaries with such material, which originated, as we have stated, with the People of the Torah who lived in the desert and were not capable of verifying the information they transmitted. However, they were famous and highly esteemed because they were people of rank in their religion and religious group. Therefore, their interpretation has been accepted from that time onward. (Ibn Khaldun, *Muqaddima* 6.10) [IBN KHALDUN 1967: 2:445–446]

37. The Clear and the Ambiguous in the Quran

We have already seen the Bible commenting upon itself and Jesus giving instruction to his disciples on how they were to understand his teaching. The Quran too issued a warning about the problems and dangers in understanding the words of God, and so provided as well an inviting peg upon which later commentators might hang their own theories concerning exegesis.

He has sent down this Book which contains some clear verses that are categorical [or "are from the Mother of the Book"] and others allegorical [or "ambiguous"]. But those who are twisted in mind look for verses allegorical [or "ambiguous"], seeking deviation and giving them interpretations of their own; but none knows their meaning except God; and those who are steeped in knowledge affirm: "We believe in them as all of them are from the Lord"; but only those who have wisdom understand. (Quran 3:7)

The following comments on these verses were written by Zamakhshari in 1134 C.E.

"Categorical verses," namely those whose diction and meaning are sufficiently clear that they are preserved from the possibility of differing interpretations and ambiguity. "And others that are ambiguous," namely those verses that are ambiguous in that they allow differing interpretations.

"The Mother of the Book": that is, the origin of the Book, since the ambiguous verses must be traced back to it and harmonized with it. Examples of such ambiguity include the following: "The vision reaches Him not, but He reaches the vision; He is All-subtle, All-aware" (6:103); or "Upon that day their faces shall be radiant, gazing upon their Lord" (75:22); or "God does not command indecency!" (7:28) compared with "And when We desire to destroy a city, We command its men who live at ease, and they commit ungodliness therein. Then the command is realized against it, and We destroy it utterly" (17:16).

If one then asks whether the (meaning of the) entire Quran might not be (clearly) determined, I answer that men would (then) depend on it since it would be so easily accessible, and thus they would neglect what they lack, namely, research and meditation through reflection and inference. If they did that, then they would be neglecting the only way by which we can attain to a knowledge of God and His unity. Again, the ambiguous verses present a test and a means of distinguishing between those who stand firm in the truth and those who are uncertain regarding it. And great advantages, including the noble sciences and the profit of higher orders of being, are granted by God when scholars stimulate each other and so develop their natural skills, discovering the meanings of the ambiguous verses and harmonizing these with the (clearly) determined verses. Further, if the believer is firmly convinced that no disagreement or self-contradiction can exist in God's words, and then he notices something that appears at least to be a contradiction, and he then diligently searches out some way of harmonizing it (with the clear verses), treating it according to a uniform principle, and by reflecting on it comes to an insight about himself and other things, and with God's inspiration he comes to an understanding of the harmony that exists between the ambiguous verses and the (clearly) determined verses, then his certainty grows and the intensity of his conviction increases.

"As for those whose heart is swerving": These are the people who introduce innovations.

"They follow the ambiguous part," that is, they confine their attention to the ambiguous verses, which give free rein to innovations without harmonizing them with the (clearly) determined verses. But these (same verses) likewise permit an interpretation which agrees with the views of the people of truth.

The following interpretation depends on how one divides—in our parlance, punctuates—the text: to wit, whether or not there should be a pause or semicolon after "except God." In Zamakhshari's first interpretation it is not in fact so punctuated, though he concedes the possibility.

"And none knows its interpretation except God and those firmly rooted in knowledge," namely, only God and His servants who have firmly rooted knowledge, that is to say, those who are firm in knowledge and so "bite with a sharp tooth," come to the correct interpretation, according to which one must necessarily explain it. Some, however, place a pause after "except God" and begin a new sentence with "And those firmly rooted in knowledge . . . say." Thus they interpret the ambiguous verses as those whose understanding God reserves to Himself alone as well as the recognition of whatever wisdom is contained in them, as, for example, the exact number of the executioners in hell and similar questions. The first reading is the correct one, and the next sentence begins with "they say," setting forth the situation of those who have a firmly rooted knowledge, namely, in the following sense: Those who know the meaning say "we believe in it," that is, in the ambiguous verses.

"All of them are from our Lord": that is, all the ambiguous verse as well as all the (clearly) determined verse (in the Quran) is from Him. Or (to put it another way), not only the ambiguous verses in the Book but also the (clearly) determined verses are from God, the Wise One, in whose words there is no contradiction and in whose Book there is no discrepancy. (Zamakhshari, *The Unveiler of the Realities, ad loc.*)

One who preferred to read and punctuate this text as Zamakhshari had was the most straightforward Aristotelian produced in Islam, the Spanish philosopher Ibn Rushd, or Averroes (d. 1198 C.E.). In his Decisive Treatise *he develops the argument that, since there is no absolute Muslim consensus on which scriptural verses should be read literally and which allegorically, a certain latitude should be permitted in exegesis (see below). He then turns to this same verse, Sura 3:7.*

It is evident from what we have said (to this point) that a unanimous agreement cannot be established in (theoretical) questions of this kind, because of the reports that many of the believers of the first generation (of Muslims), as well as others, have said that there are allegorical interpretations which ought not to be expressed except to those who are qualified to receive allegories. These are those who "are firmly rooted in knowledge." For we prefer to place a stop after God's words "and those who are firmly rooted and knowledge" (and not before it), because if the scholars did not understand allegorical interpretation (but only God), there would be no superiority in their assent which would oblige them to a belief in Him not found among the unlearned. God has described them as those who believe in Him, and this can only refer to a belief which is based on (scientific or philosophical) demonstration; and this belief only occurs together with the science of allegorical interpretation. For the unlearned believers are those whose belief in Him is not based on demonstration; and if this belief which God has attributed to the scholars (in Quran 3:7) is peculiar to them, it must come through demonstration, and if it comes through demonstration, it only occurs together with the science of allegorical interpretation. For God the Exalted has informed us that those (verses) have an allegorical interpretation which is the truth, and demonstration can only be of the truth. That being the case, it is not possible for general unanimity to be established about allegorical interpretations, which God has made peculiar to scholars. This is self-evident to any fair-minded person. (Averroes, *The Decisive Treatise* 10)

[AVERROES 1961: 53–54]

38. The Outer and Inner Meanings of the Quran

A thinker whose opinions recur throughout the work of Averroes is Ghazali (d. 1111 C.E.), the earlier Baghdad theologian and lawyer whose scathing attack on the rationalist philosophy that was attracting some Muslim thinkers in the tenth and eleventh centuries was, despite its spirited defense by Averroes, the likely cause of its eventual repudiation in Islam. Ghazali too is willing to admit the allegorical interpretation of Scripture, though with considerably more caution than Averroes.

. . . The Prophet said: "Whoever interprets the Quran according to his own opinion will have his place in Gehenna." The people who are acquainted with only the outer sense of exegesis have for this reason discredited the mystics to the extent that these latter practice exegesis, because they explain the wording of the Quran in a manner other than according to the tradition of Ibn Abbas and the (traditional) commentators; and they further maintain that what is involved (in such interpretation) is a matter of unbelief. If the advocates of traditional exegesis are correct, then the understanding of the Quran consists in nothing else than knowing its external meaning. But if they are not right, then what is the meaning of the Prophet's words: "Whoever interprets the Quran according to his own opinion will have his place in Gehenna"?

It should be noted that whenever someone maintains that the Quran has no meaning other than that expressed by the external method of exegesis, then in so doing he is expressing his own limitations. With this avowal about himself he expresses something which is doubtless correct (for his own situation), but he is mistaken in thinking that the entire creation is to be regarded on his level, that is, restricted by his limitations and situation. The commentaries and traditions show that the meanings contained in the Quran exhibit a wide scope for experts in the field. Thus, Ali [the cousin and son-in-law of the Prophet and the fourth Caliph of Islam] said (that a specific meaning can be grasped) only when God grants to someone an understanding of the Quran. But if nothing else is involved except the traditional interpretation, this is not "understanding." Further, the Prophet said that the Quran had a literal meaning, an inner meaning, an end point and a starting point of understanding. . . . According to the opinion of some scholars, every verse can be understood in sixty thousand ways, and that what still remains unexhausted (of its meaning) is still more numerous. Others have maintained that the Quran contains seventy-seven thousand and two hundred (kinds of) knowledge. . . .

Ibn Masʿud said: Whoever wishes to obtain knowledge of his ancestors and descendants should meditate upon the Quran. This knowledge does not appear, however, if one restricts the interpretation of the Quran to its outer meaning. Generally speaking, every kind of knowledge is included in the categories of actions and attributes, and the description of the nature of the actions and attributes of God is contained in the Quran. These kinds of knowledge have no end; yet, in the Quran is found (only) an indication of their general aspects. Thereby the degrees of the deeper penetration into the particulars of knowledge are traced back to the (actual) understanding of the Quran. The mere outer aspect of interpretation gives no hint of this knowledge. Rather, the fact is that the Quran contains indications and hints, which certain select people with (correct) understanding can grasp, concerning all that remains obscure in the more abstract way of thinking and about which men disagree regarding the theoretical sciences and rational ideas. How can the interpretation and explanation of the outer meaning of the Quran be adequate for this?

There are, according to Ghazali, additional reasons why one should not be limited to the mere literal meaning of God's word.

The Companions of the Prophet and the commentaors disagree on the interpretation of certain verses and put forth differing statements about them which cannot be brought into harmony with one another. That all these statement were heard issuing from the mouth of the Messenger of God is patently absurd. One was obliged to understand one of these statements of the Messenger of God in order to refute the rest, and then it becomes clear that, as concerns the meaning (of the passage of the Quran in question), every exegete has expressed what appeared to him to be evident through his inferential reasoning. This went so far that seven different kinds of interpretations, which cannot be brought into harmony with one another, have been advanced concerning the letters at the beginning of (some of) the suras.

There arises, however, the danger of personal bias.

The prohibition (against interpretation according to personal opinion cited at the outset) involves the following two reasons for its having been sent down: The first is that someone may have a (personal) opinion about something, and through his nature as well as his inclination he may harbor a bias toward it and then interpret the Quran accordingly in order thereby to find arguments to prove that his view is the correct one. Moreover, the meaning (which he links to his view) would not at all have appeared to him from the Quran if he did not have some preconceived opinion and bias. Sometimes this happens consciously, as perhaps in the case of those who use individual verses of the Quran as arguments in support of a heretical innovation and thus know that this is not in accordance with what is meant by the verse. They want rather to deceive their opponents. Sometimes, however, it (also) happens unconsciously. For instance, when a verse admits various meanings, a man inclines in his understanding to what best accords with his own opinion and inclination and thus interprets according to his "individual opinion." That is, it is a person's "individual opinion" which drives one to such an interpretation.

Finally, there is the question of the notorious ambiguity of the Arabic language.

The second reason is that someone may come to an interpretation of the Quran prematurely on the basis of the literal meaning of the Arabic, without the assistance of "hearing" (from earlier sources) and the Prophetic tradition on what is involved in the passages of the Quran which are difficult to understand, on the obscure and ambiguous expressions which are found in the Quran, and on the abbreviations, omissions, implications, anticipations and allusions which are contained in it. Whoever has not mastered the outer aspect of exegesis, but proceeds hastily to conclusions on the meaning (of the Quran) solely on the basis of his understanding of the Arabic language, he commits many errors and aligns himself thereby to the group of those who interpret the Quran according to individual opinion. Prophetic tradition and the "hearing" are indispensable for the outer aspects of exegesis, first of all in order to make one secure thereby against the opportunities for error, and also in order to extend the endeavor to understand and to reach conclusions. (Ghazali, *Revivification of the Sciences of Religion* 1.268)

39. Ghazali on the Sciences of Revelation

It is evident, then, from the differing opinions in the commentaries written on the subject—to say nothing of the received opinion that each verse of the Book "can be understood in sixty thousand ways"—that Muslims found a somewhat greater number of ambiguities in the Quran than the few classical instances cited by the exegetes. The whole range of learning that would eventually be brought to bear on elucidating them is illustrated in textbook fashion by Ghazali.

The praiseworthy sciences have roots, branches, preliminaries and completions. They [that is, the sciences of revelation] comprise, therefore, four kinds.

The "roots," of which there are (in this instance) four, constitute the first kind: (They are) the Book of God, the custom of the Prophet, the consensus of the (Muslim) community and the traditions concerning the Companions of the Prophet [that is, his contemporaries]. The consensus of the community is a "root" because it furnishes indications of the custom of the Prophet; as a "root" it is ranked third. The same is true of the traditions (of the Companions), which likewise provide indications of the custom of the Prophet. The Companions witnessed the inspiration and the sending down (of the Quran) and were able to comprehend much, through a combination of circumstances, which others were not able to observe. Sometimes the explicit statements (of revelation) do not contain something which can be observed through a combination of circumstances. For this reason the men of learning found it beneficial to follow the example of the Companions of the Prophet and to be guided by the traditions regarding them.

The "branches" constitute the second kind. This group deals with that which one comprehends on the basis of the "roots" mentioned above—and indeed cannot be gleaned from the external wording alone—through which the mind is awakened and understanding is thus expanded, so that one comprehends other meanings that are beyond the external wording. Thus one comprehends from the words of the Prophet, "the judge may not judge in anger," that he also would not judge when hungry, needing to urinate, or in the pains of sickness. The "branches" comprise two subtypes, the first of which deals with the requisites of the present world. This subtype is contained in the books of jurisprudence and is entrusted to the lawyers, who are thus the men of learning responsible for the present world. The second subtype deals with the requisites of the hereafter, thus the knowledge of the circumstances of the heart, its praiseworthy and blameworthy characteristics, that which is pleasing to God and that which is abhorrent to Him. . . .

The "preliminaries" constitute the third kind. They are the tools (of scriptural exegesis) such as lexicography and grammar, which are naturally one tool for gaining knowledge of the Book of God and the custom of His Prophet. In themselves lexicography and grammar do not belong to the sciences of revelation; however, one must become engrossed in them for the sake of revelation because the latter appears in the Arabic language. Since no revelation comes forth without language, the mastery of the language concerned becomes necessary as a tool. Among the tools of this kind belong also the skill of writing; however this is not unconditionally required since the Messenger of God was unlettered. If a man were able to retain in his memory everything he hears, then the skill of writing would become unnecessary. Yet, since people are not able to do this, in most cases the skill of writing is essential.

The "completions," that is, in relation to the study of the Quran, constitute the fourth kind. This groups contains the following divisions: (1) that which is connected with the external wording, such as the study of the (various) readings and of the phonetics; (2) that which is connected with the meaning of the contents, such as traditional exegesis, where one must also rely on tradition since the language alone does not yield the meaning; and (3), that which is connected with the "decisions" of the Quran, such as a knowledge of the abrogating and abrogated (verses), the general and the particular, the definite and the probable, as well as the kind and manner, in the same way that one makes one decision in relation to others.

It is already apparent from the listing of the "roots" above that the extra-Quranic traditions attributed to the Prophet rank directly after the Quran itself as part of

God's revelation. They too have their own proper sciences, as Ghazali now explains, and as we shall see in more detail in Chapter 3 below.

The "completions" relating to the traditions of the Prophet and the historical narratives consist of: (1) the study of the authorities, including their names and relationships, as well as the names and characteristics of the Companions of the Prophet; (2) the study of the reliability of the transmitters (of those traditions); (3) the study of the circumstances under which the transmitters lived, in order to be able to distinguish between those who are unreliable and those who are reliable; and (4) the study of the life spans of the transmitters, through which that which is transmitted with defective chains of authorities can be distinguished from that which exhibits unbroken chains. (Ghazali, *Revivification of the Sciences of Religion* 1.254)

40. Truth and Symbol

Thus far the diverse levels of meaning in Scripture flow from the inexhaustibility of God's wisdom. For some, however, there existed the possibility of deliberate conceal-ment on the part of the prophet, chiefly by reason of the inability of the masses for whom Scripture is intended to comprehend any more than mere symbols of the truths that lie beyond.

It is not necessary for the prophet to trouble their minds with any part of the knowledge of God, save that He is One, True and has no like; as for going beyond this doctrine, so as to charge them to believe in God's existence as not to be defined spatially or verbally divisible, as being neither outside the world nor within it, or anything of that sort—to do this would impose a great strain upon them and would confuse the religious system which they already follow. . . . Not every man is ready to understand metaphysics [or theology], and in any case it would not be proper for any man to disclose that he is in possession of a truth which he conceals from the masses; indeed, he must not allow himself to hint at any such thing.

The prophet's duty is to teach men to know the majesty and might of God by means of symbols and parables drawn from things which they regard as mighty and majestic, imparting to them simply this much, that God has no equal, no like and no partner. Similarly he must establish in them a belief in an afterlife in a manner that comes within the range of their imagination and will be satisfying to their souls; he will liken the happiness and misery to be experienced there in terms which they can understand and conceive. As for the truth of these matters, he will only adumbrate it to them very briefly, saying that it is something which "eye has not seen nor ear heard." . . . God certainly knows the beneficent aspect of all this, and it is always right to take what God knows exactly for what it implies. There is therefore no harm in his discourse being interspersed with sundry hints and allusions, to attract those naturally qualified for speculation to undertake philosophical research into the nature of religious observances and their utility in terms of this world and the next. (Avicenna, *Book of Deliverance*) [AVICENNA 1951: 44–45]

This is not a program for exegesis, however. Unlike the masses, the philosopher has little need for the material figures of Scripture; indeed, he would be ill advised to elicit those naked truths so carefully and consciously hidden away from the simple believers.

It has been said that a condition the prophet must adhere to is that his words should be symbols and his expressions hints. Or as Plato states in the *Laws*: Whoever does not understand the apostle's symbols will not attain the Divine Kingdom. [No such sentiments are found in our versions of Plato's *Laws*.] Moreover, the foremost Greek philosophers and prophets made use in their books of symbols and signs in which they hid their secret doctrine, men like Pythagoras, Plato and Socrates. As for Plato, he blamed Aristotle for divulging wisdom and making knowledge manifest, so that Aristotle had to reply: "Even though I had done this, I have still left in my books many a pitfall which only the initiated among the wise and learned can understand." Moreover, how could the prophet Muhammad, may God's prayers and peace be upon him, bring knowledge to the uncouth nomad, not to say to the whole human race, considering that he was sent as a Messenger to all? Political guidance, on the other hand, comes easily to prophets; also the imposition of obligations on people. (Avicenna, *On the Proof of Prophecies* 124) [LERNER & MAHDI 1972: 116]

According to both Farabi and Avicenna, as we have seen in Chapter 1 above, the philosopher and the prophet are both privy to the same God-given truths, but the latter receives the additional responsibility of transmitting them in appropriate forms to the masses. These forms are the material figures and symbols that shadow the higher reality of Truth, as Farabi explains.

The principles of the beings, their ranks of order, happiness and the rulership of virtuous cities are either cognized and intellected by man or he imagines them. To cognize them is to have their essences, as they really are, imprinted on man's soul. To imagine them is to have imprinted on man's soul their images, representations of them, or matters that are imitations of them. . . . Most men, either by nature or by habit, are unable to comprehend and cognize these things; these are the men for whom one ought to represent the manner in which the principles of the beings, their ranks of order, the Active Intellect and the Supreme Rulership [that is, prophecy] exist through things which are imitations of them. Now while the meanings and essences of these things are one (among all nations) and immutable, the matters by which they are imitated are many and varied. Some imitate them more closely, while others do so only remotely.

There is an unmistakable conclusion that follows from this line of reasoning, and Farabi does not hesitate to draw it: the truths of philosophy are universal and unequivocal; those of religion are relative, culturally determined, and limited by the understanding of the recipients.

Therefore it is possible to imitate these things for each group and each nation using matters that are different in each case. Consequently, there may be a number of virtuous nations and virtuous cities whose religions are different, even though they all pursue the very same kind of happiness. For religion is but the impressions of these things, or the impressions of their images, imprinted on the soul. Because it is difficult for the multitude to comprehend these things themselves as they are, the attempt was made to teach them these things in other ways, which are the ways of imitation. Hence these things are imitated [or symbolized by the prophets] for each group or nation through the matters that are best known to them; and it may very well be that the best known to the one may not be the best known to the other.

Most men who strive for happiness follow after an imagined not a cognized form of happiness. Similarly, most men accept such principles as are accepted and followed, and are magnified and considered majestic, in the form of (material) images, not of cognitions. Now the ones who follow after happiness and they cognize it and accept the principles as they cognize them, these are the wise men [that is, the philosophers]. And the ones in whose souls such things are found in the form of (material) images, and who accept them and follow after them as such, these are the believers. (al-Farabi, *The Political Regime* 55–56)   [LERNER & MAHDI 1972: 40–41]

41. Allegorical Interpretation as a Resolution of Apparent Contradictions

The Spanish philosopher Ibn Rushd, or Averroes (d. 1198 C.E.), begins his tract entitled The Decisive Treatise Determining the Nature of the Connection between Religion and Philosophy *by demonstrating that the Quran not only permits but even commands the study of philosophy. Whatever the virtues of this exercise, the fact remained that for most Muslims there was a conflict between what they were told in the Book of God and what they read in the Greek and Muslim philosophers. It is to that point that Averroes then turns.*

Now since this religion is true and summons to the study which leads to the knowledge of the Truth, we the Muslim community know definitively that demonstrative study [that is, philosophy] does not lead to (conclusions) conflicting with what Scripture has given us; for truth does not oppose truth but accords with it and bears witness to it.

This being so, whenever demonstrative study leads to any manner of knowledge about any being, that being is inevitably either unmentioned or mentioned in Scripture. If it is unmentioned, there is no contradiction, and it is the same case as an act whose category is unmentioned so that the (Muslim) lawyer has to infer it by reasoning from Scripture. If Scripture does speak about it, the apparent meaning of the words inevitably either accords or conflicts with the conclusions of (philosophical) demonstration about it. If this apparent meaning accords, there is no conflict. If it conflicts, there is a call for allegorical interpretation. The meaning of "allegorical interpretation" is: the extension of the significance of an expression from real to metaphorical significance, without forsaking therein the standard metaphorical practices of Arabic, such as calling a thing by the name of something resembling it or a cause or a consequence or accompaniment of it, or other such things as are enumerated in accounts of the kinds of metaphorical speech.

. . . Muslims are unanimous in holding that it is not obligatory either to take all the expressions of Scripture in their apparent [or external] meaning or to extend them all from the apparent meaning by means of allegorical interpretation. They disagree (only) over which of them should and which should not be so interpreted: the Ash'arites [that is, certain dialectical theologians] for instance give an allegorical interpretation to the verse about God's directing Himself (Quran 2:29) and the Prophetic tradition about His descent (into this world), while the Hanbalites [that is, fundamentalist lawyers and traditionists] take them in their apparent meaning. . . .

It may be objected: There are some things in Scripture which the Muslims have unanimously agreed to take in their apparent meaning, others (which they have agreed) to interpret allegorically, and others about which they have disagreed; is it permissible, then, that demonstration should lead to interpreting allegorically what they [that is, the Muslims] have agreed to take in its apparent meaning, or to taking in its apparent meaning what they have agreed to interpret allegorically? We reply: If unanimous agreement is established by a method which is certain, such (a result) is not sound; but if (the existence of) agreement on those things is a matter of opinion, then it may be sound. This is why Abu Hamid (al-Ghazali) and Abu'l-Ma'ali (al-Juwayni) and other leaders of thought said that no one should be definitely called an unbeliever for violating unanimity on a point of interpretation in matters like these.

For Averroes, that unanimity which absolutely confines one to either a literal or an allegorical interpretation of a verse of Scripture is only rarely achieved, particularly under the stringent conditions he posits. The absence of consensus of course gives considerable latitude to the exegete.

That unanimity on theoretical matters is never determined with certainty, as it can be on practical [or behavioral] matters, may be shown to you by the fact that it is not possible for unanimity to be determined on any question at any period unless that period is strictly limited by us, and all the scholars existing in that period are known to us, that is, known as individuals and in their total number, and the doctrine of each one of them on the question has been handed down to us on unassailable authority. And in addition to all this, unless we are sure that the scholars existing at the time were in agreement that there is not both an apparent and an inner meaning in Scripture, that knowledge of any question ought not to be kept secret from anyone, and that there is only one way for people to understand Scripture. But it is recorded in tradition that many of the first believers used to hold that Scripture had both an apparent and an inner meaning, and that the inner meaning ought not to be learned by anyone who is not a man of learning in this field and who is incapable of understanding it. . . . So how can it possibly be conceived that a unanimous agreement can be handed down to us about a single theoretical question, when we know definitely that not a single period has been without scholars who held that there are things in Scripture whose true meaning should not be learned by all people? (Averroes, *The Decisive Treatise* 7–9)

[AVERROES 1961: 50–53]

3. Scripture and Tradition

Their possession of the Word of God in a written form—that is, a scriptural one—was but one of the shared traits of the "People of the Book." Side by side with those written texts there was another source of revelation, equally ancient, equally authentic, and equally authoritative in the lives of the believers—so authoritative, in fact, that a Jew would readily confirm that there existed not one but two Torahs.

1. "How Many Torahs Do You Have?"

Our Rabbis taught: It happened once that a certain non-Jew came to Shammai and said: "How many Torahs do you have?" He said, "Two: the written Torah and the Torah transmitted by mouth." "I believe you with respect to the Written, but not with respect to the Oral Torah; make me a proselyte on condition that you instruct me on the Written Torah (only)." But Shammai scolded him and repulsed him in anger. When the same man went to Hillel, the latter accepted him as a proselyte. On the first day he taught him his Alef, beth, gimmel, daleths; the following day he reversed their order. "But yesterday you didn't teach me thus," the man protested. "Must you then not trust me? Then trust me with respect to the Oral Torah too." (BT.Shabbat 31a)

2. What Moses Received on Sinai

God said to Moses: "Write these things, for it is by means of these things that I have made a covenant with Israel" (Exod. 34:27). When God was about to give the Torah, He recited it to Moses in proper order, namely, the Scriptures, Mishna, Haggada and Talmud, for God pronounced all these words: God revealed to Moses even the answers to questions which distinguished scholars are destined to ask their teachers in the future, for He said all these things. Then, when God had finished,

He said to Moses, "Go and teach it to My sons." . . . Moses said, "Lord, You write it for them." God said, "I did indeed wish to give it all to them in writing, but it was revealed that the Gentiles would in the future have dominion over them, and will claim the Torah as theirs; then would my children be like the Gentiles. Therefore, give them the Scriptures in writing, and the Mishna, Haggada and Talmud orally, for it is they which separate Israel and the Gentiles." (*Tanhuma* 58b)

3. The Unwritten Law as the Distinctive Mark of Israel

In this passage from Tanhuma, *the Gentiles who "in the future will have dominion over them," that is, over the Children of Israel, and "will claim the Torah as theirs" are manifestly the Christians. As the Lord foretold, the same Christians who had expropriated the "Old Testament" for their own purposes refused to accept the oral law of the Mishna, Haggada, and Talmud, which thus became the distinctive marks of the true Israel.*

God gave the Israelites two Laws, the Written Law and the Oral Law. He gave them the Written Law with its 613 ordinances to fill them with commandments and to cause them to become virtuous, as it is said, "the Lord was pleased for His righteousness' sake to increase the Law and make it glorious." And He gave them the Oral Law to distinguish them from other nations. It was not given in writing so that the Gentiles might not falsify it, as they had with the Written Law, and say that they are the true Israel. Therefore it says, "If I were to write for him the many things of My Law, they would be counted as strange" (Hos. 8:12). The "many things" are the Mishna, which is larger than the Law. (*Numbers Rabbah* 14:10)

Rabbi Judah, son of Rabbi Shalom, remarked: Moses wanted the Oral Law to be written as well (as the Torah). But God foresaw that the Gentiles would one day translate the Torah and read it in Greek and say, "They [the Jews] are not (the true) Israel." So God said to Moses, "The Gentiles will say, 'We are (the true) Israel, we are the sons of God,' and Israel will say, 'We are the sons of God. And now the scales are evenly balanced.' " So God said to the Gentiles, "Why do you claim to be My sons? I know only him who has My mystery in his possession; he is My son." Then the Gentiles ask, "What is Your mystery?" God replied, "It is the Mishna." (*Pesikta Rabbati* 14b)

From his perspective long after both these passages had been composed, and long after most of the Jewish tradition had been committed to writing, Maimonides (d.

*1204 C.E.) had very mixed reflections on this matter of writing or not writing things
down.*

Know that many sciences devoted to establishing the truth . . . that
have existed in our religious community have perished because the length
of time that has passed, because of our being dominated by the pagan
nations, and because, as we have made clear, it is not permitted to divulge
these matters to all people. For the only thing it is permitted to divulge
to all people are the texts of the (scriptural) books. You already know that
even jurisprudence was not put down in writing in olden times because
of the precept, which is widely known to the nation: "Words that I have
communicated to you orally you are not allowed to put down in writing"
(BT.Gittin 6ob). This precept shows extreme wisdom with regard to the
Law, for it was meant to prevent what ultimately came about in this respect: I mean the multiplicity of opinions, the variety of schools, the con-
fusions occurring in the expression of what is put down in writing, the
negligence that accompanies what is written down, the divisions of the
people, who are separated into sects, and the introduction of confusion
with regard to actions. All these matters should be within the authority
of the Great Court of Law, as we have explained in our juridical compilations [that is, the *Mishneh Torah*], and as the text of the Torah shows
(Deut. 17:8–12).

*Maimonides passes from legal matters to the question of esoteric learning, like the
"Work of Creation" (see Chapter 2 above) and the "Work of the Chariot."*

Now if there was insistence that jurisprudence should not, in view
of the harm that would be caused by such a procedure, be perpetuated
in a written compilation accessible to all people, all the more could none
of the mysteries of the Torah be set down in writing and be made accessible to the people. On the contrary, they were transmitted by a few men
belonging to the elite to a few of the same kind, as I explained to you from
their saying: "The mysteries of the Torah may only be transmitted to a
counselor, wise in crafts . . . " (BT.Hagigah 14a). This was the cause that
necessitated the disappearance of those great roots (of knowledge) from
the (Jewish) nation. You will not find anything of them except slight
indications and pointers occurring in the Talmud and the commentaries
on Scripture. These are a few kernels of grain, which are overlaid by many
layers of husks, so that people were occupied with these layers of husks
and thought that beneath them there was no kernel at all. (Maimonides,
Guide of the Perplexed 1:71)

4. The Transmission of the Oral Law

If Moses received the entirety of the Law on Sinai, part in writing and part orally, how did the latter descend through many generations of Jews until it finally found written form in the Mishna of Rabbi Judah the Prince about 200 C.E.? Modern scholars offer different answers to that question, but the tradition itself supplies its own answer. Most of the Mishna is relentlessly legal in content, but one of its tractates, the Pirke Aboth, or "Sayings of the Fathers," is a collection of aphorisms. At its very beginning it presents the "chain" by which the Oral Law, here called simply "the Torah," passed from Moses to Rabbi Judah.

Moses received the Torah from Sinai and committed it to Joshua, and Joshua to the Elders, and the Elders to the Prophets, and the Prophets committed it to the men of the Great Assembly. They said three things: Be deliberate in judgment, raise many disciples and make a fence about the Law.

Simon the Just was of the remnants of the Great Assembly. He used to say: By three things is the world sustained: by the Torah, by the (Temple) service and by deeds of loving kindness.

Antigonos of Sokho received (the Torah) from Simon the Just. He used to say: Be not slaves that minister to the master for the sake of receiving a bounty, but be like slaves who minister to a master not for the sake of receiving a bounty; and let the fear of heaven be upon you.

Yosi ben Yoezer of Zeredah and Yosi ben Yohanan of Jerusalem received (the Torah) from them. Yosi ben Yoezer of Zeredah said: Let your house be a meeting place for the Sages and sit amidst the dust of their feet and drink in their words thirstily.

Yosi ben Yohanan of Jerusalem said: Let your house be opened wide and let the needy be members of your household; and talk not much with womankind. They said this of a man's own wife: how much more of his fellow's wife! Hence the Sages have said: He that talks much with womankind brings evil upon himself and neglects the study of the Law and at the last will inherit Gehenna. (M.Pirke Aboth 1:1–5)

The text continues through its list of rabbis, now given in "pairs," who received and transmitted "the Torah" from their predecessors: Joshua ben Perahiah and Nittai the Arbelite; Judah ben Tabbai and Simeon ben Shetah; Shemiah and Abtalion; Hillel and Shammai; Gamaliel and his son Simeon. Some of these scholars of the Law are known. The first of them, Simon the Just, lived about 200 B.C.E.; Simeon ben Shetah appears at the end of the Maccabean period, about 80 B.C.E.; and Hillel and Shammai were slightly older contemporaries of Jesus. This was merely the starting point of a great deal of discussion and speculation, but the tradition was maintained much as it had been enunciated in the Pirke Aboth. It is still present, though much filled out, in this classic presentation of the history of the Oral Law that stands at the beginning of Maimonides' Mishneh Torah.

All the precepts which Moses received on Sinai were given together with their interpretation, as it is said, "And I will give you the tablets of stone, and the law, and the commandment" (Exod. 24:12). The "law" here refers to the Written Law, while the "commandment," refers to its interpretation. God bade us to fulfill the Law in accordance with "the commandment." This commandment alludes to what is called the Oral Law. The whole of the Law was written by Moses our teacher before his death, in his own hand. He gave (a copy of) the scroll to each tribe and deposited one in the Ark for a testimony, as it is said, "Take this book of the law and put it by the side of the Ark of the Covenant of the Lord your God, that it may be there for a witness against you" (Deut. 31:26). "The commandment," which is the interpretation of the Law, he did not write down but gave orders concerning it to the Elders, to Joshua, and to the rest of Israel, as it is said, "All this which I command to you, that you shall do; you shall not add to nor diminish from it" (Deut. 4:2). For this reason it is called the Oral Law.

Though the Oral Law was not committed to writing, Moses taught it in its entirety in his court, to the seventy elders as well as to Eleazer, Phineas, and Joshua—all three of whom received it from Moses. To Joshua, his disciple, Moses delivered the Oral Law and charged him concerning it. So too Joshua, throughout his life, taught orally. Many elders received the Oral Law from Joshua. Eli received it from the elders and from Phineas. Samuel from Eli and his court. David from Samuel and his court. (Maimonides, *Mishneh Torah*, Introduction)

5. The Pharisees and the Oral Tradition

We have few means of verifying the earliest stages of either the Pirke Aboth's version of events or Maimonides' more extended narrative. Where the existence of an oral law, the "traditions of the fathers" as it is also called, comes into firmer focus is with the appearance on the scene of the Jewish party known as the Pharisees, present in Palestinian Judaism at least from the reign of the Hasmonean John Hyrcanus (134–104 B.C.E.). Josephus, who is our chief source for the events of the century immediately preceding and following the life of Jesus, pauses occasionally in his narrative to characterize the Pharisees, among whom he counted himself: "In my nineteenth year I began to govern my life by the rule of the Pharisees, a sect

having points of resemblance to that which the Greeks call the Stoic school"
(Life 12).

The Pharisees had passed on to the people certain regulations handed down by former generations and not recorded in the Laws of Moses, for which reason they are rejected by the Sadducees, who hold that only those regulations should be considered valid which were written down (in Scripture), and those which were handed down by former generations need not be observed. . . . The Sadducees have the confidence of the wealthy alone but no following among the populace, while the Pharisees have the support of the masses. (Josephus, *Antiquities* 13.10.5–7)

In the course of both the Antiquities *and the* Jewish War, *Josephus cites examples of the Pharisees' piety and their determined dedication to the Law, written and oral, even in the face of grave consequences. This one occurs near the end of the lifetime of Herod, Israel's ruler from 37 to 4 B.C.E. The "unrivaled interpreters of the ancestral laws" may well be the Pharisees, though Josephus himself does not call them such in the text.*

Certain popular figures rose up against him [that is, Herod] for the following reason. Judas, the son of Saripheus, and Matthias, the son of Margalothus, were the most learned of the Jews and unrivaled interpreters of the ancestral laws, and men especially dear to the people because they educated the youth, for all those who made an effort to acquire virtue used to spend time with them day after day.

When these scholars learned that the king's illness could not be cured, they aroused the youth by telling them they should pull down all the works built by the king in violation of the Laws of their Fathers and so obtain from the Law the reward of their pious efforts. It was indeed because of his audacity in making these things in disregard of the Law's provisions, they said, that all those misfortunes, with which he had become familiar to a degree uncommon among mankind, had happened to him, in particular his illness.

Now Herod had set about doing certain things that were contrary to the Law, and for these he had been reproached by Judas and Matthias and their followers. For the king had erected over the great gate of the Temple, as a votive offering and at great cost, a great golden eagle, although the Law forbids those who propose to live in accordance with it to think of setting up images or to make dedications of (the likenesses of) any living things. So these scholars ordered their disciples to pull the eagle down, saying that even if there should be some danger of their being doomed to death, still to those about to die for the preservation and safeguarding of their fathers' way of life, the virtue acquired by them in death would be far more advantageous than the pleasure of living. (Josephus, *Antiquities* 17.6.2)

According to Josephus, the Pharisees were closely allied to the throne during the Hasmonean period until a falling-out with John Hyrcanus on the question of his legitimacy as High Priest (Antiquities 13.10.5–7). The Talmud tells of just such a falling-out over priestly legitimacy. Although the not very historically minded rabbis set it in the reign of Hyrcanus' successor, Alexander Janneus, the account is revealing of the later rabbinic attitude toward those frequently mentioned Perushim, or "Separatists," who are ostensibly and nominally the Pharisees. Clearly here, at least, they are the same "Sages" whom the rabbis identified as their spiritual predecessors. The point of departure for the incident that follows was a rumor that Janneus' mother had been an alien captive, a fact that would have rendered him disqualified for the High Priesthood:

Subsequently the charge (of illegitimacy) was investigated, but not sustained, and the Sages of Israel departed in anger. Then said Eleazer ben Po'irah to King Yannai: "O King Yannai, that is the law for even the humblest man in Israel, and you, a King and a High Priest, shall that be your law too?" "Then what shall I do?" (asked the king). "If you will take my advice, trample them down." "But (if I do,) what shall happen with the Torah?" "Behold it is rolled up and lying in the corner; whoever wishes to study it, let him go and study it." Said Rabbi Nahman ben Isaac: "Immediately a spirit of heresy was instilled in him, for he should have replied, 'That is well for the Written Torah, but what of the Oral Law?' "

Straightway the evil burst forth through Eleazer son of Po'irah, all the Sages of Israel were massacred, and the world was desolate until Simon ben Shetah came and restored the Torah to its pristine glory. (B1.Kiddushin 66a)

6. Jesus and the Pharisees on the Oral Law

Josephus, in addition to writing for a Gentile audience, was also generalizing on the subject of the Pharisaic party. The Gospels too may have been intended in part for Gentiles, but the discussions between Jesus and the Pharisees recorded in them are often quite specific and concrete about points of Jewish observance as embodied in the "ancient tradition" of the Oral Law.

Jesus was approached by a group of Pharisees and lawyers from Jerusalem with the question: "Why do your disciples break the ancient tradition? They do not wash their hands before meals." [Mark 7:3–4 adds by way of explanation: "For the Pharisees and the Jews in general never eat without washing their hands in obedience to an old established tradition; and on coming from the marketplace they never eat without first washing. And there are many other points on which they have a traditional rule to maintain, for example, washing of cups and jugs and copper bowls."] He answered them. "Why do you break God's commandment in the interest of your tradition? For God said, 'Honor your father and your mother,' and 'The man who curses his father and his mother must suffer death.' But you say, 'If a man says to his father or his mother, "Anything of mine which might have been used for your benefit is set apart for God,"' then he must not honor his father and his mother.' You have made God's law null and void out of respect for your tradition. What hypocrisy! Isaiah was right when he prophesied about you: 'This people pays me lip service but their heart is far from me; their worship of me is in vain, for they teach as doctrines the commandments of men.' "

He called the crowd and said to them, "Listen to me and understand this: a man is defiled not by what goes into his mouth, but by what comes out of it."

Then the disciples came to him and said, "Do you know that the Pharisees have taken great offense at what you have been saying?" His answer was: "Any plant that is not of my heavenly Father's planting will be rooted up. Leave them alone; they are blind guides, and if one blind man guides another, both will fall into a ditch." (Matthew 15:1–14)

On the issue of washing the hands, a number of the Pharisees' enactments are embodied in both the Mishna and the Talmud. Indeed, an entire tract of the Mishna, "Hands" (Yadaim), is given over to the subject, a section of which we have seen in Chapter 1 above in connection with the sanctity of canonical Scripture.

The hands are susceptible to uncleanness, and they are rendered clean (by pouring water over them) up to the wrist. Thus, if a man poured the first water up to the wrist, and the second water above the wrist, and the water flowed back to the hand, the hand becomes clean; but if he poured both the first water and the second water above the wrist, and the water flowed back on the hand, the hand remains unclean. . . .

If there is a doubt whether an act of work was done with the water or not, or whether it was with the prescribed quantity or not, or whether it was unclean or clean, its condition of doubt is deemed clean, for they have said: If there is doubt about the hands, whether they have contracted uncleanness or have conveyed uncleanness or have become clean, they are deemed clean. . . . (M.Yadaim 2:3–4)

7. A History of the Tradition

We are given another extended version of the transmission of the Oral Law in The Khazar King, *written by Judah Halevi ca. 1130–1140 C.E.*

Prophecy lasted about forty years during the Second Temple among those elders who had the assistance of the Shekina [that is, the spirit of God] from the First Temple. Individually acquired prophecy had ceased with the removal of the Shekina (at the destruction of the First Temple) and appeared only in extraordinary times or on account of great force, as that of Abraham, Moses, the expected Messiah, Elijah and their equals. In them the Shekina found a worthy abode, and their very existence helped their contemporaries to gain the degree of prophecy. The people, after their return (from exile), still had Haggai, Zechariah, Ezra and others.

Forty years later these prophets were succeeded by an assembly of Sages, called men of the Great Assembly. They were too numerous to be counted. They had returned with Zerubbabel and inherited their tradition from the prophets, as it is said: "The prophets handed down the Law to the Men of the Great Assembly" (M.Pirke Aboth 1:1).

The next generation was that of the High Priest Simon the Just and his disciples and friends. He was followed by Antigonos of Sokho of great fame. His disciples were Zadok and Boethus, who were the originators of the sects called after them Sadduceans and Boethusans. The next was Yosi ben Yoezer, "the most pious among priests," and Joseph ben Yohanan and their friends. . . . Rabbi Yosi was followed by Joshua ben Porahyah, whose history is known. *Among his disciples was Jesus the Nazarene*, and Nittai of Arbela was his contemporary. After him came Judah ben Tabbai and Simon ben Shetah, with the friends of both. At this period arose the doctrine of the Karaites [see below] in consequence of an incident between the Sages and King (Alexander) Janneus, who was a priest. . . .

The next generation was that of Shemayah and Abtalion, whose disciples were Hillel and Shammai. Hillel was famous for his learning and his gentleness. He was a descendant of David and lived one hundred and twenty years. He had thousands of disciples. . . . The greatest of them was Jonathan ben Uzziel and the least of them was Yohanan ben Zakkai, who left unstudied no verse in the Bible, nor Mishna, Talmud, Haggada, explanatory rules of the Sages and Scribes, nor any word of the law code. Rabbi Yohanan lived a hundred and twenty years like his master and saw the Second Temple.

We have now reached the generation of rabbis in the era of the Temple destruction in 70 C.E. With them begin the attributions, all of them spurious, of written treatises and, notably, the earliest mystical works.

Among his [that is, Yohanan ben Zakkai] disciples was Rabbi Eliezer ben Hyrcanus, the author of the "Chapters of Rabbi Eliezer," a famous work on astronomy, calculation of the spheres and earth and other profound astronomical subjects. His pupil was Rabbi Ishmael ben Elisha, the High Priest. He is the author of works entitled "Hekhaloth," "Hakharath Panim" and the "Science of the Chariot" because he was initiated in the secrets of this science (of mysticism), being worthy of a degree near prophecy. . . . Another pupil of his was the famous Rabbi Joshua, the same embroiled in the famous affair with Rabbi Gamaliel; further Rabbi Yosi and Rabbi Eleazer ban Arakh.

Besides these famous men and many Sages, priests and Levites whose calling was the study of the Law, there flourished undisturbed in the same period the seventy learned members of the Sanhedrin on whose authority officials were appointed or deposed. . . . In the next generation after the destruction of the Temple, there lived Rabbi Akiba and Rabbi Tarfon and Rabbi Yosi of Galilee with their friends. . . . In the next generation lived Rabbi Meir, Rabbi Judah, Rabbi Simon ben Azzai and Rabbi Hananiah ben Teradion and their friends. They were followed by "Rabbi," that is, Rabbi Judah the Prince, our teacher. His contemporaries were Rabbi Nathan, Rabbi Joshua ben Korah, and many others who were the last teachers of the Mishna, also called *Tannaim*. They were followed by the *Amoraim*, who are the authorities of the Talmud.

The Mishna was compiled in the year 530 of the era of the Documents [that is, of the Seleucid era, which began in 312 B.C.E.], which corresponds to the 120th year after the destruction of the (Second) Temple (in 70 C.E.), and 530 years after the termination of prophecy. (Judah Halevi, *The Khazar King* 3.65–67) [HALEVI 1905: 186–191]

8. The Mishna

Thus the Oral Law passed in an unbroken chain from Moses down to the generation of Rabbi Judah, "the Prince," who about 200 C.E. collected and arranged it, and for the first time committed it to writing as the Mishna. Maimonides describes the process of its composition.

Rabbi Judah, our sainted teacher, compiled the Mishna. From the time of Moses to that of our sainted teacher, there had been composed no work from which the Oral Law was publicly taught. Rather, in each generation, the head of the then existing court or the prophet of that era wrote down for his private use an aide-mémoire of the traditions he had heard from his teachers, and which he taught orally in public. In like manner students too transcribed, each according to his ability, the exposition of the Torah and its laws as he heard them, as well as whatever new matter evolved in each generation, material which had not been handed down by tradition but had been deduced by application of the thirteen hermeneutical rules and had been adopted by the Supreme Court. This was the usage current until the time of (Rabbi Judah) our teacher, the saint.

Rabbi Judah gathered together all the traditions, enactments, interpretations, and expositions for every portion of the Torah, material that had either come down from Moses our teacher or had been deduced by the courts in successive generations. All this material was redacted in the Mishna, which was diligently taught in public, and so became generally known among the Jewish people. Copies of it were made and widely disseminated, so that the Oral Law might not be forgotten in Israel.

Why did our saintly teacher behave so rather than leaving matters as they were before? Because he noticed that the number of students was diminishing, fresh disasters were continually occurring, the wicked government was constantly extending its domain and increasing its power, and Israelites were wandering and emigrating to distant countries. So he composed a work to serve as a handbook for all, the contents of which could be studied quickly and not forgotten. Throughout his life, Rabbi Judah and his colleagues busied themselves in giving public instruction in the Mishna. (Maimonides, *Mishneh Torah*, introduction)

How little a "handbook" the Mishna of Rabbi Judah actually is may be seen from its opening. The first division is called "Seeds," and the first tractate, Berakoth or "Blessings," begins thus.

From what time in the evening may the (prayer called) "O hear" be recited? From the time when the priests enter (the Temple) to eat their grain offerings until the end of the first watch. So Rabbi Eliezer. But the Sages say: Until midnight. Rabban Gamaliel says: Until the rise of dawn. His sons once returned after (after midnight) from a wedding feast. They said to him: "We have not recited the 'O hear.' " He said to them: "If the dawn has not risen, you are still bound to recite it. Moreover, wherever the Sages prescribe 'Until midnight' the duty of fulfillment lasts until the rise of dawn." The duty of burning the fat pieces and members (of the animal offerings) lasts until the rise of dawn; and for all that must be consumed "the same day," the duty lasts till the rise of dawn. Why then have the Sages said "Until midnight"? To keep a man far from transgression. (M.Berakoth 1:1)

9. The Talmud

We resume the thread of Maimonides' historical narrative in the introduction of his Mishneh Torah.

All the Sages . . . were the great men of each successive generation, some of them were heads of schools, some Exilarchs, and some were members of the Great Sanhedrin; besides them are thousands and tens of thousands of disciples and fellow students. Ravina and Rav Ashi closed the list of the Sages of the Talmud. It was Rav Ashi who compiled the Babylonian Talmud in the land of Shinar [Babylon, that is, modern Iraq] about a century after Rabbi Yohanan had compiled the Palestinian Talmud. These two Talmuds contain an exposition of the text of the Mishna and an explanation of its obscurities and whatever new subject matter had been added by the various courts from the day of (Rabbi Judah) our saintly teacher, the saint, until the compilation of the Talmud. (Maimonides, *Mishneh Torah*, introduction)

The Talmuds, then, are expositions and a "completion" (gemara) of the Mishna, one done by the rabbis in "Babylonia," that is, Iraq, and the other by their counterparts in Galilee, and finished between 500 and 600 C.E. To illustrate, there follows the text of the Babylonian Talmud elucidating the subject matter of the Mishnaic passage (M.Berakoth 1:1) cited above.

On what does the Mishna authority base himself that he begins: "From what time?" Furthermore, why does he deal with the evening "O hear"? Let him begin with the morning one. The Mishna authority bases himself on the Scripture, where it is written, "(And you shall recite them) . . . when you lie down and when you rise up" (Deut. 6:7), and he states thus: When does the time of the recital of the "O hear" of lying down begin? When the priests enter to eat their grain offerings. And if you like, I can answer: He learns (the priority of evening) from the account of the creation of the world, where it is written, "And there was evening and there was morning, one day" (Gen 1:5). . . .

The Master said: "From the time that the priests enter to eat their grain offerings." When do the priests eat grain offerings? From the time of the appearance of the stars. Let him then say: "From the time of the appearance of the stars." This very thing he wants to teach us, in passing, that the priest may eat the grain offerings from the time of the appearance of the stars. And he also wants to teach us that the expiatory offering is not indispensable, as has been taught: "And when the sun sets, we are clean," the setting of the sun is indispensable (as a condition of purification) to eat the grain offering, but the expiatory offering is not indispensable to enable him to eat the grain offerings. But how do we know that these words "and the sun sets" mean the setting of the sun, and this "we are clean" means that the day clears away? It means perhaps: And when the sun (of the next morning) appears, and "we are clean" means that the man becomes clean. Rabbah, the son of Rabbi Shilah explains: In that case the text would have to read "he becomes clean." What is the meaning of "we are clean"? The day clears away, conformably to the common expression. The sun has set and the day has cleared away. This explanation of Rabbah son of Rabbi Shilah is unknown in the West [that is, in the Palestinian schools], and they raised the question. . . .

The Master said: "From the time that the priests enter to eat the grain offerings." They pointed to a contradiction. From what time may one recite the "O hear" in the evening? From the time the poor man comes home to eat his bread with salt till he rises from his meal. The last clause certainly contradicts the Mishna. Does the first clause also contradict the Mishna? No, the poor man and the priest have the same time.

They pointed to (another) contradiction: From what time may one begin to recite the "O hear" in the evening? From the time the people come home to eat their meal on a Sabbath eve. These are the words of Rabbi Meir. But the Sages say: From the time that the priests are entitled to eat their grain offering. A sign for the matter is the appearance of the stars. And though there is no real proof of it [that is, that the day ends with the appearance of the stars], there is a hint for it. For it is written: "So we continued in the work, half the men holding the spears, from daybreak until the stars came out" (Neh. 4:21). And it says further, "to act as a guard for us at night and as a working party by day" (Neh. 4:22). Why this second citation? If you object and say that the night really begins with the setting of the sun, but that they (the guards) stayed late and came early, (I shall reply): Come and hear the other verse: "To act as a guard for us at night and a working party by day."

Now it is assumed that the "poor man" and "the people" (of these citations) have the same time for their evening meal. And if say that the poor man and the priest also have the same time, then the Sages would be saying the same thing as Rabbi Meir? Hence you must conclude that the "poor man" and the priest have the same time, but the "poor man" and "the people" do not have the same for their evening meal.

But do the priest and the "poor man" really have the same time for supper? They pointed to a contradiction: From what time may one begin to recite the "O hear"? From the time that the Sabbath day becomes hallowed on the Sabbath eve. These are the words of Rabbi Eliezer. Rabbi Joshua says: From the time the priests are ritually clean to eat their grain offering. Rabbi Meir says: From the time the priests take their ritual bath in order to eat their grain offerings. Said Rabbi Judah to him: When the priests take their ritual bath it is still daytime! . . . The objection of Rabbi Judah to Rabbi Meir, was it well founded? Rabbi Meir may reply as follows: Do you think I am referring to the twilight as defined by you? I am referring to the twilight as defined by Rabbi Yosi. For Rabbi Yosi says: The twilight is the twinkling of an eye. The one enters and the other departs and one cannot exactly fix it (that is, the precise point between day and night). . . .

"Until the end of the first watch": . . . Rabbi Isaac ben Samuel says in the name of Rab: The night has three watches, and at each watch the Holy One, blessed be He, sits and roars like a lion and says: Woe to the children, on account of whose sins I destroyed My House and burnt My Temple and exiled them among the nations of the world.

It is worth recalling that when these discussions were recorded it had been many years since there had been a Temple, a functioning priesthood, or sacrifice in ruined Jerusalem, as we are now suddenly and innocently reminded.

It has been taught: Rabbi Yosi says, I was once traveling on the road, and I entered into one of the ruins of Jerusalem to pray. Elijah of blessed memory appeared and waited for me at the door until I finished my prayer. After I finished my prayer, he said to me: Peace be upon you, my master! And I replied, Peace be with you, my master and teacher! And he said to me, My son, why did you go into this ruin? I replied, To pray. He said to me, You ought to have prayed on the road. I said, I feared lest passersby might interrupt me. He said to me, (In that case) you should have said an abbreviated prayer. Thus I learned from him three things: One must not go into a ruin; one may say a prayer on the road; and if one does say his prayer on the road, he recites an abbreviated prayer.

He [Elijah] further said to me: My son, what sound did you hear in this ruin? I replied, I heard a divine voice, cooing like a dove and saying: Woe to the children on account of whose sins I destroyed My House and burnt My Temple and exiled them among the nations of the world! And he said to me: By your life and by your head! Not in this moment alone does this voice so exclaim, but thrice each day does it exclaim thus! And more than that, whenever the Israelites go into synagogues and school-houses and respond, "May His great name be blessed," the Holy One, blessed be He, shakes His head and says: Happy is the king who is thus praised in his house! Woe to the father who had to banish his children, and woe to the children who had to be banished from the table of their father!

Our Rabbis taught: There are three reasons why one must not go into a ruin. (BT.Berakoth 2a–3a)

And more, much more.

10. Safeguarding the Torah

Among those whom the Mishna (M.Sanhedrin 10:1) says will have no share in the afterlife is "he who maintains that the Torah is not divinely revealed." But there is more in the imprecation than what appears at first glance, as the rabbinical discussion of the passage in the Babylonian Talmud reveals. Once the operative scriptural verse has been identified, in this case Numbers 15:31, we can see its application extended beyond the question of revelation to the integrity of the text of the Torah, and finally to the Oral Law and its interpretation.

Our Rabbis taught (regarding the verse) "Because he has despised the word of the Lord, and has broken His commandments, that soul is and will be cut off" (Num. 15:31) that the phrase "despised the word of the Lord" refers to he who maintains that Torah is not from heaven. Another interpretation refers it to an Epikoros; another to one who gives an interpretation of the Torah (not in accordance with the legal prescriptions). "And has broken His commandments": this means one who abolishes the covenant of the flesh [that is, circumcision]. "That soul is and will be cut off": the first "is cut off" implies in this world; the second, "will be cut off," in the next. Hence Rabbi Eliezer of Modin taught: He who defiles the sacred food, despises the festivals, abolishes the covenant of our father Abraham, gives an interpretation of the Torah not in accordance with the legal prescriptions and publicly shames his neighbor, even if he has learning and good deeds to his credit, has no share in the future world.

Another earlier opinion taught: "Because he has despised the word of the Lord," this refers to him who maintains that the Torah is not from heaven. And even if he asserts that the whole Torah is from heaven, excepting a particular verse, which he maintains was not uttered by God but by Moses himself, he too is included in the reference. And even if he admits that the whole Torah is from heaven, excepting a single point, deduction a minori ad majus or inference by analogy [that is, two of the rules of rabbinic exegesis], he is still included in "because he has despised the word of the Lord."

It has been taught: Rabbi Meir used to say: He who studies the Torah but does not teach it is alluded to in "he has despised the word of the Lord." Rabbi Nathan said: It refers to whoever pays no heed to the Mishna. Rabbi Nehorai said: Whoever can engage in the study of the Torah and fails to do so. (BT.Sanhedrin 99a–b)

11. God Is Overruled by a Majority of the Rabbis

The following is only an anecdote, albeit a celebrated one, from the Babylonian Talmud. It reveals something of the complex relationship between the Torah and the Oral Law, God's own words and the rabbis' interpretation of them. The context is a debate concerning whether a certain kind of oven was subject to ritual impurity. A majority of the scholars said it was; Rabbi Eliezer ben Hyrkanos insisted it was not.

On that day Rabbi Eliezer brought forward all the arguments in the world, but they were not accepted. He said to them, "If my ruling is correct, let this carob tree prove it." Thereupon the carob tree was up-rooted (and moved) a hundred cubits from its place, some even say four hundred cubits. The other Sages replied, "No proof may be adduced from a carob tree." Then he said, "If my ruling is correct, let this stream of water prove it." Whereupon the stream of water flowed backward. They replied, "No proof may be adduced from a stream of water." Then he said, "If my ruling is correct, let the walls of the yeshiva prove it." Whereupon the walls of the yeshiva began to totter. But Rabbi Joshua rebuked the walls and said, "When scholars are engaged in legal dispute, what concern is it of yours?" Thus the walls did not topple, in honor of Rabbi Joshua, but neither did they return to their upright position, in honor of Rabbi Eliezer, and to this day they stand inclined. Then he said, "If my ruling is correct, let it be proved from heaven." Whereupon a heavenly voice was heard saying, "Why do you dispute with Rabbi Eliezer? His rulings are always correct." But Rabbi Joshua said, "It is not in heaven" (Deut. 30:12). What did he mean by that? Rabbi Jeremiah replied, "The Torah has already been given at Mount Sinai [and thus is no longer in heaven]. We pay no heed to any heavenly voice, because already on Mount Sinai You wrote in the Torah 'One must incline after the majority' (Exod. 23:2)."

Rabbi Nathan (later) met the prophet Elijah and asked him: "What did the Holy One, blessed be He, do at that moment?" He replied, "God smiled and said, 'My children have defeated Me, My children have defeated Me.' " (BT.Baba Metzia 59b)

12. Codifying the Oral Law

By the beginning of the Middle Ages there was a daunting body of comment and homily on the Oral Torah, much of it legal in nature. Since this was, in the eyes of observant Jews, as binding as the Torah prescriptions themselves, some order had to be put into it, a task that Maimonides proposed to himself sometime about 1177.

I, Moses, son of Maimon the Sefardi, relying on the help of God, blessed be He, resolved myself intently to study all these works, with a view toward assembling the results obtained from them on the question of what is forbidden or permitted, clean or unclean, and the other rules of the Torah—all in plain language and terse style, so that thus the entire Oral Law might become systematically known to all. I would not cite difficulties and solutions or different points of view, one person saying so and another something else, but restrict myself to clear and reasonable statements in accordance with the conclusions drawn from all these compilations and commentaries that have appeared from the time of our Holy Master [that is, Rabbi Judah the Prince] down to the present time, so that all the rules shall be accessible to young and old, whether these pertain to the (scriptural) laws or to the ordinances established by the Sages and prophets, so that there would be no need for any other work to ascertain any of the laws of Israel, but that this work might serve as a compendium of the entire Oral Law, including the ordinances, customs and decrees instituted from the days of our teacher Moses till the compilation of the Talmud, as expounded for us by the Geonim in all the works composed by them since the completion of the Talmud. Hence I have called my work *Mishneh Torah* [that is, "Repetition of the Law"], for the reason that a person who first reads the Written Law and then this compilation will know from it the whole of the Oral Law, without having to consult in the meantime any other book.

I have decided to arrange this compendium in large divisions of the laws according to their various topics. These divisions are distributed in chapters according to subject matter. Each chapter is then subdivided into smaller sections so that they may be systematically memorized. Among the laws on the various topics, some consist of rules in connection with a single biblical precept. This would be the case when such a precept is rich in traditional matter and forms a single topic. Other sections include rules referring to several precepts when these all belong to one topic. For the work follows the order of topics and is not planned according to the number of precepts, as will be explained to the reader.

The total number of precepts that are obligatory for all generations is 613. Of these, 248 are positive, their mnemonic is the number of bones in the body; 365 are negative, and their mnemonic is the number of days in the solar year. (Maimonides, *Mishneh Torah*, introduction)

The result was the Mishneh Torah. *Although most later Jews found it impressive indeed, not all of Maimonides' contemporaries were equally moved. Maimonides was constrained to write to one critic, a judge in Alexandria, and explain his work.*

You should know that every author of a book—whether it deals with the laws of the Torah or with other kinds of wisdom, whether it was composed by one of the ancient wise men among the nations of the world or by physicians—always adopts one of two ways [that is, structures or styles]: either that of the monolithic code or that of the discursive commentary. In a monolithic code, only the correct subject matter is recorded, without any questions, without any answers and without any proofs, in the way which Rabbi Judah adopted when he composed the Mishna. The discursive commentary, in contrast, records both the correct subject matter and other opinions which contradict it, as well as questions on it in all its aspects, answers and proofs as to why one opinion is true and another false, or why one opinion is proper and another improper; this method, in turn, is that of the Talmud, which is a discursive commentary upon the Mishna. Moreover, if someone should object to my distinction between the code and the commentary, and claim that because the names of the Rabbis are cited in the Mishna—as when one Rabbi holds one opinion about a law and another Rabbi holds a contradictory one—this kind of citation of names constitutes proof, it is necessary for me to point out that this is not a proof; a proof explains why one Rabbi holds a certain opinion, while another Rabbi might hold a contradictory one.

You should also understand that if I have caused the names of any Tannaim to be forgotten by recording the correct legal prescription without qualification and anonymously, I have only followed the style of Rabbi

Judah here. He too did this before me, for every legal prescription which he recorded without qualification and anonymously was originated by other scholars, yet even those other Rabbis had not originated the legal prescriptions themselves but had received them from still others, and these others from still others, all the way back to Moses our teacher. And just as the Tannaim and Amoraim did not bother to record the names of all sages from the time of Moses to their own day, because then there would be no end to the citations of names, so I also have not bothered to cite their names. . . .

. . . For this reason I also described in my introduction [to the *Mishneh Torah*] the transmission of the law from one High Court and its chief judge to the succeeding High Court and its chief judge, in order to prove that the tradition of the law did not consist in the traditions of individuals but of the traditions of multitudes. And for this same reason my endeavor and purpose in composing my work was that every ruling (*halakha*) should be cited unqualifiedly [or anonymously], even if in fact it is the opinion of an individual, but it should not be reported in the name of So-and-So. This would destroy the position of the heretics (*minim*) who rejected the entire Oral Law because they saw it transmitted in the name of So-and-So and imagined that this law had never been formulated before, so that the individual had originated it on his own. (Maimonides, *Letter to R. Phineas ben Meshullam*) [TWERSKY 1980: 33–35]

13. The Debate on the Oral Law

Neither before nor after the redaction of the Mishna did all Jews accept the principle of a divinely revealed, continuously transmitted, and authoritative Oral Law. The debate appears to have begun in Maccabean times, possibly when the thesis of the Oral Law began to be advanced in its most rigorous form. For that reason, perhaps, the Mishna had to insist so strongly not merely on the authority but even on the priority of the Oral Law.

Greater stringency applies to the observance of the words of the Scribes than to (the observance of) the words of the (written) Law. If a man said, "There is no obligation to wear phylacteries," so that he transgresses the words of the Law, he is not culpable; (but if he said), "There should be in them [that is, the phylacteries] five partitions," so that he adds to the words of the Scribes, he is culpable. (M.Sanhedrin 11:3)

The dispute is also recorded, now more openly, by Maimonides, though without much sympathy for the opponents or their motives. He is commenting on Mishna

Pirke Aboth 1:3, already quoted above, where the name Antigonos of Sokho occurs.

This sage [Antigonos] has two disciples, one named Zadok and the other Boethus. When they heard him deliver this statement, "Be not like servants etc.," they departed from him. The one said to his colleague, "Behold, the master expressly stated that man has neither reward nor punishment nor is there any expectation at all." (They said this) because they did not understand his intention. The one lent support to his colleague and they departed from the community and forsook the Torah.

A sect banded around one, and another sect around his colleague. The sages termed them "Sadducees and Boethusans." Since they were unable to consolidate the masses according to what they perceived on the faith—for this evil belief divided the consolidated; it certainly did not consolidate the divided—they feigned belief in the matter of the Written Torah because they could not falsify it before the multitude. For had they brought forth their disbelief in the words of the Torah from their own mouths, they [that is, the people] would have killed them. Therefore each said to his party that he believes in the (written) Torah but disputes the (oral) tradition since it is not authentic. They said this in order to exempt themselves from the precepts of the tradition and the decrees and ordinances inasmuch as they could not thrust everything aside, both the written (Torah) and the tradition. Moreover, the path of interpretation was thus broadened for them. Since the interpretation became a matter of their choice, each, according to his intention, could be lenient in what he might wish and stringent in what he might wish. This was possible because he did not believe at all in the fundamental principle. They, however, sought to deceive in matters which were accepted only by some people.

From the time that these evil sects went forth, they have been termed "Karaites" in these lands, meaning to say, Egypt. However, their appellation according to the sages is "Sadducees and Boethusans." They are the ones who began to contest and to interpret all the passages (of the Torah) according to what appeared to them, without at all hearkening to a sage; the reverse of what the One to be blessed stated, ". . . according to the Torah which they shall instruct you and according to the judgment which they shall tell you, you shall do; you shall not turn aside either to the right or to the left from the sentence which they shall declare to you" (Deut. 17:11). (Maimonides, *Commentary on the Mishna*, Aboth 1:3)

[MAIMONIDES 1968]

14. A Jewish Schism over the Oral Tradition

The dispute between the Sadducees and Boethusans on the one side and the Pharisees on the other had long been settled by the time Maimonides was writing at the end of the twelfth century. The history of the controversy was still of interest in Jewish circles, however, because the two points of view in support of and in opposition to the Oral Law were still being sustained. The rabbinic successors to the Pharisees remained faithful to that Law, as their writings from Mishna to Midrash all testify, while the attack upon the oral tradition was mounted from the eighth century onward by a group that called themselves Karaites or "Partisans of Scripture." This is how one Karaite of the early tenth century, Jacob al-Qirqisani, covered the same historical ground as Mishna Pirke Aboth had in the third century and Maimonides would in the late twelfth. Qirqisani takes as given the identification of the Pharisees with the rabbis of his own and an earlier time—the latter, like the former, here qualified as "Rabbanites."

After the Samaritans there appeared the Chiefs of the Community [that is, the men of the Great Assembly], who are the original Rabbanites; this was in the days of the Second Temple. The first of them to be recorded was Simeon, whom they call Simeon the Righteous; they say that he was one of the remaining members of the Great Synagogue. These latter, they say, lived in the days of Ezra and Nehemiah. The Rabbanites [that is, the Pharisees] acknowledged the authority of the Chiefs of the Community solely because they followed the practices and indulgences inherited from Jereboam. In particular they [the Rabbanites] sustained and confirmed these practices, supplied them with argumentative proofs, and wrote down the interpretation of them in the Mishna and in other works. At times one or another of them did set forth the true meaning of a biblical ordinance, but they [the Rabbanites] invariably banished him and sought to do him injury, as was, for example, the case of Gamaliel, who fixed the date of holy days on the basis of the appearance of the new moon, or of Eliezer the son of Hyrkanos, who disagreed with them on the matter of uncleanness of vessels, the construction of which had not been completed; they excommunicated him and kept away from him, despite miraculous proofs of the truth of his opinion. . . .

After the Rabbanites there appeared the Sadducees founded by Zadok and Boethus, who were, according to the Rabbanites, disciples of Antigonos (of Sokho), a successor of Simeon the Righteous and had thus received their learning from the latter. Zadok was the first to expose the errors of the Rabbanites. He openly disagreed with them and he discovered part of the truth; he also composed a book in which he reproved and attacked them. However, he produced no proof of anything that he claimed but merely set it forth in the manner of an assertion.

Jesus too is brought into the lists against the Rabbanites.

Next there appeared Yeshuʿa [that is, Jesus], who the Rabbanites say was the son of Pandera; he is known as Jesus the son of Mary. He lived in the days of Joshua, the son of Perahiah, who is said to have been the maternal uncle of Jesus. This took place in the reign of Augustus Caesar, the emperor of Rome, that is, in the time of the Second Temple. The Rabbanites plotted against Jesus until they put him to death by crucifixion.

Later Qirqisani reaches Islamic times and the beginning of the Karaite movement under Anan ben David.

There appeared Anan (ben David), who is styled the Chief of the Dispersion; this occurred in the days of the Caliph Abu Jaʿfar al-Mansur [754–775 C.E.]. He [Anan] was the first to make clear a great deal of the truth about the divine ordinances. He was learned in the lore of the Rabbanites, and not one of them could gainsay his erudition. It is reported that Hay, the president of the Rabbanite assembly, together with his father, translated the book of Anan from the Aramaic into Hebrew and found nothing in it for which they could not discover the source in Rabbanite lore, excepting his view concerning the firstborn and the difference between a firstling conceived while its mother was owned by a Gentile. . . . The Rabbanites tried their utmost to assassinate Anan, but God prevented them from doing so. (Qirqisani, *Book of Lights*)

[NEMOY 1952: 49–52]

15. Saadya on Scripture and Tradition

The Karaite center was in Iraq, where they took up the weapons of learning and polemic against the "Rabbanites" across a broad front. The principal champion of these latter was Saadya (d. 942 C.E.), the learned Egyptian scholar of Scripture and philosophy who had become Gaon, or head, of the chief rabbinic academy in Iraq. Saadya wrote a number of tracts against the Karaites, who returned the compliment for centuries afterward. Here, in his summa in Arabic entitled The Book of Doctrines and Beliefs, *he outlines his position on the two traditions of the Written and the Oral Law and offers his own utilitarian defense of the latter.*

I will now explain the character of the Holy Scriptures. I declare that God included in His Book a brief record of all that happened in past times

in the form of narratives intended to instruct us in the right way of obedience toward him. He further included His laws, and added promises of
reward for their obedience. Thus Scripture became a source of everlasting
benefit. For all the books of the prophets and the learned books of all
nations, numerous though they are, comprise only three principal elements: (1) a list of commandments and prohibitions, which forms one
point; (2) the reward and punishment which are the fruits of the former;
and (3) an account of those who rendered good service to their country
and prospered, as well as those who dealt corruptly and perished. For the
instruction necessary for a good life is complete only if these three elements are combined. . . .

I say further that the Wise, may He be exalted and glorified, knew
that His laws and the stories of His wondrous signs would, through the
passage of time, require people to hand them down to posterity, so that
they might become as evident to later generations as they were to the
earlier ones. Therefore, He prepared in our minds a place for the acceptance of reliable tradition, and in our souls a quiet corner for trusting it
so that His Scriptures and stories should remain safely with us.

I deem it proper to mention a few points in regard to the truth of
tradition. Unless men had the confidence that there exists in the world
such a thing as a true report, no man would build any expectation on any
report he might be told about success in any branch of commerce, or of
progress in any art [which we naturally believe], since it is gain which man
requires and for which he exerts his strength. Nor would he fear what he
should guard against, be it the dangerous state of a road, or a proclamation prohibiting a certain action. But if a man has neither hopes nor fears,
all his affairs will come to grief. Unless it is established that there is such
a thing as true reports in this world, people will not pay heed to the
command of their ruler or his prohibition, except at such time as they see
him with their own eyes and hear his words with their own ears; and
when no longer in his presence, they will cease to accept his commands
and prohibitions.

If things were like this, all management of affairs would be rendered
impossible and many people would perish. And unless there is a true
tradition in this world, a man would not be able to know if a certain
property was owned by his father . . . nor would a man know that he is
the son of his mother, let alone that he is the son of his father. . . .

Scripture already declares that reliable tradition is as true as the
things perceived by sight. Thus it says, "For pass over to the isles of the
Kittites, and see, and send to Kedar, and consider diligently" (Jer. 2:10).

Why does it add the words "and consider diligently" in connection with the matter of report? The answer is because a report [or tradition] is, unlike sense perception, liable to be falsified in two ways, either through a wrong idea or through willful distortion. For this reason Scripture warns, "and consider diligently." Having considered deeply how we can have faith in tradition seeing that there are these two ways (of possible falsification), I found, by way of reason, that wrong ideas and willful distortions can occur and remain unnoticed only if they emanate from individuals, whereas, in a large collective group, the underlying ideas of the individuals who compose it will never be in agreement with one another, and if they willfully decide and agree on inventing a story, this will not remain unnoticed among their people; and whenever their story is put out, there will be related, at the same time, the story of how they came to agree upon it. And when a tradition is safe against these two possibilities (of falsification), there is no third way in which it could possibly be falsified. And if the Tradition of our Fathers is viewed from the aspect of these principles, it will appear sound and safe against any attack, and true, and firmly established. (Saadya, *Book of Doctrines and Beliefs* 3.5) [SAADYA 1945: 109–111]

16. A Karaite Rejoinder to Saadya on the Oral Law

Only one of the many Karaite replies to Saadya will be cited here, that by Salmon ben Jeroham, a somewhat older contemporary of the Egyptian scholar. It is called The Book of the Wars of the Lord *and is written in rhymed quatrains.*

He stated in his misleading discourse,
And he did utter the assertion,
That the Almighty chose to reveal himself to Moses
At Mount Sinai, to give him two Laws for His chosen people
The commandments of the one Law were set down in writing,
While the commandments of the other were kept upon the tongue.
Moreover, they were both to be, into everlasting eternity,
An heirloom for the congregation of the seed of the perfect ones.
My spirit advised me to reply to him in this matter,
And to place my answer among my congregation in a written epistle,
      In order to remove the stumbling block, and to clear the path of
stones,

So that the flock of Israel would not go astray into the waterless
desert of heresy.
(Salmon ben Jeroham, *Wars of the Lord*, canto 1, 8–10) [NEMOY 1952: 72–73]

You say that the Rock has given Israel two Laws,
One which is written, and one which was preserved in your mouths.
If this is as you say,
Then indeed your deeds are but falsehood and rebellion against God.
The Holy One has given you an Oral Law
So you can recite it orally,
For, say you, He had deemed it, in His wisdom, a laudable command.
Why, then, did you write it down in ornate script?
Had the Merciful One wished to write it down,
He would have had it written down by Moses.
Now did He not give it to you to be studied orally,
And had He not ordained it not to be inscribed in a book?
Yet they altered God's alleged words and wrote it down,
And instead of studying it orally they transferred it into writing.
How, then, can their words be believed, seeing that they have
                    offended grievously?
They cannot withdraw from this contradictory path.
They wrote down both Laws, thus contemning the commandment of
                    the Almighty.
Where, then, is the Oral Law in which they place their trust?
        Their words have become void and meaningless,
        And out of their own mouths have they testified that they have
drawn God's wrath upon themselves.
(Ibid., canto 1, 18–22) [NEMOY 1952: 74–75]

I have also seen in the Talmud—
Which you Rabbanites regard as if it were your main supporting column,
And which is made by you a partner of the Law of Moses,
And is held beloved and desirable in your hearts—
The bellowing of the School of Shammai against the School of Hillel,
                    to controvert their words,
As well as that of the School of Hillel against the School of Shammai,
                    to refute their interpretations of law.
This one invokes blessings, and that one heaps curses upon their heads,
Yet both are an abomination in the sight of the Lord.
The words of which one of the two shall we accept,

And the views of which one of the two shall we condemn,
Seeing that each of them has attracted a great congregation of adherents,
    And each one of them turns to say, "I am the captain of the ship"?
(Ibid., canto 3, 2) [NEMOY 1952: 79]

17. The Written and the Oral Tradition
in the Church

The authentic writings of the Apostles and others of that first generation of Chris-
tians constitute one form of the Christian tradition—its Torah, so to speak. But
there is more: the unwritten traditions that have no less authority in the life of the
Church. Ignatius, for example, the early bishop of Antioch (d. 107 C.E.), grew
impatient with those who had to be shown everything in writing "in the archives,"
here probably the Bible.

I have heard some saying, "Unless I find it in the archives, I will not
believe it in the Gospel." And when I say, "It is in Scripture," they reply,
"That is precisely the question." As far as I am concerned, Jesus Christ
is my "archive" and the inviolable documents are his cross and his death
and his resurrection. (Ignatius, *Letter to the Philadelphians* 8.2)

One extended treatment of the theme of the unwritten tradition is found in the tract
On the Holy Spirit *written by the Cappadocian bishop Basil (d. 379 C.E.). It should*
be noted that all of his examples are drawn from the liturgical practices of the
Church, and the language suggests a comparison with the pagan "mystery religions"
and their secret rites.

Of the beliefs and public teachings preserved in the Church, some
we have from written tradition and others we have received as delivered
to us "in a mystery" by the tradition of the Apostles; and both of these
have in relation to true piety the same binding force. And these no one
will deny, at least no one who is versed even moderately in the institutions of the Church. For were we to reject such unwritten customs as
having no great force, we should unintentionally injure the Gospels in
their very vitals; or rather, reduce our public definition to a mere name
and nothing more. For example, to take the first and most general instance, who is there who has taught us in writing to sign with the cross
those who have trusted in the name of our Lord Jesus Christ? What
writing has taught us to turn to the East in our prayers? Which of the
saints has left us in writing the words at the invocation and at the display-
ing of the bread in the Eucharist and the cup of the blessing? For we are
not, as is well known, content with what the Apostle or the Gospel has

recorded; but both before and after, we say other words because of their importance for the (Eucharistic) Mystery, and these we derive from unwritten teaching. Moreover, we bless the water of baptism and the oil of the chrism, and, besides these, the one who is baptized. On the basis of what writings? Is it not from the silent and mystical tradition? What written word teaches the anointing with oil itself? And how is it that a man is baptized three times? And as to other baptismal customs, from what scriptural authority comes the renunciation of Satan and his angels? Does not this come from the unpublished and secret teaching which our fathers guarded in silence, shielded from curious meddling and inquisitive investigation, since they had learned the lesson that the reverence of the mysteries is best preserved in silence? How was it proper to parade in public the teaching of those things which it was not permitted the uninitiated to look at? (Basil, *On the Holy Spirit* 27)

18. The Apostolic Tradition as the Criterion of Truth

The tradition, therefore, of the Apostles, which is apparent throughout the world, is something which all who wish to see the facts can clearly perceive in every church; and we are able to count up those who were appointed bishops by the Apostles and to show their successors to our own time, who neither taught nor knew anything resembling these men's (heretical) ravings. For if the Apostles had known hidden mysteries which they used to teach the perfect, apart from and without the knowledge of the rest, they would have delivered them especially to those to whom they were committing the churches themselves. For they desired them to be very perfect and blameless in all things, and were also leaving them as their own successors, delivering over to them their own proper place of teaching; for if these latter should act rightly, great advantage would result, but if they fell away, the most disastrous calamity would occur. (Ireneus, *Against the Heresies* 3.3.1)

The Apostles first bore witness to the faith of Christ Jesus throughout Judea; they founded churches there, and then went out into the world and preached to the Gentiles the same doctrine of the same faith. They likewise founded churches in every city, from which the other churches derived the shoot of faith and the seeds of doctrine, yes, and are still deriving them, in order to become churches. It is through them that these churches are themselves apostolic, in that they are the offspring of apostolic churches. Every kind of thing must be judged by reference to its origin. Therefore so many and so great churches are all one, being from the first Church which is from the Apostles. . . .

It is therefore on this ground that we put forward our ruling, namely that if Jesus Christ sent out the Apostles to preach, no others are to be accepted as preachers save those whom Christ appointed, since "No one knows the Father except the Son and he to whom the Son has revealed Him" (Luke 10:22). And the Son seems not to have revealed him to any but the Apostles whom he sent out to preach, assuredly to preach what he had revealed to them. But what they preached, namely what Christ revealed to them, this, on my ruling, ought to be established solely through those same churches which the Apostles themselves founded by preaching to them as well by the living voice, as the phrase goes, as by their letters (to them) afterwards. If this is so, it follows immediately that all teaching which agrees with those apostolic churches, the sources and the origins of the Faith, must be judged the truth, since it preserves without doubt what the churches received from the Apostles, the Apostles from Christ, and Christ from God. (Tertullian, *A Ruling on Heretics* 20–21)

If there are any heresies who presume to place themselves in the Apostolic age, that they may thereby seem to have been handed down by the Apostles because they existed at the time of the Apostles, we can say: Let them produce the originals of their churches; let them unfold the roll of their bishops running down in due succession from the beginning in such manner that that first bishop of theirs shall be able to show for his ordainer or predecessor some one of the Apostles or of Apostolic men, a man, moreover, who remained steadfast with the Apostles. For in this manner the Apostolic churches transmit their registers; as the church of Smyrna which records that Polycarp was placed therein by John; as also the church of Rome which makes Clement to have been ordained in like manner by Peter. In exactly the same way the other churches likewise exhibit their several notables, whom, since they were appointed to their episcopal places by the Apostles, they regard as transmitters of the Apostolic seed. (Ibid. 32)

The fully developed position on the role of tradition, the written and the oral, as a criterion of Christian truth is found in the Commonitorium *written by Vincent of Lerins in Gaul in 434* C.E.

I have often inquired earnestly and attentively of many men eminent for their sanctity and learning, how and by what sure and, so to speak, universal rule I might be able to distinguish the truth of the Catholic faith from the falsehood of heretical depravity, and I have always, and from almost all received an answer to this effect: That whether I or anyone else should wish to detect the frauds of heretics as they arise, or to avoid their snares, and to continue sound and complete in the faith, we must with the help of the Lord fortify our faith in two ways: first, by the authority of the divine Law, and then, by the tradition of the Catholic Church.

But at this point some will perhaps ask, since the canon of Scripture is complete and sufficient for everything, indeed, more than sufficient, what need is there to add to it the authority of the Church's interpretation? For this reason, because, owing to the depth of Holy Scripture, all do not accept it in one and the same sense, but one understands its words in one way, another in another way, so that there are almost as many opinions as there are men. . . . Therefore it is most necessary, on account of so much intricacy and such various errors, that the rule of right understanding of the prophets and Apostles should be framed in accordance with the standard of ecclesiastical and Catholic interpretation. (Vincent of Lerins, *Commonitorium* 2)

Vincent then explains how the tradition is expressed.

With regard to the tradition of the Church, two precautions have to be rigorously and thoroughly observed, adhered to by everyone who does not wish to become a heretic: first, it must be ascertained whether there exists from ancient times a decree established by all the bishops of the Catholic Church with the authority of a universal council; and second, should a new question arise for which no decree can be found, one must return to those Fathers who remained in their own times and places in the unity of communion and faith and were therefore regarded as teaching "probable" doctrine. If we can discover what they held in full agreement and consent, then we can conclude without hesitation that this is the true and Catholic doctrine of the Church.

That tradition, though it had through the watchful care of the Church remained unaltered down to the present time, has nonetheless undergone "development."

The Church of Christ, the careful and watchful guardian of the teachings deposited in her charge, never changes anything in them, never diminishes, never adds; does not cut off what is necessary, does not add what is superfluous, does not lose her own and does not appropriate another's, but while dealing faithfully and judiciously with ancient teaching, keeps this one objective carefully in view: if there is anything which the past has left shapeless and rudimentary, to shape and polish it; if anything is already reduced to shape and polished, to consolidate and strengthen it; if anything is already ratified and defined, to keep and guard it. Finally, what other objectives have councils (of the Church) ever aimed at in their decrees than to provide that what was before believed in simplicity should in the future be believed intelligently; that what was before preached coldly, should in the future be preached earnestly; that what was before practiced negligently, should henceforth be practiced with doubled solicitude? (Ibid. 25)

19. Jahiz on the Usefulness of Tradition

Al-Jahiz (d. 886 C.E.) offered his Muslim readers of the ninth century this explanation of the presence of a large body of traditions from the Prophet that were circulating in Islam.

God knows that man cannot of himself provide for his own needs, and does not intuitively understand the consequences of things without the benefit of the example of messengers, the books of his ancestors, and information about past ages and rulers. And so God has assigned to each generation the natural duty of instructing the next, and has made each succeeding generation the criterion of the truth of the information handed down to it. For hearing many unusual traditions and strange ideas makes the mind more acute, enriches the soul, and gives food for thought and incentive to look further ahead. More knowledge received orally means more ideas, more ideas mean more thought, more thought means more wisdom, and more wisdom means more sensible actions. . . .

Since God did not create men in the image of Jesus, son of Mary, John, son of Zachariah, and Adam, father of humankind, but rather He created them imperfect and unfit to provide for their own needs . . . He sent His Messengers to them and set up His Prophets among them, saying, "Man should have no argument against God after the Messengers" (Quran 4:163). But most men were not eyewitnesses to the proofs of His Messengers, nor did God allow them to be present at the miracles of His Prophets, to hear their arguments or to see their manner of working. And so it was needful that those who were present tell those who were absent, and that they attend to the teaching of the former; and He needed to vary the characters and the motives of those who were doing the transmitting, to show to their hearers and the faithful generally that a large number of people with differing motives and contrasting claims could not all have

invented a false tradition on the same subject without collusion and con-
spiring on the subject. . . . For if they had, it would be known and spoken
of abroad . . . and men would have the greatest of proofs against God, as
He said, "That man should have no argument against God after the Messengers"; for He would be enjoining on them obedience to His Messengers, faith in His Prophets and His Books, and belief in His heaven and
His hell, without giving them proof of tradition or the possibility of
avoiding error. But God is far above such. (Jahiz, *The Proofs of Prophecy*
125–126)

20. Scripture, Tradition, and the Law in Islam

This mildly rationalizing and utilitarian view of tradition in general and Islamic
tradition in particular may have interested the more sophisticated readers of the
cultured and clever Jahiz. For most Muslims, however, "the tradition" or "the
traditions" had quite another import: by Jahiz' day they already provided the basis
of a great deal of Muslim belief and practice. In Arabic "a tradition" (hadith) and
"the tradition" (sunna) mean two different things, neither entirely synonymous
with what is understood by the English term "tradition." "A tradition," when it is
used in its technical sense, means a report of some saying or deed of the Prophet that
is transmitted on the witness and authority of one of the men or women around him,
the "Companions of the Prophet," as they came to be called. It will generally be
called here "a Prophetic tradition." "The tradition" is actually "the tradition of the
Prophet," that is, his customary behavior, his teaching, or his example, as it is
reflected in those just mentioned reports. "The tradition of the Prophet" was as
authoritative as the Quran for Muslims, from both a legal and a doctrinal point of
view, as indeed some Prophetic traditions themselves assert.

Al-Irbad al-Sariya declared that God's Messenger got up and said:
"Does any of you, while reclining on his couch, imagine that God has
prohibited only what is to be found in the Quran? By God, I have commanded, exhorted and prohibited various matters as numerous as what
is found in the Quran, or more numerous." (Baghawi, *Mishkat al-Masabih*
6.1.2)

Aisha said: God's Messenger did a certain thing and gave permission
for it to be done, but some people abstained from it. When God's Messenger heard of it, he delivered a sermon, and after extolling God he said:
"What is the matter with people who abstain from a thing which I do?
By God, I am the one of them who knows most about God and fears Him
most." Bukhari and Muslim transmit this tradition. (Ibid. 6.1.1)

That the earliest Muslims followed the example of their Prophet, "who knows most about God," would seem to need little argument or demonstration. But there were other means of defining moral and legal action for a Muslim: adherence to local custom, for example, or even resort to some kind of analogical reasoning to elicit expanded or additional legal prescriptions from the Quran's "clear declarations." It was in this more polemical context that the role of "the Prophetic tradition" began to be argued in Islam. The earliest and most powerful case for the role of the Prophet's own authentic words and deeds, his "tradition," as the primary instrument for understanding the legal material in the Quran was made by the pioneer Egyptian Muslim jurist al-Shafi i (d. 820 C.E.) in his* Treatise on the Roots of Jurisprudence. *The argument begins, as always, with the Book itself.*

Shafi*i said: God has placed His Apostle—(in relation) to His religion, His commands and His Book—in the position made clear by Him as a distinguishing standard of His religion by imposing the duty of obedience to him as well as prohibiting disobedience to him. He has made his merits evident by associating belief in His Apostle with belief in Him. . . . He said:

"They alone are true believers who believe in God and His Apostle, and when they are with him on a matter of common concern, do not depart without obtaining his leave" (Quran 24:62).

Thus God prescribed that the perfect beginning of the faith to which all things are subordinate shall be belief in Him and then in His Apostle. For if a person believes only in Him and not in His Apostle, the name of the perfect faith will never apply to him until he believes in His Apostle together with Him. (Shafi*i, *Treatise*)   [SHAFI'I 1961: 109–110]

*From this principle that belief in God is necessarily accompanied by belief in the Apostle of God, Shafi*i *proceeds to bind the notion of the Prophet's custom into the scriptural proof. This he does by understanding the concept of "wisdom," where it occurs in the phrase "the Book and the Wisdom," as a reference to the words and deeds of the Prophet himself.*

Shafi*i said: God has imposed the duty on men to obey His divine commands as well as the tradition of His Apostle. For He said in His Book:

"Send to them, O Lord, an Apostle from among them to impart Your messages to them, and teach them the Book and the Wisdom, and correct them in every way; and indeed, You are mighty and wise" (Quran 2:129).

*After citing a number of almost identical passages, Shafi*i *continues.*

So God mentioned His Book, which is the Quran, and Wisdom, and I have heard that those who are learned in the Quran, whom I approve, hold that Wisdom is the tradition of the Prophet of God, which is like what God Himself said; but God knows best! For the Quran is mentioned first, followed by Wisdom; then God mentioned His favor to mankind by teaching them the Quran and Wisdom. So it is not permissible for Wisdom to be called here anything save the tradition of the Apostle of God. For Wisdom is closely linked with the Book of God, and God has imposed the duty of obedience to His Apostle, and imposed on men the obligation to obey his orders. So it is not permissible to regard anything as a duty save that set forth in the Quran and the tradition of the Prophet. (Shafi'i, *Treatise*) [SHAFI'I 1961: 110–122]

That what Muhammad said and did reflected nothing but the will of God, Shafi'i easily demonstrates by reference to passages like the following.

O Prophet, fear God and do not follow the unbelievers and the hypocrites. But follow what is revealed to you from your Lord. Verily, God is All-knowing, All-wise. Truly, God is aware of the things you do. (Quran 33:1–2)

O Apostle, announce what has reached you from your Lord, for if you do not, you will not have delivered His message. God will preserve you from the mischief of men; for God does not guide those who do not believe. (Quran 5:67)

In certifying that the Prophet guides mankind along a straightforward path—the path of God—and that he delivers His message and obeys His commands, as we have stated before, and in ordering obedience to him and in emphasizing all this in the (divine) communications just cited, God has given evidence to mankind that they should accept the judgment of the Apostle and obey his orders. (Shafi'i, *Treatise*) [SHAFI'I 1961: 118]

Shafi'i's argument has now reached a crucial juncture.

Shafi'i said: Whatever the Apostle has decreed that is not based on any (textual) command from God, he has done so by God's command. . . . For the Apostle had laid down a tradition (on matters) for which there is a text in the Book of God as well as for others concerning which there is no specific text. But what he has laid down in the Prophetic tradition God has ordered us to obey, and He regards our obedience to him [Muhammad] as obedience to Himself, and refusal to obey him as disobedience to Him for which no man will be forgiven; nor is an excuse for failure to obey the Prophet's tradition possible owing to what I have already stated and what the Prophet himself has said:

"Sufyan told us from Salim Abu al-Nadr, a freed slave of Umar ibn Ubaydallah, who heard Ubaydallah ibn Abi Rafi' related from his father that the Apostle had said: 'Let me find no one of you reclining on his couch, and when confronted with an order of permission or prohibition from me, say: I do not know (if this is permitted or prohibited); we will follow only what we find in the Book of God.' " (Shafi'i, *Treatise*)
[SHAFI'I 1961: 118–119]

So both the Prophetic tradition and the discrete reports that constituted it were carefully studied by Muslim scholars, as Ibn Khaldun explains in his Prolegomenon to History, *written in 1377 C.E.*

It should be known that the sciences with which people concern themselves in cities and which they acquire and pass on through instruction are of two kinds: one that is natural to man and to which he is guided by his own ability to think, and a traditional kind that he learns from those who invented it.

The first kind comprises the philosophical sciences. They are the ones with which man can become acquainted through the very nature of his ability to think and in whose objects, problems, arguments and methods of instruction he is guided by his human perceptions, so that he is made aware of the distinction between what is correct and what is wrong in them by his own speculation and research, inasmuch as he is a thinking human being.

The second kind comprises the traditional, conventional sciences. All of them depend upon information based on the authority of the given religious law. There is no place in the intellect for them, save that the intellect may be used in connection with them to relate problems of detail with basic principles. Particulars that constantly come into being are not included in the general tradition by the mere fact of its existence. Therefore, such particulars need to be related (to the general principles) by some kind of analogical reasoning. However, such analogical reasoning is derived from the (traditional) information, while the character of the basic principle, which is traditional, remains valid [that is, unchanged]. Thus analogical reasoning of this type reverts to being tradition itself, because it is derived from it.

It is clear from Ibn Khaldun's remarks that he is not using "traditional" in the sense of "ordinary," "usual," or "the way things have always been done," but rather in the original sense of "handed down" and so, somewhat more awkwardly in English, of the "traditioned" sciences, where it is not so much a question of a science that had been handed down as of a science using "traditioned" data. All those data

derive, as he next indicates, from the twin source of the Quran and the reported, or
"traditioned," behavior of the Prophet.

The basis of all the traditional [that is, "traditioned"] sciences is the
legal material of the Quran and the customary behavior of the Prophet,
which is the law given us by God and His Messenger, as well as the
sciences connected with that material, by means of which we are enabled
to use it. This, further, requires as auxiliary sciences the sciences of the
Arabic language [that is, grammar, rhetoric, lexicography, etc.]. Arabic is
the language of Islam and the Quran was revealed in it.

The different kinds of traditional sciences are numerous, because it
is the duty of the responsible Muslim to know the legal obligations God
placed upon him and upon his fellow men. They are derived from the
Quran and the reported behavior of the Prophet, either from the text
itself or through general consensus, or a combination of the two. Thus he
must first study the explicit wording of the Quran. This is the science of
Quran interpretation [see Chapter 2 above]. Then he must study the
Quran, both with reference to the manner in which it has been transmitted and related on the authority of the Prophet who brought it from God,
and with reference to the differences in the readings of the Quran readers. This is the science of Quran reading [see Chapter 1 above].

Then he must study the manner in which the "tradition of the
Prophet" is connected with its originator [that is, Muhammad], and he
must discuss the transmitters who have handed it down. He must know
their circumstances and their probity, so that the information he receives
from them may be trusted and so that one may be able to know the part
of it in accordance with whose implications one must act. These are the
sciences of Prophetic tradition.

Then the process of evolving the laws from their basic principles
requires some normative guidance to provide us with the knowledge of
how that process takes place. This is the science of the principles of
jurisprudence. After one knows the principles of jurisprudence, one can
enjoy, as its result, the knowledge of the divine laws that govern the
actions of all Muslims. This is jurisprudence proper [see Chapter 5
below].

Furthermore, the duties of the Muslim may concern either the body
or the heart. The duties of the heart are concerned with faith and the
distinction between what is to be believed and what is not to be believed.
This concerns the articles of faith which deal with the essence and the
attributes of God, the events of the Resurrection, Paradise, punishment

and predestination, and entails discussion and defense of these subjects with the help of intellectual arguments. This is speculative theology. (Ibn Khaldun, *Muqaddima* 6.9) [IBN KHALDUN 1967: 2:436–438]

21. The Inspiration of the Prophetic Traditions

As we have already seen in Chapter 1 above, there was no doubt that the Quran was the inspired word of God. Likewise, for the Prophetic traditions, there is some internal testimony in a few reports that at least some of the words of Muhammad were the result, and enjoyed the authority of, a divine inspiration. The following is reported on the authority of the Prophet's companion Ubayda.

The descent of inspiration was troublesome to the Prophet. His face would go ashen in color. One day inspiration came down on him [possibly just after the revelation of Sura 4:15] and he showed the usual signs of distress. When he recovered, he said: "Take it from me! God has appointed a way for the women: the non-virgin with the non-virgin and the virgin with the virgin. The non-virgin, one hundred strokes and death by stoning; the virgin, one hundred strokes and banishment for a year. (Bayhaqi, *The Great Tradition*) [Cited by BURTON 1977: 74]

The theologian al-Ghazali puts the Muslim position on the Prophetic traditions succinctly.

God does not have two words, one in the Quranic style which we are bidden to recite publicly, and called the Quran, while the other word is not Quran. God has but one word which differs only in the mode of its expression. On occasions God indicates His word by the Quran; on others, by words in another style, not publicly recited, and called the Prophetic tradition. Both are mediated by the Prophet. (Ghazali, *Mustasfa* 1.125) [Cited by BURTON 1977: 57]

22. Transmission of the Prophetic Traditions

Muslim tradition is unanimously agreed that parts at least of the Quran were written down, whether "on palm leaves or flat stones or in the hearts of men," during the Prophet's own lifetime. There is no such unanimity concerning the Prophetic traditions, as these two widely circulated reports testify.

Abdullah ibn Umar reported: "We said, 'O Prophet of God, we hear from you traditions which we cannot remember. May we not write them down?' 'By all means write them down,' he said."

Abu Hurayra reported: "The Prophet of God came to us while we were writing down traditions and said, 'What is this you are writing down?' We said, 'Traditions which we hear from you.' Said he, 'A book other than the Book of God! Do you not know that it was nothing but the writing of books other than the Book of God that led astray the peoples who were before you?' We said, 'Are we to relate traditions from you, O Prophet of God?' He replied, 'Relate traditions from me; there is no objection to that. But he who intentionally speaks falsely on my authority will find a place in hell.' " [Cited by GUILLAUME 1924: 15–16]

23. Tendentious and Sectarian Traditions

That some people were in fact speaking falsely on the authority of the Prophet must have been apparent to everyone who looked into the matter of the Prophetic traditions. The reported words of the Prophet were important not merely for understanding the legal material in the Quran but also for settling various historical claims. The Shi'ites, for example, those partisans of the Imamate of Ali, bolstered their claims to rulership in Islam not merely by charging that the text of the Quran had been deliberately tampered with (see Chapter 1 above); they also interpreted the extant text in a different fashion. How can one determine the truth or falsity of such a claim is the question posed by the essayist al-Jahiz (d. 886 C.E.) in his tract called The Uthmanis.

The radical Shi'ites claim that God revealed several verses regarding Ali, notably the following: "Obey God, obey God's Messenger and those in authority among you" (Quran 4:62), in which "those in authority" refers to Ali and his descendants. In truth, if traditionists were agreed that this verse refers to Ali and his descendants, then we must accept it; but if it [that is, this reported interpretation] is spurious, transmitted on weak authority, it is not only weak but exceptional, and you cannot account it part of your evidence. A Prophetic tradition can derive from a single reliable source and be transmitted on equally sound authority, but it is still reckoned "exceptional" unless it is widely known and a matter of common knowledge. On the other hand, a tradition can be transmitted by two or three persons regarded by traditionists as weak authorities, and in that case it is weak by reason of the weakness of its transmitters; but it still cannot be described as "exceptional" as long as it is transmitted by three authorities. The only sure proof lies in traditions that are transmitted in such a fashion that deliberate forgery or conspiracy to forge can be ruled out. These are the accepted Prophetic traditions.

A tradition is accepted not merely because of the number and reliability of its transmitters, but because it has been transmitted by a number of authorities whose motives and inclinations are so different that they could not have possibly conspired together to utter a forged Prophetic tradition. Then the compiler must satisfy himself that these different authorities transmitted the tradition through an equal number of transmitters of equally different motives and tendencies. If the final version then corresponds with the original, conviction is inescapable and doubt and suspicion are excluded.

Turning to the claim that in the verse "Obey . . . " God was referring to Ali to the exclusion of all the (other) Emigrants, the report on which this interpretation rests does not fulfill these conditions or fit this description. Indeed, the commentators suggest that it refers rather to the Prophet's officers and governors, to Muslims in general or to the leaders of expeditions . . . and that it is an injunction to the people to obey the commanders of the army and submit to the civil administration (of the community). (Jahiz, *The Uthmanis* 115)

24. The Criticism of Traditions

Nor was sectarianism the only cause for the multiplication of Prophetic traditions, some of them of very doubtful authenticity. Within less than a hundred years after the death of Muhammad the "traditions of the Prophet" were being invoked ever more frequently and systematically in the elaboration of Islamic law. This new approach to Islamic law, which is typified in the Muslim jurisprudent al-Shafi'i (d. 820 C.E.), created a new demand for traditions, and the supply soon began to rise to meet it.

Some idea of the enormous number of traditions that were eventually credited to the Prophet may be gotten from the fact that when Muslim scholars sat down to collect these reports, one of them, al-Bukhari (d. 870 C.E.), had reputedly accumulated 600,000 such, of which only 7,275 were included in his anthology, a number that may perhaps be reduced to 4,000 or even 2,762 when repetitions are eliminated. Another scholar, Abu Dawud, used only 4,800 out of his collection of some 500,000 Prophetic traditions in his anthology.

One Muslim response to this unchecked growth in the number of Prophetic traditions was, as Jahiz had done, to develop a more critical attitude toward these reports and to attempt to separate, if not the authentic from the spurious, then the "sound" from the "weak." The chief method of proceeding was to scrutinize the chain of transmitters that each tradition now self-consciously bore as a sign of its authenticity. Ibn Khaldun (d. 1406 C.E.) describes the fully developed science of

tradition criticism in the survey of Islamic sciences that he incorporated into his
Prolegomenon to History.

The purpose of the discipline is a noble one. It is concerned with the knowledge of how to preserve the traditions transmitted on the authority of the Master of the religious law [that is, Muhammad], until it is definite which are to be accepted and which are to be rejected.

It should be known that the men around Muhammad and the men of the second generation who transmitted the traditions were well known in the cities of Islam. There were transmitters in the Hijaz, in Basra and Kufa [the early Muslim garrison towns in Iraq], and then in Egypt and Syria. They were famous in their time. The transmitters in the Hijaz had fewer links in their chains of transmitters and they were sounder, because they were reluctant to accept (as reliable transmitters) those who were obscure and whose conditions were not known. . . .

At the beginning, knowledge of the religious law was entirely based on (oral) tradition. It involved no speculation, no use of opinion, and no intricate reasoning. The early Muslims occupied themselves with it, selecting the sound material, and thus eventually perfected it. Malik wrote the *Kitab al-Muwatta* according to the Hijazi tradition, in which he laid down the principal laws on the basis of sound, generally agreed-upon (material). He arranged the work according to juridical categories. (Ibn Khaldun, *Muqaddima* 6.11) [IBN KHALDUN 1967: 2:452–453]

Another of the sciences of tradition is the knowledge of the norms that leading tradition scholars have invented in order to know the chains of transmitters, the (individual) transmitters, their names, how the transmission took place, their conditions, their classes, and their different technical terminologies. This is because general consensus makes it obligatory to act in accordance with information established on the authority of the Messenger of God. This requires probability for the assumption that the information is true. Thus the independent student must verify all the means by which it is possible to make such an assumption.

He may do this by scrutinizing the chains of transmitters of traditions. For that purpose one may use such knowledge of the probity, accuracy, thoroughness and lack of carelessness or negligence as the most reliable Muslims describe a transmitter as possessing. Then, there are the differences in rank that exist among the transmitters. Further, there is the way the transmission took place. The transmitter may have heard the *shaykh* (dictate the tradition), or he may have read it (from a book) in his presence, or he may have heard it read (by another) in the presence of the *shaykh*, or the *shaykh* may have written it down for him, or he may have obtained the approval of the *shaykh* for written material, or he may have obtained his permission to teach certain materials. (Ibid.)

[IBN KHALDUN 1967: 2:448–449]

25. The Categories of Traditions

This careful scrutiny of the transmitters of any given tradition allowed the scholar to categorize the tradition in question and to rate it according to the criteria he had set up.

There are differences with regard to the soundness or acceptability of the transmitted material. The highest grade of transmitted material is called "sound" (by the tradition scholars). Next comes "good." The lowest grade is "weak." The classification of traditions also includes "missing the original transmitter on Muhammad's authority," "missing one link," "missing two links," "affected with some infirmity," "unique," "unusual" and "unique and suspect." In some cases there is a difference of opinion as to whether such traditions should be rejected. In other cases, there is general agreement that they should be rejected. The same is the case with traditions with sound chains. In some instances there is general agreement as to their acceptability and soundness, whereas, in other instances, there are differences of opinion. Tradition scholars differ greatly in their explanation of these terms. (Ibn Khaldun, *Muqaddima* 6.11)

[IBN KHALDUN 1967: 2:449–450]

26. The Companions of the Prophet

The traditions on the excellence of the generation of Muhammad's contemporaries was not simply an exercise in piety. It was these worthies who were the eyewitness generation and so stood behind every tradition attributed to the Prophet. And it was their character rather than the acuity of their sight or hearing that guaranteed what they transmitted.

The best of mankind after these [that is, after the early Caliphs and the veterans of the Battle of Badr] are the Companions of God's Messenger from the period during which he was among them. Anyone who knew him for a year or a month or a day or an hour, or even saw him, is of the Companions, to the extent that he was with him, took precedence with him, heeded his words and regarded him. The least of these in companionhood is better than the generation which did not see him. If they should come before God with all their works like those who were the associates of the Prophet—God bless him and give him peace—and beheld him and listened to him, the one who saw him with his own eye and believed in him even for a single hour is better for his association than all who followed after, even if they should have performed all the (requisite) good works. (Ahmad ibn Hanbal, *Creed*) [WILLIAMS 1971: 31]

27. Contradictory Traditions

Careful scrutiny of the external transmission mechanisms of a Prophetic tradition was not the only way of investigating Prophetic traditions in Islam. Some attention was also given to the matter of the tradition itself, particularly to the question of contradictory traditions. Al-Shafiʿi himself addressed the problem.

As to contradictory Prophetic traditions where no indications exist to specify which is the abrogating and which is the abrogated tradition, they are all in accord with one another and contradiction does not really exist among them. For the Apostle of God, being an Arab by tongue and by country, may have laid down a general rule intended to be general and another general rule intended to be particular. . . . Or a certain question may have been asked to which he gave a concise answer, leading some of the transmitters to relate the tradition in detail and others in brief, rendering the meaning of the tradition partly clear and partly vague. Or (it may happen) that the transmitter of a certain tradition related the answer he heard from the Prophet without knowing what the question had been, for had he known the question he would have understood the answer clearly from the reasoning on which the answer was based.

The Prophet may have likewise laid down a tradition covering a particular situation and another covering a different one, but some of those who related what they had heard failed to distinguish between the two differing situations for which he had laid down the traditions. . . . He may have also provided a tradition consisting of an order or permission or prohibition, the wording of which was general, and he may have provided a second specifying tradition which made it evident that his order of prohibition was not intended to prohibit what he made lawful, nor that his order of permission made lawful what he prohibited. For all possibilities of this kind parallel examples exist in the Book of God. (Shafiʿi, *Treatise*) [SHAFIʿI 1961: 180–181]

28. The Canonical Collections

We return to Ibn Khaldun's survey of the science of tradition. He now describes the five collections of traditions that had gained the cachet of authority in Islam.

There was Muhammad ibn Isma'il al-Bukhari [d. 870 C.E.], the leading tradition scholar of his time. In his *Musnad al-Sahih* he widened the area of tradition and published the orthodox traditions according to subject. He combined all the different ways of the Hijazis, Iraqis and Syrians, accepting the material upon which they all agreed, but excluding the material concerning which there were differences of opinion. He repeated a given tradition in every chapter upon which the contents of that particular tradition had some bearing. Therefore his traditions were repeated in several chapters, because a single tradition may deal with several subjects, as we have indicated. His work thus comprised 7,200 traditions, of which 3,000 are repeated. In each chapter he kept separate the (different) recensions (of the same tradition), with the different chains of transmitters belonging to each.

Then came the imam Muslim [d. 875 C.E.]. . . . He composed his *Musnad al-Sahih*, in which he followed Bukhari, in that he transmitted the material that was generally agreed upon, but he omitted the repetitions and he did not keep the (different) recensions and chains of transmitters separate. He arranged his work according to juridical categories and the chapter headings of jurisprudence.

How elaborate these judicial categories were may be seen from a glance at Bukhari's Sahih. The whole work is divided into ninety-seven "books." The first contain traditions on the beginning of revelation, on faith and knowledge. The next thirty books are given over to traditions connected with ablution, prayer, alms, pilgrimage, and fasting. These are followed by twenty-two books on matters of business, trusteeship, and in general with conditions of employment and various legal matters. There are three books of traditions on fighting for the faith and dealing with subject peoples, followed by one on the beginning of creation. The next four collect traditions on the Prophets and the admirable traits of various contemporaries of Muhammad, including some account of the Prophet's life up to the Hijra. The next book follows his career at Medina. There are two books with exegetical traditions on the Quran. The three following deal with marriage, divorce, and the maintenance due to one's family. From here to book ninety-five various subjects are treated, among them food, drink, clothing, seemly behavior, medicine, invitations, vows, the expiation of broken vows, blood revenge, persecution, the interpretation of visions, civil strife, and the trials before the end of the world. Book 96 stresses the importance

adhering to the Quran and the Sunna, and the last book, which is fairly lengthy,
addresses itself chiefly to theological questions on the subject of the Unity of God.
We return once more to the text of Ibn Khaldun.

Scholars have corrected the two authors [that is, Bukhari and Mus-
lim], noting the cases of sound traditions not (included in their works).
They have mentioned cases where they have neglected (to include traditions which, according to) the conditions governing the inclusion of traditions in their works (should have been included).

Abu Dawud [d. 888 C.E.] . . . al-Tirmidhi [d. 892C.E.] . . . and al-
Nasa'i [d. 915 C.E.] wrote tradition works which included more than
merely "sound" traditions. Their intention was to include all traditions
that amply fulfilled the conditions making them actionable traditions.
They were either traditions with few links in the chain of transmitters,
which makes them sound, as is generally acknowledged, or they were
lesser traditions, such as (the category of) "good" traditions and others.
It was to serve as a guide to orthodox practice. (Ibn Khaldun, *Muqaddima*
6.11) [IBN KHALDUN 1967: 2:454–455]

29. A Tradition Summa: The "Forty" of al-Nawawi

These four great collections of Prophetic traditions, each of which included thousands
of separate reports, were made and arranged primarily for the benefit of lawyers,
who required a convenient way of finding Prophetic precedents. Their size and
complexity made them hardly useful for most Muslims. The needs of piety were met
by subsequent smaller collections called "The Forty," since, as one Prophetic tradi-
tion reported, there would be a special blessing on whoever assembled that number
of reports from the Prophet. One of the best known was the "Forty Sound Prophetic
Traditions" of al-Nawawi (d. 1278 C.E.), which served as a kind of catechism in
many parts of the Islamic world.

It has come to us on the authority of Ali ibn Abi Talib . . . Ibn Umar
and Ibn Abbas and Anas ibn Malik and Abu Hurayra and Abu Sa'id
al-Khudri, with whom may God be pleased, through many channels and
varied lines of transmission, that the Apostle of God, upon whom may be
God's blessing and peace, said: "Whoever preserves for my community
forty traditions concerning matters of this religion, God will raise him up
on the Last Day in the company of the jurists and the theologians." . . .

The theologians, with whom may God be pleased, have composed
innumerable works on this matter (of the Forty Traditions). . . . And now

I have sought God's help in assembling forty Prophetic traditions in imitation of those predecessors, the outstanding traditionists and scholars of Islam. The theologians have agreed that it is permissible to use a weak tradition when it concerns a matter of a meritorious work, yet in spite of this I have not relied on that but rather on the saying of him [that is, Muhammad], upon whom be God's blessing and peace, in the genuine Prophetic traditions: "Let him among us who (was present and) saw, inform him who was absent," and on his saying: "May God brighten life for any man who hears what I say, pays heed to it, and passes it on just as he has heard it."

Among the theologians are some who have assembled forty Prophetic traditions concerning the principles of religion, while others (have made their collections) with reference to the derivative matters of religion. Some about the Holy War, some about ascetic practices, some about rules of conduct, some about practical sermonizing. All these are pious purposes, so may God be pleased with such as have purposed them. My thought, however, was to assemble forty more important than any of these, to wit, the forty traditions which would include all the above mentioned (subjects), and each tradition of which would set forth one of the great points of religious belief, those which the theologians have referred to as "the pivot of Islam" or "the half of Islam" or "the third thereof," or some such title. Then I shall insist that each of the forty be a "sound" Prophetic tradition, for the most part such as will be found in the books called *The Sound* by al-Bukhari and Muslim. I shall record them without their chains of transmitters in order to make it easier to memorize them and make them more generally profitable, if God so wills, and after them I shall add explanations of any obscure expression in them. (Nawawi, *The Forty Traditions*) [JEFFERY 1962: 142–144]

4. The Law of God

1. Moses Receives the Torah

The Covenant had been concluded with Abraham, as the Book of Genesis explains, but it was not until the days of Moses, when the Israelites had been led out of Egypt into the wilderness, that the Law was given to Israel.

On the third new moon after the Israelites had gone forth from the land of Egypt, on that very day, they entered the wilderness of Sinai. Having journeyed from Rephidim, they entered the wilderness of Sinai and encamped in the wilderness. Israel encamped there in front of the mountain, and Moses went up to God. The Lord called to him from the mountain, saying: "Thus shall you say to the house of Jacob and declare to the children of Israel: 'You have seen what I did to the Egyptians, how I bore you on eagles' wings and brought you to Me. Now, then, if you will obey Me faithfully and keep My Covenant, you shall be My treasured possession among all the peoples. Indeed, all the earth is Mine, but you shall be to Me a kingdom of priests and a holy nation.' These are the words that you shall speak to the children of Israel."

Moses came and summoned the elders of the people and put before them all the words that the Lord had commanded him. All the people answered as one, saying, "All that the Lord has spoken we will do." And Moses brought back the people's words to the Lord. And the Lord said to Moses, "I will come to you in a thick cloud, in order that the people may hear when I speak with you and so trust you ever after." Then Moses reported the people's words to the Lord, and the Lord said to Moses, "Go to the people and warn them to stay pure today and tomorrow. Let them wash their clothes. Let them be ready for the third day; for on the third day the Lord will come down, in the sight of all the people, on Mount Sinai. You shall set up bounds for the people round about, saying, 'Beware of going up on the mountain or touching the borders of it. Whoever touches the mountain shall be put to death; no hand shall touch him, but he shall be either stoned or shot; beast or man, he shall not live.' When the ram's horn sounds a long blast, they may go up on the mountain. . . ."

On the third day, as morning dawned, there was thunder and lightning and a dense cloud upon the mountain, and a very loud blast of the horn; and all the people who were in the camp trembled. Moses led the people out of the camp toward God, and they took their places at the foot of the mountain.

Now Mount Sinai was all in smoke, and the Lord had come down upon it in fire; the smoke rose like the smoke of a kiln, and the whole mountain trembled violently. The blare of the horn grew louder and louder. As Moses spoke, God answered him in thunder. The Lord came down upon Mount Sinai, on the top of the mountain, and the Lord called Moses to the top of the mountain and Moses went up. The Lord said to Moses, "Go down, warn the people not to break through to the Lord to gaze, lest many of them perish. The priests also who come near the Lord must purify themselves, lest the Lord break out against them." But Moses said to the Lord, "The people cannot come up to Mount Sinai, for You warned us, saying, 'Set bounds about the mountain and sanctify it.' " So the Lord said to him, "Go down and come back together with Aaron; but let not the priests or the people break through to come up to the Lord, lest He break out against them." And Moses went down to the people and spoke to them.

God spoke all these words, saying:

"I am the Lord your God who brought you out of the land of Egypt, the house of bondage. You shall have no other gods beside Me.

"You shall not make for yourself a sculpted image, or any likeness of what is in the heavens above, or on the earth below, or in the waters under the earth. You shall not bow down to them or worship them. For I, the Lord your God, am an impassioned God, visiting the guilt of the fathers upon the children, upon the third and upon the fourth generations of those who reject Me, but showing kindness to the thousandth generation of those who love Me and keep My commandments.

"You shall not swear falsely by the name of the Lord your God; for the Lord will not clear one who swears falsely by His name.

"Remember the sabbath day and keep it holy. Six days you shall labor and do all your work, but the seventh day is a sabbath of the Lord your God; you shall not do any work—you, your son or daughter, your male or female slave, or your cattle, or the stranger who is within your settlements. For in six days the Lord made heaven and earth and sea, and all that is in them, and He rested on the seventh day; therefore the Lord blessed the sabbath and hallowed it.

"Honor your father and your mother, that you may long endure on the land which the Lord your God is giving you.

"You shall not murder.

"You shall not commit adultery.

"You shall not steal.

"You shall not bear false evidence against your neighbor.

"You shall not covet your neighbor's house; you shall not covet your neighbor's wife, his male or female slave, or his ox or his ass, or anything that is your neighbor's."

All the people witnessed the thunder and the lightning, the blare of the horn and the mountain smoking; and when the people saw it they fell back, and stood at a distance. "You speak to us," they said to Moses, "and we shall obey; but let not God speak to us lest we die." Moses answered the people, "Do not be afraid; for God has come only in order to test you, and that the fear of Him may be ever with you, so that you do not go astray." So the people remained at a distance, while Moses approached the thick cloud where God was. (Exodus 19:1–20:18)

2. "The Covenant Is in These Words"

As the Exodus narrative proceeds, an increased emphasis is placed on the written *quality of the Covenant and, apparently in passing, on a distinction that many later interpreters found useful between God's "commands" and His "rules."*

Moses went and repeated to the people all the commands of the Lord and all the rules; and all the people answered with one voice and said, "All the things the Lord has commanded we will do!" Moses then wrote down the commands of the Lord.

Early in the morning, he set up an altar at the foot of the mountain, with twelve pillars for the twelve tribes of Israel. He designated some young men from among the Israelites, and they offered burnt offerings and sacrificed bulls as offerings of well-being to the Lord. Moses took one part of the blood and put it in basins, and the other part of the blood he dashed against the altar. Then he took the record of the Covenant and read it aloud to the people. And they said, "All the Lord has spoken, we will do." Moses took the blood and dashed it on the people and said, "This is the blood of the Covenant which the Lord now makes with you concerning all these commands." (Exodus 24:3–8)

The Lord said to Moses, "Come up to me on the mountain, wait there and I will give you the stone tablets with the teachings and commandments which I have inscribed to instruct them." So Moses and his attendant Joshua arose, and Moses ascended the mountain of God. To the elders he had said, "Wait here for us until we return to you. You have Aaron and Hur with you; let anyone who has a legal matter approach them."

When Moses had ascended the mountain, the cloud covered the mountain. The Presence of the Lord abode on Mount Sinai, and the cloud hid it for six days. On the seventh day He called to Moses from the midst of the cloud. Now the Presence of the Lord appeared in the sight of the Israelites as a consuming fire on the top of the mountain. Moses went inside the cloud and ascended the mountain; and Moses remained on the mountain forty days and forty nights. (Exodus 24:12–18)

The Lord gives the tablets to Moses.

Moses turned and went down from the mountain bearing the two tablets of the Pact, tablets inscribed on both their surfaces; they were inscribed on the one side and the other. The tablets were God's work, and the writing was God's writing, incised upon the tablets. (Exodus 32:15–16)

Even before he reaches the camp of the Israelites, Moses hears the sounds of the orgiastic worship of a golden calf the Israelites had made Aaron set up in his absence. In a fit of anger he smashes the tablets of the Law. After the people have been punished and the worship of the True God restored—and Moses makes the extraordinary request of being allowed to gaze on the very Presence of God—the leader of the Israelites once again prepares to ascend the mountain.

The Lord said to Moses, "Carve two tablets of stone like the first, and I will inscribe upon the tablets the words that were on the first tablets, which you shattered. Be ready by morning, and in the morning come up to Mount Sinai and present yourself there to Me, on the top of the mountain; neither shall the flocks and the herds graze at the foot of the mountain."

So Moses carved two stone tablets like the first, and early in the morning he went up on Mount Sinai, as the Lord had commanded him, taking the two stone tablets with him. The Lord came down in the cloud; He stood with him there, and proclaimed the name Lord [that is, YHWH]. The Lord passed before him and proclaimed "The Lord! the Lord! a God compassionate and gracious, slow to anger, abounding in kindness and faithfulness, extending kindness to the thousandth generation, forgiving iniquity, transgression and sin; yet He does not remit all punishment, but visits the iniquity of fathers upon children and children's children, upon the third and fourth generations."

Moses hastened to bow low to the ground in homage, and said, "If I have gained Your favor, O Lord, let the Lord go in our midst, even though this is a stiff-necked people. Pardon our iniquity and our sin, and take us for Your own."

The Lord said: "Hereby I make a Covenant. Before all your people I shall work such wonders as have not been wrought in all the world or in any nation; and all the people who are with you will see how awesome are the Lord's deeds." (Exodus 34:1–10)

The Lord then gives a series of admonitions and advisements (Exod. 34:10–26), and the narrative concludes.

The Lord said to Moses, "Write down these commandments, for in accordance with these commandments I make a Covenant with you and Israel." And Moses was there with the Lord forty days and forty nights; he ate no bread and he drank no water; and he wrote down on the tablets the terms of the Covenant, the Ten Commandments. (Exodus 34:27–28)

3. Moses on Sinai: The Quranic Version

As we have already seen, the Quran pays particular attention to the sojourn of the Israelites in Egypt. One of the longer versions of those events occurs in Sura 7, which resumes its narrative after the escape of Moses and his people across the Red Sea.

When We brought the children of Israel across the sea, and they came to a people who were devoted to their idols, they [that is, the Israelites] said, "Moses, make us a god like theirs." "You are ignorant," he replied. "These people and their ways will surely be destroyed, for false is what they practice. Do you want me to seek for you," he said, "a god other than the God, when He has exalted you over all the nations of the world? Remember the day when he saved you from the people of the Pharaoh who oppressed and afflicted you, and slew your sons and spared your women. In this was a great trial from your Lord."

We made an appointment of thirty nights with Moses (on Mount Sinai), to which we added ten more; so the term set by the Lord was completed in forty nights. Moses said to Aaron, his brother, "Deputize for me among my people. Dispose rightly, and do not follow the way of the authors of evil."

When Moses arrived at the appointed time and his Lord spoke to him, he said, "My Lord, reveal Yourself to me, that I may behold You." "You cannot behold me," he said, "but look at the mountain. If it remains firm in its place, you may then behold Me." But when the Lord appeared on the mountain in His effulgence, it crumbled to a heap of dust, and Moses fell unconscious. When he came to, he said, "All glory be to You! I turn to You in repentance, and I am the first to believe." He said, "O Moses, I raised you above all men by sending my messages and speaking to you."

And We wrote down on tablets admonitions and clear explanations of all things for Moses, and ordered him, "Hold fast to them and command the people to observe the best in them." (Quran 7:138–145)

4. That Moses Was the Best of Lawgivers and His the Best Constitution

Thus Moses received God's Law for His people on Sinai, not merely the written Torah but, as later generations of Jews understood it, the oral Law as well. No one had any doubts that it was the voice of God that had spoken. Where there was some hesitation perhaps was in the role of Moses in the process. Generally speaking, the Jewish tradition gave to Moses a larger share in this deposit of law and precept than Christianity was willing to concede to the Evangelists who wrote down the Gospels or the Muslims to Muhammad. Philo, for example, who had, or chose, in the first century to compete with the sophisticated legal and philosophical theories of the Greeks and the Romans, saw Moses as the ideal legislator, the peer, indeed the superior, of Lycurgus and Pythagoras.

That Moses himself was the best of all lawgivers everywhere, either among the Greeks or the barbarians, and that his laws are the most excellent and truly come from God, since they neglect nothing that is necessary, the following is the clearest proof. If anyone examines the legal usages of other peoples he will find that they have been shaken by innumerable causes—wars, tyrannies or other undesirable events that befall them by the stroke of fortune's turnings. Frequently it is luxury, flowing to excess through unstinting supplies and superfluities, that has destroyed the laws, since the multitudes are unable to bear "an excess of good things" and grow insolent through satiety, and insolence is the antagonist of law. But Moses' laws alone, firm, unshaken, unswerving, stamped as it were by the seals of nature itself, remain solid from the day that they were first enacted to now, and there is hope that they will remain for all future ages as though immortal, so long as the sun and the moon and the entire heaven and universe exist. In any case, though the (Jewish) nation has experienced so many changes both by way of success and the reverse, nothing, not even the smallest part of his ordinances, has been disturbed; since all have clearly accorded high honor to their venerable and godlike character. . . .

But this is not yet the marvel of it, though it may rightly be thought a great matter in itself, that the (Mosaic) laws should have been observed through all time. More wonderful, I believe, is the fact that not only Jews but all other peoples, and particularly those that have taken greater stock of virtue, have grown devout to the point of approving and honoring our laws. In this they have obtained a singular honor, which belongs to no other code. The following is the proof. Among the Greek and barbarian states, there is virtually none that honors the institutions of any other. Indeed, scarcely does any state hold fast lastingly to its own, as it adapts them to meet the vicissitudes of times and circumstances. . . . Virtually all people from the rising of the sun to its setting, every country, nation and state, are hostile to foreign institutions and believe that they increase the approbation of their own by showing disdain for those of others. This is not the case with ours. They draw the attention and win over all barbarians, Greeks, mainlanders and islanders, nations east and west, Europe, Asia, the entire inhabited world from end to end. (Philo, *Life of Moses* 2.12–20) [PHILO 1901. 270–271]

Much the same point regarding Moses and his "constitution" is made, albeit in a more legally nuanced and in perhaps a more Roman than Greek fashion, by the historian Josephus. It occurs in his rejoinder, written in the last years of the first Christian century, to Philo's old Egyptian antagonist Apion and so was directed to a Gentile audience for whom the notion that the law came directly from God would not have been very persuasive.

There is endless variety in the details of the customs and laws which prevail in the world at large. To give but a summary enumeration: some people have entrusted the supreme political power to monarchies, others to oligarchies, yet others to the masses. Our lawgiver [that is, Moses], however, was attracted by none of these forms of polities, but he gave to his constitution the form of what, if a somewhat forced expression be permitted, may be called a "theocracy," placing all sovereignty and authority in the hands of God. To Him he persuaded all to look, as the author of all blessings, both those which are common to all mankind and those which they had won for themselves by prayer in the crises of history. He convinced them that no single action, no secret thought, could be hid from Him. He represented Him as One, uncreated and immutable to all eternity, in beauty surpassing all mortal thought, made known to us by His power, although the nature of His real being passes knowledge.

That the wisest of the Greeks learned to adopt these conceptions of God from principles with which Moses supplied them, I am not now concerned to urge; but they have borne abundant testimony to the excellence of these doctrines, and to their consonance with the nature and majesty of God. In fact, Pythagoras, Anaxagoras, Plato, the Stoics who succeeded him, and indeed nearly all the philosophers appear to have held similar views concerning the nature of God. These, however, addressed their philosophy to the few, and did not venture to divulge their true beliefs to the masses, who had their own preconceived opinions; whereas our lawgiver, by making practice square with precept, not only convinced his own contemporaries but so firmly planted this belief concerning God in their descendants to all future generations that it cannot be moved. The cause of his success was that the very nature of his legislation made it far more useful than any other; for he did not make religion a department of virtue, but the various virtues—I mean justice, temperance, fortitude and mutual harmony in all things between the members of the community—departments of religion. Religion governs all our actions and occupations and speech; none of these things did our lawgiver leave unexamined or indeterminate.

Josephus then turns to more general considerations and to this remarkable appreciation of the Mosaic polity, or rather, its Pharisaic understanding.

All schemes of education and moral training fall into two categories: instruction is imparted in one case by precept, in the other by the practical exercise of the character. All other legislators, differing in their opinions, selected the particular method which each preferred and neglected the other. . . . Our legislator, on the other hand, took great care to combine both systems. He did not leave training in morals inarticulate; nor did he permit the letter of the law to remain inoperative. Starting from the very beginning with the food which we partake from infancy and the private life of the home, he left nothing, however insignificant, to the discretion and caprice of the individual. What meats a man should abstain from and what he may enjoy, with what persons he should associate, what period should be devoted respectively to strenuous labor and to rest—for all this our leader made the Law the standard and the rule, that we might live under it as a father and a master, and be guilty of no sin through willfulness or ignorance.

For ignorance he left no pretext. He appointed the Law to be the most excellent and necessary form of instruction, ordaining not that it should be heard once for all, or twice, or on several occasions, but that every week men should desert their other occupations and listen to the Law, and obtain a thorough and accurate knowledge of it, a practice which all other legislators seem to have neglected. Indeed, most men, so far from living in accordance with their own laws, hardly know what they are. Only when they have done wrong do they learn from others that they have transgressed the law. Even those of them who hold the highest and most important offices admit their ignorance, for they employ professional legal experts as assessors and leave them in charge of the administration of affairs. But should anyone of our nation be questioned about the laws, he would repeat them all more readily than his own name. The result, then, of our thorough grounding in the laws from the first dawn of intelligence is that we have them, as it were, engraved on our souls. A transgressor is a rarity, evasion of punishment by excuses an impossibility.

To this cause above all do we owe our admirable harmony. Unity and identity of religious belief, perfect uniformity in habits and customs, produce a very beautiful concord in human character. Among us alone will be heard no contradictory statements about God, such as are common among other nations, not only on the lips of ordinary individuals under the impulse of some passing mood, but even boldly propounded by philosophers, some putting forward crushing arguments against the very existence of God, others depriving Him of His providential care for mankind. Among us alone will be seen no difference in the conduct of our lives. With us, all act alike, all profess the same doctrine about God, one which is in harmony with the Law and affirms that all things are under His eye. Even our womenfolk and dependents would tell you that piety must be the motive of all our occupations in life. (Josephus, *Against Apion* 2.16–19)

Our earliest imitators were the Greek philosophers, who, though ostensibly observing the laws of their own countries, yet in their conduct and philosophy were Moses' disciples, holding similar views about God and advocating the simple life and friendly communion between man and man. But that is not all. The masses have long since shown a keen desire to adopt our religious observances; and there is not one city, Greek or barbarian, to which our custom of abstaining from work on the seventh day has not spread, and where the fasts and the lighting of lamps and many of our prohibitions in the matter of food are not observed. Moreover, they attempt to imitate our unanimity, our liberal charities, our devoted labor in the crafts, our endurance under persecution on behalf of our laws. The greatest miracle of all is that our Law holds out no seductive bait of sensual pleasure, but has exercised this influence through its own inherent merits; and as God permeates the universe, so the Law has found its way among all mankind. (Ibid. 2.38)

5. The Precepts of the Law and the Great Commandment

The rabbis had little need and even less desire to construct the kinds of arguments we have just seen Philo and Josephus making for their Gentile readers. The rabbis' concerns were quite different.

Rabbi Hananiah ben Akashya says: The Holy One, blessed be He, was minded to grant merit to Israel. Therefore He multiplied for them the Law and the commandments, as it is written, "It pleased the Lord, for the furtherance of His justice, to make His Law a law of surpassing majesty" (Isa. 42:21). (M.Makkoth 3:16)

Rabbi Simlai said: 613 commandments were given to Moses, 365 negative commandments, answering to the number of the days of the year, and 248 positive commandments, answering to the number of man's members. Then David came and reduced them to 11 [cf. Ps. 15]. Then came Isaiah and reduced them to six [cf. Isa. 33:15]. Then came Micah and reduced them to three [cf. Mic. 6:8]. Then Isaiah came again and reduced the three to two, as it is said, "Keep judgment and do righteousness." Then came Amos and reduced them to one, as it is said, "Seek Me and live." Or, one may say, then came Habakkuk and reduced them to one, as it is said, "The righteous shall live by his faith." (BT.Makkoth 23b–24a)

It happened that a certain non-Jew came before Shammai and said to him, "I wish you to make me a proselyte, but on condition that you teach me the whole Torah while I stand on one foot." Thereupon Shammai drove him off with the builder's cubit measure that he held in his hand. When the same man approached Hillel, the latter said to him, "What is hateful to you, do not do to your neighbor: that is the whole Torah, while all the rest is commentary on it; go and learn it." (BT.Shabbat 31a)

At about the same time, a similar question was posed to another rabbi in the Gospels, perhaps by one of Hillel's own students.

Then one of the lawyers, who had been listening to the discussion and had noted how well he [that is, Jesus] answered, came forward and asked him: "Which commandment is first of all?" Jesus answered, "Hear, O Israel, the Lord our God is the only Lord; love the Lord your God with all your heart, with all your soul, with all your mind and with all your strength (Deut. 6:5). The second is this: Love your neighbor as yourself (Lev. 19:18). There is no other commandment greater than these." The lawyer said to him, "Well said, Master. You are right in saying that God is one and beside Him there is no other. And to love Him with all your heart, all your understanding and all your strength, and to love your neighbor as yourself—that is far more than any burnt offerings or sacrifices." When Jesus saw how sensibly he answered, he said to him, "You are not far from the kingdom of God." (Mark 12:28–34)

Paul, another lawyer, had studied with Hillel's successor, Gamaliel. He is even more terse in his résumé of the Law.

He who loves his neighbor has satisfied every claim of the Law. For the commandments, "Thou shall not commit adultery, thou shall not kill, thou shall not steal, thou shall not covet," and any other commandments there may be, are all summed up in one rule, "Love your neighbor as yourself." Love cannot wrong a neighbor; therefore the whole Law is summed up in love. (Paul, *To the Romans* 13:9–10)

6. There Was, There Will Be, Only One Law

Both the Christians and the Muslims eventually claimed to possess a new and more perfect version of God's Law. Maimonides (1135–1204 C.E.), who had experienced both claims, saw it as part of his task to demonstrate that there was not, nor could there be, any such thing as a new Torah.

Nothing similar to the call addressed to us by Moses our Master has been made before him by any one of those we know who lived in the time between Adam and him; nor was a call similar to that one made by one of our prophets after him. Correspondingly it is a fundamental principle of our Law that there will never be another Law. Hence, according to our opinion, there never has been a Law and there never will be a Law except the one that is the Law of Moses our Master.

The explanation of this, according to what is literally stated in the prophetic books and is found in the tradition, is as follows. Not one of the prophets—such as the Patriarchs, Shem, Eber, Noah, Methuselah and Enoch—who came before Moses our Master has ever said to a class of people: God has sent me to you and has commanded me to say to you such and such things; He has forbidden you to do such and such things and has commanded you to do such and such things. This is a thing that is not attested to by any text in the Torah and that does not figure in any true tradition. These men received only prophetic revelation from God. . . . He who received a great overflow, as for instance Abraham, assembled the people and called them by the way of teaching and instruction to adhere to the truths that he had grasped. Thus Abraham taught the people and explained to them by means of speculative proofs that the world had but one deity, that He had created all the things that are other than Himself, and that none of the forms and no created thing in general ought to be worshiped. This is what he instructed the people in, attracting them by means of eloquent speeches and by means of the benefits conferred upon them. But he never said: God has sent me to you and has given me commandments and prohibitions. Even when the commandment of circumcision was laid upon him, his sons, and those who belonged to him, he circumcised them alone and did not use the form of the prophetic call to exhort the people to do this. . . .

As for the prophets from among us who came after Moses our Master, you know the text of all their stories and the fact that their function was that of preachers who called upon the people to obey the Law of Moses, threatened those who rejected it, and held out promises to those who were firm in observing it.

That there never was such a Law, or such a prophet, either before or after Moses is argued in this passage from an analysis of the texts of Scripture itself. That there never will be is handled differently. Here the argument is based on an analogy with contemporary theories about the physical constitution of living things: that health, for example, is the result of the equilibrium of the humors within the body. Such an argument came easily to the mind of Maimonides, a Spanish biblical and Talmudic scholar who passed much of his later career as court physician to the Muslim rulers of Egypt. Maimonides continues the argument.

We likewise believe that things will always be this way. As it says: "It is not in heaven etc." (Deut. 30:12) . . . "for us and our children forever" (Deut. 29:28). And that is as it ought to be. For when a thing is as perfect as it is possible to be within its species, it is impossible that within that species there should be found another thing that does not fall short of that perfection either because of excess or deficiency. Thus in comparison with a temperament whose composition is of the greatest equibalance possible in the species in question, all other temperaments are not composed in accordance with this equibalance because of either deficiency or excess. Things are similar with regard to this Law, as is clear from its equibalance. For it says: "Just statutes and judgments" (Deut. 4:8). Now you know that the meaning of "just" is equibalanced. For these are manners of worship in which there is no burden and excess, such as monastic life and pilgrimage and similar things, nor any deficiency necessarily leading to greed and being engrossed in the indulgence of appetites, so that in consequence the perfection of man is diminished with respect to his moral habits and to his speculation, which is the case with regard to all the other laws of the religious communities of the past. (Maimonides, *Guide of the Perplexed* 2.39) [MAIMONIDES 1963: 379–380]

The Jewish position was of course well known to the Christians. Here is one Muslim response, by the theologian al-Nasafi (d. 1114 C.E.). If the conclusions would not have been at all acceptable, the terms of Nasafi's argument might have appealed to the physician Maimonides.

The Jews—may God curse them—teach that abrogation of religious Law is not possible, but according to truly orthodox people (in the Muslim community) it is possible. The Jews offer proof and say that the fact that something is commanded (by God) necessarily means that it is helpful, and the fact that something is forbidden (by God) necessarily means that it is harmful. If that is so, then the fact that God has given commands and prohibitions in the Torah indicates that it is concerned with something helpful (to humanity). If then it is possible for Him (later) to forbid something He had commanded in the Torah, that would mean that in the Torah He had commanded something harmful. But that cannot be, for God is wise, He knows the final outcome of affairs, and it is not possible that His action should be described as foolish.

In reply to this we teach that if God gives commands about some matter, that necessarily means it would be helpful at that time, but it does not mean that it would necessarily be helpful at all times. An example is that of food and drink, which are assuredly helpful in a state of hunger but are not necessarily helpful in a state of satiety. Another example is that of the physician who orders for the sick person different medicines at different times, yet that involves no introduction of a new opinion, but is to ensure real helpfulness at that particular time.

By way of confirmation Nasafi concludes with the traditional Muslim view of the revelation of Law (see Chapter 1 above), namely, that between Moses and Muham-

mad revealed Books of Law had been given to David, that is, the Book of Psalms, and to Jesus, that is, the Gospel. Nasafi continues.

So it is here. God is more compassionate to His servants than is a tender physician, and when He appointed the Torah as a religious Law in the time of Moses—on whom be peace—that was something helpful, and (continued to be) until the completion of the Mosaic dispensation. Then (after the completion of the Mosaic dispensation) the helpfulness was in the Psalter until the completion of the Davidic dispensation. Then (after that) the helpfulness was in the Gospel until the completion of the Christian dispensation. Finally, the helpfulness was in the Quran in this age of our Prophet Muhammad—upon whom be God's blessing and peace. (Nasafi, *Sea of Discourse on Theology*)

[JEFFERY 1962: 450–451]

7. The Laws after Moses

If there was no Law after Moses, there was nonetheless a great deal of legal material that evolved, in one fashion or another, out of that original deposit.

The two Talmuds, the Tosefta, the Sifra and the Sifre, and the To-seftot are the sources from all of which it is elucidated what is forbidden and what is permitted, what is unclean and what is clean, what is a penal violation and what involves no penalty, what is fit to be used and what is unfit for use, all in accordance with the traditions received by the sages from their predecessors in an unbroken succession up to the teachings of Moses as he received them on Sinai. From these sources too are ascertained the decrees, instituted by the sages and the prophets, in each generation, to serve as a protective fence about the Law, in accordance with Moses' express injunction, "You shall keep My charge" (Lev. 18:30), that is, "Ordain a charge to preserve My charge." From these sources a clear conception is also obtained of the customs and ordinances, either formally introduced in various generations by their respective authorities or that come into use with their sanction; from these it is forbidden to depart, as it is said, "You shall not turn aside from the sentence which they shall declare to you, to the right hand nor to the left" (Deut. 17:11). So too these works contain the clearly established judgments and rules not received by Moses, but which the Supreme Court of each generation deduced by applying the hermeneutical principles for the interpretation of the Law, and which were decided by those venerable authorities to be the law, all of which, accumulated from the days of Moses to his own time, Rav Ashi put together in the Gemara [that is, the Talmud]. (Maimonides, *Mishneh Torah*, introduction)

Precisely the same point had been made earlier by Judah Halevi in his dialogue entitled The Khazar King, *written ca. 1130–1140 C.E.*

Some of our laws originate, in certain circumstances, "from the place which the Lord shall choose." Prophecy lasted about forty years of the Second Temple. Jeremiah in his prophetic speeches commended the people of the Second Temple for their piety, learning and fear of God. If we did not rely on men like these, on whom should we rely? We see that prescriptions given after Moses' death became law. Thus Solomon hallowed "the middle of the court" (1 Kings 8:64ff.), slaughtered sacrifices on a place other than the altar, and celebrated "the feast seven days and seven nights." David and Samuel appointed the order of the Temple choir, which became a fixed law. Solomon both added to the sanctuary built in the desert and omitted things from it. Ezra imposed the tax of one-third of a shekel on the community of the Second Temple (Neh. 10:33). A stone paving was put in the place of the Ark, hiding it behind a curtain, because they knew that the Ark had been buried in that place.

The objection is then raised that there is a biblical injunction concerning the Law, that "You shall not add thereto nor diminish from it" (Deut. 13:1). How is that to be answered?

This was said only to the masses, that they should not conjecture and theorize and contrive laws according to their own conception. . . . They were recommended to the post-Mosaic prophets, the priests and the judges, as it is written: "I will raise them up a prophet . . . and he will speak to them all that I shall command them" (Deut. 18:18). With regard to the priests and the judges, it is said that their decisions are binding. The words, "You shall not add etc." refer to "that which I commanded you through Moses" as well as any "prophet from among the brethren" who fulfills the conditions of a prophet. They further refer to regulations laid down in common by priests and judges "from the place which the Lord shall choose." For they (too) have divine assistance and would never, on account of their large number, concur in anything which contradicts the Law. Much less likelihood was there of erroneous views because they had inherited vast learning, for the reception of which they were naturally endowed. (Judah Halevi, *The Khazar King* 3.40–41)

[HALEVI 1905: 172–173]

8. How the Law Worked

For most of their history, whether they were under foreign domination or native rulers, the Jews lived under what might be called the Mosaic constitution, the Torah viewed as a body of operational law administered by a court. That court was called the Great Sanhedrin and sat in Jerusalem under the presidency of the High Priest until 70 C.E. But it was not the only religious court in Palestine; there were lesser Sanhedrins, which may have been local bodies or those with limited competence. That there was, in any event, a judicial system with the right of appeal rather than a single court of Jewish law in Greco-Roman times in Palestine is attested to by the Mishna tractate Sanhedrin.

There were three courts (in Jerusalem): one used to sit at the (eastern?) gate of the Temple mount, one used to sit at the gate of the Temple Court (of the Israelites), and one used to sit in the Chamber of Hewn Stone (M.Middoth 5:4). They [that is, local judges from the provinces] used to come first to the court that was at the gate of the Temple Mount, and one would say, "This was the way I interpreted (the Law) and that the way my colleagues interpreted; and in this way I taught and in that my colleagues." If the members of that court had heard of a (precedential) tradition, they told it to them, otherwise they [that is, the appellants] took themselves to the court that was at the gate of the Temple Court. [Here the process is repeated. If no precedent is found in tradition, they proceed upwards.] . . . They come to the Great Court that was in the Chamber of Hewn Stone, whence the Law goes forth to all Israel, as it is written, "From that place which the Lord shall choose" (Deut. 17:10).

When that passage was written, much of the earlier legal system had been swept away in the debacle that overwhelmed Jerusalem. But the work of legal discussion and enlargement went on, chiefly in Galilee, and found its expression in the Mishna. Rabbi Judah's redaction of the Mishna was completed sometime about 200 C.E., and for the next three centuries scholars in the schools of Palestine, notably at Tiberias, and in those of Iraq worked at elucidating and refining it. The work of each group was eventually collected in a gemara or "completion." The gemara of the "Babylonians" of Iraq was connected with the name of Rav Ashi (d. 427 C.E.), and it was, according to Maimonides, a fortuitous event, since the fortunes of the Jewish community were rapidly changing in those days.

After the Court of Rav Ashi, who compiled the ["Babylonian"] Gemara which was finally completed in the days of his son, an extraordinarily great dispersion of Israel throughout the world took place. The people emigrated to remote parts and distant isles. The prevalence of

wars and the march of armies made travel insecure. The study of the
Torah declined. The Jewish people did not flock to the schools in their
thousands and tens of thousands as heretofore; but in each city and country individuals who felt the divine call gathered together and occupied
themselves with the Torah, studied all the works of the sages, and from
these learned the method of legal interpretation.

The extraordinary flexibility of the system is now emphasized.

If a court established in any country after the time of the Talmud
made decrees or ordinances or introduced customs for those residing in
its particular country or for residents of other countries, its enactments
did not obtain the acceptance of all Israel because of the remoteness of
Jewish settlements and the difficulties of travel. And as the court of any
particular country consisted of individuals (whose authority was not universally recognized), while the Supreme Court of seventy-one members
had, several years before the compilation of the Talmud, ceased to exist,
no compulsion is exercised on those living in one country to observe the
customs of another country; nor is any court directed to issue a decree
that had been issued by another court in the same country. So too, if one
of the Gaons [described below] taught that a certain judgment was correct, and it became clear at a later date that this was not in accordance
with the views of the Gemara, the earlier authority is not necessarily
followed but the view is adopted which seems more reasonable, whether
it be that of an earlier or later authority.

But there is, for all that, a cohesive center.

The foregoing observations refer to rules, decrees, ordinances and
customs that originated after the Talmud had been compiled. But whatever is already mentioned in the Babylonian Talmud is binding on all
Israel. And every city and country is bound to observe all the customs
observed by the sages of the Gemara, promulgate their decrees and uphold their institutions, on the ground that all the customs, decrees and
institutions mentioned in the Talmud received the assent of all Israel, and
those sages who instituted the ordinances, issued the decrees, introduced
the customs, gave the decisions and taught that a certain ruling was
correct, constituted the total body or the majority of Israel's wise men.
They were the leaders who received from each other traditions concerning the fundamentals of Judaism in an unbroken succession back to Moses
our teacher, upon whom be peace. (Maimonides, *Mishneh Torah*, Introduction)

The closure of the Talmud did not end the work of either the jurisprudents or the judges. The former continued to study the materials from the oral tradition that Maimonides was to excerpt and arrange in his Mishneh Torah, while the latter, pressed by requests for judgment on the basis of the laws, were in effect creating new ones. Maimonides explains.

The sages who arose after the completion of the Talmud, studied it deeply and became famous for their wisdom, are called Gaons. All these Gaons who flourished in the land of Israel, Babylon, Spain and France taught the method of the Talmud, elucidated its obscurities and expounded the various topics with which it deals. For its method is exceedingly profound. . . . Many requests were made to the Gaons of the day by residents of different cities, asking for explanations of difficulties in the Talmud. These the Gaons answered, according to their ability. Those who had put the questions collected the responses which they made into books for study. The Gaons also, at different periods, composed commentaries on the Talmud. . . . They also made compilations of settled rules as to things permitted or forbidden, as to infractions which were penal or were not liable to a penalty. All these dealt with matters in regard to which compendia were needed, that could be studied by one not capable of penetrating to the depths of the Talmud. This is the godly work in which all the Gaons of Israel engaged, from the completion of the Talmud to the present date which is the eighth year of the eleventh century after the destruction of the Second Temple [that is, 1177 C.E.]. (Maimonides, *Mishneh Torah*, Introduction)

9. The Codification of Torah Law

As we have already seen in Chapter 3 above, Maimonides' major legal undertaking was the Mishneh Torah, his codification of "Jewish Law," where that term is understood as embracing all the prescriptions from Moses to the completion of the Talmud. To Torah in the narrower sense—the written Law given to Moses on Mount Sinai—he devoted far less attention. He did codify it after a fashion, but almost as an afterthought in the wake of the Mishneh Torah and chiefly because he disagreed with certain of his predecessors on which commandments belonged to that number of 613. He describes this later project.

At the completion of our earlier well-known work, which included a commentary on the whole of the Mishna [that is, the *Mishneh Torah*], our objective in writing it was achieved with an explanation of the substance of each and every legal prescription in the Mishna, since our intention there was not to include for every commandment an exhaustive discussion of the law embracing everything that is necessary (to know) of the prohibited and the permissible, liable and free; that much is clear to whoever studies the work. I then decided that it would be advisable to compile a compendium which would include all the laws in the Torah and its regulations, with nothing omitted. In this compendium I would try, as is my custom, to avoid mentioning differences of opinion and rejected teachings, and include there only the established law, so that this compendium would embrace all the laws of the Torah of Moses our teacher, whether they have a bearing in the time of exile or not. . . .

When I first had the idea for this work (of the *Mishneh Torah*), and set to writing it by giving an initial brief list of all the commandments by running through them in the Introduction, I was overcome with a feeling of distress, which in fact I have experienced for a number of years, and which was as follows. Scholars who are engaged in enumerating the commandments, or in writing anything whatsoever on the subject, have all come forward with such strange theories that I could hardly describe their magnitude. . . . Therefore I thought it advisable to precede what I mentioned with a treatise in which I would explain the enumeration of the commandments (of the Torah) and how they are to be counted. To that end I would bring proofs from the verses of the Torah and from the words of the sages, of blessed memory, concerning their interpretation, and I would also precede it with a discussion of the principles that are to guide us in enumerating the commandments. . . . Thus I will explain all the commandments, listing them one after the other, bringing proof wherever there is a doubt, or where one not skilled in the Laws of the Torah might possibly have some unfounded opinion; these I will remove and further explain everything about which there is some doubt. (Maimonides, *Book of the Commandments*, Introduction)

10. Two Classes of Laws: The Rational and the Revelational

Philo was among the first Jews to explore the path that led through the Greek and Roman theories of law and of cognition, both of which had contributed, as we have seen, to his own understanding of Torah and of the role of Moses in the revelation and the promulgation of the Law. History was not kind to Philo. The Christians expropriated a good deal of his thinking to their own ends, to which it was most congenial. Perhaps more important, the political disasters that descended upon the Jews under Roman sovereignty made the project of recasting Judaism in the then current Hellenic mode an extremely unappetizing one to many religious Jews. The revival of that enterprise had to wait nine centuries, for the passage of the Jews from Roman to Christian to Muslim sovereignty in the Near East and the extraordinary revival of Greek learning in tenth-century Baghdad. That time and that milieu prompted one Jewish scholar, the Gaon Saadya, to cast another look at the legacy of Hellenism. In his Book of Doctrines and Beliefs *(933 C.E.) Saadya attempts to put speculative reason in the service of the Law.*

After these introductory remarks, I now come to the subject proper. I declare that our Lord, may He be exalted and glorified, has informed us through the words of His prophets that He wishes us to lead a religious life by following the religion which He instituted for us. This religion contains laws which He has prescribed for us and which it is our duty to keep and fulfill in sincerity, as it is said, "This day the Lord your God commanded you to do these statutes and ordinances; you shall, therefore, observe and do them with all your heart and all your soul" (Deut. 26:16). His messengers established these laws for us by wondrous signs and miracles, and we commenced to keep and fulfill them forthwith. Later we found that speculation confirms the necessity of the Law for us. It would, however, not have been appropriate to leave us to our own devices.

It is desirable that I should explain which matters and aspects (of the Law) speculation confirms as necessary. I maintain that reason bids us respond to every benefactor either by returning his kindness, if he is in need of it, or by offering our thanks, if he is not in need of recompense. Now since this is a dictate of reason itself, it would not have been fitting for the Creator, be He exalted and glorified, to waive this right in respect of Himself, but it was necessary that He should command His creatures to worship Him and to render thanks to Him for having created them. Reason further lays down that the wise man should not permit himself to be vilified and treated with contempt. It is similarly necessary that the Creator should forbid His servants to treat Him in this way. Reason further prescribes that human beings should be forbidden to trespass upon one another's rights by any sort of aggression. It is likewise necessary that the Wise One should not permit them to act in such a way. Reason, furthermore, permits a wise man to employ a workman for any kind of work and pay him his wages for the sole purpose of allowing him to earn something, since this is a matter which results in benefit to the workman and causes no harm to the employer.

Saadya then shows that these four objectives that reason dictates are in fact the substance of the Law laid down by God in the Torah. They constitute what he later calls the class of "Rational Laws," those both revealed and confirmed by reason. He then turns to a second category, the "Revelational Laws."

The Second Class of Law consists of matters regarding which reason passes no judgment in the way of either approval or disapproval so far as their essence is concerned. But our Lord has given us an abundance of such commandments and prohibitions in order to increase our reward and happiness through them, as is said: "The Lord was pleased, for His righteousness' sake, to make the Law great and glorious" (Isa. 42:21). . . .

The Second Class of Law [that is, "Revelational Laws"] concerns such matters as are of a neutral character from the point of view of reason, but which the Law has made the objects of commandment in some cases and prohibitions in others, leaving the rest in their neutral state. Instances are the distinguishing of Sabbath and Festivals from ordinary days; the selection of certain individuals to be prophets and leaders; the prohibition to eat certain foodstuffs; the avoidance of sexual intercourse with certain people; the abstention enforced during periods of impurity. The great motive for the observance of these principles and the laws derived and branching out from them is, of course, the command of our Lord and the promotion of our happiness resulting from it, but I find for most of them also some minor and partial motives of a useful character.

Saadya, then, is not quite willing to surrender this class of Laws to a purely arbitrary choice on God's part; they too have some practical and so reasonable—end. He takes up the question of the Torah's dietary laws. Although they cannot be demonstrated as necessary by human reason alone, they do serve some sensible utilitarian purpose.

The prohibition not to eat certain animals has this advantage (for example): It makes it impossible to liken any of the animals to the Creator, since it is unthinkable that one should permit oneself either to eat or to declare as impure what one likens to God. Also it prevents people from worshiping any of the animals, since it is unthinkable that one should worship either what serves as food or what one declares as impure. . . .

If one examines most of the "Revelational Laws" in the above fashion, one will find in them a great number of partial motives and reasons of usefulness. But the wisdom of the Creator and His knowledge is above everything human beings can attain, as is said, "For the heavens are higher than the earth, as are My ways higher than your ways" (Isa. 55:9). (Saadya, *Book of Doctrines and Beliefs* 3.2)

[SAADYA 1945: 94–105]

11. Maimonides and Aquinas on the
Purposes of the Law

Why was the Law given? The question was not often raised among the rabbis, except perhaps when some of its provisions were attacked by non-Jews, as we shall see. But once the Jews, like the Christians and Muslims, were exposed to philosophy and its claims to be a source of truth and certitude, the issue of the intent and purpose of the Law had to be addressed by anyone who took that claim seriously. One who did address it was Maimonides, who in addition to his training in Torah and Mishna was a profound student of Hellenic philosophy, whether in its Greek or its Islamic versions. He resumes the same theme taken up in his Letter to the Yemen.

The Law as a whole aims at two things: the welfare of the soul and the welfare of the body. As for the welfare of the soul, it consists in the multitude's acquiring correct opinions corresponding to their respective capacity. Therefore some of those opinions are set forth explicitly and some are set forth in parables. For it is not within the nature of the common multitude that its capacity should suffice for apprehending that subject matter as it is. As for the welfare of the body, it comes about by the improvement of their ways of living with one another. This is achieved through two things. One of them is the abolition of their wronging each other. This is tantamount to every individual among the people not being permitted to act according to his will and up to the limits of his power, but being forced to do what is useful to the whole. The second thing consists in the acquisition by every human individual of moral qualities that are useful for life in society so that the affairs of the city may be ordered. (Maimonides, *Guide of the Perplexed* 3.27) [MAIMONIDES 1963: 510]

The Law, then, in Maimonides' view, as in Plato's before him, provides truth for the "multitude" and inculcates the virtues of temperance and justice. Clearly, Maimonides viewed human perfection as essentially political; that is, it was to be achieved by a life in society. Regarding the first objective, the correct opinions that the Law seeks to inculcate, Maimonedes notes:

. . .You should know that in regard to correct opinions through which the ultimate perfection may be achieved, the Law has communicated only their end and issued a call to believe in them in a summary way, that is, to believe in the existence of the deity, may He be exalted, His unity, His knowledge, His power, His will, His eternity. All these points are ultimate ends, which can be made clear in detail and through definitions only after one knows many opinions. In the same way the Law also issues a call to adopt certain beliefs, belief in which is necessary for the sake of political welfare. . . .

What results from what we have now stated as a premise regarding this subject is that whenever a commandment, be it a prescription or a prohibition, requires abolishing reciprocal wrongdoing, or urging to a noble moral quality leading to a good social relationship, or communicating a correct opinion that ought to be believed either on account of itself or because it is necessary for the abolition of reciprocal wrongdoing or for the acquisition of a noble moral quality, such a commandment has a clear cause and is of manifest utility. No question concerning the end need be posed with regard to such commandments. For no one was ever so perplexed for a day as to ask why we were commanded by the Law that God is one, or why we were forbidden to kill and to steal, or why we were forbidden to exercise vengeance and retaliation, or why we were ordered to love each other.

Thus there is no discussion of laws that seem to conform to the dictates of right reason, what another tradition called the "natural law." Where the problem arose was in that category Saadya had called "Revelational Law."

The matter about which people are perplexed and opinions disagree—that some say there is no utility in them except the fact of the mere command, whereas others saw there is a utility in such commandments that is hidden from us—are the commandments from whose external meaning it does not appear that they are useful according to one of the three notions we have mentioned: I mean to say that they neither communicate an opinion nor inculcate a moral quality nor abolish reciprocal wrongdoing. Apparently these commandments are not related to the welfare of the soul, as they do not communicate a belief, or to the welfare of the body, as they do not communicate rules useful for the governance of the household. Such, for example, are the prohibitions of mingled stuff, of the mingling of diverse species, and of meat (boiled) in milk and the commandment concerning the covering of blood, the heifer whose neck was broken, and the firstling of an ass and others of the same kind. However, you will hear my explanation for all of them and my exposition of the correct and demonstrated causes for all of them. (Maimonides, *Guide* 3.28) [MAIMONIDES 1963: 512–513]

Thomas Aquinas (d. 1274 C.E.), a Christian theologian at the University of Paris, was the inheritor and student of a natural law tradition, which reached him by way of the Stoics, Cicero, and Augustine. In that context, he places his discussion of the Torah—the Christians' "Old Law"—in his Summa Theologica.

It belongs to the divine law to direct men to one another and to God. Now each of these belongs, from a universal point of view, to the dictates of the natural law, to which dictates the moral precepts are to be referred; yet each of them has to be determined by divine or human law because naturally known principles are common, both in speculative and practical matters. Accordingly, just as the determination of the common principle about divine worship is effected by ceremonial precepts, so the determination of the common principle of that justice which is to be observed among men is effected by the judicial precepts.

We must therefore distinguish three kinds of precepts in the Old Law, to wit, the moral precepts, which are dictated by the natural law; ceremonial precepts, which are determinations of the divine worship; and judicial precepts, which are determinations of the justice to be maintained among men. Therefore the Apostle (Paul), after saying that "the Law is holy," adds that "the commandment is just, and holy, and good" (Rom. 7:12): "just" in respect to the judicial precepts; "holy" with regard to the ceremonial precepts, since that is holy which is consecrated to God; and "good," that is, conducive to virtue, as to the moral precepts. (Aquinas, *Summa Theologica* I/2, ques. 99, art. 4) [AQUINAS 1945: 822]

But if the moral precepts of the Torah are "dictated by natural law" and so in accordance with reason, what need was there for the revelation of such precepts and their incorporation into the Mosaic Law?

It was fitting that the divine law should come to man's assistance not only in those things for which reason is insufficient, but also in those things in which human reason may happen to be impeded. Now as to the most common principles of the natural law, the human reason could not err universally in moral matters; but through being habituated to sin, it became darkened as to what ought to be done in the particular. But with regard to the other moral precepts, which are conclusions drawn from the common principles of the moral law, the reason of man went astray, to the extent of judging to be lawful things which are evils in themselves. Hence there was need for the authority of the divine law to rescue men from both these defects. Thus among the articles of faith not only are those things set forth to which reason cannot reach, such as the Trinity of the Godhead, but also those things to which right reason can attain, such as that God is one; and this in order to remove the manifold errors in which reason is liable to err. (Ibid., ques. 99, art. 2, ad 2)

[AQUINAS 1945: 2:819]

The Old Law showed forth the precepts of the natural law, and added certain precepts of its own. Accordingly, as to those precepts of the natural law contained in the Old Law, all were bound to observe them, not because they belong to the Old Law but because they belong to the natural law. But as to those precepts that were added to the Old Law, they were not binding on any save the Jewish people alone.

The reason for this is because the Old Law was given to the Jewish people that they might receive a prerogative of holiness, in reverence for Christ who was to be born of that people. Now when any laws are enacted for the special sanctification of certain ones, these are binding on them alone. Thus clerics who are set aside for the service of God are bound to certain obligations to which the laity are not bound, and religious are likewise bound by their profession to certain works of perfection to which the secular clergy are not bound. In like manner, this people were bound to certain special observances to which other peoples were not bound. (Ibid., ques. 98, art. 5) [AQUINAS 1945: 2:814]

12. The Example of Circumcision

From an early period it was the practice of circumcision, that seal of the Covenant, that most exercised those Jews who attempted to rationalize the Law, not least because it was used to precisely the opposite end by polemicists among the Gentiles. Both the charge and the retort are already present in Philo in the first century C.E.

The general categories of the special laws, the so-called Ten Commandments, have been carefully investigated in the preceding treatise. Following the sequence of our work, we must now examine the particular ordinances. I shall begin with that which is an object of derision among many people. The circumcision of the genital organs is held in ridicule, though it is most zealously practiced by many other nations, especially by the Egyptians, a people that appears to be populous, ancient and philosophical in the highest degree. It would therefore be proper to let go of the childish banter and investigate more wisely and seriously the causes thanks to which this custom has prevailed, and not hastily pass judgment on the recklessness of great nations. They should reflect that it is unnatural that so many thousands in every generation undergo cutting and mutilate their own bodies and those of their nearest kin while suffering severe pains (without reason), and that there are many conditions that impel them to maintain and discharge a practice introduced by the ancients. The principal reasons are four in number.

The first is that it secures release from the severe and virtually incurable malady of the foreskin called carbuncle, which, I believe, gets its name from the fact that it involves a chronic inflammation and which is more prone to befall those who retain the foreskin. Second, it furthers the cleanliness of the whole body as befits a consecrated order, wherefore the Egyptian priests go even further and have their bodies shaved. For some impurities that ought to be purged collect gradually and retract in the hair and the foreskin. Third, it assures the resemblance of the circumcised member to the heart. For as both are prepared for generation, the cardial pneuma for the generation of thought, the reproductive organ for living creatures, the earliest men deemed it right to assimilate the manifest and visible organ through which sensible things are naturally engendered to the unseen and superior organ by which intelligible things are produced. The fourth and most essential reason is its predisposition to increase fecundity, for it is said that the sperm has free passage without being scattered or flowing into the folds of the foreskin, and consequently the circumcised nations appear to be the most prolific and populous.

Philo is willing to accept these medical and sociological reasons for circumcision on the authority of others more knowledgeable than himself. But he is a philosopher and so has his own reasons that persuade to the purposefulness of circumcision.

These are the explanations that have reached us from the antiquarian studies of inspired men who researched the Mosaic writings with the utmost care. As for myself, in addition to what has been said, I believe that circumcision is a symbol of two things that are particularly essential. One is the excision of pleasures that bewitch the mind. For since among the love-lures of pleasure the prize is carried off by the union of man and woman, the legislators thought it right to dock the organ that serves such intercourse, thus intimating that circumcision signifies the excision of excessive and superfluous pleasure, not of one pleasure alone, but through the one that is most violent also of all the others.

The other reason is that a man should know himself and expel from his soul the grievous malady of conceit. For there are some who boast of their ability to fashion, like good sculptors, the fairest of creatures, man, and puffed up with pride, have deified themselves, ignoring the true Cause of all created things, though they could find a corrective for their delusions in their own acquaintances. For many man among them are sterile and many women barren, whose relations are without issue and who grow old childless. This evil opinion must therefore be excised from the mind together with all others that are not God-loving. (Philo, *The Special Laws* 1.1–11) [PHILO 1981: 277–278]

The moral purpose of the Law, the acquisition of moral qualities, is likewise illustrated by Maimonides' remarks on circumcision.

Similarly, with regard to circumcision, one of the reasons for it is, in my opinion, the wish to bring about a decrease in sexual intercourse and a weakening of the organ in question, so that this activity might be diminished and the organ be in as quiet a state as possible. It has been thought that circumcision perfects what is a congenital defect. This gave the possibility to everyone to raise an objection and say: How can natural things be defective so that they need to be perfected from the outside, all the more because we know how useful the foreskin is for that member? In fact this commandment has not been prescribed with a view to perfecting a congenital defect but to perfecting a moral defect. The bodily pain caused to that member is the real purpose of circumcision. None of the activities necessary for the preservation of the individual is harmed thereby, nor is procreation rendered impossible, but violent concupiscence and lust that goes beyond what is needed are diminished. The fact that circumcision weakens the faculty of sexual excitement and sometimes perhaps diminishes the pleasure is indubitable. For if at birth this member has been made to bleed and has had its covering taken away from it, it must indubitably be weakened.

The Sages, may their memory be blessed, have explicitly stated: "It is hard for a woman with whom an uncircumcised man has had sexual intercourse to separate from him" (Genesis Rabbah 80). In my opinion this is the strongest of the reasons for circumcision. Who first began to perform this act if not Abraham, who was celebrated for his chastity, as has been mentioned by the Sages, may their memory be blessed, with reference to his dictum: "Behold, now I know that you are a fair woman to look upon" (Gen. 12:11).

Maimonides then passes to the social benefits of circumcision.

According to me circumcision has another very important meaning, namely, that all people professing, that is, those who believe in the unity of God, should have a bodily sign uniting them so that one who does not belong to them should not be able to claim that he is one of them, while being a stranger. For he would do this in order to profit by them and to deceive the people who profess this religion. Now a man does not perform this act (of circumcision) upon himself or upon a son unless it be in consequence of a genuine belief. For it is not like an incision in the leg or a burn in the arm, but is a very, very hard thing.

It is also well known what degree of mutual love and mutual help exists between people who all bear the same sign, which forms for them a sort of covenant or alliance. Circumcision is a covenant made by Abraham our father with a view to the belief in the unity of God. This covenant imposes the obligation to believe in the unity of God: "To be a God to you and to your seed after you" (Gen. 17:7). This is also a strong reason, as strong as the first, which may be adduced to account for circumcision; perhaps it is even stronger than the first.

Finally, it is the voice of the physician and the student of human psychology that we hear.

The perfection and perpetuation of this Law can be achieved only if circumcision is performed in childhood. For this there are three wise reasons. The first is that if the child were let alone until he grew up, he would sometimes not perform it. The second is that a child does not suffer as much pain as a grown-up man because his membrane is still soft and his imagination weak; for a grown-up man would regard the thing, which he would imagine before it occurred, as terrible and hard. The third is that the parents of the child that is just born take lightly matters concerning it, for up to that time the imaginative form that compels the parents to love it is not yet consolidated. For this imaginative form increases through habitual contact and grows with the growth of the child, then it begins to decrease and disappear. For the love of the father and the mother for the child when it has just been born is not like their love for it when it is one year old, and their love for it when it is one year old is not like their love when it is six years old. Consequently, if the child were left uncircumcised for two or three years, this would necessitate the abandonment of circumcision because of the father's love and affection for his child. At the time of its birth, on the other hand, this imaginative form is very weak, especially as far as concerns the father, upon whom (the fulfillment of) this commandment is imposed. (Maimonides, *Guide of the Perplexed* 3.49) [MAIMONIDES 1963: 609–610]

When we turn to Aquinas on the same subject, we find that he has built his explanation around Paul's letter to the Romans. He displays borrowings from Maimonides, though with some very different emphases and typical Christian additions.

The chief literal reason for circumcision was in order that man might profess his belief in one God. And because Abraham was the first to sever himself from the infidels by going out from his house and his kindred, for this reason he was the first to receive circumcision. This reason is set forth by the Apostle (Paul) thus: "He received a sign of circumcision, a seal of the justice of the faith which he had, being uncircumcised," because, namely, we are told that "to Abraham faith was reputed unto righteousness," for the reason that "against hope he believed in hope," that is, against the hope that is of nature he believed in the hope that is of grace, "that he might be the father of many nations," when he was an old man, and his wife an old and barren woman (Rom. 4:9ff.). And in order that this declaration and imitation of Abraham's faith might be fixed firmly in the heart of the Jews, they received in their flesh such a sign as they could not forget; and so it is written: "My covenant shall be in your flesh for a perpetual Covenant" (Gen. 16:13). This was done on the eighth day, because until then a child is very tender, and so might be seriously injured. . . . And it was not delayed after that time, lest some might refuse the sign of circumcision because of the pain; and also lest the parents, whose love for their children increases as they become used to their presence and as they grow older, might withdraw their children from circumcision.

A second reason may have been the weakening of concupiscence in that member. A third motive may have been to revile the worship of Venus and Priapus, which gave honor to that part of the body. . . . The Lord's prohibition (against self-mutilation) extended only to cutting oneself in honor of idols, and such was not the circumcision of which we have been speaking.

The figurative reason for circumcision was that it foreshadowed the removal of corruption, which was to be brought about by Christ, and will be perfectly fulfilled in the eighth age, which is the age of those who rise from the dead. And since all corruption of guilt and punishment comes to us, by reason of our carnal origin, from the sin of our first parent, therefore circumcision was applied to the generative member. (Aquinas, *Summa Theologica* I/2, ques. 102, art. 5, ad 1) [AQUINAS 1945: 2:885–886]

13. Rules without Reason

The case of circumcision was by no means the first occasion that questions had arisen about certain prescriptions of the Law. We shall return to Maimonides, and particularly to his suggestions on the origins of the prohibition of mixing meat and milk. In the fourth and fifth Christian centuries, perhaps under the stimulus of Greek and Christian polemic, the rabbis had begun to make a distinction between God's com-

mandments or judgments on the one hand and his "statutes" on the other. Each had
the binding force of law, but for different reasons.

It says in Leviticus 18:4, "You shall observe My judgments and execute my statutes." The Rabbis teach: "My judgments" are those things
which, if they had not been written, would have had to be written, such
as (commandments against) idolatry, unchastity, bloodshed, robbery,
blasphemy. "My statutes": these are the things to which Satan and the
Gentiles raise objections, such as not eating pig, not wearing linen and
woolen together, the law of levirate marriage, the scapegoat. Should you
say, "These are empty things," the Scripture adds, "I am the Lord, I have
made decrees; you are not at liberty to criticize them." (BT.Yoma 67b)

The point is made even more directly in the conclusion of the following anecdote,
which has to do with the ritual of the red heifer described in Numbers 19:1–10.

A heathen said to Yohanan ben Zakkai, "What you do (in the matter
of the red heifer) seems like sorcery. You take a red cow and kill it, and
burn the corpse and crush its ashes, and then preserve them. Then if one
of you becomes unclean by touching a dead body, you sprinkle on the
man two or three drops of the water into which the ashes have been cast,
and you say to him, 'You are clean.' " Rabbi Yohanan said to him, "Has
the demon of madness ever entered into you?" He said, "No." "Have you
ever seen a man into whom that demon had entered?" "Yes," he replied.
"And what do they do to him?" The man answered, "They take roots and
make a smoke underneath the man, then they sprinkle water on him and
the demon flies away from him." Rabbi Yohanan said to him, "Let your
ears hear what your mouth has just said" [that is, you are refuted out of
your own mouth]. . . . When the heathen had gone, his disciples said to
Rabbi Yohanan, "You beat him with a feeble reed, but what is your
answer to us?" Rabbi Yohanan said, "The dead body does not really defile;
the water does not really purify; but God has said, 'I have ordained an
ordinance, I have decreed a decree; it is not permitted for you to transgress it.' " (*Numbers Rabbah* 19:8)

Rabbi Yohanan's conclusion could not, surely, have much pleased Maimonides.

There is a group of human beings who consider it a grievous thing
that causes should be given for any law; what would please them most is
that the intellect would not find a meaning for the commandments and
prohibitions. What compels them to feel thus is a sickness that they find
in their souls, a sickness to which they are unable to give utterance and
of which they cannot furnish a satisfactory account. For they think that

if those laws were useful in this existence and had been given to us for that reason, it would be as if they derived from the reflection and the understanding of some intelligent being. If, however, there is a thing for which the intellect could not find any meaning at all and that does not lead to something useful, it indubitably derives from God; for the reflection of man would not lead to such a thing. It is as if, according to these people of weak intellects, man were more perfect than his Maker; for man speaks and acts in a manner that leads to some intended end, whereas the deity does not act thus but commands us to do things that are not useful to us and forbids us to do things that are not harmful to us. But He is far exalted above this; the contrary is the case, the whole purpose consisting in what is useful to us, as we have explained on the basis of the dictum: "For our good always, that He might preserve us alive, as it is at this day" (Deut. 6:24). (Maimonides, *Guide of the Perplexed* 3.31) [MAIMONIDES 1963: 524]

As we have already seen, Maimonides had an attentive reader in the Christian theologian Thomas Aquinas. For Aquinas too, the prescriptions of the Mosaic Law had their reasons. One of them was characteristically Christian: the prefiguring of the New Law in the Old. Thus for him there was not only a literal cause for the sacrifice of the red cow but an elaborate figurative one as well.

The figurative reason for this sacrifice was that the red cow signified Christ in respect of his assumed weakness, denoted by the female sex, while the color of the cow designated the blood of his passion. And the "red cow was of full age" because all Christ's works were perfect; "in which there was no blemish; and which had not carried the yoke" because Christ was innocent and he did not carry the yoke of sin. It was commanded to be taken to Moses because they blamed Christ for transgressing the Law of Moses by violating the Sabbath. And the cow was commanded to be brought to Eleazer the priest because Christ was delivered into the hands of the priests to be slain. It was immolated "outside the camp" because Christ suffered outside the (city) gate. And the priest dipped "his finger in her blood" because in this separation (of the blood from the red cow), symbolized by the finger, the mystery of Christ's passion should be considered and imitated.

The blood was sprinkled "over against . . . the tabernacle," which denotes the synagogue, to signify either the condemnation of the unbelieving Jews or the purification of the believers; and this "seven times" in token either of the seven gifts of the Holy Spirit or of the seven days wherein all time is comprised. . . . The ashes of the burning were gathered by "a man that is clean" because the relics of the Passion came into the possession of the Gentiles, who were not guilty of Christ's death. The ashes were put into water for the purpose of expiation because baptism receives from Christ's Passion the power of washing away sins. The priest who immolated and burned the cow, and he who burned, and he who gathered together the ashes were all unclean, as also he that sprinkled the water. This was the case either because the Jews became unclean through putting Christ to death, whereby our sins are expiated, and this "until evening," that is, until the end of the world when the remnants of Israel will be converted; or else because they who handle sacred things with a view to the cleansing of others contract certain uncleannesses, as Gregory says, and this "until evening," that is, until the end of his life. (Aquinas, *Summa Theologica* I/2, ques. 102, art. 5, ad 5) [AQUINAS 1945: 2:891–892]

14. The Divine Ruse of the Law

In his search for the causes behind apparently arbitrary commandments in the Torah, Maimonides frequently had resort to the explanation that they were promulgated to discourage idolatry. But the "wily graciousness" of God had another intent in mind.

The deity made a wily and gracious arrangement with regard to all the individuals of the living beings that suck. For when born, such individuals are extremely soft and cannot feed on dry food. Accordingly breasts were prepared for them so that they should produce milk with a view to their receiving humid food, which is similar to the composition of their bodies, until their limbs gradually and little by little became dry and solid. Many things in our Law are similar to this very governance on the part of Him who governs, may He be glorified and exalted. For a sudden transition from one opposite to another is impossible. Therefore man, according to his nature, is not capable of abandoning suddenly all to which he was accustomed. And therefore God sent Moses our Master to make of us "a kingdom of priests and a holy nation" (Exod. 19:6). . . . And at that time the way of life generally accepted and customary in the whole world and the universal service on which we were brought up consisted in offering various species of living beings in the temples in which images were set up, in worshiping the latter, and in burning incense before them. . . .

His wisdom, May He be exalted, and his gracious ruse, which is manifest in regard to all His creatures, did not require that He give us a Law prescribing the rejection, abandonment and abolition of all these kinds of worship. For one could not then conceive the acceptance of (such a Law), considering the nature of man, which always likes that to which it is accustomed. . . . Therefore He, may He be exalted, suffered the above-mentioned kinds of worship to remain, but transferred them from created or imaginary and unreal beings to His own name, may He be exalted, commanding us to practice them with regard to Him, may He be exalted. Thus He commanded us to build a Temple for Him . . . to have an altar for His name . . . to have sacrifice offered up to Him . . . to bow down in worship before Him and to burn incense before Him. And He forbade the performance of any of these actions with a view to someone else. . . . And He singled out priests for the service of His sanctuary. . . . And because of their employment in the Temple and the sacrifices in it, it was necessary to fix for them dues that would be sufficient for them, namely, the dues of the Levites and the priests. Through this divine ruse it came about that the memory of idolatry was effaced and the grandest and true foundation of our belief, namely the existence and the oneness of the deity, was firmly established, while at the same time the souls had no feeling of repugnance and were not repelled because of the abolition of the modes of worship to which they were accustomed and than which no other mode of worship was known at that time.

I know that on thinking about this at first your soul will necessarily have a feeling of repugnance toward this notion and will feel aggrieved because of it, and you will ask me in your heart and say to me: How is it possible that none of the commandments, prohibitions, and great actions—which are very precisely set forth and prescribed for fixed seasons—should be intended for its own sake but for the sake of something else, as if this was a ruse invented for our benefit by God in order to achieve His first intention? What was there to prevent Him, may He be exalted, from giving us a Law in accordance with His first intention and from procuring us the capacity to accept this? Hear then the reply to your question that will put an end to this sickness in your heart and reveal to you the true reality of that to which I have drawn your attention. It is to the effect that the text of the Torah tells a quite similar story, namely, in its dictum: "God led them not by the way of the land of the Philistines, although it was near . . . " and so on. "But God led the people about, by way of the wilderness of the Red Sea" (Exod. 13:17–18). Just as God perplexed them in anticipation of what their bodies were naturally incapable of bearing—turning them away from the high road toward which they had been going, toward another road so that the first intention should be achieved—so did He in anticipation of what the soul is naturally incapable of receiving prescribe the laws that we have mentioned so that the first intention should be achieved, namely, the apprehension of Him, may He be exalted, and the rejection of idolatry. . . .

As for your question: What was there to prevent God from giving us a Law in accordance with His first intention and from procuring us the capacity to accept this? . . . One may say to you: Inasmuch as God's first intention and His will are that we should believe in this Law and that we should perform the actions prescribed by it, why did He not procure us the capacity always to accept this intention and to act in accordance with it, instead of using a ruse with regard to us, declaring that He will procure us benefits if we obey Him and will take vengeance on us if we disobey Him and performing in deed all those acts of benefiting and all those acts of vengeance? For this too is a ruse used by Him with regard to us in order to achieve His first intention with respect to us. What was there to prevent Him from causing the inclination to accomplish the acts of obedience willed by Him and to avoid the acts of disobedience abhorred by Him, to be a natural disposition fixed in us?

There is one and the same general answer to (these) questions and to all others that belong to the same class: Though all miracles change the nature of some individual being, God does not change at all the nature of human individuals by means of miracles. . . . It is because of this that there are commandments and prohibitions, rewards and punishments. . . . We do not say this because we believe that the changing of the nature of any human individual is difficult for Him, may He be exalted; rather it is possible and fully within His capacity. But according to the foundations of the Law, of the Torah, He has never willed to do it, nor shall He ever will it. For were it His will that the nature of any human individual should be changed because of what He, may He be exalted, wills from that individual, sending of prophets and all giving of a Law would have been useless.

In the end, however, Maimonides is forced to concede that there are some commandments whose precise cause is concealed from us by reason of our ignorance of the historical circumstances or the form of the idolatry they were intended to cure or ameliorate.

In the case of most of the statutes whose reason is hidden from us, everything serves to keep people away from idolatry. The fact that there are particulars the reason for which is hidden from me and the utility for which I do not understand, is due to the circumstance that things known by hearsay are not like things that one has seen. . . . If we knew the particulars of those (idolatrous) practices and heard details concerning those (pagan) opinions, we would become clear concerning the wisdom manifested in the details of the practices prescribed in the commandments concerning the sacrifices and the forms of uncleanness and other matters whose reason cannot, to my mind, be easily grasped. . . .

Consider how great was the extent of this corruption and whether or not it was fitting to spend one's efforts in putting an end to it. Most of the commandments serve, therefore, as we have made clear, to put an end to those opinions and to lighten the grave and oppressive burdens, the toil and the fatigue, that those people imposed upon themselves in their cult. Accordingly, every commandment or prohibition of the Law whose reason is hidden from you constitutes a cure for one of those diseases, which today—thank God—we do not know any more. (Maimonides, *Guide of the Perplexed* 3.49) [MAIMONIDES 1963: 612]

15. Crimes and Their Penalties in the Torah

Inserted in the middle of the account of the giving of the Law in Exodus 20:22– 23:33 is a series of regulations, many of which appear to bear upon the life of a settled agricultural community. That would date them after the Israelite entry into Canaan, but they are attached here to the Sinai covenant. Some have to do with criminal acts and carry the death penalty.

21:15–17: He who strikes his mother or father shall be put to death. He who kidnaps a man, whether he has sold him or is still holding him, shall be put to death. He who insults his father or mother shall be put to death.

22:17–20: You shall not let live a sorceress. Whoever lies with a beast shall be put to death. Whoever sacrifices to any god other than the Lord alone shall be proscribed.

"Proscription," according to Leviticus 27:29, is death. Note too the general principle enunciated in Exodus 21:23–25.

If . . . damage ensues (from an act), the penalty shall be life for life, eye for eye, tooth for tooth, hand for hand, foot for foot, burn for burn, wound for wound, bruise for bruise.

Some of the regulations pertain to cult, including this obligation to pilgrimage.

23:14–17: Three times a year you shall hold a (pilgrimage) festival for Me. You shall celebrate the (pilgrimage) feast of Unleavened Bread [Passover]—eating unleavened bread for seven days as I have commanded you—at the set time in the month of Abib, for in it you went forth from Egypt; and none shall come before Me empty-handed. You shall celebrate the (pilgrimage) feast of Harvest [Shabuoth or "Weeks," celebrated fifty days after Passover and so called in Greek "Pentecost"] of the firstfruits of your work, of what you sow in the field, and the (pilgrimage) feast of Ingathering [Sukkoth or "Booths"] at the end of the year, when you gather in the results of your work on the land. These three times a year all your males shall appear before the Sovereign, the Lord.

16. Crimes and Their Penalties in the Quran

As for the thief, whether man or woman, cut off his hand as a punishment from God for what he has done. (Quran 5:38)

Thus the Quran too has its list of crimes and the punishments specified for each. In such cases of Quranically prescribed penalties there was, of course, no room for a judge's discretion, no matter how harsh the punishment might seem. The following legal definitions of certain crimes—the Quran does not so much define the crimes as name them—and their prescribed penalties is from a manual written by the jurisprudent al-Nawawi (d. 1277 C.E.).

Crimes punishable by amputation: For theft the amount necessitating punishment by amputation is (at least) of equal value to a quarter of a (gold) dinar. Two persons stealing together must have stolen twice the minimum amount. There is no amputation if what was stolen was impurity [which cannot constitute property], such as wine, or a pig or dog, or the skin of an animal not ritually slaughtered. But if the container of the wine was worth the minimum amount, amputation follows.

Theft by a minor, an insane person, or one forced against his will is not punished by cutting off the hand, but cutting may be performed on members of a "protected community" [e.g., a Jew or a Christian] subject to our laws. The right hand is cut off for the first offense, even if more than one theft was involved, the left foot for the second, the left hand for the third, and the right foot for the fourth. . . .

Sins not punishable by a prescribed penalty or expiation may be punished by imprisonment, beating, slapping, or threatening. The nature of this is at the discretion of the ruler or his deputy. (Nawawi, *The Goal of Seekers*) [WILLIAMS 1971: 151]

17. The Quran on Jewish Infidelity to the Law

In many instances, then, the Quran simply legislated without a glance backward at those other revealed Books. In at least one case, however, that regarding adultery, Muhammad appears simply to have affirmed the Torah. Moreover, the general theme of Jewish infidelity to the Law given them by God as part of the Covenant is often reflected upon in the Quran.

Remember when We made a Covenant with the people of Israel and said, "Worship no one but God and be good to parents and your kin and to orphans and the needy, and speak of goodness to men, and observe your devotional obligations and pay the alms tithe," you went back on your word, except only a few, and paid no heed.

And remember when We made a Covenant with you whereby you agreed you will neither shed blood among you nor turn your people out of their homes, you promised and are a witness to it too.

But you still kill one another and you turn a party of your people from their homes, assisting one another against them with guilt and oppression. Yet, when they are brought to you as captives, you ransom them, though forbidden it was to drive them away. Do you, then, believe a part of the Book and reject a part? There is no other award for them who so act but disgrace in the world, and on the Day of Judgment, the severest of punishment; for God is not heedless of all you do. (Quran 2.83–85)

18. Muslim and Christian Infidelity to the Torah

The Jews living under Islam were certainly aware of the Muslims' claim to be the inheritors of the true Torah tradition. One reaction to that claim occurs in the dialogue called The Khazar King, *written by Judah Halevi, a Jew from Muslim Spain, sometime about 1130–1140 C.E. Although he recognizes that Islam bears a closer affinity to Judaism than does Christianity, Halevi is not about to surrender the heritage of the Law to Muslims. The point of departure is a remark by the "Rabbi" of the dialogue that Jerusalem is "a divine place, and the law coming forth from it is the true religion." The king of the Khazars, who is making inquiry into the religious claims of Judaism, Christianity, and Islam, then turns to those latter groups.*

The Khazar King: Certainly if later religions admit the truth and do not dispute it, then they all respect the place [that is Jerusalem], and call it the stepping-stone of the prophets, the gate of heaven, the place of the gathering of the souls (on the Day of Judgment). They further admit the existence of prophecy in Israel, whose forefathers were distinguished in a like manner. Finally they believe in the work of creation, the flood, and nearly all that is contained in the Torah. They also perform pilgrimages to this hallowed place.

The Rabbi: I would compare them to proselytes who did not accept the whole Law in all its branches, but only the fundamental principles, if their actions did not belie their words. Their veneration of the land of prophecy consists chiefly in words, and at the same time they also revere places sacred to idols. Such is the case in places in which an assembly happened to meet, but in which no sign of God became visible. Retaining the relics of ancient idolatry and feast days, they changed nothing but the forms. These were indeed demolished (by Muhammad), but the relics were not removed. I might almost say that the verse in the Bible, occurring repeatedly: "You shall not serve strange gods, wood and stone" (Deut. 28:36, 64), contains an allusion to those who worship the wood (of the Cross) and those who worship the stone (of the Ka῾ba at Mecca). We, through our sins, incline daily more toward them.

It is true that they, like the people of Abimelech and Nineveh, believe in God, but they philosophize concerning God's ways. The leader of each of these parties [that is, the Muslims and the Christians] maintained that he had found the divine light at its source, to wit, in the Holy Land, and that there he ascended to heaven, and commanded that all the inhabitants of the globe should be guided in the right path. They turned their faces toward that land in prayer, but before long they [that is, the Muslims] changed and turned toward (Mecca) the place where the greatest number of their people lived. . . .

The Khazar King: But the followers of other religions approach you more nearly than the philosophers?

The Rabbi: They are as far removed from us as the followers of a religion from a philosopher. The former seek God not only for the sake of knowing him but also for other benefits which they derive therefrom. The philosopher, however, only seeks Him that he may be able to describe Him accurately in detail, as he would describe the earth. . . . Ignorance of God would be no more injurious than would ignorance concerning the earth be injurious to those who consider it flat. . . . We cannot blame philosophers for missing the mark, since they only arrived at this knowledge by way of speculation, and the result could not have been different. The most sincere among them speak to the followers of a revealed religion in the words of Socrates: "My friends, I will not contest your theology. I say, however, that I cannot grasp it; I only understand human wisdom."

The speculative religions [that is, Christianity and Islam], on the other hand, are now as far removed from us as they were formerly near. If this were not so, Jeroboam and his party would be nearer to us, even though they worshiped idols, since they were Israelites inasmuch as they practiced circumcision, observed the Sabbath and other regulations, with few exceptions which administrative emergencies forced them to neglect. They [that is, the Muslims] acknowledged the God of Israel who delivered them from Egypt, in the same way as did the worshipers of the golden calf in the desert [that is, the Christians]. The former class is at best superior to the latter inasmuch as they [the Muslims] prohibited images. Since, however, they altered the direction of prayer and sought the Divine Influence where it is not to be found [that is, in Mecca], altering at the same time the majority of ceremonial laws, they wandered far from the straight path. (Judah Halevi, *The Khazar King* 4.10–13)
[HALEVI 1905: 215–219]

19. Maimonides on the Counterfeit Children of Abraham

The rather careful argument of The Khazar King *yields to more direct polemic in a letter written by Maimonides to the Jews of the Yemen. In the latter half of the twelfth century this community was not so much perplexed as persecuted and had in its midst both apostates and messianic claimants. The times called not for demonstration but encouragement and support, which Maimonides attempted to provide. He touched, among other things, upon the alleged resemblance of Christianity and Islam to the religion of the Jews.*

Our religion differs as much from other religions for which there are alleged resemblances as a living man endowed with the faculty of reason is unlike a statue which is ever so well carved out of marble, wood, bronze or silver. When a person ignorant of divine wisdom or of God's works sees the statue that superficially resembles a man in its contours, form, features, and color, he believes that the structure of the parts of a statue is like the constitution of a man, because he is deficient in understanding concerning the inner organization of both. But the informed person who knows the interior of both is cognizant of the fact that the internal structure of the statue betrays no skillful workmanship at all, whereas the inward parts of man are truly marvelously made, a testimony to the wisdom of the Creator, such as the prolongation of the nerves in the muscles and their ramifications, the branching out of the sinews and their intersections. . . .

Likewise a person ignorant of the secret meaning of Scripture and the deeper significance of the Law would be led to believe that our religion has something in common with another if he makes a comparison between the two. For he will note that in the Torah there are prohibitions and commandments, just as in other religions there are permitted and interdicted acts, both contain a system of religious observances, positive and negative precepts, sanctioned by reward and punishment.

If he could only fathom the inner intent of the Law, then he would realize that the essence of the true religion lies in the deeper meaning of its positive and negative precepts, every one of which will aid man in his striving after perfection, and remove every impediment to the attainment of excellence. These commands will enable the masses and the elite to acquire moral and intellectual qualities, each according to his ability. Thus the godly community becomes pre-eminent, reaching a twofold perfection. By the first perfection I mean man's spending his life in this world under the most agreeable and congenial conditions. The second perfection would constitute the achievement of intellectual objectives, each in accordance with his native powers.

The tenets of other religions which resemble those of Scripture have no deeper meaning, but are superficial imitations, copied from and patterned after it. They modeled their religions upon ours in order to glorify themselves and indulge their fancy that they are similar to so-and-so. However, their counterfeiting is an open secret to the learned. Consequently they become objects of derision and ridicule, just as one smiles at an ape when it imitates the actions of men. (Maimonides, *Letter to the Yemen*)

20. The Observance of the Sabbath

The Israelites have been led from Egypt by Moses. To sustain them in the desert, God sends down like a miraculous dew in the night a food called manna, which the Israelites collect. The events that follow take place before Sinai.

So they gathered it [that is, the manna] every morning, each as much as he needed to eat; for when the sun grew hot, it would melt. On the sixth day they gathered double the amount of food, two omers for each; and when all the chieftains came and told Moses, he said to them, "This is what the Lord meant: Tomorrow is a day of rest, a holy sabbath to the Lord. Bake what you would bake and boil what you would boil; and all that is left put aside to be kept until the morning." So they put it aside until morning, as Moses had ordered; and it did not turn foul, and there were no maggots in it. Then Moses said, "Eat it today, for today is a sabbath of the Lord; you will not find it today on the plain. Six days you shall gather it; on the seventh day, the sabbath, there will be none."

Yet some of the people went out on the seventh day to gather it [that is, the manna] but they found nothing. And the Lord said to Moses, "How long will you men refuse to obey My commandment and My instructions? Mark that the Lord has given you the sabbath; therefore He gives you two days' food on the sixth day. Let everyone remain where he is: let no man leave his place on the seventh day." And the people remained inactive on the seventh day. (Exodus 16:21–30)

Thus the Sabbath became one of the Israelites' holy days (Lev. 23:2–3), and its observance was incorporated into the Torah legislation given to Moses on Sinai as part of the Ten Commandments. The Exodus version (Exod. 20:8:1–17) of the commandment and the form it assumes in Deuteronomy (Deut. 5:6–21) offer interesting variations on both its origins and its intent.

Remember the sabbath day and keep it holy. Six days you shall labor and do all your work. But the seventh day is a sabbath of the Lord your God: you shall not do any work—you, your son or your daughter, your male or female slave, or your cattle, or the stranger who is within your settlements. For in six days the Lord made heaven and earth and sea, and all that is in them, and He rested on the seventh day; therefore the Lord blessed the sabbath day and hallowed it. (Exodus 20:8–11)

Observe the sabbath day and keep it holy, as the Lord your God has commanded you. Six days you shall labor and do all your work, but the seventh day is a sabbath of the Lord your God: you shall not do any work—you, your son or your daughter, your male or female slave, your ox or your ass, or any of your cattle, or the stranger in your settlements, so that your male and female slaves may rest as you do. Remember that you were a slave in the land of Egypt and the Lord your God freed you from there with a mighty hand and an outstretched arm, therefore the Lord your God commanded you to keep holy the sabbath day. (Deuteronomy 5:12–15)

21. The Sabbath and the
Humanitarian Intent of the Mosaic Law

If we follow the account in Deuteronomy literally, the reason for the injunction to observe the Sabbath was to serve as a remembrance of the Israelites' bondage in Egypt and God's gracious release of them from their ignoble condition of slavery. Such a literal reading did not satisfy all students of Scripture, however. For Philo, among others, God and His lawgiver Moses had other and somewhat more profound lessons in mind.

But it seems that Moses added the other injunctions because of the less obedient who pay little attention to his commandments, and required not only free men to cease from work on the Sabbath, but allowed the same to menservants and handmaids, proclaiming to them security and virtual freedom after every six days, in order to teach both master and servant an admirable lesson. The masters must become accustomed to working with their own hands, not waiting for the services and ministrations of their household slaves, so that if any adverse circumstances should prevail in the course of the vicissitudes of human affairs, they may not through inexperience of personal labor be distressed from the start and renounce the tasks enjoined on them, but use the different parts of their body with greater agility and act with vigor and ease. The servants, on the other hand, should not despair of higher hopes, but possessing in the relaxation that comes after every six days an ember or spark of freedom, look for their complete release if they remain true and loyal to their masters. From the occasional submission of free men to perform the services of slaves and the possibility for the slaves to share in a sense of security, the result will be that human life will advance toward the higher perfection of virtue, when both the seemingly illustrious and the obscurer sort remember equality and owe each other a necessary debt.

But it is not to the servants alone that the Law has granted the Sabbath rest, but also to the cattle. The servants are indeed free by nature, for no man is naturally a slave, but the irrational animals have been made ready for the need and service of men and rank as slaves. (Philo, *The Special Laws* 2.66–69) [PHILO 1981: 238–239]

Nor is this humanitarian purpose limited to the Sabbath regulation.

With these considerations in view, the expounder of the laws proclaimed a day of rest for the land (through the sabbath-year commandment) and restrained the husbandman from his work after every six-year period. But he introduced this regulation not only for the reason just mentioned but also because of his customary humanity, which he thinks fit to interweave into every part of his legislation, thereby impressing on the readers of Sacred Scripture sociable and kindly character traits. For he commands them not to shut off any field during the sabbath-year. All vineyards and olive groves are to be left open, and similarly other properties, whether of sown crops or trees, so that the poor may freely use the wild-growing fruits as much, if not more so, than the proprietors. Thus, on the one hand, he did not allow the masters to till their fields with the aim of sparing them the distress of providing the expenditure (for cultivation) and receiving no profits in return, and, on the other hand, he thought it fit that the needy for that period of time at any rate should enjoy as their own what seemed to belong to others, thus delivering them from any beggerly mien and the reproaches attached to mendicants. Is it not proper that we cherish laws filled with such gentleness, by which the rich are instructed to distribute and share what they have and the poor are exhorted not to be haunting the homes of the affluent on every occasion under the necessity of remedying their indigence, but at times also to derive profit from fruits that, as I said, grow wild and which they can regard as their own? (Ibid. 2.104–107) [PHILO 1981: 239]

22. Maimonides on the Sabbath

The association of the Sabbath now with the work of creation and now with the exodus from Egypt did not escape the commentators on the Law. Maimonides reflects on the reasons in his Guide of the Perplexed *and finds that they verify his own views on the purposes of the Law.*

Perhaps it has already become clear to you what is the cause of the Lord's establishing the Sabbath so firmly and ordaining death by stoning for breaking it. The Master of the Prophets [Moses] has put people to death because of it. It comes third after the existence of the deity and the denial of dualism. For the prohibition of the worship of anything except Him only aims at the belief in His unity. You know from what I have said that opinions do not last unless they are accompanied by actions that strengthen them, make them generally known, and perpetuate them among the multitude. For this reason we are ordered by the Law to exalt this day, in order that the principle of the creation of the world in time be established and universally known in the world, through the fact that all people refrain from working on one and the same day. If it is asked,

What is the cause of this? the answer is: "For in six days the Lord made" (Exod. 20:1).

For this commandment two different causes are given, corresponding to two different effects. In the first Decalog, the cause for exalting the Sabbath is stated as follows: "For in six days the Lord etc." In Deuteronomy, on the other hand, it is said: "Remember that you were slaves in Egypt. . . . For that reason the Lord your God commanded you to keep holy the sabbath day" (Deut. 5:15). This is correct. For the effect, according to the first statement is to regard that day as noble and exalted. . . . This is the effect consequent upon the cause stated in the words: "For in six days etc." However, the order given us by the Law with regard to it and the commandment ordaining us in particular to keep it are an effect consequent upon the cause that we had been slaves in Egypt where we did not work according to our free choice and when we wished and where we had not the power to refrain from working. Therefore we have been commanded inactivity and rest so that we should conjoin two things: the belief in a true opinion—namely the creation of the world in time, which, at the first go and with the slightest of speculations, shows that the deity exists—and the memory of the benefit God bestowed upon us by giving us rest from the burdens of the Egyptians. Accordingly the Sabbath is, as it were, of universal benefit, both with reference to a true speculative opinion and to the well-being of the state of the body. (Maimonides, *Guide* 2.31) [MAIMONIDES 1963: 359–360]

23. Mountains Hanging by a Hair: The Sabbath Prescriptions

(The rules about) release from vows float in the air and have nothing to support them. The rules about the Sabbath, festival offerings and sacrilege are as mountains hanging by a hair, for Scripture is slight but the rules many. (M.Hagigah 1:8)

In the light of the prescriptions as they are set down in Exodus and Deuteronomy, the activities specifically prohibited on the Sabbath appear to be limited to laboring, going abroad, and cooking. But questions must have arisen. In the following case we can note the extension of the commandment, though once again on the basis of a divine decree, to an activity that had been either licit or of indifferent notice up to that point.

During the time that the Israelites were in the wilderness a man was found gathering sticks on the sabbath day. Those who had caught him in the act brought him to Moses and Aaron and all the community, and they kept him in custody, because it was not clearly known what was to be done with him. The Lord said to Moses, "The man must be put to death; he must be stoned by all the community outside the camp." So they took him outside the camp and all stoned him to death, as the Lord had commanded Moses. (Numbers 15:32–36)

There must have been continuous legal discussion of the Sabbath prescriptions over the following centuries. Although most of the debates are invisible to us, some of the development is apparent in the Book of Jubilees, a retelling of the early books of the Bible with a marked emphasis on and extension of the legal material there. It was written in Hebrew, probably by a Pharisee, sometime between 135 and 105 B.C.E. It ends with a redefinition—in the text it is Moses speaking to the people—of the Sabbath regulations.

And behold the commandments about the sabbaths, and all the rules and regulations I have written down for you. Six days you shall work, but on the seventh day is the sabbath of the Lord your God: on it you shall do no work, neither you nor your sons, nor your slave boys nor your slave girls, nor any of your cattle, nor the alien who is among you. And the man who does any work on it shall die: whoever desecrates that day, whoever lies with a woman, or whoever talks on it about anything he intends to do (what, for example, he will buy or sell the next day), and whoever draws water on it because he did not remember to draw it on the sixth day, and whoever lifts any load to carry it out of his tent or out of his house, shall die. You shall do no work whatever on the sabbath: only what you have prepared for yourself on the sixth day shall you eat and drink, so that you may eat and drink and rest and keep sabbath from all work on that day, and bless the Lord your God who has given you a festal day and a holy day. . . . And any man who does any work on the sabbath days, or goes on a journey, or tills a field (whether at home or elsewhere), and whoever lights a fire, or loads any beast, or travels by ship on the sea, and whoever shoots or kills anything or slaughters a beast or a bird, or who-ever catches an animal or a bird or a fish, or whoever fasts or makes war on the sabbath—the man who does any of these things on the sabbath shall die, so that the sons of Israel may observe the sabbaths in accordance with the commandments concerning the sabbaths of the land, as it is written on the tablets which He gave into my hands to write out for you the laws of the seasons, and the seasons according to the division of their days. (Jubilees 50:6–13)

By about 200 C.E., the time of the writing down of the Mishna, which devotes an entire tractate to the observance of the Sabbath, the list of prohibited Sabbath activities had been spelled out by the rabbis in enormous detail.

There are thirty-nine main categories of work (outlawed by the Sabbath prohibition against "daily work"): planting, plowing, reaping, binding sheaves, threshing, winnowing, cleaning crops, grinding, sifting, kneading, baking, shearing wool, washing, beating or dyeing it, spinning, weaving, making two loops, plaiting or braiding, separating two threads, tying (a knot), loosening (a knot), sewing two stitches, tearing in order to sew two stitches, hunting a deer or any other animal, slaughtering or flaying or salting the deer, curing its skin, scraping or cutting it up, writing two letters, erasing in order to write two letters, building, pulling down, putting out a fire, lighting a fire, striking with a hammer, and taking anything from one domain to another. These are the main categories of work, thirty-nine in all. (M.Shabbat 7:2)

If a non-Jew lights a lamp on the Sabbath, a Jew may make use of the light. But if he lights it for the sake of the Jew, it is forbidden. If a non-Jew fills a trough with water for his cattle, a Jew may water his own cattle afterwards. But if the non-Jew does it for the Jew, it is forbidden. If a non-Jew sets up a gangplank to go down from a ship, a Jew may go down after him. But if he does it for a Jew, it is forbidden. Rabban Gamaliel and some elders were once traveling on a ship, and a non-Jew set up a gangplank to go down from it. Rabban Gamaliel and the elders did go down by it. (M.Shabbat 16:8)

24. Jesus on the Sabbath

According to the Mishna, reaping, winnowing, and grinding are among the many activities forbidden on the Sabbath. The Talmud discusses another case that had arisen: was it permitted for an individual to pluck grain, rub it in his own hand and eat it?

One may pluck (grain) with the hand and eat (on the Sabbath), but one may not pluck with an implement; and one may rub and eat (grain on the Sabbath), but one may not rub with an implement. These are the words of Rabbi Akiba, but other Sages say that one may rub with one's finger tips and eat, but one may not run a quantity with the hand and eat. (BT.Shabbat 128a–b)

Rabbi Akiba lived in the early second century C.E., but that the rabbinic controversy on this point was at least a century older and that Jesus was embroiled in it, we can read in the Gospel.

One Sabbath he (Jesus) and his disciples were going through the grain fields, and his disciples were plucking the ears of grain, rubbing them in their hands and eating them. Some of the Pharisees said, "Why are you doing what is forbidden on the Sabbath?" Jesus answered, "So you have not read [1 Sam. 21:1–7] what David did when he and his men were hungry? He went into the House of God and took the sacred bread to eat and gave it to his men, though priests alone are allowed to eat it, and no one else." He also said, "The Son of Man is sovereign even over the Sabbath." (Luke 6:1–5)

The two other Synoptics end the same story somewhat differently.

(Jesus continued) have you not read in the Law that the priests in the Temple break the Sabbath and it is not held against them? I tell you, there is something greater than the Temple here. If you had known what that text means, "I require mercy, not sacrifice" (Hos. 6:6), you would not have condemned the innocent. For the Son of Man is sovereign over the Sabbath. (Matthew 12:3–8)

He also said to them [the Pharisees], "the Sabbath was made for the sake of man and not man for the Sabbath: therefore the Son of Man is sovereign even over the Sabbath." (Mark 2:27–28)

In all three of the Synoptics the incident of plucking the kernels of grain on the Sabbath is followed by another instance that brought Jesus into conflict with the Pharisees. The possibility that the prohibitions against certain activities on the Sabbath could be overridden by other, higher considerations already emerges from the first case, and the Mishna makes it explicit.

Rabbi Mattathiah ben Heresh said: If a man has a pain in his throat, they may drop medicine in his mouth on the Sabbath, since there is doubt whether his life is in danger, and whenever there is doubt that life is in danger this overrides the Sabbath. If a building falls down on a man (on the Sabbath) and there is doubt whether he is there or not, or whether he is alive or dead, or whether he is a Gentile or an Israelite, they may clear away the ruin from above him. If they find him alive, they may clear it away (still more) from above him; but if dead, they leave him. (M.Yoma 8:6–7)

Thus the principle was established, but the conditions and circumstances of Sabbath assistance were by no means fixed. According to Mishna Shabbat 22:6 it was not permitted to set a broken limb on the Sabbath or to attend to a sprain, presumably because these were not life-threatening ills. The same general rule probably held with regard to domestic animals: if an animal fell into a pit, it might be made

*comfortable but not removed, except if its life were threatened—if the pit were filled
with water, for example. It must have been that type of debate, then, that lay
behind the only cure that Jesus performed on the Sabbath, one that, since it was
effected simply by a word, involved no "work" in any defined sense of that term.*

He [Jesus] went to another place and entered their synagogue. A
man was there with a withered arm, and they asked Jesus, "Is it permitted
to heal on the Sabbath?" They wanted to frame a charge against him. But
he said to them, "Suppose you had one sheep, which fell into a ditch [or
well] on the Sabbath; is there not one of you who would catch hold of it
and lift it out? And surely a man is worth more than a sheep! It is therefore permitted to do good on the Sabbath." Turning to the man, he said,
"Stretch out your arm." He stretched it out, and it was made sound again
like the other. But the Pharisees on leaving the synagogue laid a plot to
do away with him. (Matthew 12:9–14)

25. A Gate in the Fence around the Law: The Erub

*One of the more widely discussed Sabbath prohibitions was the limitation on travel.
"Let each man stay where he is; no one may stir from his home on the seventh day,"
Exodus 16:29 commands. Using Numbers 35:1–5 as their guide, the rabbis defined
a "Sabbath's journey"—the distance comprised by one's domicile or "domain" and
so a legitimate area of movement—as 2,000 cubits. There was, however, one alle-
viation granted by the rabbis to the Mosaic Law by redefining "domain" through
the introduction of the notion of an erub, a "mixture" or "fusion" of the boundaries of one's domain or even of an entire town to permit freer movement within it
on the Sabbath. This extension was accomplished in one of two ways: by preparing
food beforehand and depositing it in the newly "acquired" locality; or by joining
the places together with a continuous link, a rope, for example. An entire treatise
of the Mishna was devoted to this transparent legal contrivance, and the question
was put to the rabbi who spoke for Judah Halevi in The Khazar King: "How can
we make lawful a thing which God has forbidden by means so paltry and artificial?"*

Heaven forbid that all these pious men and Sages should concur in
untying one of the knots of the Divine Law. Their intention was to make
it tighter and therefore they said: Build a fence around the Law. Part of
this (fence building) is the rabbinic prohibition of carrying things out of
private to public ground and vice versa, a prohibition not of Mosaic
origin. In constructing this fence they introduced this license to prevent
their religious zeal from ranking with the Torah and at the same time to
give people some liberty in moving about. This liberty was gained in a

perfectly lawful way and takes the form of the *Erub*, and marks a line between what is entirely legal, the fence itself, and the secluded part inside the latter. (Judah Halevi, *The Khazar King* 3.51) [HALEVI 1905: 180]

26. The Dietary Laws

You shall not eat anything abhorrent. These are the animals that you may eat: the ox, the sheep, the goat, the deer, the gazelle, the roe buck, the wild goat, the ibex, the antelope, the mountain sheep, and any other animal that has true hoofs which are cleft in two and brings up the cud—such you may eat. But the following, which do not bring up the cud or have true hoofs which are cleft through, you may not eat: the camel, the hare, and the daman—for though they bring up the cud, they have no true hoofs—they are unclean for you; also the swine—for although it has true hoofs, it does not bring up the cud—is unclean for you. You shall not eat of their flesh or touch their carcasses.

These you may eat of, all that live in the water: you may eat anything that has fins and scales. But you may not eat anything that has no fins and scales: it is unclean for you.

You may eat any clean bird. The following you may not eat: the eagle, the vulture and the black vulture; the kite, the falcon, and the buzzard of any variety; every variety of raven; the ostrich, the nighthawk, the sea gull, the hawk of any variety, the little owl, the great owl, and the white owl; the pelican, the bustard, and the cormorant; the stork, any variety of heron, the hoopoe, the bat.

All winged swarming creatures are unclean for you; they may not be eaten. You may eat only clean winged creatures.

You shall not eat anything that has died a natural death. You shall give it to the stranger in your community to eat, or you may sell it to a foreigner. For you are a people consecrated to the Lord your God. (Deuteronomy 14:3–21)

And the Lord spoke to Moses, saying: "Speak to the Israelite people thus: 'You shall eat no fat of ox or sheep or goat. Fat from animals that died (a natural death) or were torn by beasts may be put to any use, but you must not eat it. If anyone eats the fat of animals from which offerings by fire may be made to the Lord, the person who eats it shall be cut off from his kin. And you must not consume any blood, either of bird or of animal, in any of your settlements. Anyone who eats blood shall be cut off from his kin.' " (Leviticus 7:22–27)

The reasons for these prohibitions—and the more specific list in Leviticus 11—have been often discussed in ancient as well as modern times. Here will be cited only two of the many opinions on the subject: one from the beginning of the Christian era, that of the Alexandrian philosopher Philo, who offers a symbolic interpretation; and the other a medieval viewpoint, that of the physician and lawyer Moses Maimonides.

It might perhaps be assumed to be just that all wild beasts that feed on human flesh should suffer from men the same treatment that the beasts inflict on them. But Moses is of the opinion that we should abstain from the enjoyment of these, even though they provide a most pleasant and delectable feast, since he is considering what is appropriate for a civilized soul. For though it is fitting for the perpetrators of such acts to suffer the like, it is not proper for the sufferers to retaliate, lest they become unconsciously brutalized by the savage passion of anger. So cautious is he in this regard that, wishing to have full scope to restrain the impulse for the food just mentioned, he also forbade the use of other carnivores, distinguishing the herbivores as constituting gentle herds, since they are naturally tame and live on the gentle fruits the earth produces and do not engage in scheming against others. They are ten in number . . . for since Moses always held fast to the science of arithmology, which he acutely perceived to be of the greatest import in all that exists, he never legislated any law, great or small, without including and as it were adjusting to his enactments the appropriate number. But of all the numbers from the monad on up, ten is the most perfect, and, as Moses says, most holy and sacred, and with it he marks the kinds of clean animals whose use he wished to assign to the members of his commonwealth.

He subjoins a general test and a verification of the ten species of animals, employing two signs, the parted hoof and chewing the cud. Animals lacking both or one of these are unclean. Now both these signs are symbols of the methods of teaching and learning most conducive to knowledge, by which the better is distinguished from the worse with a view to avoiding confusion. For just as the ruminant animal after chewing up the food fixes it in the gullet, again after a while draws it up and masticates it and then transfers it to the belly, in like manner the student, after receiving from the teacher through his ears the principles and intuitions of wisdom, prolongs the learning process since he cannot straightway apprehend and grasp them with acumen, till by repeating in his memory, through constant exercises which function like the glue of conceptions, he firmly stamps their impression in his soul.

But there appears to be no advantage in having a firm apprehension
of ideas unless there is in addition a discrimination and a distinction
between them with a view to our choosing what we ought and avoiding
their opposites, of which the parted hoof is the symbol. For the path of
life is twofold, one branch leading to vice, the other to virtue, and we
must learn to turn away from one and never abandon the other. For this
reason all animals that are either solid-hoofed or many-hoofed are unclean, the former because they hint at the notion that the good and the
bad have one and the same nature, like concave and convex and an uphill
and downhill road; the latter because they display before our lives many
roads, or rather dead ends, to deceive us, for with a multitude of roads
it is no easy matter to perceive the best and most efficient path. (Philo,
The Special Laws 4.103–110) [PHILO 1981: 282–283]

For the physician Maimonides the reasons for the prohibition are what we might call
nutritional or hygienic.

Among all those (foods) forbidden us, only pork and fat may be
imagined not to be harmful. But this is not so, for pork is more humid
than is proper and contains more superfluous matter. The major reason
why the Law abhors it [the pig] is its being very dirty and feeding on dirty
things. You know to what extent the Law insists upon the need to remove
filth out of sight, even in the field and in a military camp, and all the more
within cities. Now if swine were used as food, marketplaces and even
houses would have been dirtier than latrines, as may be seen at present
in the country of the Franks [that is, the European Christians]. You know
the dictum of the Sages, may their memory be blessed: "The mouth of a
swine is like walking excrement."

The fat of the intestines also makes us full, spoils the digestion, and
produces cold and thick blood. It is more suitable to burn it. Blood, on
the one hand, and carcasses of beasts that have died, on the other, are also
difficult to digest and constitute a harmful nourishment. It is well known
that a beast that has been wounded is close to being a carcass. (Maimonides, *Guide of the Perplexed* 3.48) [MAIMONIDES 1963: 598]

27. From Torah to Code on a Point of Law

You shall not boil a kid in its mother's milk. (Exodus 23:19)

This single dietary injunction, repeated at Exodus 34:26 and Deuteronomy 14:21,
provides us with an opportunity to follow the progressive elaboration and interpreta-

tion of a Torah prescription. We begin with the Mishna, where the discussion is already well under way.

No flesh may be cooked in milk excepting the flesh of fish and locusts; and no flesh may be served up on the table together with cheese excepting the flesh of fish and locusts. If a man vowed to abstain from flesh, he is permitted the flesh of fish and locusts. A fowl may be served up on the table together with cheese, but it may not be eaten with it. So the School of Shammai. And the School of Hillel say: It may neither be served nor eaten with it. Rabbi Yosi said: This is one of the cases where the School of Shammai followed the more lenient and the School of Hillel the more stringent ruling. Of what manner of table did they speak? Of a table whereat men eat; but on a table whereon food is (merely) set out, a man may put the one beside the other without scruple. (M.Hullin 8:1)

In its comments on this Mishnaic text the gemara *of the Babylonian Talmud reviews the debate on the subject.*

. . . Agra, the father-in-law of Rabbi Abba, recited: a fowl and cheese may be eaten without restriction. He recited it and he himself explained it thus: it means without washing the hands or cleansing the mouth (between the eating of one and the other).

Rabbi Isaac the son of Rabbi Mesharsheya once visited the house of Rabbi Ashi. He was served with cheese which he ate and then was served with meat which he also ate without washing his hands (between the courses). They said to him: Has not Agra the father-in-law of Rabbi Abba recited that fowl and cheese may be eaten without restriction? A fowl and cheese, yes; but meat and cheese, no! He replied: That is the rule only at night, but by day I can see (that my hands are clean).

It was taught: the School of Shammai say: One must clean (the mouth between meat and cheese courses); the School of Hillel say: One must rinse it. Now what is meant by "one must clean" and "one must rinse"? If one says that it means this, that the School of Shammai say that one must clean the mouth but not rinse it and the School of Hillel say one must rinse the mouth but not clean it, then the statement of Rabbi Zera, to wit, "cleaning the mouth must be done with bread only," would agree with the view of the School of Shammai, would it not? But if you say that it means this, that the School of Shammai say that one must clean the mouth and not rinse it and the School of Hillel say that one must *also* rinse it, then it is a case where the School of Shammai adopt the lenient ruling and the School of Hillel the strict ruling. Why then is this not taught among the cases in which the School of Shammai adopt the lenient ruling

and the School of Hillel the strict ruling? Rather this must be the interpretation: the School of Shammai say that one *must* clean, and this is also
the law with regard to rinsing. And the School of Hillel say that one *must*
rinse, and this is also the law with regard to cleaning. One (school) mentions one requirement, the other (school) another, but they do not really
differ.

The above-cited text stated: Rabbi Zera said: "cleaning the mouth
must be done with bread only." This means only with wheaten bread but
not with barley bread. And even with wheaten bread it is allowed only if
it is cold and not if it is still warm, because of smearing. And it must be
soft and not hard. The law is, cleaning the mouth may be done with
everything except flour, dates, and vegetables.

Rabbi Assi inquired of Rabbi Yohanan: "How long must one wait
between flesh and cheese courses?" He replied: "Nothing at all." But this
cannot be, for Rabbi Hisda said: "If a person ate flesh, he is forbidden to
eat (after it) cheese. If he ate cheese, he is permitted to eat after it flesh."
This indeed was the question: how long must one wait between cheese
and flesh? And he replied: "Nothing at all."

The (above-cited) text (stated): Rabbi Hisda said: "If a person ate
flesh, he is forbidden to eat (after it) cheese, if he ate cheese, he is permitted to eat (after it) flesh." Rabbi Aha b. Joseph asked Rabbi Hisda:
"What about the flesh that is (caught) between the teeth?" He quoted (in
reply) the verse, "While the flesh was yet between their teeth" (Num.
11:33).

Mar Ukba said: "In this matter I am what vinegar is to wine compared to my father. For if my father were to eat flesh now, he would not
eat cheese until this very hour tomorrow, whereas I do not eat cheese
(after flesh) in the same meal, but I do eat it at my next meal." (BT.Hullin
104b–105a)

*Maimonides summed up the state of the question as it was understood in the twelfth
century.*

One who has eaten cheese or milk first is permitted to eat meat immediately afterwards, but he must rinse his hands and cleanse his mouth
between the cheese and the meat. With what shall he cleanse his mouth?
With bread or fruit which he chews and swallows or spits out. And the
mouth may be cleaned with all things except dates, flour or vegetables,
for these do not clean well.

With regard to what (sort of) meat are these rules stated? With
regard to the meat of domesticated or wild animals. But if one ate the

meat of fowl after eating cheese or milk, he is not obligated to either cleanse his mouth or wash his hands.

One who had eaten meat first, whether of animals or of fowl, is forbidden to take milk until he has waited (a period) corresponding to the interval of another meal, which is something like six hours, because of the meat between the teeth which was not dislodged in cleaning. (Maimonides, *Mishneh Torah*: "Laws of Prohibited Foods" 9, 26–28)

One of the earliest attempts to order and codify the rabbinic discussions, the Shulhan Aruch *of Joseph Karo (1488–1575 C.E.), sets forth the law this way.*

If one has eaten meat, even of a wild animal or fowl, he may not eat cheese afterwards until he has waited for six hours. And even if he has waited the required period, if there is meat between his teeth, he must dislodge it. One who chews for an infant must also wait.

If one has eaten cheese, he is permitted to eat meat immediately afterwards, so long as he inspects his hands to see that nothing of the cheese has stuck to them. And if it is night, and he cannot inspect them well, he must wash them, and cleanse his mouth and rinse it. The cleaning consists in chewing bread and cleansing his mouth well with it; he may do the same with anything he wishes, except flour, dates or vegetables, since they adhere to the back of the mouth and do not clean well. Afterwards he should wash his mouth with water or wine. What meat is being referred to here? The flesh of domesticated or wild animals. But if one chooses to eat fowl after cheese, in that case he need not clean (the mouth) or wash (the hands).

If one has eaten a meat-cooked dish, he is permitted to eat a dairy-cooked dish afterwards, and hand washing between them is optional. But if one decides to eat cheese itself after a meat-cooked dish or meat itself after a dairy-cooked dish, the hands must be washed. (*Shulhan Aruch* Yorei De'ah 89)

Finally, in his Guide of the Perplexed *Maimonides returns to the question of meat cooked in milk and offers an opinion of why it was legislated in the first place.*

As for the prohibition against eating meat (boiled) in milk, it is in my opinion not improbable that—in addition to this being undoubtedly very gross food and very filling—idolatry had something to do with it. Perhaps such food was eaten at one of the ceremonies of their cult or at one of their festivals. A confirmation of this may, in my opinion, be found in the fact that the prohibition against eating meat (boiled) in milk, when it is mentioned for the first two times (in the Bible), occurs near the commandment concerning pilgrimage: "Three times a year. . . ." It is as if it is said, When you go on pilgrimage and enter the House of the Lord your God, do not cook there in the way they used to. According to me this is the most probable view regarding the reason for this prohibition. (Maimonides, *Guide* 3.48) [MAIMONIDES 1963: 599]

28. Jesus and the Dietary Laws

The dietary laws were a lively subject of debate in Jesus' day and milieu, or so it would appear from the frequency with which the Pharisees tested him on various aspects of the question. In at least one place Jesus appears to give the answer direct.

Then Peter said, "Tell us what the parable means?" Jesus answered, "Are you still as dull as the rest? Do you not see that whatever goes in by the mouth passes into the stomach and is discharged into the drain? But what comes out of the mouth has its origins in the heart, and that is what defiles a man. Wicked thoughts, murder, adultery, fornication, theft, perjury, slander—these all proceed from the heart; and these are the things that defile a man; but to eat without first washing his hands, that cannot defile him." (Matthew 15:15–20)

Mark, when he tells the same story, adds by way of editorial comment (7:19): "Thus he [that is, Jesus] declared all foods clean." If Mark did indeed receive his Gospel tradition from Peter (see Chapter 1 above), he may have had a privileged understanding of this text from his source, but only well after the event. Peter, it is clear, did not know that Jesus had declared all foods clean by these words, not at any rate until after Jesus' Ascension, when he had a private vision on the matter.

At Caesarea there was a man named Cornelius, a centurion of the Italian Cohort, as it was called. He was a religious man, and he and his whole family joined in the worship of God. He gave generously to help the Jewish people, and was regular in his prayers to God. One day about three in the afternoon he had a vision in which he clearly saw an angel of God, who came into his room and said, "Cornelius!" He stared at him in terror. "What is it, my lord?" he asked. The angel said, "Your prayers and acts of charity have gone up to heaven to speak for you before God. And now send you to Joppa for a man named Simon, also called Peter; he is lodging with another Simon, a tanner whose house is by the sea." So when the angel who was speaking with him had gone, he summoned two of his servants and a military orderly who was a religious man, told them the whole story and sent them to Joppa.

Next day, while they were still on their way and approaching the city, about noon Peter went up on the roof to pray. He grew hungry and wanted something to eat. While they were getting it ready, he fell into a trance. He saw a rift in the sky and a thing coming down that looked like a great sheet of sail cloth. It was slung by the four corners and was being lowered to the ground. In it he saw creatures of every kind, whatever walks or crawls or flies. Then there was a voice which said to him, "Up, Peter, kill and eat." But Peter said, "No, Lord, no: I have never eaten anything profane or unclean." The voice came again a second time: "It is not for you to call profane what God counts clean." This happened three times; and then the thing was taken up again into the sky. (Acts 10:1–16)

The climax, and perhaps the point of this story, occurs somewhat later in Acts, when the authorities of the nascent Church in Jerusalem are asked to rule on the matter of Gentile membership in their fellowship. Should such new believers in the Messiahship of Jesus—men and women who neither knew nor observed Jewish circumcision or Jewish dietary restrictions—be admitted to baptism and community membership? Peter cited his experience, and then James, "the brother of the Lord," spoke for all.

It is the decision of the Holy Spirit, and our decision, to lay no further burden on you beyond these essentials: you are to abstain from meat that has been offered to idols, from blood, from anything that has been strangled, and from fornication. If you keep yourselves free from these things, you will be doing right. (Acts 15:28–29)

29. Clean and Unclean in the Christian Conscience

James' ruling was apparently a decision without a sequel. Paul never refers to it in his letters, and the Gentile Christians seem not to have concerned themselves with the issue of Jewish dietary restrictions thereafter. But they were of concern to some, the Jewish Christians, for example, who still had to resolve for themselves the dietary issue and the larger question of the prescriptions of the Mosaic Law. We have already seen one method of dealing with the Law in Christian circles, through an allegorizing exegesis, in the so-called Letter of Barnabas, which presents a remarkable specimen of the technique precisely as applied to the dietary code in Leviticus. Then the appropriate conclusion is drawn.

In these dietary laws, then, Moses was taking three moral maxims and expounding them spiritually; though the Jews, with their carnal instincts, took him to be referring literally to foodstuffs. . . . Moses did say, however, that "you may eat anything that has cloven hoofs and chews the cud" (Lev. 11:3). Why does he say this? Because when a creature of that

kind is given provender, it shows its recognition of the giver and takes evident pleasure in him while refreshing itself. So Moses, contemplating what the Lord required, gave it this apt turn of expression. For what these words of his mean is "seek the company of men who fear the Lord; who muse in their hearts on the purport of every word they have received; who receive the statutes of the Lord on their lips and observe them; who know that meditation is a delight; who do in fact 'chew the cud' of the Lord's word." And the "cloven hoof"? That means that a good man is at one and the same time walking in this present world and also anticipating the holiness of eternity. So you see what a master of lawgiving Moses was. His own people did not see or understand these things— how could they?—but we understand his directions rightly, and interpret them as the Lord intended. Indeed, it was to aid our comprehension of them that He "circumcised" our ears and hearts. (*Letter of Barnabas* 10)
[STANIFORTH 1968: 208]

By his allegorical method the author of the Letter of Barnabas *has helped free the Christian from the literal observance of the Law while maintaining the validity of the Mosaic revelation. His moralizing treatment of Leviticus 11 had a long afterlife in the Christian tradition. What is odder to note, however, is the persistence of the older Mosaic tradition of clean and unclean foods.*

Adamnan (ca. 621–704 C.E.) was a potent figure in the establishment of Christianity in Scotland and Ireland in the seventh century. The following canons or disciplinary statutes were passed by one of the Irish church councils of that era and then circulated under his name. Their concern with purity and contamination is little different from that of the Jews.

1. Marine animals cast upon shores, the nature of whose death we do not know, are to be taken for food in good faith, unless they are decomposed.

2. Cattle that fall from a rock, if their blood has been shed, are to be taken; if not, but if their bones and their blood has not come out, they are to be rejected as if they were carrion.

3. Animals that have died in the water are carrion since their blood remains within them. . . .

14. Things that are drowned in water are not to be eaten, since the Lord has prohibited the eating of flesh that contains blood (Lev. 17:10–14; Deut. 12:16, 12:23) for in the flesh of an animal drowned in water the blood remains coagulated. This the Lord prohibits, not because in those days men ate raw flesh, since it would be none too sweet, but because they had been eating drowned and carrion flesh. And the Law written in

metrical fashion says, "Thou shalt not eat carrion flesh" (cf. Lev. 5:2, 17:15).

30. The Quran and the Prophet on Dietary Laws

The matter of clean and unclean foods that was being discussed in Ireland in the seventh century was also the subject of pronouncements, much to the same end, in Arabia of the same era.

Forbidden to you (for food) is carrion and blood and the flesh of the swine, and whatsoever has been killed in the name of some other God, and whatever has been strangled, or killed by a blow or a fall, or a goring, or that which has been mauled by wild beasts, unless slaughtered while still alive; and that which has been slaughtered at altars is forbidden. . . . If one of you is driven by hunger (to eat the forbidden), without the evil intent of sinning, then God is forgiving and kind.

They ask you (Muhammad), what is lawful for them. Say: "All things are lawful for you that are clean, and what the trained hunting animals take for you, as you have trained them in the light of God's teachings, but read over them the name of God, and fear God, for God is swift in the reckoning." (Quran 5:3–4)

There are as well a great many Prophetic traditions on the subject.

Abu Thaʿalaba al-Kushani reported that he said: "Prophet of God, we are in a land belonging to folk who are People of the Book, so may we eat out of their vessels? In a hunting region I hunt with my bow, my dog which is trained and my dog which is not trained, so what is right for me?" Muhammad replied: "Regarding what you have mentioned about the vessels of the People of the Book, if you can get anything else, do not eat out of them; but if you cannot, wash them and eat out of them. Eat what you have hunted with your bow when you have mentioned God's name; eat what you have caught with your trained dog when you have mentioned God's name; eat what you have caught by your untrained dog (only) when you are present at the kill." This tradition was transmitted by Bukhari and Muslim. (Baghawi, *Mishkat al-Masabih* 19.1.1)

Abu Hurayra reported God's Messenger as saying: "Eating any fanged beast of prey is prohibited." Muslim transmitted this tradition.

Ibn Abbas said God's Messenger prohibited every beast of prey with a fang and every bird with a talon. Bukhari and Muslim have transmitted this tradition.

Jabir said that on the day of Khaybar God's Messenger forbade the flesh of domestic asses but permitted horseflesh. Bukhari and Muslim have transmitted this tradition. (Ibid. 19.3.1)

There are also, typically, traditions on the etiquette of eating.

Ibn Umar reported God's Messenger as saying: "When any of you eats, he should eat with his right hand, and when he drinks, he should drink with his right hand." Muslim transmitted this tradition.

He (also) reported God's Messenger as saying: "None of you must ever eat or drink with his left hand, for the devil eats and drinks with his left hand." Muslim transmitted this tradition. (Ibid. 20.1.1)

There was little debate on the general thrust of these Quranic verses and Prophetic traditions. One had to descend to a much lower level of specificity to encounter the "controversial questions." The Quran, for example, includes these verses.

O believers, eat what is good of the food We have given you, and be grateful to God, if indeed you are obedient to Him. Forbidden to you are carrion and blood, and the flesh of swine, and that which has been consecrated [or killed] in the name of any other god. If one is obliged by necessity to eat it without intending to transgress, or reverting to it, he is not guilty of sin; for God is forgiving and kind. (Quran 2:172–173)

No one was likely to commend the eating of swine in the light of such scriptural testimony, but there did arise certain secondary issues, which appear in Razi's Quran commentary.

As to swine, there are certain complex questions. The community is in agreement that all parts of the swine are forbidden. God here refers to the flesh (and not the other parts) of the swine since the chief use (of the swine) has to do with its flesh. This manner of speaking is similar to the words of God: "O believers, when proclamation is made for prayer on the day of assembly [that is, Friday], hasten to the recollection of God and leave off your bargaining" (Sura 62:9), where God specifically forbade bargaining because it represented the main occupation of the people. Thus, though the bristles of the swine are not included in the precise wording (in this verse), they (too) are unanimously regarded as forbidden and impure. There is, however, a difference of opinion concerning whether one may use them in sewing. Abu Hanifa and Muhammad al-Shaybani consider it permissible, while al-Shafi'i does not. Abu Yusuf said, "I regard sewing with swine bristles as objectionable"; but it is also related (elsewhere) that he regarded it as permissible. The arguments of Abu Hanifa and Muhammad al-Shaybani are as follows. We note that the use of swine bristles is conceded to the shoemakers among the Muslims and is not explicitly condemned. There (even) exists an urgent necessity for it. When al-Shafi'i says that the blood of fleas does not contaminate the clothing because it is difficult to protect oneself from it, why then, by the same reasoning, are not swine bristles permissible since one sews with them? (Razi, *Great Commentary*, *ad loc.*)

31. "What I Tell You Is This"

Whether or not Peter had simply failed to understand his master's teachings on the matter of the dietary laws, Jesus certainly had no hesitation about revising, expanding, or, in the case of divorce, abrogating Torah prescriptions, and in his own name.

You have learned that they were told, "Do not commit adultery." But what I tell you is this: If a man looks upon a woman with a lustful eye, he has already committed adultery in his heart. (Matthew 5:27–28)

Again, you have learned that our forefathers were told, "Do not break your oath," and, "Oaths sworn to the Lord must be kept." But what I tell you is this: You are not to swear at all—not by heaven, for it is God's throne, nor by earth, for it is His footstool, nor by Jerusalem, for it is the city of the great King, nor by your own head, because you cannot turn one hair on it white or black. Plain "Yes" or "No" is all you need to say; anything beyond that comes from the devil. (Matthew 5:33–37)

You have learned that they were told, "Eye for eye, tooth for tooth." But what I tell you is this: Do not set yourself against the man who wrongs you. If someone slaps you on the right cheek, turn and offer him your left. If a man wants to sue you for your shirt, let him have your coat as well. If a man in authority makes you go one mile, go with him two. Give when you are asked to give; and do not turn your back on a man who wants to borrow. (Matthew 5:38–42)

You have learned that they were told, "Love your neighbor, hate your enemy." But what I tell you is this: Love your enemies and pray for your prosecutors, only so can you be children of your heavenly Father, who makes His sun rise on good and bad alike and sends the rain on the honest and the dishonest. If you love only those who love you, what reward can you expect? Surely the tax gatherers do as much as that. And if you greet only your brothers, what is there extraordinary in that? Even the heathen do as much. There must be no limit to your goodness, as your heavenly Father's goodness knows no bounds. (Matthew 5:43–48)

32. Contract or Sacrament: The Case of Divorce

One instance where Jesus clearly separated himself from the Torah tradition was in the matter of divorce, and that issue provides an opportunity for comparing the three religious traditions on a single point of religious law. The classical biblical text on the subject occurs in Deuteronomy, where the law is not stated as a general prescription on the grounds or manner of divorce but rather as the solution of a rather involved case of divorce and remarriage and a contemplated third marriage to the original spouse.

A man takes a wife and possesses her. She fails to please him because he finds something obnoxious [or "indecent"] about her, and he writes her a bill of divorcement, hands it to her, and sends her away from his house; (let us suppose) she leaves his household and becomes the wife of another man; then this latter man (also) rejects her, writes her a bill of divorcement, hands it to her and sends her away from his house; or it may be the man who married her last dies. (Whatever the case) the first husband who divorced her shall not take her to wife again, since she has been defiled (for him)—for that would be abhorrent to the Lord. You must not bring sin upon the land which the Lord your God has given you as a heritage. (Deuteronomy 24:1–4)

The issue of divorce arises in Matthew's Gospel—again not so much as a matter of principle as a detached correction of Torah law amidst a number of "but what I tell you . . ." instructions.

They [that is, the Israelites] were told, "A man who divorces his wife must give her a note of dismissal." But what I tell you is this: If a man divorces his wife for any cause other than unchastity, he involves her in adultery, and anyone who marries a divorced woman commits adultery. (Matthew 5:31–32)

Later, however, the more general question of the grounds for divorce is put to Jesus, why or under what circumstances we do not know, except that it was to test him.

Some Pharisees came and tested him [that is, Jesus] by asking, "Is it lawful for a man to divorce his wife on any and every ground?" He asked in return, "Have you never read that the Creator made them from the beginning male and female?" And he added, "For this reason a man shall leave his father and mother, and the two shall become one flesh. It follows that they are no longer two individuals: they are one flesh. What God has joined together, man must not separate." "Why then," they objected, "did Moses lay it down that a man might divorce his wife by note of dismissal?" He answered, "It was because your minds were closed that Moses gave you permission to divorce your wives; but it was not like that when all began. I tell you, if a man divorces his wife for any cause other than unchastity, and marries another, he commits adultery." (Matthew 19:3–9)

The "note of dismissal" (in Hebrew get; *pl.* gittin) *is the subject of an entire tractate in the Mishna, most of which is devoted to the circumstances governing the validity of such a document.*

The essential formula in the bill of divorce is, "Behold, you are free to marry any man." Rabbi Judah says (that it is): "Let this be from me your writ of divorce and letter of dismissal and deed of liberation, that you may be free to marry whomsoever you will." (M.Gittin 9:3)

If a man throws a bill of divorce to his wife while she is within her house or her courtyard, she is divorced. But if he throws it to her while she is in his house or his courtyard, even though he is with her in bed, she is not divorced; but if he throws it into her bosom or her basket, she is divorced. (Ibid. 8:1)

A few passages range a little more widely and touch briefly upon some of the grounds for the action.

If a man put away his wife because of her evil reputation, he may not take her back; and if because of a vow [see M.Ketuboth 7:1ff.], he may not take her back. . . . If a man put away his wife because she was barren, Rabbi Judah says: He may not take her back. But the Sages say: He may take her back. (Ibid. 4:7–8)

In this passage all the differing interpretations of the grounds for divorce rely on exactly the same verse, Deuteronomy 24:1.

The School of Shammai say: A man may not divorce his wife unless he found unchastity in her, for it is written [in Deut. 24:1], "because he has found in her indecency in anything." And the School of Hillel say: He may divorce her even if she spoiled a dish for him, for it is written, "because he has found in her indecency in anything." Rabbi Akiba says: He may divorce her even if he found another fairer than she, for it is written [in the same passage], "she does not win his favor." (Ibid. 9:10)

Some grounds for divorce are so grave that they preclude the return of the property given in the woman's dowry:

These are they who are put away without their marriage settlement: a wife that transgresses the Law of Moses and Jewish custom. What constitutes a transgression of the Law of Moses? If a wife gives her husband untithed food [Num. 18:21ff.], or has intercourse with him while she is unclean [Lev. 18:19], or does not set apart dough offering [Num. 15:18], or utters a vow and does not fulfill it [Deut. 23:21]. And what constitutes a transgression of Jewish custom? If she goes out with her hair unbound, or spins in the street, or speaks with any man. Abba Saul says: Also if she is a scold. And who is deemed a scold? Whoever speaks inside her house and can be heard by her neighbors. (M.Ketuboth 7:6)

Although this text appears to recognize the distinction between religious grounds for divorce ("transgression of the Law of Moses") and more personal and secular reasons (incompatibility, "transgression of Jewish custom"), Jewish thinking about marriage and its dissolution remained contractual and its primary concerns were with validity and equity. Jesus moved it onto other ground by referring its institution in effect to God Himself, but it was Paul above all who shaped Christian thinking about marriage and provided the theological ground that made divorce unthinkable. For the Christian, marriage was eventually formalized as a sacrament, an outward sign that brought divine grace (see Chapter 5 below). This passage in Paul's letter to the Ephesians is crucial in that evolution.

Husbands, love your wives as Christ also loved the Church and gave himself up for it, to consecrate it, cleansing it by water and word, so that he might present the Church to himself all glorious, with no stain or wrinkle or anything of the sort, but holy and without blemish. In the same way men also are bound to love their wives, as they love their own bodies. In loving his wife, a man loves himself. For no one ever hated his own body: on the contrary, he provides and cares for it; and that is how Christ treats the Church, because it is his body, of which we are living parts. Thus it is that, in the words of Scripture, "a man shall leave his father and mother and shall be joined to his wife, and the two shall become one flesh." It is a great truth that is hidden here. I for my part refer it to Christ and to the Church, but it applies also individually; each of you must love his wife as his very self, and the wife must see to it that she pays her husband all respect. (Paul, *To the Ephesians* 5:25–33)

The Pauline view must soon have become standard. Ignatius of Antioch (d. 107 C.E.) counseled that "bridegrooms and brides ought to be married with the recognition of the bishop so that the marriage takes place according to the Lord and not according to lust" (To Polycarp 5:1). By the time Augustine came to write On Marriage and Concupiscence *in 419 C.E., Jesus' remarks on marriage had been joined to his presence at the marriage feast at Cana (John 2:1–11), and both connected with Paul's reflections in his letter to the Ephesians.*

Since it is not only fecundity, whose fruit is in offspring, nor only modesty, whose restraint is faith, but also a kind of sacrament of matrimony is commended to the married faithful, so that the Apostle says, "Husbands, love your wives, just as Christ loved the Church." There is no doubt that this is indeed a sacrament, that a man and woman united in marriage remain together inseparably for as long as they live, nor can one spouse rid himself of the other, except in cases of fornication. . . . If someone should do this [that is, get a divorce], he is not breaking the laws of this age, where divorce and remarriage are permitted, which the Lord testified that holy Moses granted to the Israelites because of the hardness of their hearts, but rather he is guilty, according to the law of the Gospel, of adultery, just as is his wife, if she marries another. . . . There remains something conjugal between those partners as long as they live, which neither separation nor intercourse with others can delete.

In marriages the nuptial goods are cherished: offspring, faith, the sacrament. But not merely that a child should be born, but that he should be reborn, for he is born simply for punishment if he is not reborn to life. And faith, not of the type that the unbelievers possess in their appetite for the flesh. . . . And the sacrament, which they do not lose by separation and adultery but preserve as spouses in concord and chastity. (Augustine, *On Marriage and Concupiscence* 1.10.17)

Augustine's remark on "the laws of this age" acknowledge the presence of another legal system with which the Christians of the Gentile world had to cope: the Roman divorce laws. According to Jewish law, only the man could initiate divorce. Jesus too had spoken of a man's being prohibited from divorcing his wife and so presumably, as Mark 10:12 seems to add, of a wife's being prohibited from divorcing her husband. Roman law, on the other hand, permitted either spouse to divorce the other. Jerome (d. 419 C.E.) took up the Roman notion of the equality of the sexes before the civil law and extended it more broadly into the moral law.

The Lord has commanded that a wife should not be put away except for fornication; and that when she has been put away [that is, divorced], she ought to remain unmarried. Whatever is given as a commandment to men logically applies to women also. For it cannot be that while an adulterous wife is divorced, an incontinent husband must be kept. . . . The laws of Caesar are different, it is true, from the laws of Christ; Papinian [the Roman jurist] commands one thing, our Paul another. Among the Romans the (marriage) bonds are loosed in the case of immodesty on the part of men. But with us, what is unlawful for women is also unlawful for men, and both are bound by the same conditions of service. (Jerome, *Letter 78*)

33. Divorce in Islamic Law

Like the Jewish tradition, Muslim law recognized without debate the possibility of dissolving a marriage contract and devoted most of its attention to regulating and defining the grounds for such action—how it was to be performed in a valid fashion, and what were its legal consequences. Of these latter, it was the establishment of paternity after the divorce and the conditions of the marriage settlement that attracted the most concern. The Quran is already quite detailed on the matter.

Those who swear to keep away from their wives (with intent to divorce) have four months of grace; then if they reconcile (during this period), surely God is forgiving and kind. And if they are bent on divorce, God hears all and knows everything. (Quran 2:226–227)

If the husband's waiting period is intended to prevent rash or hasty action, that prescribed for the wife is to ensure that, if she is pregnant, the father will be established.

Women who are divorced have to wait for three monthly periods, and if they believe in God and the Last Day, they must not hide unlawfully what God has formed within their wombs. Their husbands would do well to take them back in that period, if they wish to be reconciled. Women also have recognized rights as men have, though men are over them in rank. But God is all-mighty and all-wise.

Divorce must be pronounced twice, and then a woman must either be retained in honor or released in kindness. And it is not lawful for you [that is, the husbands] to take anything of what you have given them. . . .

Divorce is (still revokable) after two pronouncements, after which they must either keep them [that is, the men's wives] honorably or part with them in a decent way. You are not allowed to take away the least (part) of what you have given your wives, unless both of you fear that you would not be able to keep within the limits set by God. . . .

If a man pronounces divorce again [that is, for the third time], she becomes unlawful for him (for remarriage) until she has married another man. Then if this latter divorces her, there is no harm if the (original) pair unite again if they think they will keep within the bounds set by God and made clear for those who understand.

When you have divorced your wives, and they have reached the end of the period of waiting, then either keep them honorably or let them go with honor, and do not detain them with the intent of harassing lest you should transgress. (Quran 2:228–231)

What seems to be chiefly envisioned here is the restraint of the financial manipulation of women, perhaps through prolonging the procedure of pronouncing the triple formula of divorce, since only the husband could initiate the divorce, or even of coercing the women to buy themselves out of the contract. A number of Prophetic traditions show other sides of the intent and process of divorce in Islam.

Thawban reported God's Messenger as saying, "If any woman asks her husband to divorce her without some very good reason, the odor of Paradise will be forbidden her."

Ibn Umar reported the Prophet as saying, "The lawful thing which God hates most is divorce."

Abu Hurayra reported God's Messenger as saying, "There are three things which, whether undertaken seriously or lightly, are treated seriously: marriage, divorce, and taking back a wife before a divorce is final."

On the triple repetition of the divorce formula, which was obviously not intended to be done on a single occasion, Prophetic tradition relates the following.

Mahmud ibn Labib told that when God's Messenger was informed about a man who divorced his wife by declaring it three times without any interval between them, he arose in anger and said, "Is sport being made of the Book of God Who is great and glorious even while I am among you?" At that a man got up and said, "Messenger of God, shall I kill him?" (Baghawi, *Mishkat al-Masabih* 12.12.3)

5. The New Covenants

1. Jesus as the Fulfillment of the Law

As we have seen in the previous chapter, Matthew's Gospel presents a number of dicta whereby Jesus appears to be modifying or even abrogating the Mosaic Law. They are preceded, moreover, by Jesus' own most sweeping statement of the connection between his Messianic mission and the Mosaic Law.

Do not suppose that I have come to abolish the Law and the prophets. I did not come to abolish but to complete. I tell you this: so long as heaven and earth endure, not a letter, not a stroke will disappear from the Law until all that must happen has happened. If any man therefore sets aside the least of God's commandments and teaches others to do the same, he will have the lowest place in the kingdom of heaven, whereas anyone who keeps the Law and teaches others so, will stand high in the kingdom of Heaven. I tell you, unless you show yourselves far better men than the Pharisees and the doctors of the Law, you cannot enter the kingdom of heaven. (Matthew 5:17–20)

The fully developed Christian tradition, if it struggled to understand other implications of this passage, had no difficulty with the notion that Jesus was himself the fulfillment and perfection of the Mosaic Law.

Now Christ fulfilled the precepts of the Old Law both in his works and in his teaching. In his works, because he was willing to be circumcised and to fulfill the other legal observances which were binding for the time being. . . . In his teaching he fulfilled the precepts of the Law in three ways. First, by explaining the true sense of the Law. This is clear in the case of murder and adultery, the prohibition of which the Scribes and Pharisees thought to refer only to the exterior act; and so our Lord fulfilled the Law by showing that the prohibition extended also to the interior acts of sin. Secondly, our Lord fulfilled the precepts of the Law by prescribing the safest way to comply with the statutes of the Old Law.

Thus the Old Law forbade perjury, and this is more safely avoided by abstaining altogether from swearing, save in cases of urgency. Thirdly, our Lord fulfilled the precepts of the Law by adding some counsels of perfection, and this is clearly seen in Matthew 19:21, where our Lord said to the man who affirmed that he had kept all the precepts of the Old Law: "One thing is lacking to you: if you will be perfect, go, sell whatever you have and give to the poor, and then you will have riches in heaven; and come, follow me." (Aquinas, *Summa Theologica* I/2, ques. 107, art. 2) [AQUINAS 1945: 2:961]

2. Paul on Torah, Sin, and Redemption

Aquinas in the thirteenth Christian century is at ease with this critical Gospel text on the connection of Jesus and the Law. By then, the separation between Jews and Christians had long since been absolute. But in the days immediately following the death of Jesus, when the community of his followers was made up entirely of Jews, the issue was quite different. It was Paul, in the forefront of the mission to the Gentiles, who attempted to work out the theology of the new relationship between belief in Jesus and the Law of Moses.

It was through one man that sin entered the world, and through sin, death; and thus death pervaded the whole human race, inasmuch as all men have sinned. For sin was already in the world before there was Law, though in the absence of Law no reckoning is kept of sin. But death held sway from Adam to Moses, even over those who had not sinned as Adam did, by disobeying a direct command—and Adam foreshadows the Man who was to come.

But God's act of grace is out of all proportion to Adam's wrongdoing. For if the wrongdoing of that one man brought death upon so many, its effect is vastly exceeded by the grace of God and the gift that came to so many by the grace of one man, Jesus Christ. . . .

It follows, then, that as the issue of one misdeed was condemnation for all men, so the issue of one just act is acquittal and life for all men. For as through the disobedience of one man the many were made sinners, so through the obedience of one man the many will be made righteous.

Law intruded into this process to multiply lawbreaking. But where sin was thus multiplied, grace immeasurably exceeded, in order that, as sin established its reign by way of death, so God's grace might establish its reign in righteousness and issue in eternal life through Jesus Christ our Lord. . . .

For if we have become incorporate with him in a death like his, we shall also be one with him in a resurrection like his. We know that the man we once were was crucified with Christ for the destruction of the sinful self, so that we may no longer be the slaves of sin, since a dead man is no longer answerable for his sin. But if we thus died with Christ, we also believe that we shall come to life with him. We know that Christ, once raised from the dead, is never to die again; he is no longer under the dominion of death. For in dying as he died, he died to sin, once for all, and in living as he lives, he lives in God. In the same way you must regard yourselves as dead to sin and alive to God, in union with Christ Jesus. . . .

You cannot be unaware, my friends—I am speaking to those who have some knowledge of law—that a person is subject to the law so long as he is alive and no longer. For example, a married woman is by law bound to her husband while he lives; but if he dies, she is discharged from the obligations of the marriage law. . . . So you, my friends, have died to the Law by becoming identified with the body of Christ and accordingly you have found another husband in him who rose from the dead, so that we may bear fruit for God. While we lived on the level of our lower nature, the sinful passions evoked by the Law worked in our bodies, to bear fruit for death. But now, having died to that which held us bound, we are discharged from the Law, to serve God in a new way, the way of the spirit, in contrast to the old way, the way of a written code.

What follows? Is the Law identical with sin? Of course not. But except through Law I would never have become acquainted with sin. For example, I should never have known what it was to covet, if the Law had not said, "Thou shall not covet." Through that commandment sin found its opportunity, and produced in me all kinds of wrong desires. In the absence of Law, sin is dead thing. There was a time when, in the absence of Law, I was fully alive; but when the commandment came, sin sprang to life and I died. The commandment which should have lead to life proved in my experience to lead to death, because sin found its opportunity in the commandment, seduced me, and through the commandment killed me.

Therefore the Law is in itself holy, and the commandment is holy and just and good. Are we to say then that this good thing was death to me? By no means. It was sin that killed me, and thereby sin exposed its true character: it used a good thing to bring about my death, and so, through the commandment, sin became more sinful than ever.

We know that the Law is spiritual; but I am not: I am unspiritual, the purchased slave of sin. I do not ever acknowledge my own actions as mine, for what I do is not what I want to do, but what I detest. But if what I do is against my will, it means that I agree with the Law and hold it admirable. But as things are, it is no longer I who perform the action, but the sin that lodges in me. For I know that nothing good lodges in me—in my unspiritual nature, I mean—for the will to do good is there, the deed is not. The good which I want to do, I fail to do; but what I do is the evil which is against my will; and if what I do is against my will, clearly it is no longer I who am the agent, but sin has made its lodging in me.

I discover this principle, then: that when I want to do the right, only the wrong is within my reach. In my inmost self I delight in the Law of God, but I perceive that there is in my bodily members a different law, fighting against the Law that my reason approves and making me a prisoner under the law that is in my members, the law of sin. Miserable creature that I am, who is there to rescue me out of this body doomed to death? God alone, through Jesus Christ our Lord! Thanks be to God! In a word, then, I myself, subject to God's Law as a rational being, am yet, in my unspiritual nature, a slave to the law of sin.

The conclusion of the matter is this: there is no condemnation for those who are united with Christ Jesus, because in Christ Jesus the life-giving law of the spirit has set you free from the law of sin and death. What the Law could never do, because our lower nature had robbed it of its potency, God has done: by sending his own Son in a form like that of our own sinful nature, and as a sacrifice for sin, He has passed judgment against sin within that very nature, so that the commandment of the Law might find fulfillment in us, whose conduct, no longer under the control of our lower nature, is directed by the Spirit. (Paul, *To the Romans* 5:12–8:4)

The same issue is addressed more succinctly in Paul's letter to the Galatians.

You may take it, then, that it is the men of faith who are Abraham's sons. And Scripture, foreseeing that God would justify the Gentiles through faith, declared the Gospel to Abraham beforehand: "In you all nations shall find blessing." Thus it is the men of faith who share the blessing with faithful Abraham.

On the other hand, those who rely on obedience to the Law are under a curse, for Scripture says: "A curse is on all who do not persevere in doing everything that is written in the Book of the Law" (Deut. 27:26).

It is evident that no one is ever justified before God in terms of the Law; because we read "he shall gain life who is justifid through faith" (Hab. 2:4). Now Law is not at all a matter of having faith: we read, "he who does this shall gain life by what he does" (Lev. 18:5).

Christ brought us freedom from the curse of the Law by becoming for our sake an accursed thing; for Scripture says, "A curse is on everyone who is hanged on a gibbet" (Deut. 21:23). And the purpose of it all was that the blessing of Abraham should in Jesus Christ be extended to the Gentiles, so that we might receive the promised Spirit through faith. . . .

Does the Law then contradict the promises? No, never! If a law had been given which had power to bestow life, then indeed righteousness would have come from keeping the Law. But Scripture has declared the whole world to be prisoners in subjection to sin, so that faith in Jesus Christ may be the ground in which the promised blessing is given, and given to those who have such faith.

Before this faith came, we were close prisoners in the custody of the Law, pending the revelation of faith. Thus the Law was a kind of tutor in charge of us until Christ should come when we should be justified through faith; and now that faith has come, the tutor's charge is at an end. (Paul, *To the Galatians* 3:7–25)

We return, finally, to Aquinas.

The end of every law is to make men just and virtuous. Consequently, the end of the Old Law was the justification of men. The Law, however, could not accomplish this, but foreshadowed it by certain ceremonial actions and promised it in words. And in this respect the New Law fulfills the Old by justifying men through the power of Christ's Passion. This is what the Apostle (Paul) says: "What the Law could not do . . . God sending His own Son in the likeness of the sinful flesh . . . has condemned sin in the flesh, that the justification of the Law might be fulfilled in us" (Rom. 8:3–4). And in this respect the New Law gives what the Old Law promised, according to 2 Cor. 1:20: "He," that is, Christ, "is the Yes pronounced upon God's promises, every one of them." Again, in this respect is also fulfilled what the Old Law foreshadowed. Hence it is written concerning the ceremonial precepts that they were "a shadow of things to come, but the body is of Christ" (Col. 2:17); in other words, the reality is found in Christ. Therefore the New Law is called the law of reality, whereas the Old Law is called the law of shadow or of figure. (Aquinas, *Summa Theologica* I/2, ques. 107, art. 2) [AQUINAS 1945: 2:961]

3. The Rabbis on Justification through the Law

If Paul had serious doubts whether anyone could be justified by Torah Law, no matter how carefully observed, the rabbis had no hesitation on the subject. Their chain of reflections takes its starting point from this text in the Mishna.

Anyone who fills one *mitzvah* [that is, a commandment of the Law], God benefits him and lengthens his days and he inherits the land. And everyone who does not fulfill one *mitzvah*, it shall be ill with him and he shall not have length of days and he shall not inherit the land. (M.Kiddushin 1:10)

This is a minimum-maximum case; but in their commentaries on the passage, the Sages broadened the discussion.

About this it is written, "One sinner destroys much good" (Eccles. 9:18). A man should always regard himself as half innocent and half guilty: if he performs one *mitzvah*, happy is he for weighing himself down in the scale of innocence; if he commits one transgression, woe to him for weighing himself down in the scale of guilt. About this one it was written, "One sinner destroys much good." Because of a single sin which he committed, much good is lost to him. Rabbi Simeon ben Eleazer said: Since the individual is judged according to the majority (of his deeds, good and bad), and the world is judged according to its majority, a man should always regard himself as half innocent and half guilty. (Tosefta Kiddushin 1:10)

And in the Jerusalem Talmud:

Ben Azzai gave an interpretation of this verse: "Dead flies makes the perfumer's ointment give off an evil odor" (Eccles. 10:1). One deduces from the use of the singular verb [though the subject is plural] that just as a single fly may infect the perfumer's ointment, so the man who commits only one sin loses thus the merit of his good works. Rabbi Akiba gave an interpretation of this verse: "Therefore Sheol has enlarged its appetite and opened its mouth beyond measure" (Isa. 5:14). It is not written here "beyond measures" but "beyond measure." (It refers to) whoever does not have one *mitzvah* which can prove in his favor (and so make the scales incline) to the side of innocence. This he said with regard to the world to come. But in this world, if even 999 angels declare him guilty and one angel declares him innocent, the Holy One, blessed be He, inclines (the scale) to the side of innocence. (JT.Kiddushin 61d)

4. "The Laws of the Torah Shall Never Be Abrogated"

There is no sign in the passage just cited that the rabbis were arguing, however indirectly, against some Pauline theory of redemption. But when the Jewish theologian Saadya wrote, in Arabic, his Book of Doctrines and Beliefs *in 933 C.E., he was confronted with two distinct and prevalent claims that the Torah had been abrogated—one by the Christians, as we have seen, and another advanced by Islam, in whose very bosom Saadya lived and worked. The issue must have been very much on his mind in the mixed and catholic society of tenth-century Baghdad.*

Having dealt with these matters (of Scripture and tradition), I deem it right to add to my remarks a word on the abrogation of the Law, since this seems to be the place for it. I declare that the Children of Israel, according to an accepted tradition, were told by the Prophets that the laws of the Torah shall never be abrogated. They assert that they heard this in clear terms which allowed no room for misunderstanding or allegorical interpretation. I therefore searched in the Scriptures and found support for this tradition. First, in regard to most of the laws it is written that they are "a covenant forever" and "for your generation." There is, furthermore, a phrase which occurs in the Torah, "Moses commanded us a law, an inheritance of the congregation of Jacob" (Deut. 33:4). Moreover, our people, the Children of Israel, are a people only by virtue of our laws, and since the Creator has declared that our people should exist as long as heaven and earth exist, it necessarily follows that our Law should continue to exist as long as heaven and earth are in being, and this is what He says: "Thus says the Lord . . . if these ordinances depart from before Me, then the seed of Israel also shall cease from being a nation before me forever" (Jer. 31:36).

I found that in the last period of prophecy God exhorted His people that they should keep the Law of Moses until the Day of Judgment, which will be preceded by the advent of Elijah. He says, "Remember the Law of Moses, My servant, which I commanded to him in Horeb for all of Israel, even statutes and ordinances. Behold, I will send you Elijah the prophet before the coming of the great and terrible Day of the Lord" (Mal. 3:22–23).

Then, perhaps with an eye toward the Christians and Muslims, Saadya continues.

Some people say that in the same way as the reason for believing in Moses was his performance of wonders and miracles, so it follows that the reason for believing in some other prophet would be the performance of wonders and miracles by the latter. I was greatly astonished when I heard this remark. For the reason for our belief in Moses lies not in the wonders and miracles only, but the reason for our belief in him and all other prophets lies in the fact that they admonished us in the first place to do what was right, and only after we had heard the prophet's message and found it was right did we ask him to produce miracles in support of it. If he performed them, we believed in him. But if we hear his call and find it, at the outset, wrong, we do not ask him for miracles, for no miracle can demonstrate the impossible. . . .

So it is with anyone who claims to be a prophet. If he tells us, "My Lord commands you to fast today," we ask him for a sign of his prophecy, and if we see it, we believe it and shall fast. But if he says, "My Lord commands you to commit adultery and steal," or, "He announces to you that He will flood the world again," or, "He informs you that He created heaven and earth (literally) in one year," we shall not ask him for a sign because he brings us a message which neither reason nor tradition can sanction. (Saadya, *Book of Doctrines and Beliefs* 3.6) [SAADYA 1945: 111–114]

5. Augustine on Symbol and Reality in the Law

Augustine too wrote on the question of reality and the Law, though in a different context than Aquinas. In On Christian Instruction, *Augustine's remarks flow from his general linguistic, or better rhetorical, theory of sign and thing, of symbol and reality, which he was in the course of applying to the interpretation of Scripture (see Chapter 2 above). For him the Old Testament was symbol, a visible or "carnal" sign of the spiritual reality of the New. To mistake one for the other was to suffer bondage to a sign, a condition shared by both the Jews and the pagans. But the "slavery" of the Old Testament permitted certain nuances.*

He who produces or worships any symbol, unaware of what it means, is enslaved to a sign. On the other hand, he who either uses or esteems a beneficial sign, divinely established, whose efficacy and meaning he knows, does not worship this visible and transitory sign; he worships rather that reality to which all such symbols must be ascribed. Besides, such a man is spiritual and free even during the period of his slavery, when it is not yet advisable to unveil to his mind, carnal as it is, those signs by whose yoke it is to be completely subdued. Such spiritual men are those who were the patriarchs, prophets and all those among the people of Israel, through whom the Holy Spirit gave us the remedies and comforts of the Scriptures. At present, since the evidence of our freedom has been made so clearly apparent in the Resurrection of the Lord, we are not burdened by the heavy labor of even those signs which we understand now. The Lord himself and the Apostolic tradition have transmitted a few observances instead of many, and these are very easy to fulfill, very venerable in their meaning, and most sublime in practice. Examples of these are Baptism and the celebration of the Body and Blood of the Lord. When anyone who has been instructed observes these practices, he understands to what they refer, so that he does not venerate them in a carnal slavery, but rather in a spiritual liberty. (Augustine, *On Christian Instruction* 3.9) [AUGUSTINE 1947: 128]

6. The Law of Fear and the Law of Love

Aquinas approaches the distinction between the Israelites' "Old Law" and the Christians' "New" from another perspective.

(In one respect) the New Law is not distinct from the Old Law because they both have the same end, namely man's subjection to God; and there is but one God of the New and of the Old Testament, according to Romans 3:30: "It is one God that justifies circumcision by faith and uncircumcision through faith." But from another point of view, the New Law is distinct from the Old Law because the Old Law is like a pedagogue of children, as the Apostle (Paul) says (Gal. 3:24), whereas the New Law is the law of perfection, since it is the law of charity, of which the Apostle says that it is "the bond of perfection" (Col. 3:14). . . .

All the differences assigned between the Old and New Laws are gathered from their relative perfection and imperfection. For the precepts of every law prescribe acts of virtue. Now the imperfect, who as yet are not possessed of the habit of virtue, are directed in one way to perform virtuous acts, while those who are perfected by the possession of virtuous habits are directed in another way. For those who as yet are not endowed with virtuous habits are directed in the performance of virtuous acts by reason of some outward cause, for instance by the threat of punishment or the promise of some extrinsic rewards, such as honor, riches or the like. Hence the Old Law, which was given to men who were imperfect, that is, who had not as yet received spiritual grace, was called the Law of Fear, inasmuch as it induced men to observe its commandments by threatening them with penalties; and it is likewise spoken of as containing temporal promises. On the other hand, those who are possessed of (the habit of) virtue are inclined to do virtuous deeds through love of virtue and not because of some extrinsic punishment or reward. Hence the New Law, which derives its pre-eminence from the spiritual grace instilled into our hearts, is called the Law of Love; and it is described as containing spiritual and eternal promises, which are objects of the virtues, chiefly of charity. Accordingly, such persons are inclined of themselves to these objects, not as to something foreign, but as to something of their own. For this reason, too, the Old Law has been described as restraining the hand, not the will, since when a man refrains from some sins through fear of being punished, his will does not shrink absolutely from sin, as does the will of a man who refrains from sin through love of righteousness. Hence the New Law, which is the Law of Love, is said to restrain the will. (Aquinas, *Summa Theologica* I/2, ques. 107)

[AQUINAS 1945: 2:958–960]

7. When Did the Ceremonial Precepts of the Torah Cease To Be Binding on Christians?

These are general distinctions between the Old Law and the New. Aquinas also takes up here and elsewhere the question of the ceremonial and liturgical prescriptions laid out in such detail in the Torah.

All ceremonies are professions of faith, in which the interior worship of God consists. Now man can make profession of his inward faith by deeds as well as by words; and in either profession [that is, by deeds or words], if he make a false declaration he sins mortally. Now, though our faith in Christ is the same as that of the (biblical) fathers of old, yet, since they came before Christ, whereas we came after him, the same faith is expressed in different words by us and by them. . . . Consequently, just as it would be a mortal sin now for anyone, in making a profession of faith, to say that Christ is yet to be born, which the fathers of old said devoutly and truthfully, so too it would be a mortal sin now to observe those ceremonies which the fathers of old fulfilled with devotion and sincerity. (Aquinas, *Summa Theologica* I/2, ques. 103, art. 4)

[AQUINAS 1945: 2:915]

The argument is apparently simple. But Aquinas had also to address the glaringly obvious example of the first generation of Christians, indeed, of the Apostles themselves, who continued to observe the Mosaic Law. Here the going is more complex.

On this point there seems to have been a difference of opinion between Jerome and Augustine. For Jerome distinguished two periods of time (*Against Faustus* 19.16). One was the time previous to Christ's Passion, during which the legal ceremonies (of the Mosaic Law) were neither dead, since they were obligatory and did expiate in their own fashion; nor deadly, since it was not sinful to observe them. But immediately after Christ's Passion they began to be not only dead, so as no longer to be either effectual or binding, but also deadly, so that whoever observed them was guilty of mortal sin. Hence he maintained that after the Passion the Apostles never observed the legal ceremonies in real earnest but only by a kind of pious pretense, lest, namely, they should scandalize the Jews and hinder their conversion. This pretense, however, is to be understood not as if they did not in reality perform those actions but in the sense that they performed them without the intention of observing the ceremonies of the Law, just as a man might cut away his foreskin for health's sake and not with the intention of observing legal circumcision.

But since it seems unbecoming that the Apostles, in order to avoid scandal, should have hidden things pertaining to the truth of life and doctrine, and that they should have made use of pretense in things pertaining to the salvation of the faithful, therefore Augustine more fittingly distinguished three periods of time (*Letter* 82.2). One was the time that preceded the Passion of Christ, during which the legal ceremonies (of the Mosaic Law) were neither dead nor deadly; another period was after the publication of the Gospel, during which the legal ceremonies are both dead and deadly. The third is a middle period, to wit, from the Passion of Christ to the publication of the Gospel, during which the legal ceremonies were indeed dead because they had neither effect nor binding force; but they were not deadly because it was lawful for Jewish converts to Christianity to observe them, provided they did not put their trust in them so as to hold them to be necessary for salvation, as though faith in Christ could not justify without the legal observances. On the other hand, there was no reason why those who were converted from paganism to Christianity should observe them. Hence Paul circumcised Timothy, who was born of a Jewish mother; but he was unwilling to circumcise Titus, who had been born a Gentile.

The reason why the Holy Spirit did not wish the converted Jews to be debarred at once from observing the legal ceremonies, while converted pagans were forbidden to observe the rites of paganism, was in order to show that there was a difference between those rites. For pagan ceremonial was rejected as absolutely unlawful and as prohibited by God for all time, whereas the legal ceremonial (of the Mosaic Law) ceased as being fulfilled through Christ's Passion, being (originally) instituted by God as a prefiguring of Christ.

According to Jerome, Peter withdrew himself from the (company of the) Gentiles (in Antioch) (Gal. 2:12) in order to avoid giving scandal to the Jews, of whom he was the Apostle. Hence he did not sin at all in acting thus. On the other hand, Paul in like manner made a pretense of blaming him (for acting thus) in order to avoid scandalizing the Gentiles, whose Apostle he was. But Augustine disapproves of this solution. For in canonical Scripture [to wit, Gal. 2:12], wherein we must not hold anything to be false, Paul says that Peter was to be blamed. Consequently it is true that Peter was at fault and Paul blamed him in very truth and not with pretense. Peter, however, did not sin by observing the legal ceremonial for the time being, since this was lawful for him who was a converted Jew. But he did sin by excessive minuteness in the observance of the legal rites lest he should scandalize the Jews, with the result that he gave scandal to the Gentiles.

Finally, Aquinas turns to the ruling of the Apostles in Jerusalem whereby Gentile converts are to "abstain from things polluted by contact with idols, from fornication, from anything that has been strangled and from blood" (Acts 15:28–29).

Some have held that this prohibition of the Apostles is not to be taken literally but spiritually. . . . Others maintain that these foods were forbidden literally, not to prevent the observance of legal ceremonies (of the Mosaic Law) but in order to prevent gluttony. . . . We must follow a third opinion and hold that these foods were forbidden literally, not with the purpose of forcing compliance with the legal ceremonies but in order to further the union of Gentiles and Jews living side by side. For blood and things strangled were loathsome to the Jews by ancient custom, and the Jews might have suspected the Gentiles of relapse into idolatry if the latter had partaken of things offered to idols. Hence the things were prohibited for the time being, during which the Gentiles and the Jews were to become united together. But as time went on, with the lapse of the cause, the effect lapsed also, when the truth of the Gospel teaching was divulged, wherein our Lord taught that "not that which enters the mouth defiles a man" (Matt. 15:11), and that "nothing is to be rejected that is received with thanksgiving" (1 Tim. 4:4). (Aquinas, *Summa Theologica* I/2, ques. 103, art. 4, ad 1–3) [AQUINAS 1945: 2:916–918]

8. Old Testament Morality in New Testament Times

For the Christians the difference between the Old and the New Dispensation was not merely that of the abrogation of the precepts of the Old Law. The Christian had to face, as did the Jew, the issue of practices apparently condoned, or at least permitted, in the Bible narrative that were no longer regarded as moral. Augustine advises the Christian reader of the Old Testament on how these are to be understood.

We must also be careful not to think that what is understood in the Old Testament, because of the circumstances of those times, as neither a vice nor a crime, even though it is interpreted not figuratively but literally, can be applied to these times as a mode of life. No one will do this unless he is dominated by a lust which seeks protection even in the very Scriptures by which it should be destroyed. The unhappy man does not realize that those things have been set before his mind for this useful purpose, namely, that men of good hope may understand with profit that a practice which they scorn can have a good use, and one which they adopt can lead to damnation, if charity motivates the use of the first practice, and lust the use of the second.

What lies behind the discussion, as it often does in these circumstances, is the polygamy of the biblical patriarchs.

Thus, even if it were then possible, because of the circumstances, for anyone to possess many wives chastely, it is now possible for another man to be lustful with only one. I have more regard for a man who makes use of the fruitfulness of many wives for the sake of another purpose than for the man who indulges in carnal pleasures with only one wife for the sake of that pleasure. In the first case, a benefit in harmony with the circumstances of the time is sought, in the second instance, lust concerned with temporary sensual pleasure is gratified. Those to whom the Apostle (Paul) "by way of concession" allowed carnal intercourse with one wife because of their "lack of self-control" (1 Cor. 7:2, 6) are less advanced on the road to God than those who, although they had several wives, looked only toward the begetting of children in this union, just as a wise man looks only to the health of his body in the matter of food and drink. And so, if they [that is, biblical polygamists] had been living at the time of the Lord's coming, when the time had come to gather the stones and not to scatter them, they would at once have made themselves eunuchs "for the kingdom of heaven's sake." For there is no difficulty in denying ourselves something, unless there is lust in enjoying it. (Augustine, *On Christian Instruction* 3.18) [AUGUSTINE 1947: 137–139]

And, more generally on the moral differences between the Old and New Testaments:

Although all or nearly all the deeds which are recorded in the Old Testament must be regarded not only in their literal sense but figuratively as well, the reader should interpret as a symbol even those acts which he has taken literally if those who have done them are praised (in the Bible), even though their actions differ from the custom of good men who have kept the divine commands since the coming of the Lord. However, he should not carry that same action over into his own conduct, for there are many deeds which were performed in accordance with duty at that time which can be performed now only through lust.

On the other hand, when he reads of the sins of noble men (in the Bible), even though he can observe and verify in them some figures of future events, he may still apply the proper meaning of the action to this end, namely, that he will by no means venture to boast about his own virtuous deeds nor, because of his own uprightness, look down upon those others as if they were sinners. . . . The sins of those men have been written down for a reason and that is that the following passage of the Apostle (Paul) might be everywhere taken into account: "Therefore let him who thinks he stands take heed lest he fall" (1 Cor. 10:20). There is practically no page of the Holy Books which does not cry out that "God resists the proud but gives grace to the humble" (James 4:6). (Ibid. 3.22–23)   [AUGUSTINE 1947: 142–143]

9. Priests and Sin

In both the biblical and the Christian tradition the priesthood serves not merely as the instrument of sacrifice but as the agent of cleansing and reconciliation. "Sins are forgiven," Ambrose said, "through the office of the priest and the sacred ministry" (On Cain and Abel 2.4.15). In the following passage Jerome compares the cleansing powers of the Christian priesthood with its Jewish prototype. His point of departure is the role of the Jewish priest in certifying the disease of leprosy. The text in Leviticus 13:1ff. lists and classifies the symptoms in great detail. If, in the judgment of the priest, the symptoms are those of a malignant condition, he pronounces the afflicted person unclean.

As for the person with a leprous affection, his clothes shall be rent, his head left bare, and he shall cover over his upper lip; and he shall call out "Unclean! Unclean!" He shall be unclean as long as the disease is on him. Being unclean, he shall dwell apart; his dwelling shall be outside the camp. (Leviticus 13:45–46)

Conversely, there might be grounds for thinking that the disease had been healed.
Here the procedure for ritual purification is more elaborate.

This shall be the ritual for a leper at the time that he is to be cleansed. When it is reported to the priest, the priest shall go outside the camp. If the priest sees that the leper has been cured of his scaly affection, the priest shall order two live clean birds, cedar wood, crimson stuff, and hyssop to be brought for him who is to be cleansed. The priest shall order one of the birds slaughtered over fresh water in an earthen vessel; and he shall take the live bird, along with the cedar wood, the crimson stuff and the hyssop, and dip them together with the live bird in the blood of the bird that was slaughtered over the fresh water. He shall then sprinkle it seven times on him who is to be cleansed of the eruption and cleanse him; and he shall set the live bird free in the open country.

The one to be cleansed shall wash his clothes, shave off all his hair, and bathe in water; then he shall be clean. After that he may enter the camp but must remain outside his tent for seven days. On the seventh day he shall shave off all the hair of his head, his beard and his eyebrows. When he has shaved off all his hair, he shall wash his clothes and bathe his body in water. On the eighth day he shall take two male lambs without blemish, one ewe lamb in its first year without blemish, three-tenths of a measure of choice flour with oil mixed in for a meal offering, and one measure of oil. These shall be presented before the Lord.

The offering ritual is then described in great detail.

. . . Thus the priest shall make expiation for him before the Lord. The priest shall then offer the sin offering and make expiation for the one being cleansed of his uncleanness. Lastly, the burnt offering shall be slaughtered, and the priest shall offer the burnt offering and the meal offering on the altar, and the priest shall make expiation for him. Then he shall be clean. (Leviticus 14:1–20)

Precisely such an instance is encountered in the Gospels.

After he had come from the hill he [that is, Jesus] was followed by a great crowd. And now a leper approached him, bowed low, and said, "Sir, if only you will, you can cleanse me." Jesus stretched out his hand, touched him and said, "Indeed, I will; be clean again." And his leprosy was cured immediately. Then Jesus said to him, "Be sure to tell nobody; but go and show yourself to the priest, and make the offering laid down by Moses for your cleansing; that will certify the cure." (Matthew 8:1–4)

We turn now to Jerome, commenting on this passage from the Gospel of Matthew.

We read of lepers in Leviticus, where they are ordered to show themselves to the priests; then, if they have leprosy, they are rendered unclean by the priests; not that the priests make them lepers and unclean but because they have some knowledge of the leper and the non-leprous and can distinguish who is clean and who is unclean. Thus just as in that instance the priest renders the leper clean or unclean, so too among us the bishop or the presbyter, not those who are unsound or diseased, but by reason of his office, when he has heard the types of sins committed, knows who is to be bound and who is to be released. (Jerome, *Commentary on Matthew* 16.19)

For the biblical society, leprosy was an actual physical complaint, a disease poised in the shared zone between physical and ritual impurity. For the Christians, however, with their diminished sense of ritual impurity, the connection between sin and disease shaded off into one of their favorite metaphors, the priest as the physician of souls. The same canon of the Fourth Lateran Council of 1215 that prescribed annual confession for all Latin Christians also stipulated the following.

The priest, moreover, shall be discreet and cautious, so that in the manner of a skillful physician he may pour wine and oil upon the wounds of the injured, diligently searching out the circumstances of both the sinner and of the sin, that from these he may prudently understand what manner of advice he ought to offer him and what sort of remedy he ought to apply, employing various measures in order to heal the sick. (Acts of the Fourth Lateran Council) [MCNEILL & GAMER 1938: 414]

By the time of the Fourth Lateran Council the invocation of the priest as physician was, in fact, a metaphor. Both the society at large and the Church had generally separated physical and moral defects, as was obviously not the case with cited instances of leprosy and in this Gospel passage.

As he went on his way Jesus saw a man blind from his birth. His disciples put the question, "Rabbi, who sinned, this man or his parents? Why was he born blind?" "It is not that this man or his parents sinned," Jesus answered; "he was born blind so that God's power might be displayed in curing him." (John 9:1–3)

10. On the Nature of Sin

The anonymous disciples who posed the question to Jesus were making two assumptions: first, that the man's physical defect of blindness was possibly the result of a moral defect, sin; and second, that the effects of sin, in this case blindness, could still be felt in the next generation after its commission, that "the sins of the fathers are visited upon their children, to the third and fourth generation," as a celebrated text of Exodus 20:5 has it. Both assumptions were of capital concern to Christian theologians wrestling with the problem of sin, guilt, and punishment. Thomas Aquinas (d. 1277 C.E.) takes up both. First, on physical defects as a punishment for sin, dealt with under the rubric "Whether death and other bodily defects are the result of sin," Thomas holds that they are the result not of actual sins committed by the person suffering them but of original sin.

The sin of our first parent [that is, Adam] is the cause of death and all such defects in human nature, insofar as by the sin of our first parent the original justice was taken away, by which were not only the lower parts of the soul held together under the control of reason, without any disorder whatever, but also the whole body was held together in subjection to the soul, without any defect. . . . Therefore, when original justice was forfeited through the sin of our first parent, just as human nature was stricken in the soul by the disorder among the powers, so also it became subject to (physical) corruption by reason of disorder in the body.

Now the withdrawal of original justice has the character of punishment, even as the withdrawal of grace has. Consequently, death and all consequent physical defects are punishments of original sin. And although these defects are not intended by the sinner, nevertheless they are ordered according to the justice of God, Who inflicts them as punishments. (Aquinas, *Summa Theologica* I/2, ques. 85, art. 5) [AQUINAS 1945: 2:701]

Are all punishments and defects, birth defects for example, as in the case of the man born blind, the result of sin?

Sometimes a thing seems penal yet has not the nature of punishment absolutely. For punishment is a species of evil and evil is a privation of good. And since man's good is manifold, namely, the good of the soul, the good of the body, and external goods, it happens sometimes that a man suffers the loss of a lesser good that he may profit from a greater; as when he suffers a loss of money for the sake of bodily health, or the loss of both for the sake of spiritual health and the glory of God. In both cases the loss is an evil to a man, not absolutely, but relatively; and hence it does not answer to the name of punishment in the absolute sense, but of medicinal punishment. . . . And since such are not punishments properly speaking, they are not referred to sin as their cause except in a restricted sense; because the very fact that human nature needs treatment with penal medicines is due to the corruption of nature, which is itself the punishment of original sin. . . .

Such defects in those who are born with them, or from which children suffer, are the effects and punishments of original sin, as we have stated above. . . . As for the fact that they are not equally in all, this is due to the diversity of nature which is left to itself, as was stated above. (Aquinas, *Summa Theologica* I/2, ques. 87, art. 7) [AQUINAS 1945: 2:717–718]

And finally, what of the question of inherited guilt, the one raised by the text in Exodus 20:5, to which may be added, as Thomas does, a New Testament parallel. Jesus is reported speaking to the Pharisees.

You snakes, you vipers' brood, how can you escape being condemned to hell? . . . On you will fall all the innocent blood spilt on the ground, from innocent Abel to Zechariah son of Berachiah, whom you murdered between the sanctuary and the altar. Believe me, this generation will bear the guilt of all. (Matthew 23:35–36)

Both passages [Thomas begins] should be referred, apparently, to temporal or bodily punishments, insofar as children are the property of their parents, and descendants of their forefathers. Or, if the reference is to spiritual punishment, they must be understood in reference to the imitation of sin. . . . The sins of the fathers are said to be punished in their children because the latter are more prone to sin through being brought up amid their parents' crimes, both by becoming accustomed to them, and by imitating their parents' example, conforming to their authority, as it were. Moreover, they deserve heavier punishment if, seeing the punishment of their parents, they fail to mend their ways. (Aquinas, *Summa Theologica* I/2, ques. 87, art. 8) [AQUINAS 1945: 2:719–720]

11. Penalties and Penances

Although Paul's new, Christ-centered view of the Law shifted the focus away from the Pharisaic and rabbinic emphasis on observance to the Christian's justification through faith, his letters are likewise filled with admonitions to the new Christians to avoid the practices prevalent in the pagan culture and society that surrounded those early believers. Paul was not legislating; he was simply stating the obvious in condemning murder, fornication, slander, lying, and blasphemy—all crimes overtly and incontestably against the Law of God revealed on Sinai. In the generations immediately after Paul the list of such sins grows into a swelling catalogue of Christian "commandments," like this early example from the anonymous second-century work called the Teaching of the Apostles.

You shall not kill; you shall not commit adultery, sodomy or fornication; you shall not steal; you shall not use magic; you shall not traffic

with drugs or procure abortions or kill the newborn child; you shall not
covet your neighbor's goods; you shall not forswear yourself; you shall
not bear false witness, or slander or bear malice. You shall not be double-
minded or doubled-tongued, for a double tongue is a snare of death. Your
word shall not be false or empty, but fulfilled in deed. You shall not be
coveteous, or extortionate, or hypocritical, or spiteful or arrogant. You
shall hate no man; but some you shall rebuke and for some you shall pray
and some you shall love more than your own soul.

My child, flee from all evil and from all that resembles it. Be not
wrathful, for wrath leads to murder; nor a zealot, nor contentious, nor
quick to anger; for from all these things murders are begotten. Be not
lustful, for lust leads to fornication; nor a filthy talker nor one of high
looks; for from all these things adulteries are begotten. Be not an augur,
for it leads to idolatry, nor an enchanter, nor a mathematician [that is, an
astrologer], nor one who practices lustrations, nor so much as look upon
these things; for from all these things idolatry is begotten. Be not a liar,
for the lie leads to theft; nor a lover of money, nor vainglorious; for from
all these things thefts are begotten. (*Teaching of the Apostles* 2)

*Here too there is little to distinguish a Christian's morality from that of a Torah-
observant Jew of the same era, save for the obvious absence of matters of ritual
purity. Regarding penalties, the Torah is generally explicit on the subject of crimes
against God's Law and their punishment. The punishments, as we have seen, were
often severe, but we have little certitude of how often or how rigorously they were
carried out to the letter: the same Jews who stoned Stephen to death for blasphemy
in 30 C.E. claimed a few weeks before that they had lost the right to capital
punishment in the case of Jesus (John 18:28–32).*

*Temple sacrifice presented the alternative of atoning for sin through sacrifice
rather than paying for it with blood or property. But with the final destruction of
the Temple in 70 C.E., the possibility of sacrifice, and with it that of sacrificial
atonement, becomes moot. There remained, of course, excommunication as a form
of retribution for sin, but as we observed, it seems to have been little used in practice.
The emphasis in Jewish moral teaching swung markedly and distinctly in the direction of the avoidance of sin.*

*The Christians of Paul's day were just beginning to experiment with the notion
of excommunication, as we shall see in the next chapter, and they certainly had no
authority to impose capital punishment. But there was for the Christians a more
powerful precedent than the Jewish one. Jesus himself announced his power to forgive
sin, and he passed this power "to bind and to loose" to his Apostles after him:
"Whatsoever you shall bind on earth shall be bound in heaven, and whatsoever you
shall loose on earth shall be loosed in heaven" (Matt. 16:19). That passage was*

generally understood to mean that the reconciliation of the sinner, and the terms of repentance, rested in the hands of the Church. There remained to be resolved, however, the task of laying out those terms: the definition and distinction of sins and what constituted the penalty or penance for each. The Church's synods and councils eventually took up the first task. The disciplinary canons attached to each council's dogmatic findings constituted a growing body of ecclesiastical statute law, in the first instance regulating the behavior of clerics but gradually extending over the whole body of Christians, as shall be seen below. The matter of penance, however, of prescribing the penalties attached to specific sins, was left in a considerably more unregulated state. Often it was left to individual discretion or local practice to fix such penances. One source of authority on the matter were the bishops, whose guidance was often sought and whose responses to queries, because of the prestige and orthodoxy of the authors, carried weight far beyond their immediate jurisdiction. One such was Basil (ca. 330–379 C.E.), the enormously influential Anatolian bishop whose severe penitential prescriptions often took on the force of law for the Church.

Those who are guilty of sodomy or bestiality, as well as murderers, sorcerers, adulterers and idolaters, all deserve the same penalty. . . . We should receive those who have repented over the course of thirty years. Ignorance, voluntary confession and the long lapse of time provide grounds for forgiveness. (Basil, *Letter* 188)

An intentional homicide, when he repents, should be excommunicated for twenty years. . . . On the completion of this period he will be permitted to share in the sacrament. . . . The unintentional homicide will be excommunicated for ten years. . . . The adulterer for fifteen years; fornicators for seven years. . . . Whoever has denied Christ should weep and remain in penance for his whole life long; he may be given the sacrament only at the moment of death. (Basil, *Letter* 217)

Basil's penances reflect an era when public penance, administered once in a lifetime, was still the norm. But from the sixth century onward, confession, penance, and the reconciliation of the Christian sinner were increasingly a private matter between priest and penitent. It was the parish priest, then, who required guidance on sins, their cures and penalties. This is one early attempt to provide such guidance, from the beginning of the sixth century.

Those who become drunk from ignorance (shall do penance for) fifteen days; from negligence, forty days; from contempt, three forty-day periods. One who constrains another to get drunk for the sake of good fellowship shall do the same penance as the drunken man. One who under the influence of hatred or wantonness constrains others to drunkenness that he may basely put them to confusion or ridicule, if he has not done adequate penance, shall do penance as a slayer of souls. (*Excerpts from the Book of David*) [MCNEILL & GAMER 1938: 172]

The approach taken in the examples just cited look chiefly toward intent in imposing penance for sin. Equally often the quality or condition of the sinner or the victim determined the severity of the penalty, as in the following, a "penitential," or book of penances, compiled for the guidance of confessors sometime about 830 C.E. by one Halitgar of Cambrai. In these handbooks, which become common in Europe from the sixth century onward, the offenses are normally broken down by topic. The following are from the section called "On Fornication."

6. If anyone [that is, a cleric] commits fornication as did the Sodomites, he shall do penance for ten years, three of them on bread and water.

7. If any cleric commits adultery, that is, if he begets a child with the wife or the betrothed of another, he shall do penance for seven years; however, if he does not beget a child and the act does not come to the notice of men, if he is a cleric he shall do penance for three years, one of these on bread and water; if a deacon or a monk, he shall do penance for seven years, three of these on bread and water; a bishop, twelve years, five on bread and water.

9. If anyone commits fornication with a nun or with one who is vowed to God, let him be aware that he has committed adultery; therefore he shall do penance as stated above.

10. If anyone commits fornication by himself or with a beast of burden or with any quadruped, he shall do penance for three years; if he has clerical rank or a monastic vow, he shall do penance for seven years.

These and some following prescriptions in this section have to do with the sexual offenses of clerics. The Penitential then turns to similar sins committed by laymen.

13. If any layman commits fornication as the Sodomites did, he shall do penance for seven years.

14. If anyone begets a child of the wife of another, that is, commits adultery and violates his neighbor's bed, he shall do penance for three years and abstain from juicy foods and from his own wife, giving in addition to the husband the price of his wife's violated honor.

15. If anyone wishes to commit adultery and cannot, that is, he is not accepted, he shall do penance for forty days.

16. If anyone commits fornication with a woman, that is, with widows and girls: if with a widow, he shall do penance for a year; if with a girl, he shall do penance for two years.

17. If any unstained youth is joined to a virgin, if the parents are willing, she shall become his wife; nevertheless, they shall do penance for one year and then become man and wife.

18. If anyone commits fornication with a beast, he shall do penance for one year. If he has not a wife, he shall do penance for half a year.

19. If anyone violates a virgin or a widow, he shall do penance for three years. . . .

21. If any one of the women who have committed fornication slays those who are born or attempts to commit abortion, the original regulation forbids communion to the end of her life. What is actually laid down they may mitigate somewhat in practice. We determine they shall do penance for a period of ten years, according to rank, as the regulations state. (Halitgar, *Penitential*) [MCNEILL & GAMER 1938: 302–304]

The "penance" envisioned in these prescriptions is normally some form of fasting or abstinence, typically a diet of bread and water from rising until mid-afternoon. At first it seems probable that the penitent underwent a continuous fast for a prescribed time, with the exception of Sundays and holy days. But from the eighth century onward, the penitential fast was often prescribed for a definite time of the year or of the week, especially the three quadragesimae, or quarantines, and the "required weekdays." The three quarantines corresponded to the three principal festivals of the year, preceding Easter and Christmas (that is, the Advent and Lenten fasts) but following Pentecost. The "required weekdays" were Monday, Wednesday, and Friday. Earlier, all sorts of variations were possible, as in this early sixth-century example.

The penance of a presbyter, a deacon, a subdeacon or a virgin who falls, as well as anyone who puts a man to death, who commits fornication with beasts or with his sister or with another's wife, or who plans to slay a man with poisons, is three years. During the first year he shall lie upon the ground; during the second his head shall be laid upon a stone; during the third, upon a board; and he shall eat only bread and water and salt and some pease porridge. Others prefer thirty periods of three days, or (penances) with special fasts, with food and bed as aforesaid, with food at Nones [that is, about three in the afternoon], until the second year. Another penance is for three years, but with a half-pint of beer or milk with bread and salt every second night with the ration of dinner; and they ought to so supplicate God regularly in the twelve hours of the nights and of the days. (*Excerpts from the Book of David*) [MCNEILL & GAMER 1938: 173–174]

The alternative penances in the text just cited are either early examples of or steps on the way toward a system of "equivalents" that shows up in the penitentials and elsewhere. The commutation of penances may be an attempt at lightening some by intensifying and compressing them. This is a seventh-century example from the disciplinary statutes of the Irish Church and has to do with clerics.

3. The equivalent of a year (of penance): three days with a dead saint in a tomb without food or drink and without sleep, but with a garment about him and with the chanting of psalms and with the prayer of the hours. . . .

4. The equivalent of a year: a three-day period in a church without food, drink, sleep or a garment, and without a seat; and the chanting of psalms with the canticles and the prayer of the hours. . . .

8. The equivalent of a year: forty days on bread and water and a special [that is, an all-day] fast in each week and forty psalms and sixty genuflections and the praying of the hours.

9. The equivalent of a year: fifty days in a long special fast and sixty psalms and genuflections and the praying of the hours.

10. The equivalent of a year: forty days on water and grain and two special fasts each week and forty psalms and genuflections and prayer every hour.

11. The equivalent of a year: a hundred days on bread and water and prayer every hour.

12. All these fasts are without flesh and wine—except a little beer—in another's church during the time. (*The Irish Canons*)

[MCNEILL & GAMER 1938: 123–124]

It was not unknown for penances to be commuted or "redeemed" by monetary payments.

If anyone is not able to fast and has the means to redeem himself, if he is rich, for (every) seven weeks of penance he shall give twenty solidi. But if he has not sufficient means, he shall give ten solidi. But if he is very poor, he shall give three solidi. But let no one be startled because we have commanded to give twenty solidi or a smaller amount, since if he is rich it is easier for him to give twenty solidi than for a poor man to give three solidi. But let everyone give attention to the cause to which he is under obligation, whether it is to be spent on the redemption of captives, or upon the sacred altar, or for poor Christians. And know this, my brethren, that when men or women slaves come to you seeking penance, you are not to be hard on them or compel them to fast as much as the rich, since men and women slaves are not in their own power; therefore lay upon them a moderate penance. (Halitgar, *Penitential*)

[MCNEILL & GAMER 1938: 299]

12. Canons and Canon Law

The first collection and arrangement by topic of the disciplinary canons enacted by the Church councils took place in the sixth century, at the same time as and under the influence of Emperor Justinian's codification of Roman civil law. And just as in the civil process, codification did not end the enactment of new ecclesiastical canons or the making of new collections. Sometime about 1140 C.E. there was a major new addition to the literature, the Decretum, *or more properly* The Concord of Discordant Canons, *by the jurist Gratian. Here for the first time there was an attempt at jurisprudence in addition to mere collection and arrangement. The scholastic and systematic quality of the work is immediately apparent.*

PART I, DISTINCTION III

Part I. All these examples belong to the secular law, but because a civil decree is one thing and an ecclesiastical decree another, and since the civil law is called public or civil, we must inquire by what name an ecclesiastical decree is called. An ecclesiastical decree is denoted by the term "canon." And a canon is defined by Isidore (of Seville) in his *Etymologies*, Book VI, as follows:

Chapter I: What a canon is:
It is called "canon" in Greek, "rule" in Latin
Chapter II: Why is it called a rule?
It is called a rule because it leads correctly and it leads no one astray. Others have said it is a rule either because it governs, or because it provides the norm for right living, or it corrects what is crooked and evil.

Part II. Further, some of the canons are decrees of the pontiffs, others the statutes of councils. Some councils are universal, some are provincial. Some provincial councils are held by the authority of the Roman pontiff, namely, in the presence of a legate of the Holy Roman Church; others in fact by the authority of patriarchs or primates or the metropolitan of the province.

This is what must be understood about the general rules. There are also certain private laws, ecclesiastical as well as secular, which are called privileges. Isidore defines these in Book V (of his work):

Chapter III: What a privilege is:
Privileges are laws for individual persons; they are, in a sense, private laws. For it is held a privilege because it is held privately.

(Gratian, *Decretum*)

Gratian was a Roman jurist and, of course, a Western Christian writing for the Western Church. He was quite prepared, then, to accept the decretal letters of the

Popes as possessing equal weight with the decrees of the councils in the formulation of the Church's law. Here he draws, in this same connection, an interesting distinction between law and the exegesis of Scripture.

DISTINCTION XX

Part I. It follows that decretal letters must be executed by an authority equal to that of the canons of councils. Now there is a question concerning those who interpret Sacred Scripture. Are they to be followed, or are they subject to these same (decretal letters)? For the more a man depends on reason, the more authority his words would seem to possess. Indeed, many writers of (theological) works, men possessed of a superior knowledge, as if by a more ample grace of the Holy Spirit, are shown to have adhered more to reason. So it would seem that the opinions of Augustine, Jerome and other writers of treatises are to be preferred to the decrees of many of the (Roman) pontiffs.

So it might appear, but such is not necessarily the case, as Gratian argues.

Part II. It is, however, one thing to terminate cases, another to expound Sacred Scripture correctly. In settling litigation not only is wisdom necessary, but also authority. Christ, in order to say to Peter, "Whatever you bind on earth will be bound in heaven, etc.," first gave him the keys of the kingdom of heaven. In one instance he gave him the wisdom to discern between one type of leprosy and another, in the other he gave him the power to cast some out of the Church or to receive others. Since, then, all cases are terminated in either the absolution of the innocent or the condemnation of the guilty, absolution or condemnation require not only wisdom but power on the part of those presiding. It appears that the commentators on Sacred Scripture, even if they excel the (Roman) pontiffs in wisdom and are placed before them in the interpretation of Holy Scripture, nevertheless, because they have not attained to the peak of dignity of the latter, deserve, in defining legal cases, a place after them in rank. (Gratian, *Decretum*)

13. The Derivation of God's Commands: The Muslim View

The Muslim's lot was somewhat simpler than the Christian's. As has been noted, what Jesus or the early Christians understood by "Scripture" was quite simply the Bible. It was only after some time had passed that the body of Christian traditions known collectively as the "New Testament" was regarded as Scripture in its own right and attached, in the manner of a diptych, to the "Old." The Muslim, on the other hand, had neither to explain nor explain away the Torah, since the Quran was quite simply a fresh revelation of those same truths or, from a legal point of view, a restatement of the Law of God that made its earlier expressions not so much abrogated as moot. The Quran, since it is the word of God, and since it obviously includes in its contents a great many prescriptions pertaining to conduct, was also the Law of God. There is no doubt that Muslims thought so from the beginning or that the Prophet's own extra-Quranic teaching and example counted heavily in the early community's efforts at living the life of a believer. That much we can assume; it fell to later Muslims, who lived within a long-established and fully defined version of that life, to explain to themselves just how that had come about. The first example comes from a lawyer, al-Shafi'i (d. 820 C.E.), who was himself involved in defining the Islamic law.

Shafi'i said: The sum total of what God declared to His creatures in His Book, by which He invited men to worship Him according to His prior decision, falls in various categories.

One such category is what He declared to His creatures textually (in the Quran), such as the aggregate of duties owed him, namely, that they shall perform the prayer, pay the alms tax, perform the pilgrimage and observe the fast (of Ramadan); and likewise that He has forbidden disgraceful acts, in both public and private, such as the explicit prohibition of adultery, the drinking of wine, eating the flesh of dead things and blood and pork; and finally He has made clear to them how to perform the duty of ablution as well as other matters stated explicitly in the Quran.

A second category consists in those acts the obligation of which He established in His Book but whose manner of performance He made clear by the discourse of His Prophet. The number of prayers (to be said each day), and the (amount) of the alms tax and their time (of fulfillment) are cases in point, but there are similar cases revealed in His Book.

A third category consists of what the Messenger of God established by his own example or exhortation, though there is no explicit rule on them defined by God (in the Quran). For God has laid down in His Book the obligation of obedience to His Prophet and recourse to his decision. So he who accepts a duty on the authority of the Prophet of God accepts it by an obligation imposed by God.

A fourth category consists in what God commanded His creatures to seek through personal initiative (devoted to study of the Quran or the traditions of the Prophet) and by it put their obedience to the test exactly as He tried their obedience by the other duties which He ordered them to fulfill, for the Blessed and Most High said: "And we shall put you on trial in order to know those of you who strive and endure, and We will test your accounts" (Quran 47:33). (Shafiʿi, *Treatise*)

[SHAFIʿI 1961: 67–68]

The same process is described five and a half centuries later by Ibn Khaldun (d. 1406 C.E.), now writing less as a lawyer than as a self-conscious historian.

The basic sources of legal evidence are the Book, that is, the Quran, and then the Prophetic traditions, which clarify the Quran. At the time of the Prophet the laws were received directly from him. He possessed the Quranic revelation, and he explained it directly. No transmission, speculation or analogical reasoning was necessary. After the Prophet's death direct explanation was no longer possible. The Quran was preserved through a general and continuous transmission. As for the Prophetic tradition, the men around Muhammad all agree that it was necessary to act in accordance with whatever of it has reached us, as statement or practice, through a sound report that can be trusted to be truthful. It is in this sense that legal evidence is determined by the Quran and the Prophetic tradition.

Then general consensus took its place next to them. The men around Muhammad agreed to disapprove of those who held opinions different from theirs. They would not have done that without some basis for doing so, because people like the men around Muhammad do not agree upon something without a valid reason. In addition, the evidence attests the infallibility of the whole group. Thus, general consensus became a valid proof in legal matters.

Then we looked into the methods according to which the men around Muhammad and the early generations made their deductions from the Quran and the Prophetic tradition. It was found that they compared similar cases and drew conclusions from the analogy, in that they either all agreed or some of them made concessions in this connection to others. Many of the things that happened after the Prophet are not included [or are not covered] in the established texts. Therefore they compared and combined them with the established indications that are found in the texts, according to certain rules that governed their combinations. This assured the soundness of their comparison of two similar cases, so that it could be assumed that one and the same divine law covered both cases. This became another kind of legal evidence, because the early Muslims all agreed upon it. This is analogy, the fourth kind of evidence. (Ibn Khaldun, *Muqaddima* 6.13) [IBN KHALDUN 1967: 3:23–24]

14. On Consensus

Both Shafi'i and Ibn Khaldun were discussing what had come to be called the "roots of the law," that is, the sources from which authoritative legal prescriptions may be derived. The Quran is obviously one such source, and in its case the problem was not one of validation but of interpretation (see Chapter 2 above). As for the Prophetic traditions, and indeed for certain practices that find no authority in either the Quran or those same traditions, Ibn Khaldun rests heavily on the principle of consensus, which he pushes back into the "Apostolic age" of Islam, that generation of "men around Muhammad" who "agreed to disapprove of those who held opinions different from theirs." Shafi'i too had something to say about this principle of consensus, and it is not very different from what Ibn Khaldun said nearly seven centuries after him.

Al-Shafi'i said, may God have mercy on him: Someone said to me: I have understood your rule concerning the prescriptions of God and the prescriptions of the Prophet, may God bless and save him, and I have understood that whoever follows the Prophet follows God in that God has enjoined obedience to His Prophet. There is also proof of what you say, that no Muslim who knows a Quranic text or a Prophetic tradition may maintain the contrary of either of them, and I have understood that this too is a prescription of God. But what is your proof for following that on which the people are agreed when there is no text to that effect, either as a revelation from God or as a tradition handed down from the Prophet? Do you believe, as some do, that their consensus can rest only on a firm Prophetic tradition, even when that latter has not been handed down?

I answered him: That on which they are in agreement and say that it is a tradition handed down from the Prophet is as they say, if it please God. . . . We maintain what they maintain, following their authority, because we know that even though the tradition of the Prophet may be forgotten by some of them, it cannot be forgotten by all of them, and we know that all of them cannot come to agree on something contrary to the Prophetic tradition, or on any error, please God.

His anonymous questioner requires a proof, and Shafi'i cites a Prophetic tradition to him.

There are three things which cannot be resented by the heart of a Muslim: sincerity of action for God, good advice to the Muslims, and keeping close to the community of the Muslims. . . .

It was then asked, what is the meaning of the Prophet's command to keep close to the community?

Shafi'i's explanation suggests that the consensus had to do not merely with the first generation of Muslims, those "Companions of the Prophet" on whom so much of the validation of Islamic law rests, but extended into the entire community of believers.

I said [Shafi'i continued] there is but one meaning to it. . . . Since the community of the Muslims is scattered in different countries, one could not keep close to the physical community whose members were scattered, and besides, they were found together with Muslims and unbelievers, with pious men and sinners. Thus it could not mean a physical "closeness" since that was not possible, and because physical nearness would in itself effect nothing, so that there is no meaning in "cleaving to the collectivity" except in agreeing with them in what they make lawful and forbidden, and obedience in both these matters. He who maintains what the community of the Muslims maintains is keeping close to the community, and he who deviates from what the community of the Muslims maintains deviates from that community to which he is commanded to remain close. Error arises in separation. In the community there can be no total error concerning the meaning of the Book, of the Prophetic tradition, or of analogical reasoning, please God. (Shafi'i, *Treatise*)

[SHAFI'I 1961: 285–287]

15. Personal Initiative in the Law

Of all the "roots" on the law, it was the one known as "taking personal initiative" that provoked the most resistance in conservative legal circles. The Quran and the Prophetic tradition both came to be regarded as a form of God's revelation, as we have seen, and the consensus of the community could be seen as the working out of that revelation in social terms: the community could not err on God's and His Prophet's intentions, particularly since there were diffused throughout that community of Muslims so many well-attested and agreed-upon Prophetic traditions that exemplified those intentions. But "personal initiative" was a more nakedly personal judgment on the divine intention, an attempt on the part of a jurist to advance his own reasoned opinion where the Quran provided no text and the tradition and consensus no guidance. Shafi'i accepted it, but under limited circumstances and with a prescribed methodology, namely, analogy, which for him and for most jurists was the only acceptable way of exercising personal initiative in the law.

On all matters touching the Muslim there is either a binding decision (based on the Quran or the tradition) or an indication as to the right answer. If there is a decision, it should be followed; if there is no indication as to the right answer, it should be sought by personal initiative, and that is the same as analogy.

Shafiʿi chose to write his Treatise on the Roots of Jurisprudence *in the form of a dialogue. At this point his imaginary interlocutor has a great many questions and problems about this personal approach to the law.*

He asked: If the scholars apply analogy correctly, will they arrive at the right answer in the eyes of God? And will it be permissible for them to disagree through analogy? Have they been ordered to seek one or different answers for each question? What is the proof for the position that they should apply analogy on the basis of the literal rather than the implicit meaning (of a precedent), and that it is permissible for them to disagree in their answers.

Shafiʿi does not answer directly; he prefers, in his pedagogical fashion, to review the general elements in the law and our knowledge of it.

Legal knowledge is of various kinds. The first consists of the right decisions in both the literal and implied senses; the other, of the right answer in the literal sense only. The right decisions in the first instance are those based either on God's command (in the Quran) or on a tradition from the Apostle related by the public from an earlier public. These two [that is, the Quran and the Prophetic tradition] are the two sources by virtue of which the lawful is to be established as lawful and the unlawful as unlawful. This is the kind of knowledge of which no one is allowed to be either ignorant or doubtful.

Second, the legal knowledge of the specialists consists of Prophetic traditions related by a few and known only to scholars, but others are under no obligation to be familiar with it. Such knowledge may be found among all or a few of the scholars, and it is related by a reliable transmitter from the Prophet. This is the kind of knowledge which is binding on scholars to accept, and it constitutes the right decision in the literal sense insofar as we accept the validity of the testimony of two. This is right only in the literal sense, because it is possible that the evidence of the two witnesses might be false.

Third, there is legal knowledge derived from consensus.

And finally, we come to legal knowledge derived from personal initiative by way of analogy, by virtue of which right decisions are sought. Such decisions are right in the literal sense only to the person who applies the analogy but not to the majority of scholars, since nobody knows what is hidden except God.

The other asked: If legal knowledge is derived through analogy, provided it is rightly applied, should those who apply analogy agree on most of the decisions, although we may find them disagreeing on some?

Shafiʿi replied: Analogy is of two kinds: the first, if the case in question is similar in principle to the precedent, no disagreement of this kind is permitted. The second, if the case in question is similar to several precedents, analogy must be applied to the nearest in resemblance and the most appropriate. But in this instance those who apply analogy are likely to disagree (in their answers).

The other asked: Will you give examples? . . . .

Shafiʿi replied: If we were in the Sacred Mosque (at Mecca) and the Kaʿba is in sight, do you not say that we should face it in prayer with certainty? . . .

The other replied: That is right.

Shafiʿi asked: Are we not under obligation to face the Sacred House in prayer no matter where we happen to be?

That is right.

Do you hold that we could always face the Sacred House correctly?

No, he replied. Not always as correctly as when you were able to see the Sacred House; however, the duty imposed on you was fulfilled [that is, however imperfectly we may have faced the now invisible Kaʿba].

Shafiʿi asked: Is, then, our obligation to seek the unknown object different from our obligation to seek the known object?

That is right. . . . On what ground do you hold that the exercise of personal initiative is permitted?

Shafiʿi replied: It is on the basis of God's saying:

"From whatever place you come out, turn your face in the direction of the Holy Mosque; and wherever you may be, turn your faces in its direction" (Quran 2:145)

Regarding him who wishes to face the Sacred Mosque in prayer and whose residence is at a distance from it, legal knowledge instructs us that he can seek out the right direction through personal initiative on the basis of certain indications (guiding) toward it. For he who is under obligation to face the Holy House and does not know whether he is facing in the right or wrong direction may be able to face toward the right one through certain indications known to him which help him to face it as accurately as he can, just as another person may know other indications which help to orient him, though the direction found by each person may be different. . . . Let us assume that you and I know the direction of this road, and that I hold that the prayer-direction is this way and you disagree with me. Who should follow the opinion of the other?

The other replied: Neither is under an obligation to follow the other. What should each one do then?

The other replied: If I hold that neither should pray until he is certain (of the direction), both might not know it with certainty. Then either the prayer obligation should be abandoned, or the prayer-direction obligation waived so that each can pray in whatever direction he wishes. But I am not in favor of either of those two options. I am rather bound to hold that each one should pray in the direction he believes right and he would be under no obligation to do otherwise. . . .

Shafiʿi replied: You have held that prayer is permissible despite your awareness that one of them is in error; it is even possible that both of them were in error. I have added (the general principle that) such a distinction would be binding on you in the cases of legal witnesses and analogical deduction.

The other replied: I hold that such an error is inevitable but it is not intentional. . . .

Shafiʿi said: It is clear to those of you who are certain of truthful information that personal initiative should never be resorted to except in seeking an unknown object by means of certain indications, although it is permissible for those who exercise such initiative to disagree in their decisions.

The other asked: How is personal initiative to be exercised?

Shafiʿi replied: God, glorified and praised be He, has endowed men with reason by which they can distinguish between differing viewpoints, and He guides them to the truth either by (explicit) texts or by indications (through which they may exercise judgment).

Will you give an example?

God erected the Sacred House and ordered men to face it in prayer when it is in sight, and to seek its direction (by personal initiative) when they are at a distance from it. And He created for them the heaven and the earth and the sun and the moon and the stars and the seas and the mountains and the wind (as guiding indications). For God said:

"It is He who has appointed for you the stars, that by them you might be guided in the darkness of land and sea." (Quran 6:97)

And He said:

"And by landmarks and by the stars they might be guided." (Quran 16:16)

Thus God instructed men to be guided by the stars and other indicators, and by His blessing and help they know the direction of the Sacred House. . . . Thus men should seek, through the reasoning power that God has implanted in them, the direction in which He made it incumbent upon them to face in prayer. If it is thus sought, through their reasoning

power and the indications (pointing to it), men can fulfill their duty.
(Shafi'i, *Treatise*) [SHAFI'I 1961: 288–303]

If we move forward four centuries, we discover that Shafi'i's carefully wrought argument has come to rest in summary in the legal handbooks, in this instance that written by the Syrian jurist Ibn Qudama (d. 1223 C.E.). It occurs under the heading "The Conditions of Prayer" in the subsection "Facing the Prayer-Direction."

The traveler who is making a supererogatory prayer while mounted may pray in whatever direction he happens to be; likewise, the Muslim who is incapable of turning toward the Ka'ba, by reason of danger or for some other reason, should make his prayer however he is able. But outside these two cases, no prayer is meritorious unless it is made in the direction of the Ka'ba. The Muslim who is in the vicinity should turn toward the Ka'ba itself; if he is at a distance, he should pray in its direction.

The Muslim who is ignorant of the direction of the Ka'ba and is in an inhabited area, should inform himself and base himself on the prayer-niches of the Muslims (there); he is bound, in case of error, to begin the prayer over. When two Muslims must determine the direction on their own personal initiative and they are in disagreement, neither is bound to follow the other. The blind man and uneducated should follow the advice of whoever seems most worthy of confidence. (Ibn Qudama, "The Conditions of Prayer") [IBN QUDAMA 1950: 22–23]

We return to Shafi'i's Treatise, where he now sets down some summary cautions on the use of personal initiative in the law.

Nobody should apply analogy unless he is competent to do so through his knowledge of the commands of the Book of God, its prescribed duties and its ethical discipline, its abrogating and abrogated communications, its general and particular rules, and its right guidance. Its ambiguous passages should be interpreted by the tradition of the Prophet; if no tradition is found, then by the consensus of Muslims; if no consensus is possible, then by analogical deduction.

No one is competent to apply analogy unless he is conversant with the established Prophetic tradition, the opinions of his predecessors, the consensus and disagreement of the people, and has adequate knowledge of the Arab tongue. Nor is he regarded as competent in analogical reasoning unless he is sound in mind, able to distinguish between closely parallel precedents, and is not hasty in expressing an opinion unless he is certain of its correctness. Nor shall he refrain from listening to the opinions of those who may disagree with him. (Shafi'i *Treatise*) [SHAFI'I 1961: 306–307]

Shafiʿi has enumerated some of the skills required of the the Muslim lawyer if he is to exercise "personal initiative." Ibn Khaldun covers much the same ground.

The transmitted traditions which constitute the "Prophetic tradition" need verification through an investigation of the ways of transmission and the probity of the transmitters [see Chapter 3 above], so that the likelihood of the truthfulness of the transmitted information, which is the basis for the necessity to act in accordance with it, becomes clear. This is also one of the basic subjects of the discipline of jurisprudence. Added to this is the knowledge of abrogating and abrogated traditions, when two traditions are contradictory and the earlier one of the two is taught. This too is another subject of jurisprudence. After that there comes the study of the meaning of words. This is because one depends upon knowledge of the conventional meanings of single or composite utterances, for deriving ideas in general from word combinations in general. The philological norms needed in this connection are found in the sciences of grammar, inflection, syntax and style. . . .

Next, the study of analogy is a very important basis for this discipline. It helps to ascertain the correctness of both principal and special aspects of laws depending on reasoning and analogy; to examine the particular characteristic of a case on which the law is considered probably to depend, as to whether it exists in the principle; and to find out whether that characteristic exists in the special case without anything contradicting it, which would make it impossible to base the law upon it. (Ibn Khaldun, *Muqaddima* 6.13) [IBN KHALDUN 1967: 3:24–27]

16. Legal Knowledge and Legal Obligations

The Islamic law is not simply a body of theory; it is also a code of action defining which among human acts are permissible and which forbidden. In short, it imposes obligations. Shafiʿi in his Treatise *undertakes to explain how those obligations differ for various segments of the Muslim community.*

Someone asked me: What is legal knowledge and how much should men know of it?

Shafiʿi replied: Legal knowledge is of two kinds: one is for the general public, and no sober and mature person should be ignorant of it. . . . For example, that the daily prayers are five, that men owe to God to fast in the month of Ramadan, to make the pilgrimage to the Holy House whenever they are able, and to pay the legal alms in their estate; that He has prohibited usury, adultery, homicide, theft, wine, and everything of that sort which He has obligated men to comprehend, to perform, to pay in their property, and to abstain from because He has forbidden it to them.

This kind of knowledge may be found textually in the Book of God or may be found generally among the people of Islam. The public relates it from the preceding public and ascribes it to the Apostle of God, no one ever questioning its ascription or its binding force upon them. It is the kind of knowledge that admits of error neither in its narrative nor in its interpretation; it is not permissible to question it.

He asked: What is the second kind?

Shafiʿi replied: It consists of the detailed duties and rules obligatory on men, concerning which there exists neither a text in the Book of God nor, regarding most of them, a Prophetic tradition. Whenever a Prophetic tradition does exist in such a case, it is of the kind that is related by few authorities, not the public, and is subject to different interpretations arrived at by analogy.

17. The Collective Obligation

In addition to the obligation common to every individual and that binding only on specialists, Shafiʿi continues, there is a third type of legal obligation, collective in nature, which rests upon the Muslim community as a whole but not upon every individual within it.

There is a third kind of knowledge. . . . The public is incapable of knowing this kind of knowledge, nor can all specialists obtain it. But those who do obtain it should not neglect it. If some can obtain it, the others are relieved of the obligation of obtaining it, but those who do obtain it (and perform the consequent obligation), they will be rewarded.

The classic example of a "collective obligation" is that of the Holy War (see Chapter 6 below), to which Shafiʿi now turns.

God has imposed the duty of Holy War, as laid down in His Book and uttered by His Prophet's tongue. He stressed the calling to Holy War as follows:

"God has verily bought the souls and possessions of the faithful in exchange for Paradise. They fight in the way of God and kill and are killed. This is a promise incumbent on Him, as in the Torah, so the Gospel and the Quran. And who is more true to his promise than God? So rejoice at the bargain you have made with Him; for this will be triumph supreme." (Quran 9:111)

A number of other Quranic passages on the subject are cited. Then Shafi'i resumes.

These communications mean that the Holy War, and rising up in arms in particular, is obligatory for all able-bodied believers, exempting no one, just as prayer, pilgrimage and alms are performed, and no person is permitted to perform the duty for another, since performance by one will not fulfill the duty for another.

They may also mean that the duty of Holy War is a collective duty different from that of prayer: Those who perform it in a war against the polytheists will fulfill the duty and receive the supererogatory merit, thereby preventing those who remained behind from falling into error.

But God has not put the two categories of men on an equal footing, for He said:

"Such believers who sit at home—unless they have an injury—are not the equals of those who fight in the path of God with their possessions and their selves. . . . God has promised the best of things to both, and He has preferred those who fight to those who sit at home by granting them a mighty reward." (Quran 4:97)

He asked: What is the proof for your opinion that if some people perform the duty, the others would be relieved of the punishment?

It is in the communication I have just cited. . . . God said: "Yet to each God has promised the best of things." Thus God promised "the best of things" for those who stayed behind and could not go to the Holy War, although He clearly specified His preference for those who went to the Holy War over those who stayed at home. If those who stayed at home were in error, while others were fighting, they would be committing a sin, unless God forgives them, rather than receiving "the best of things." (Shafi'i, *Treatise*) [SHAFI'I 1961: 82–86]

18. The Evolution of Islamic Jurisprudence

How had this complex legal system come about? Part of Ibn Khaldun's Prolegomenon to History is given over to a description of the origin and evolution of the various sciences found in Islam. Some of these are what he calls "speculative," that is, they rely on the unaided use of the human intellect for their development and understanding. Others are "traditioned" and are essentially the elaboration of revealed data given in the Quran and the Prophetic traditions (see Chapter 3 above). The former are by and large the legacy of Hellenism in Islam, while the latter are an Arab creation and are indigenous to Islam. Primary among the "traditioned" sciences is the one called jurisprudence.

Jurisprudence is the knowledge of the classification of the laws of God, which concern the actions of all responsible Muslims, as obligatory, forbidden, recommendable, disliked, or permissible. These laws are derived from the Quran and the Prophetic traditions and from the evidence the Lawgiver [that is, Muhammad] has established for a knowledge of the laws. The laws evolved from the whole of this evidence are called jurisprudence.

Then, as he does for all the sciences under discussion, Ibn Khaldun launches into a capsule history of the discipline.

The early Muslims evolved the laws from that evidence, though unavoidably they differed in the interpretation of it. The evidence is mostly derived from texts; the texts are in Arabic. In many instances, and particularly with regard to legal concepts, there are celebrated differences among them as to the meaning implicit in the words. Furthermore, the Prophetic traditions differ widely in respect of the reliability of the recensions; their legal contents, as a rule, are contradictory. Therefore a decision is needed. This makes for differences of opinion. Furthermore, evidence not derived from texts causes still other differences of opinion. Then there are new cases which arise and are not covered by the texts. They are referred by analogy to things that are covered by the texts. All this serves to stir up unavoidable differences of opinion, and this is why differences of opinion occurred among the early Muslims and the religious leaders after them.

Moreover, not all the men around Muhammad were qualified to give legal opinions. Not all of them could serve as sources for religious practice; that was restricted to men who knew the Quran and were acquainted with the abrogating and the abrogated, the ambiguous and the unambiguous verses, and with all the rest of the evidence that can be derived from the Quran, since they have learned these matters from the Prophet directly, or from their higher-ranking colleagues who had learned it from him. These men were called "readers," that is, men who were able to read the Quran. (Ibn Khaldun, *Muqaddima* 6.14)

[IBN KHALDUN 1967: 3:3–4]

19. The Classical Schools

Ibn Khaldun now traces the evolution of the nascent Islamic legal system into distinct "schools," each with its particular point of view. The differences are not *great, save in the case of Sh*ite jurisprudence, whose principles are, for the Sunni Ibn Khaldun, "futile."*

It continued to be that way at the beginning of Islam. Then the cities of Islam grew, and illiteracy disappeared from among the Arabs because of their constant occupation with the Quran. Now the development of jurisprudence from its sources took place. Jurisprudence was perfected and came to be a craft and science. The Quran readers were no longer called Quran readers but jurists and religious scholars.

The jurists developed two different approaches to jurisprudence. One was the use of opinion [or reasoning] and analogy; it was represented by the Iraqis. The other was the use of Prophetic traditions; it was represented by the Hijazis. . . . Few traditions circulated among the Iraqis. Therefore they made much use of analogy and became skilled in it. That gave them the name of the "representatives of opinion." Their chief, around whom and whose followers their school centered, was the Imam Abu Hanifah [d. 767 C.E.]. The leader of the Hijazis was Malik ibn Anas [d. ca. 795 C.E.] and, after him, al-Shafi'i [d 820 C.E.].

Later on, a group of religious scholars disapproved of analogy and rejected its use. They were the Zahirites [literally, "partisans of the plain or 'open' sense"]. They restricted the sources of the law to the texts and the general consensus. . . . The leader of this school was Dawud ibn Ali [d. 884 C.E.] and his son and their followers. . . . The Zahirite school has become extinct today as the result of the extinction of their religious leaders and the disapproval of their adherents by the great mass of Muslims. . . .

. . . The Alids [that is, the Shi'ites] invented their own school and had their own jurisprudence. They based it on their dogma requiring abuse of some of the men around the Prophet and upon their stated opinion concerning the infallibility of the Imams and the inadmissibility of differences in their statements. All these are futile principles. The Kharijites similarly had their own school. The great mass did not approve of these schools but greatly disapproved them and abused them. Nothing is known of the opinions of these schools. Their books have not been transmitted; no trace of them can be found except in regions inhabited (by them). The books of the Shi'a are thus found in Shi'ite countries and wherever Shi'ite dynasties exist, in the West, the East and in the Yemen. The same applies to the Kharijites. . . .

Malik ibn Anas was followed by al-Shafi'i. He traveled to Iraq after

Malik's time. He met the followers of the Imam Abu Hanifah and learned
from them. He combined the approach of the Hijazis with those of the
Iraqis. He founded his own school and opposed Malik on many points.
Malik and al-Shafi'i were followed by Ahmad ibn Hanbal [d. 855 C.E.]. He
was one of the highest-ranking scholars of the Prophetic traditions. His
followers studied with those of Abu Hanifah, notwithstanding the abundant knowledge of Prophetic traditions they themselves possessed. They
founded another school. (Ibn Khaldun, *Muqaddima* 6.14)

[IBN KHALDUN 1967: 3:4–8]

20. The End of the Age of the Fathers

Just as a consensus developed among medieval Christians that the line of the "Fa-
thers of the Church" had come to an end sometime in the era of John of Damascus
(d. ca. 750 C.E.), the Muslims too reflectively closed what was called "the gate of
independent judgment" and denied later scholars the same freedom enjoyed by
earlier Muslim lawyers to derive fresh legal principles from the data of the Quran
and the Prophetic traditions. Ibn Khaldun explains why.

These four authorities [that is, Malik ibn Anas, Abu Hanifah, al-
Shafi'i, and Ahmad ibn Hanbal] are the ones recognized by tradition
in Muslim cities. Tradition-bound people obliterated all other authorities, and scholars no longer admitted any differences of opinion. The
technical terminology became very diversified, and there are obstacles
preventing people from attaining the level of independent judgment. It
was also feared that the existence of differences of opinion might affect
unqualified people whose opinion and religion could not be trusted. Thus,
scholars came to profess their inability to apply independent judgment
and had the people adopt the tradition of the authorities mentioned and
of the respective group of adherents of each. They also forbade one to
modify his traditional allegiance (to one of these four schools) because
that would imply frivolity. All that remained after basic textbooks had
been produced and the continuity of their transmissions had been established was to hand down the respective school traditions and, for each
individual adherent, to act in accordance with the traditions of his school.
Today jurisprudence means this and nothing else. The person who would
claim independent judgment nowadays would be frustrated and have no
adherents. (Ibn Khaldun, *Muqaddima* 6.12)

[IBN KHALDUN 1967: 3:8–9]

21. Abrogation in Islamic Law

*As both Shafi*c*i and Ibn Khaldun pointed out more than once, there was no more troublesome issue in Islamic law than that of abrogation, the annulment of one divine ordinance and the substitution of another in its place, "so that what is lawful may become unlawful and what is unlawful may become lawful," as Tabari says. The question is in fact raised by the Quran itself.*

When We cancel a message [or "verse"] or throw it into oblivion, We replace it with a better one or one similar. Do you not know that God has power over all things? (Quran 2:106)

When We substitute a revelation for another revelation—God knows best what He reveals—they say, you [Muhammad] have made it up. (Quran 16:101)

*This is Shafi*c*i's view of the passages and the principle behind them.*

God indeed created mankind for whatever His established knowledge desired in creating it and for whatever its destiny should be. There is no reversal at all in His judgment, He being swift of reckoning. And He revealed to them the Book that explains everything as a guide and a mercy. In it He laid down some duties which He confirmed and others which He abrogated, as a mercy to His people so as to lighten their burden and to comfort them in addition to the favors which He had begun to bestow upon them. For the fulfillment of the duties which He confirmed, He rewarded them with Paradise and with salvation from His punishment. His mercy has included all of them in what He confirmed and what He abrogated. Praise be to Him for his favors. (Shafi°i, *Treatise*) [SHAFI°I 1961: 123]

*The principle of one verse of the Quran abrogating or canceling another, for all its intrinsic interest for the theologian, was not the crucial point with regard to Islamic law, however. For the lawyers the more troublesome question was whether a tradition reported from and attributed to the Prophet could replace a Quranic prescription. At first there was resistance to the notion that one of the Prophet's sayings could invalidate a Quranic prescription, as appears in what Shafi*c*i says next.*

God has declared that He abrogated revelations of the Book only by means of other revelations in it; that the Prophetic tradition cannot abrogate the Book but that it should only follow what is laid down in the Book; and that the Prophetic tradition is intended to explain the meaning of a revelation of a general nature set forth in the Book. For God said:

"When Our clear messages are recited to them, those who do not hope to meet Us say: 'Bring a different Quran, or make amendments in this one.' Say: 'It is not for me to change it of my will. I follow only what was revealed to me. If I disobey my Lord, I fear the punishment of an awful Day.' " (Quran 10:15)

Thus God informed men that He had commanded His Prophet to obey what was revealed to him but that He did not empower him to alter (the Book) of his own accord. (Shafiʿi, *Treatise*) [SHAFIʿI 1961: 123–124]

And what of the Prophetic tradition itself? May it too be abrogated? Shafiʿi replies.

In like manner the tradition of the Prophet states: Nothing can abrogate it except another tradition of the Prophet. If God were to address to His Apostle a revelation on a matter on which Muhammad had provided a tradition different from what God had addressed to him, the Prophet would (then) provide a tradition in conformity with whatever God had revealed to him, and thus he would make clear to men that he was providing a tradition that abrogated one earlier or contrary to it. (Shafiʿi, *Treatise*) [SHAFIʿI 1961: 125]

But lawyers know that neither life nor law is so simple as that.

Someone may ask: Is it possible to assume that there was a transmitted tradition which was abrogated, while the abrogating tradition was not transmitted?

Shafiʿi replied: That is impossible. . . . Were this possible the entire Prophetic tradition might be abandoned by men, for they would then say, "Perhaps it was abrogated." No duty has ever been abrogated unless it was replaced by another. The abrogation of the prayer-direction toward Jerusalem by another in the direction of the Kaʿba is a case in point. (Shafiʿi, *Treatise*) [SHAFIʿI 1961: 126]

The importance given to those divinely certified traditions by legal scholars— Shafiʿi chief among them—eventually prevailed, and what passed into Muslim orthodoxy was the principle that Quran could be abrogated by both the Quran and the tradition of the Prophet. The argument is laid out with great clarity by Ghazali (d. 1111 C.E.).

There is no dispute concerning the view that the Prophet did not abrogate the Quran on his own authority [cf. Quran 10:15]. He did it in response to revelation [cf. Quran 53:3–4: "Nor does he speak of his own desire. It is nothing but an inspiration that is inspired"]. The abrogating text in such cases is not worded in the Quranic style.

Even if we consider the Prophet capable of abrogating the Quran on the basis of his own reflection, the authority to exercise his discretion derived from God. Thus God does the actual abrogating, operating through the medium of his Prophet. Consequently one should hold that the rulings of the Quran may (also) be abrogated by the Prophet, rather than solely by (another verse of) the Quran. Although the inspiration in these cases is not Quranic inspiration, the word of God is nonetheless one, and God's word is both the abrogating and the abrogated. God does not have two words, one in the Quranic style which we are bidden to recite publicly, and called the Quran, while the other word is not Quran. God has but one word which differs in the mode of its expression. On occasions God indicates His word by the Quran; on others, by words in another style, not publicly recited, and called the Prophetic tradition.

Both are mediated by the Prophet. In each case the abrogator is God alone who indicates the abrogation by means of His Prophet, who instructs us of the abrogation of His Book. Thus none other but the Prophet is capable of manifesting; none other but God of initiating. Were God in this manner to abrogate a verse by the instrumentality of His Prophet, and subsequently to bring another verse similar to the one that had been abrogated, He would have made good His promise (in Sura 2:106). . . . God did not mean to say that He proposed to bring a verse superior to the first. No part of the Quran is superior to another. He meant to state that He would bring a ruling superior to the first, in the sense of its being easier to perform, or richer in terms of reward. (Ghazali, *Mustasfa* 1.125)
[Cited by BURTON 1977: 57]

22. The Case of the Woman Taken in Adultery

This issue of abrogation leads us back to one of the more celebrated incidents recorded in the Gospel of John, that of the woman who was caught in adultery and was then brought to Jesus as a test case.

At daybreak he [that is, Jesus] appeared again in the Temple, and all the people gathered round him. He had taken his seat and was engaged in teaching them when the doctors of the Law and the Pharisees brought in a woman caught committing adultery. Making her stand out in the middle, they said to him: "Master, this woman was caught in the very act of adultery. In the Law of Moses it is laid down [Lev. 20:10; Deut. 22:20–21] that such women are to be stoned. What do you say about it?"

They put the question as a test, hoping to frame a charge against him. Jesus bent down and wrote with his finger on the ground. When they continued to press their question, he sat up straight and said, "That one of you who is faultless shall throw the first stone." Then once again he bent down and wrote on the ground. When they heard what he said, one by one they went away, the eldest first.

And Jesus was left alone with the woman still standing there. Jesus again sat up and said to the woman, "Where are they? Has no one condemned you?" She answered, "No one, sir." Jesus said, "Nor do I condemn you. You may go; do not sin again." (John 8:1–11)

A somewhat similar incident is told of Muhammad, though here a very different point is being made. The story occurs in a tradition going back to Umar and preserved in Bukhari's collection of "sound traditions."

(According to Umar): "They brought to the Prophet, on whom be God's blessing and peace, a Jew and a Jewess who had committed fornication. He said to them, 'What do you find in your Book?' They said, 'Our rabbis blacken the faces of the guilty and expose them to public ridicule.' Abdullah ibn Salam [a Jewish convert] said, 'Messenger of God, tell the Jews to bring the Torah.' They brought it but a Jew put his hand over the verse which prescribes stoning and began to read what came before and after it. Ibn Salam said to him, 'Raise your hand,' and there was the verse about stoning beneath his hand. The Messenger of God gave the order and they were stoned." Ibn Umar added: "They were stoned on the level ground and I saw the man leaning over the woman to shield her from the stones." (Bukhari, *Sahih* 4.300, 309)

23. An Instance of Abrogation: Stoning in Text and Tradition

One of the recurrent charges leveled by Muhammad against the Jews, and echoed in the Quran, was that of the falsification of Scripture. In the example just cited the Prophet shows his fidelity to the Torah-prescribed penalty of stoning, despite the Medinese Jews' attempt to conceal it. The Quran too is explicit on the matter of adultery and fornication, though in a somewhat unexpected way.

The adulterer and the adulteress should be flogged a hundred lashes each, and no pity for them should deter you from the law of God, if you believe in God and the Last Day, and the punishment should be witnessed by a body of believers. (Quran 24:2)

Stoning as a penalty for adultery is nowhere mentioned in the Quran, though the punishment is prescribed by the Torah and apparently practiced by Muhammad. The reconciliation was effected through a Prophetic tradition related on the authority of Ubada. In this case the divine inspiration for Muhammad's utterance is carefully underlined.

The descent of inspiration was troublesome to the Prophet. His face would go ashen in color. One day inspiration came down upon him and he showed the usual signs of distress. When he recovered he said: "Take it from me! God has appointed a way for the women: the non-virgin with the non-virgin and the virgin with the virgin. The non-virgin, one hundred strokes and death by stoning; the virgin, one hundred strokes and banishment for a year." [BURTON 1977: 74]

Put in this fashion, a Prophetic tradition would simply have abrogated the Quran. But some Muslims at least must have had reservations. Another set of traditions, this time reported of Muhammad's companion and the second Caliph of Islam, Umar ibn al-Khattab, intimated that a stoning penalty actually had been revealed as part of the Quran, though it was not in the present copies. According to Umar:

God sent Muhammad with the truth and revealed to him the Book. Part of what God revealed was the stoning verse. We used to recite it and we memorized it. The Prophet stoned and we have stoned after him. I fear that with the passage of time some will say, "we do not find stoning in the Book of God," and will therefore neglect a divine injunction which God revealed. Stoning is a just claim. [BURTON 1977: 77–78]

Why then did not Umar add it to the text of the Quran?

By Him who holds my soul in His hand! Except that men would say, "Umar has added it to the Book of God," I would write it in with my own hand: "The married man and the married woman, when they fornicate, stone them outright." [BURTON 1977: 78]

We are even told where this verse would have occurred.

Ubayy asked Zirr ibn Hubaysh, "How many verses do you recite in the sura (called) 'The Clans' (Sura 33)?" Zirr replied, "Seventy-three verses." Ubayy asked if that was all. "I have seen it," he said, "when it was the same length as (the Sura called) 'The Cow' (Sura 2). It contained the words: 'The married man and the married woman, when they fornicate, stone them outright, as an exemplary punishment from God. God is Mighty, Wise.'" [BURTON 1977: 80]

The question finally comes to rest, all controversy aside, in a jurist's manual of the

*thirteenth century, in a section on Quranically prescribed penalties. The author is
the Syrian al-Nawawi (d. 1277 C.E.).*

Fornication: This consists of introducing the male organ into the
vagina of a forbidden woman without any ambiguity or doubt, or into the
anus of a man or woman as well, according to our (Shafiʿite) school, and
it receives a prescribed penalty, regardless of whether it was done for
payment or by consent, and is applied as well for (relations with) a
woman within the forbidden degrees of kinship or marriage, even if a
marriage was performed. The guilty person must be adult, sane, and
aware that it was wrong. Drunkenness is no excuse.

1. The prescribed penalty of an adult free Muslim or member of a
"protected community" [e.g., a Jew or a Christian], who has consum-
mated a legal marriage previous to the act, is stoning to death. If one of
the two partners has not (contracted a marriage), it does not lessen the
guilt of the other.

2. The prescribed penalty of a fornicator who is not an adult and free
or who has never married is one hundred lashes and banishment for one
year, and if the Imam [that is, the ruler] designates a place of banishment,
that must be accepted.

3. For a slave the prescribed punishment is fifty lashes and banishment for half a year. (Nawawi, *The Goal of Seekers*) [WILLIAMS 1971: 150–151]

24. Controversial Questions

*Although there might be general agreement on the basic principles of the law, there
was certainly a great deal of room for debating some of its specifics. Indeed, this area
of "controversial questions" debated among the four classical schools of Islamic law
constituted an entire subspecies of the discipline of jurisprudence. It is once again
Ibn Khaldun who is writing.*

It should be known that the jurisprudence just described, which is
based upon religious evidence, involves many differences of opinion
among scholars of independent judgment. Differences of opinion result
from the different sources they use and their different outlooks, and they
are unavoidable, as we have stated before.

These differences occupied a very large space in Islam. Originally
people could adhere to any juridical authority they wished. Later on the
matter was in the hands of the four leading authorities in the Muslim
cities. They enjoyed a very high prestige. Adherence was restricted to

them, and people were thus prevented from adhering to anyone else. This situation was the result of the disappearance of independent initiative (in the law), because this was too difficult a matter and because, in the course of time, the scholarly disciplines constituting material for independent judgments had multiplied. Also, there existed nobody who might have organized a school in addition to the existing four. Thus, they were set up as the basic schools of Islam.

Differences of opinion among the adherents of these schools and the followers of their laws received equal status with differences of opinion concerning religious texts and legal principles in general. The adherents of the four schools held disputations in order to prove the correctness of their respective founders. These disputations took place according to sound principles and fast rules. Everybody argued in favor of the correctness of the school to which he adhered and which he followed. The disputations concerned all the problems of religious law and every subject of jurisprudence. . . . These disputations clarified the sources of the authorities as well as the motives of their differences and the occasions when they exercised independent judgment. (Ibn Khaldun, *Muqaddima* 6.13) [IBN KHALDUN 1967: 3:30–31]

25. Legal Reasoning on the Prohibition of Wine

Ibn Khaldun's discussion of legal principles is highly abstract and was intended to be so. How the principles he describes were actually applied and controverted may be seen in the instance of the prohibition against wine, recorded in the Quran in the following words.

They question you concerning wine and gambling. Tell them: "There is great sin and (some) profit in them. But the sin in them is greater than the benefit." (Quran 2:219)

The legal commentaries on this brief passage are long and exceedingly complex. This one comes from the Quran commentary of Fakr al-Din al-Razi (d. 1209 C.E.). He begins by attempting to determine the circumstances of this particular revelation.

Some have noted that in God's words "they question you concerning wine and gambling," exactly what the people have asked about is not made clear. It is possible that they inquired about the character and nature of wine. Or they could have asked whether it was permissible to use wine. And finally, they could have asked whether it was permissible or sinful to drink it. But since God answers by indicating the sinfulness of both (wine and gaming), the emphasis in the answer proves that the (original) questions had to do with permission and sinfulness. This verse involves many complex questions.

The first step toward a solution of those questions is to connect this verse with the other Quranic verses that seem to pertain to the same subject, a process that might reveal the evolution of the prohibition.

Four (Quranic) verses have been revealed on the subject of wine. In Mecca the following verse came down: "And (We give you) the fruits of the palms and the vines, from which you obtain an intoxicant as well as wholesome food. Surely this is a sign for people who understand" (Sura 16:67). On the basis of this it would appear that Muslims drank such drinks, since they were (apparently) permitted. Then, however, Umar, Muʿadh and a group of other Companions of the Prophet asked: "Messenger of God, give us an opinion concerning wine, since it seizes a man's mind and steals his wealth!" Then there were revealed the following words of God concerning wine: "In both are great sin and some uses for men." From that point onward some continued to drink wine, while others abstained from it. Then Abd al-Rahman ibn Awf invited some people, and they drank wine together and became drunk. One of them arose in order to perform the prayer and (incorrectly) recited: "Say: O unbelievers, I worship"—the text reads "I do not worship"—"what you worship" (Sura 109:1). At this point the following verse came down: "O believers, do not approach prayer when you are intoxicated until you are aware of what you are saying" (Sura 4:43).

Then some of the Helpers came together, and among them was Saʿd ibn Abi Waqqas. When they became drunk, they began to boast and recite poetry to each other, until finally Saʿd recited a poem that included a slander against the Helpers. Then when one of the Helpers struck Saʿd with the jawbone of a camel and inflicted a deep head wound on him, the latter complained to the Messenger of God, and Umar said: "God, give us a conclusive statement concerning wine!" Then came down the verse: "O believers, wine, games of chance, idols and divining arrows are an abomination and belong to the works of Satan. So avoid it! Perhaps you will (then) prosper. Satan desires only to bring about enmity and hatred among you, with wine and games of chance, and to bar you from the remembrance of God and from prayer. Will you then not desist?" (Sura 5:90–91). Umar added, "Will we desist, Lord?"

Al-Quffal said that the wisdom of issuing the prohibition (against drinking wine) in these stages consists in the fact that God knew that the people had been accustomed to drinking wine and drawing upon its many uses. So He also knew that it would be unbearable for them if He had prohibited wine to them all at once, and thus doubtless He used these stages as a kindness in the prohibition (against drinking wine).

But there are some who hold that God forbids wine and games of chance in the first verse in question (2:219), and that His words "Do not approach prayer when you are intoxicated" came down after it. That is, the request that the drinking of wine be forbidden during the time of prayer is connected with these words, since one who drinks wine would be performing his prayer while intoxicated. If, therefore, intoxication is forbidden, then the prohibition against drinking wine is also included. The verse (regarding the prohibition of wine) in (the sura called) "The Table" [that is, 5:90–91] came down after the verse under discussion and it represents the strongest possible form of the prohibition. According to al-Rabiʿ ibn Anas, however, the present verse (2:219) came down after the prohibition of wine.

My own view is that one should note that the present verse shows the (prior existence of the) prohibition against wine. It lacks, however, a (precise) explanation of what wine is.

What then is the present state of the question among jurists?

. . . al-Shafiʿi said that every intoxicating drink is wine; Abu Hanifah (on the other hand) said that "wine" refers specifically to a strong grape juice that develops foam (as a result of fermentation). The evidence on which Shafiʿa makes his judgment is of several different types.

The first type of evidence that Shafiʿi adduced was that of the Prophetic traditions on the subject.

1. The first (example of the argument from Prophetic tradition) is what is presented on Abu Dawud's testimony in his tradition collection entitled *Sunan*, on the authority of al-Shaʿbi, from Ibn Umar, who was reported to have said: On one particular day the prohibition against wine was revealed, and this was at a time when wine was made of five kinds of things: grapes, dates, wheat, barley and millet. At that time one understood as "wine" a liquid that clouds [the verb here is *khamara*; the noun for wine throughout is *khamr*] the mind.

From this Shafiʿi thought three kinds of conclusions might be drawn: The first is that this shows that all these (substances) were designated as wine; second, the report is the equivalent of an explicit declaration that the prohibition of wine includes the prohibition of these five kinds; third, Umar was speaking of every kind of drink that "clouds" the mind. Umar doubtless knew the correct linguistic usage, and so his tradition indicates that "wine" is a designation for all drinks that "cloud" the mind. And so forth.

2. The second example of Shafiʿi's evidence is this: Abu Dawud relates from al-Nuʿman ibn Bashir the following statement: The Messenger of God said: "Wine is made out of grapes, dates, honey, wheat and barley." From this one can draw two conclusions: first, that this is an explicit explanation that all these things fall in the category of "wine" and thus are also included in the verse that issues the prohibition against wine; and second, that it was not the intention of the lawgiver to give instructions covering all the terms (for wine and similar drinks). Thus, in the present case he had nothing else in mind but to explain that the decision which applies to wine (from grape juice) also applies to these (other types of wine). If the published decision, which refers specifically to wine (made from grape juice), pertains (generally) to the evil of drinking, then it must be applied in like manner to these (other) types of drinks. Al-Khattabi said that the reason the Messenger of God used the word "wine" specifically for these five things was not because wine is produced only from these five, but they are mentioned by name because they were well known at that time. And so the decision concerning these five applies to all that are like them, such as millet, sult and tree sap. . . .

3. Shafiʿi's third example is as follows: Abu Dawud relates also from Nafiʿ who relates from Ibn Umar: The Messenger of God said that every intoxicating drink is wine and that every type of intoxicating drink is forbidden. Al-Khattabi remarked the following: If the Messenger of God states that every type of intoxicating drink is to be considered wine, then this leads to two possible interpretations: first, the word "wine" is being used to designate all drinks that cause intoxication. . . . After the verse had proclaimed the prohibition against "wine," the people did not know the exact meaning which God meant to express by "wine," that is, whether the lawgiver was using the expression according to its usual meaning in Arabic or was producing a legal category by the creation (of a new definition of the word "wine"), as is also the case with the terms "prayer," "fast" and others; and second, the meaning of his statement is that every intoxicating drink is to be treated as sinful as wine. That is, when the Messenger of God says that this intoxicating drink is wine, the literal meaning would be that they are all actually (different kinds of) wine. Now it is clear that this is not what is meant, so one must take it as a figurative expression for whatever is the equivalent (of wine), and this remains as the authoritative decision.

4. The fourth example is this: Abu Dawud relates the following from Aisha: The Messenger of God was asked about a certain concoction and he answered: "Every drink that intoxicates is prohibited." Al-Khattabi remarked: The drink being referred to in the question was one made of honey, and thus this statement of the Messenger of God refutes every interpretation that is put forward by those who declare that such "drinks" are permitted. The statement also refutes the assertion of those who say that a small amount of an intoxicating drink is allowed. The Messenger of God was asked about only a single kind, the honey concoction, but answered with a prohibition against the (entire) class (of intoxicating drinks). This includes not only a large amount of it but a small amount. If separate classifications according to kind and amount were intended here, then the Messenger of God would have mentioned this and not neglected it.

5. The fifth example is this: Abu Dawud related from Jabir ibn Abdullah: The Messenger of God said that whatever intoxicates in large amounts is prohibited in small amounts.

6. The sixth example is this: Abu Dawud related further from al-Qasim, who related from Aisha (who said): I heard how the Messenger of God said: "Every intoxicant is forbidden. Whatever intoxicates in the amount of a bale is also forbidden in a handful." . . . Here then it is most clearly evident that sinfulness extends to all parts of (intoxicating) drinks.

7. The seventh example is this: Abu Dawud also related from Shahr ibn Hawshab who related from Umm Salama that the Messenger of God prohibited every intoxicating and debilitating drink. Al-Khattabi said that by "debilitating" is to be understood every drink that brings about weaknesses and stiffness in the joints. It doubtless includes all kinds of (intoxicating) drinks.

All these Prophetic traditions indicate that every intoxicating drink is wine and is thus prohibited.

Moreover, other types of arguments supported this conclusion, as Razi now explains. The first derives from the etymology of the word "wine" itself.

The second kind of argument which indicates that every intoxicating drink (*muskir*) is wine (*khamr*) is seen when one considers the etymology. The lexicographers mention that the basic meaning of the root *kh-m-r* is "to cover." Thus the head veil is called *khamaar* because it covers the head of a woman, while a *khamar* may be a shrub or a ground depression in a hill, which conceals somebody. . . . The etymology shows that by "wine" we are to understand anything that "veils" [or "clouds"] the mind, just as one designates wine as an intoxicant (*muskir*) because it "closes" (*sakara*) the mind.

The argument from consensus is then put forward.

The third kind of argument which indicates that by "wine" is to be understood whatever intoxicates is based on the fact that the community agrees in the following: There are three (Quranic) verses which refer to wine, in two of which it is explicitly called such (2:219 and 5:90) . . . while the third verse refers to intoxication and contains God's words: "Do not approach prayer when you are intoxicated" (4:43). This shows that by "wine" is meant intoxicants.

And finally, the case can be made from analogical reasoning.

The fourth kind of argument is as follows: The occasion for the prohibition of wine was when Umar and Muʿadh said: "Messenger of God, wine seizes the mind and steals the wealth. Give us an explanation concerning it!" Thus they asked for a judgment from God and His Messenger because wine seizes the mind. Hence it necessarily follows that all that is like wine in this sense is either wine or is equivalent to it in view of the present decision.

The fifth kind of argument is as follows: God has confirmed His prohibition of wine through His words: "Satan desires only to create enmity and hatred among you, with wine and games of chance, and to bar you from a remembrance of God and from prayer" (2:219). Doubtless such kinds of acts are motivated by intoxication. This cause is certain. Accordingly, the present verse (2:219) presents more precise evidence of the fact that the sinfulness of (the use of wine) lies in the fact that it intoxicates. Whether it is now unconditionally necessary that every intoxicating drink is wine or whether this is not so, in all cases the present decision is valid for all intoxicating drinks. Whoever thinks correctly and freely knows that these aspects (of the evidence) are given clearly and distinctly, along with the (clear) statement of the problem. (Razi, *The Great Commentary*, ad loc.)

Once the arguments had all been set forth, the fact remained that the drinking of wine was a Quranically proscribed crime. From this practical perspective the treatment of prosecution and punishment is far more succinct.

Forbidden beverages: Every drink that inebriates in a large quantity is forbidden in a small quantity. The prescribed punishment is not given to a child, an insane person or a non-Muslim subject. One may take wine in case of immediate necessity, according to our (Shafiʿite) school, e.g., to dislodge food in the throat which is choking one, if nothing else is available; one is, however, liable to punishment if he uses wine for medicine or because of thirst.

The prescribed punishment for a free person is forty blows, and that for a slave twenty; by whip, hand, sandal or a rolled-up garment. It is said that it should be with a whip. The Imam [that is, the ruler] may double the punishment if he sees fit. (Nawawi, *Guide for Seekers* 205–244)

[WILLIAMS 1971: 152]

26. The Fast of Ramadan

The fast during the month of Ramadan was one of the precepts laid down in the Quran for all believers. Here we trace the practice from the chief Quranic text, through the prophetic traditions, to the commentators.

O believers, fasting is enjoined on you, even as it was on those before you, so that you might become righteous.

Fast a certain number of days, but if someone is ill or traveling, the same number of other days (he had missed), and those who find it difficult should (as compensation) feed a poor person. For the good they do with a little hardship is better for men. And if you fast, it is good for you, if you knew.

. . . When you see a new moon you should fast for the whole month; but a person who is ill or traveling should fast on other days, as God wishes ease and not hardship for you, so that you complete the (fixed) number and give glory to God for the guidance and be grateful. . . .

You are allowed to sleep with your wives on the nights of the fast: they are your dress as you are theirs. God is aware you were cheating yourselves so He turned to you and pardoned you. So now you may have intercourse with them. Eat and drink until the white thread of dawn appears clear from the dark line, then fast until night falls; and abstain from your wives to stay in the mosques for assiduous devotion. These are the bounds fixed by God, so keep well within them. . . . (Quran 2:183–187)

We begin with some of the Prophetic traditions on the subject of the Ramadan fast.

Ibn Umar, may God be pleased with both of them (both father and son), reported God's Messenger, may peace be upon him, as saying in connection with Ramadan: Do not fast till you see the new moon and do not break fast until you see it; but if the weather is cloudy, calculate it. (Muslim, *Sahih* 6.406.2363)

Sahl ibn Saʿd said that when this verse was revealed, "Eat and drink until the white thread becomes distinct to you from the black thread," a person would take hold of a white thread and a black thread and keep eating until he could find them distinct (in the light of the dawn). It was then that God, the Majestic and Great, revealed (the rest of the phrase) "of the dawn," and then it became clear that "thread" refers to the streak of light in the dawn. (Ibid. 6.412.2397)

Ibn Umar reported that the Messenger of God, may peace be upon him, observed fasts uninterruptedly [that is, night and day] in Ramadan, and the people did this (in imitation of him). But he forbade them to do so. It was said to him: You yourself observe the fasts uninterruptedly (but you forbid us to do so). Upon this he said: I am not like you: I am fed and supplied drink (by God). (Ibid. 6.415.2427)

Abu Hurayra, may God be pleased with him, reported that a person came to the Messenger of God, may peace be upon him, and said: Messenger of God, I am undone. He [Muhammad] said: What brought about your ruin? The man said: I have had intercourse with my wife (during the day) in Ramadan. Upon this Muhammad said: Can you find a slave to set free (by way of atonement)? The man said: No. Muhammad said: Can you fast for two consecutive months? The man said: No. Muhammad said: Can you provide food for sixty poor people? The man said no. The man then sat down and there was brought to the Messenger of God, may peace be upon him, a basket which contained dates. Muhammad said: Give these dates as an alms. The man said: Am I to give to one who is poorer than I. There is no family poorer than mine between the two lava plains of Medina. The Messenger of God laughed so broadly that his back tooth showed and said. Go and give it to your family to eat. (Ibid. 6.418.2457)

Aisha, may God be pleased with her, reported that Hamza ibn Amr al-Aslami thus asked the Messenger of God, may peace be upon him: Messenger of God, I am a person devoted much to fasting. Should I fast during the journey? He said: Fast if you like and break it if you like. (Ibid. 6.421.2488)

Ibn Abbas, may God be pleased with both of them (father and son), reported that when God's Messenger, may peace be upon him, came to Medina, he found the Jews observing the fast on the day of Ashura [that is, the tenth of Muharram]. The Jews were asked about it and they said: It is the day on which God granted victory to Moses and the Banu Israʾil over the Pharaoh and we observe fast out of gratitude to Him. Upon this the Messenger of God, may peace be upon him, said: We have closer connection with Moses than you have, and he commanded (Muslims) to observe fast on this day. (Ibid. 6.423.2518)

Aisha, may God be pleased with her, reported that the Quraysh used to fast on the day of Ashura in the pre-Islamic days and the Messenger of God, may peace be upon him, also observed it. When he migrated to Medina he himself observed the fast and commanded (others) to observe it. But when fasting during the month of Ramadan was made obligatory, he said: He who wishes to observe the fast (of Ashura) may do so and he who wishes to abandon it may do so. (Ibid. 6.423.2499)

The following two traditions, reported from the same authority, show one verse of the Quran abrogating another.

Salama ibn Akwa, may God be pleased with him, reported that when this verse was revealed, "And for those who can afford it there is a ransom, the feeding of a man in need" (2:184), he who liked to fast fasted and he who liked not to observe it ate and expiated till the (following part of the) verse was revealed which abrogated it.

Salama ibn Akwa reported: During the lifetime of the Messenger of God, may peace be upon him, in one month of Ramadan he who wished to fast fasted and he who wished to break it broke it and fed a needy person as an expiation, till this (following) verse was revealed: "But whoever does good of his own accord, it is better for him." (Muslim, *Sahih* 6.428.2547–2548)

The reference to fasting as an obligation imposed upon others before Islam (2:183) elicited these remarks from the exegete Tabari (d. 923 C.E.) on the origins of the Christians' Lenten fast during the fifty days preceding Easter.

As for those who were before us, they were the Christians. The month of Ramadan was prescribed, as it was also prescribed for them neither to eat nor to drink if they wake up after they had gone to sleep. Nor were they allowed to go in to their wives during the entire month of Ramadan. The Christians found the fast of Ramadan hard to endure. Ramadan rotated from winter and summer. As they realized this, they agreed to have the fast between winter and summer. They said: "We shall add twenty days as expiation for what we have done." Thus they made their fast fifty days. Muslims continued to observe the fast in emulation of Christians until the incidents of Abu Qays ibn Sirmah al-Ansari and Umar ibn al-Khattab, when God made lawful for them [that is, the Muslims] eating, drinking and sexual intercourse until the appearance of the dawn. (Tabari, *Commentary* 3.411) [AYOUB 1984: 189]

These "incidents" are described by the commentator al-Wahidi (d. 1076 C.E.).

At first the Muslims used to eat, drink and go in to their wives (after sunset in Ramadan) so long as they had not gone to sleep. Once they slept they did not do any of these things until the following evening. It happened that Qays ibn Sirmah al-Ansari was fasting, so he came to his wife at the time of the breaking of the fast (in the evening), but she had nothing for him to eat. While she went to fetch food for him, he fell asleep. Around noon of the next day he fainted. Likewise, Umar ibn al-Khattab came in to his wife after she had slept. All this was reported to the Prophet. Then this verse (2:187) was sent down and the Muslims were pleased with it. (Wahidi, *The Occasions of Quranic Revelation* 45) [AYOUB 1984: 197]

And on the question of substituting another good work, to wit, feeding a needy person, for the fast during Ramadan:

In sum, abrogation is stipulated only in the case of one in sound health and not on a journey. This is based on God's saying, "Therefore whosoever among you witnesses the moon, let him fast (the month)." The aged one who is near death, however, is allowed not to observe the fast; nor is he obliged to make up fasting by other days. This is because his condition would not change in such a way so as to make up for the days he missed. But if he does break the fast, he should feed a poor man for every day if he has the means to do so. (Ibn Kathir, *Commentary* 1.378–379) [AYOUB 1984. 190–191]

By the time the command to fast had passed into the legal manuals it had been thoroughly discussed by Islamic lawyers, who could then pronounce on almost any conceivable complication. The following commentary from the legal manual of al-Nawawi (d. 1277 C.E.) sets out the conditions of fulfilling the obligation.

To fast one must rigorously avoid intercourse, vomiting . . . or introducing any substance into the "interior of the body." . . . It does not matter if the "interior" is inside the head or the belly or the intestines or the bladder; all can break the fast with the introduction of a substance by snuffing or eating or injection, or through incision in the belly or the head or the like. According to the soundest opinion, putting drops in the nose or the urethra breaks the fast.

It is necessary, however, that the introduction (of a substance) be through an open passage. Thus there is no harm in oil's entering the pores

by absorption, or when *kohl* [or eyeliner] is used, and its taste is afterwards perceived in the throat.

Further, the introduction must be intended, so that if a fly or a gnat
or dust of the road or flour dust entered (the body) by accident, the fast
would not be broken. It also would not be broken if saliva were swal-
lowed carelessly. But the fast is broken if saliva leaves the mouth, and one
brings it back into the mouth, or if one moistens a thread in one's mouth
and then puts it back in the mouth still moist, or if one swallows saliva
in which a foreign substance or something unclean is mixed.

If one swallows saliva in the mouth, then, he does not break the fast,
but if he swallows water from the mouth or nose remaining after the
ablutions, if it is in any quantity, he does break the fast. If food remaining
between the teeth is dislodged by saliva, it does not break the fast. (Nawawi, *Program for Students*) [WILLIAMS 1971: 113–114]

*And finally, Ghazali offers a prescription for converting a ritual obligation into a
genuinely spiritual act.*

When you fast, do not imagine that fasting is merely abstaining from
food, drink and marital intercourse. Muhammad, God bless and preserve
him, has said: "Many a one who fasts has nothing from his fasting save
hunger and thirst." Rather, perfect fasting consists in restraining all the
members from what God Most High disapproves. You must keep the eye
from looking at things disapproved, the tongue from uttering what does
not concern you, and the ear from listening to what God has forbidden—
for the hearer shares the guilt of the speaker in cases of backbiting.
Exercise the same restraint over all the members as over the stomach and
the genitals. A prophetic tradition runs: "Five things make a man break
his fast: lying, backbiting, malicious gossip, the lustful glance and the false
oath." Muhammad, God bless and preserve him, said: "Fasting is a protection; if one of you is fasting, let him avoid obscene speech, loose living
and folly; and if anyone attacks him or insults him, let him say, 'I am
fasting.'"

Then endeavor to break your fast with lawful food, and not to take
an excessive amount, eating more than you normally eat at night because
you are fasting by day; if you take the whole amount you usually take,
there is no difference between eating it at one meal at night and eating
it at two meals (one by day and one by night, as when one is not fasting).
The aim of fasting is to oppose your appetites, and to double your capacity for works of piety. (Ghazali, *The Beginning of Guidance* 27)
[GHAZALI 1953: 129–130]

27. The Menstruant

One Prophetic tradition that invites a direct comparison with Torah law is that on the subject of menstruation.

Anas said that among the Jews, when a woman menstruated, they did not eat with her, and they did not live with such in their houses, so the Prophet's companions questioned him, and God revealed the verse, "They ask you also concerning women during menstruation . . ." (Quran 2:222). The Messenger of God then said, "Do everything except have sexual intercourse." The Jews heard of that and said, "This man does not want to leave anything we do unopposed." Usayd ibn Hudayr and Abbad ibn Bishr came and said, "Messenger of God, the Jews are saying such and such. Shall we not then live with them?" The face of the Messenger of God then underwent such a change that we thought he was angry with the two men. But when they went out they encountered a gift of milk which was being brought for the Prophet; and he sent after them and offered them a drink, whereby they knew he was not angry with them. Muslim transmitted this tradition. (Baghawi, *Mishkat al-Masabih* 3.13)

This tradition suggests that there was no prior Arab custom on the subject of menstruation, or none that was an issue for Muhammad, and that the Quran's remark on it in 2:222 was prompted by someone's awareness of Jewish legislation about menstruation. The Torah indeed speaks of it, and in no uncertain terms, in the midst of a long section of Leviticus on various forms of ritual impurity.

When a woman has a discharge, her discharge being blood from her body, she shall remain in her impurity seven days; whoever touches her shall be unclean until evening. Anything that she lies on during her impurity shall be unclean; and anything she sits on shall be unclean. Anyone who touches her bedding shall wash his clothes, bathe in water and remain unclean until evening; and anyone who touches anything on which she has sat shall wash his clothes, bathe in water and remain unclean till evening. Be it the bedding or be it the object on which she has sat, on touching it he shall be unclean until evening. If a man lies with her, her impurity is communicated to him; he shall be unclean for seven days, and any bedding on which he lies shall become unclean. (Leviticus 15:19–24)

The laws of ritual purity and impurity were taken seriously indeed by the rabbis of the post-biblical period, and the Mishna has a whole series of tractates, called collectively "Cleannesses," on that subject. One of them, Niddah, or "The Menstru-

ant," *is given over to the matter of those few lines in Leviticus. As in most other tracts of the Mishna, when we enter Niddah, we come into a discussion already in progress, and the participants show their usual disinterest in informing us when or under what circumstances it began. The rabbis are discussing when the beginning of the period of impurity is calculated and what tests might be required to determine if a woman is indeed menstruating. They praise women who test themselves often and condemn men who attempt the same thing. The matter of testing is obviously important: it determines, for example, whether a woman may share in consecrated food, which will not be an issue in Islam, and the advisability of having intercourse, which will.*

Women may always be assumed clean in readiness for their husbands. When men have come from a journey their wives may be assumed clean in readiness for them. The School of Shammai say: She needs two test cloths for every act (of intercourse), or else on every occasion she should examine it by the light of a lamp. And the School of Hillel say: Two test cloths suffice her throughout the entire night. (M.Niddah 2:4)

The discussion then veers into another related subject. Menstruation and childbirth are both among the causes of a seven-day impurity. Mishna Niddah then attempts to make a determination of when a miscarriage or natural abortion issues in a true childbirth. There is first a general rule.

If a woman suffers a miscarriage and there was blood with it, (it in effect constitutes a childbirth and so) she becomes unclean; but if there was not, (there was no childbirth and so) she remains clean. (Ibid. 3:1)

More elaborate criteria govern this determination, an examination of the aborted fetus, for example.

If the abortion was a fetus filled with water or filled with blood or filled with variegated matter, she need not consider it a human being; but if its (human) parts were formed, she must remain unclean for the number of days prescribed for a male and for a female (birth). (Ibid. 3:3)

Another general rule emerges, this time on the question of when a fetus becomes a human being. The issue is still to determine postpartum ritual purity: a true human birth renders the mother ritually unclean; any other miscarriage leaves her in her original state of ritual purity.

If she suffered a miscarriage on the fortieth day, she need not consider it as a (human) infant; if on the forty-first day, she must continue (unclean for the days prescribed) both for a male and for a female (birth) and also for a menstruant. Rabbi Ishmael says: If (the miscarriage) occurs on the forty-first day, she must continue (unclean for the days prescribed) for a male birth and for a menstruant; but if on the eighty-first day, she must continue (unclean for the days prescribed) for a male and for a female birth and for a menstruant, since a male is fully fashioned after forty-one days but a female only after eighty-one days. But the Sages say: The creation of a male and the creation of a female are alike: each is (fully fashioned) after forty-one days. (Ibid. 3:7)

Finally, menstrual uncleanness is used, by way of analogy, as a type of excommuni-cation from the community of the true Israel, or at least as a disincentive to intermarriage, as here in the case of the Samaritans and the Sadducees.

The daughters of the Samaritans are (considered unclean as) men-struants from their cradle; and thus the Samaritan men convey unclean-ness to what lies beneath them in the same degree (as someone who has the flux conveys uncleanness) to what lies above him, since they have connection with menstruants. . . . The daughters of the Sadducees, if they follow in the ways of their fathers, are deemed like the women of the Samaritans; but if they have separated themselves and follow in the ways of the Israelites, they are deemed like the women of the Israelites. (Ibid. 4:1)

Without suggesting that Muhammad or his contemporaries were aware of all of it, this was the background against which Quran 2:222 was revealed.

They ask you about menstruation. Tell them: "This is a pollution. So keep away from women in this state till they are clean of it. When they are free of it, you may go in to them as God has enjoined. For God loves those who seek pardon and those who are clean." (Quran 2:222)

The Quran, then, seems to take the same view as Leviticus: menstruation is a form of ritual impurity, and a man should separate himself from a menstruating woman until the period is over and the woman has purified herself. But that the Muslims understood what has here been translated as "approach" only in sexual terms is made pointedly clear in the traditions handed down from the Prophet on this subject. They occur in the canonical tradition books grouped in a collection called "Menstru-ation," under the larger juridical category of "Purifications."

Aisha said, "The Prophet and I used to wash from one vessel when we were both ritually unclean from sex. . . . I would drink when I was menstruating, then hand it to the Prophet and he would put his mouth where mine had been and drink; and I would eat flesh from a bone when I was menstruating, then hand it to the Prophet, and he would put his mouth where mine had been. . . ." She also said: "The Prophet would recline in my lap when I was menstruating, then recite the Quran." She also said: "The Prophet said to me, 'Get me the mat from the mosque,' and when I said I was menstruating, he said, 'Your menstruation is not in your hand.' " Maymuna said: "God's Messenger used to pray in a woolen garment which was partly over him and partly over me while I was menstruating." (Baghawi, *Mishkat al-Masabih* 3.13)

There is an entire series of traditions on the theme "Sex above the Waist with a Menstruating Woman."

Aisha reported: "When anyone among us [that is, Muhammad's wives] was menstruating, the Messenger of God, may peace be upon him, asked her to tie a skirt about her and embraced her."

Umm Salama reported: "While I was lying in a bed cover with the Messenger of God, may peace be upon him, I began menstruating, so I slipped away and I picked up my menstrual clothes. Upon this the Messenger of God, may peace be upon him, said: 'Have you begun your period?' I said 'Yes' He called me and I lay down with him on the bed cover." And she further said that she and the Messenger of God used to bathe from the same vessel after sexual intercourse. (Muslim, *Sahih* 119.577, 581)

On the face of it, then, the Prophet appears to have taken menstruation rather lightly. Not so the later Muslim lawyers, who were apparently far closer to Leviticus than to the Prophetic traditions. The jurist Ibn Qudama (d. 1223 C.E.) is one example.

The menstrual periods of women involve ten prohibitions: (1) performance of prayer; (2) obligatory prayer; (3) fasting; (4) circumambulation of the Ka'ba; (5) reading the Quran; (6) touching a copy of the Quran; (7) remaining in a mosque; (8) sexual contacts; (9) formal repudiation of a wife; and (10) being reckoned in a period of voluntary continence. [IBN QUDAMA 1950: 14]

28. A Christian Appraisal of the Islamic Law

Note has already been taken in Chapter 1 above of the judgments rendered on Muhammad and the Quran by the Dominican missionary and veteran Near Eastern traveler Ricoldo di Monte Croce (d. 1320 C.E.). The same scholar and polemicist, who had studied Islam in the schools of Baghdad, offered this summary and appraisal of the Islamic law.

Let us give a brief summary of the Saracens' religious law. Contrary to what is thought, the law of the Saracens is rambling, confused, opaque, lying, irrational and violent. In the first place, it is broad, attacking both the rule of the philosophers of the world who say that it is as difficult to live a virtuous life as it is for an arrow to hit the center of a target as well as the teaching of the Great Philosopher, to wit Christ, who says that narrow is the path that leads to life. For for them the necessity of salvation means nothing except that they say "There is no god but God and Muhammad is the Messenger of God." All the Saracens hold in common that a Saracen has only to say this and he will be saved, even if he should have committed all the sins in the world. Even though they lay down many prohibitions and command many other things in their law, namely in Alcoran, nevertheless the sinner pays no penalty in the next life. It should also be noted that that expression which Muhammad expresses, as it seems to me, in a hundred different ways in the Alcoran, "There is no god but God," is admitted by all religious groups. For that proposition says no more than "There is no dog but dog," or "There is no horse but horse," etc. What the Muslims intend is that the self-evidence of the proposition "there is no god but God" also be extended to "Muhammad is the Messenger of God." But how great an injury they do to philosophical truth by linking the falsest of propositions with the truest of propositions, and how great an injury they do to God by connecting the truth of God with the lie and falsehood of Muhammad, every thoughtful man may judge for himself. And they consider themselves saved if they say that alone. Their law, then, may be called broad. And Satan cunningly foresaw this, so that those people, who are unwilling to ascend by the narrow way to happiness, might take the broad way down to hell.

And how can they observe something which they do not understand? They themselves make their law so confused by their own explanations that their God, who gave the law, almost appears stupid. For it is written there that fornication is prohibited, but every kind of buying and selling is licit and not prohibited and that each may do as he wishes with his own goods. This, then, is what the scrupulous Saracens do. They go to a house of prostitution and say to the whore: "I am filled with desire, but fornication is not permitted. So sell yourself to me." And she sells herself and once the price has been paid, he says to her: "You belong to me." When she agrees that such is indeed the case, he concludes: "According to our law I can do as I wish with my own possessions." Then he can sleep with her with peace of mind. This is indeed what Muhammad himself seems to say in Alcoran, in base and open language: "Wear out the women and it will be no sin as long as you have given the price which you promised." (Ricoldo di Monte Croce, *Itinerary*) [LAURENT 1873: 135–136]

6. One God, One Faith, One Community

1. Unity and Heresy

In the first afterglow of the Ascension and Pentecost, there was only unity and concordance among the followers of the Risen Messiah, as the Acts of the Apostles testifies.

They [the followers of Jesus] met constantly to hear the Apostles teach and to share the common life, to break bread, and to pray. A sense of awe was everywhere, and many marvels and signs were brought about through the Apostles. All whose faith had brought them together held everything in common: they would sell their property and possessions and make a general distribution as the need of each required. With one mind they kept up their daily attendance at the Temple, and, breaking bread in private houses, shared their meals with unaffected joy, as they praised God and enjoyed the favor of the people. (Acts 2:42–47)

The whole body of believers was united in heart and soul. Not a man claimed any of his possession as his own but everything was held in common, while the Apostles bore witness with great power to the resurrection of the Lord Jesus. (Acts 4:32)

That is how the earliest Christian fellowship in Jerusalem appeared to one of its close observers, himself a Christian. But on Luke's own testimony, that pristine unanimity was soon rent, not with sin but with differences of opinion. Sometimes merely administrative matters were in question, as when the "Hebrews" and the "Hellenists" differed over the welfare program in Jerusalem (Acts 6:1–6). More profoundly, Paul and the elders under James did not see eye to eye on the Gentile question. Likewise, a close reading of Paul's letters reveals discord and "divisions," as he calls them, in the communities under his care. Paul was in fact constrained to remonstrate more than once with the brethren at Corinth.

I appeal to you, my brothers, in the name of our Lord Jesus Christ: agree among yourselves and avoid divisions; be firmly joined in unity of mind and thought. I have been told, my brothers, by Chloe's people that there are quarrels among you. What I mean is this: each of you is saying, "I am Paul's man" or "I am Apollo's"; "I follow Cephas" or "I am Christ's." Surely Christ has not been divided among you. (Paul, *To the Corinthians* 1.1:10–13)

And later in the same letter:

In giving you these injunctions, I must mention a practice which I cannot commend: your meetings do more harm than good. To begin with, I am told that when you meet as a congregation you fall into sharply divided groups; and I believe there is some truth in it, for dissensions are necessary if only to show which of your members are sound. (Ibid. 1.11:17–19)

Indeed, the word "heretic" appears in Paul for the first and only time in the entire New Testament—though assuredly not with the same pointed connotation that it possessed later—when he used it in distinction to a praiseworthy "orthodoxy."

Steer clear of foolish speculations, genealogies, quarrels, and controversies over the Law; they are unprofitable and pointless. A heretic should be warned, once, and once again; after that have done with him, recognizing that a man of that sort has a distorted mind and stands self-condemned in his sin. (Paul, *To Titus* 3:9–10)

Two centuries later, when the life of those same communities was infinitely more complex and the "divisions" ran deeper and more painfully through the body of Christians, Cyprian, the bishop of Carthage, returned to Paul's remarks and enlarged them.

Heresies have often arisen and still arise for this reason, that disgruntled minds will quarrel, or disloyal troublemakers will not maintain the unity. But these things the Lord permits and endures, leaving man's freedom unimpaired, so that when our minds and hearts are tested by the touchstone of truth, the unswerving faith of those who are approved may appear in the clearest possible light. This was foretold by the Holy Spirit through the Apostle, when he says, "Dissensions are necessary if only to show which of your members are sound." Thus are the faithful approved, thus the faithless discovered; thus too, even before the day of judgment, already here below, the souls of the just and the unjust are distinguished, and the wheat is separated from the chaff. This explains why certain people, backed by their hot-headed associates, seize authority for them-

selves without any divine sanction, making themselves into bishops regardless of the rules of appointment, and since there is no one to confer
the episcopate on them, they assume the title of bishop on their own
authority. (Cyprian, *On the Unity of the Church* 10)

2. The Rule of Faith

*How manifestly Jesus intended that there should be one body of believers, and how
difficult that intention was to achieve in the face of discordant opinions on the most
fundamental questions of faith, is a commonplace theme in early Christian writing.
Almost all the early Fathers of the Church touched upon this matter of unity and
schism, and by the late second century a number of solutions had been put forward.
Both Ireneus (d. ca. 200 C.E.) and Tertullian (d. after 220 C.E.) proposed what they
called the "rule of faith," a summary statement of the essential teaching of the
Church received from Jesus Christ himself through the Apostles. It alone would
suffice for salvation since, as Tertullian put it, "there is no need of curiosity after
Christ, nor of inquiry after the Gospels."*

The Church, though dispersed throughout the whole world, even to
the ends of the earth, has received from the Apostles and their disciples
this faith: in one God, the Father Almighty, who made the heaven and the
earth and the seas and all the things that are in them; and in one Christ
Jesus, the Son of God, who took flesh for our salvation; and in the Holy
Spirit, who proclaimed through the prophets the dispensations and the
comings, and the birth from a virgin, and the suffering, and the resurrection from the dead, and the fleshly ascension of the beloved Christ Jesus,
our Lord, and his future manifestations from heaven in the glory of the
Father, "to sum up all things" (Eph. 1:10), and to rise up anew all flesh
of the human race, in order that to Christ Jesus, our Lord and God and
Savior and King, according to the will of the Invisible Father, "every knee
should bend, of things in heaven, and things on earth, and things under
the earth, and that every tongue should confess" (Phil. 2:10–11) to him
and that he should execute just judgments toward all. . . .

As I have already observed, the Church, having received this preaching and this faith, though scattered throughout the whole world, yet as
if occupying one house, carefully preserves it. She also believes those
points of doctrine as if she had but one soul and one and the same heart,
and she proclaims them, and teaches them, and hands them down, all
with perfect harmony, as if she possessed a single mouth. For, though the
languages of the world are dissimilar, yet the import of the tradition is
one and the same. For the churches which have been planted in Germany

have not believed or handed down anything different, nor do those in
Spain, nor those in Gaul, nor those in the East, nor those in Egypt, nor
those in Libya, nor those that have been established in the central regions
of the world. . . . Nor will any one of the rulers of the churches, however
highly gifted he may be in point of eloquence, teach doctrines different
from those, for no one is greater than his Master; nor, on the other hand,
will he who is deficient in expression inflict injury on the tradition. For
the faith being one and the same, neither does the one who is able to
discourse at length upon it make any addition to it, nor does one who can
say but little diminish it. (Ireneus, *Against the Heresies* 1.10.1–2)

A half-century later the bishop of Carthage in Africa had a similar vision of the
unity of the Church, though now with somewhat more emphasis on the authority
of the bishops.

This oneness we must hold to firmly and insist on, particularly those
of us who are bishops and exercise authority in the Church, so as to
demonstrate that the episcopal power is one and undivided as well. Let
none mislead the brethren with a lie, let none corrupt the true content
of the faith with a faithless perversion of the truth. The authority of the
bishops forms a unity, of which each holds his part in totality; and the
Church too forms a unity, however far she spreads and multiplies through
the offspring of her fertility, just as the sun's rays are many, yet the
strength deriving from its sturdy source is one. So too, though many
streams flow from a single spring, and its multiplicity appears to be scattered abroad by the copiousness of its swelling waters, their oneness
abides by reason of their point of origin. Try to cut off one of the sun's
rays; the unity of that body permits no such division of its light. But if you
break a branch from a tree, it can blossom no more, and if you dam up
a stream at its source, it dries up in its lower reaches. So too our Lord's
Church is radiant with light and pours her rays out over the whole world;
but it is one and the same light that is spread everywhere, and the unity
of her body suffers no division. She spreads her branches in luxuriant
growth all over the earth, she extends her abundant streams still farther;
yet one is the headwaters, one the source, one the mother who is prolific
in her offspring, generation after generation: of her womb we are born,
on her milk are we fed, from her Spirit our souls draw their breath of life.
(Cyprian, *On the Unity of the Church* 5)

God is one, and Christ is one, and his Church is one; one is the faith
and one the people harmoniously cemented together into the strong unity
of a body. This unity cannot be split asunder; that one body cannot be

divided by any cleavage of its structure, nor cut up into fragments with its vitals torn apart. Nothing that is separated from the parent stock can ever live or breathe apart; all hope of its salvation is lost. (Ibid. 23)

Cyprian looks back to what already appeared as the golden age of the community.

This common mind once prevailed in the time of the Apostles; this was the spirit in which the new community of the believers obeyed our Lord's commands and maintained charity with one another. The Scriptures are witness to it: "The crowd of those who who had come to believe acted with one mind and soul." . . . But among us that unity of mind has weakened in proportion as the generosity of our charity has crumbled away. In those days they would sell their houses and their estates and lay up for themselves treasures in heaven by giving money to the Apostles for distribution to those in need. But now we do not even give tithes on our patrimony, and whereas our Lord tells us to sell, we buy instead and accumulate. To such an extent have our people lost their steadfastness in belief. That is why our Lord has said in his Gospel, with an eye toward our times, "The Son of Man, when he comes, shall he find, do you think, faith on earth?" We see what he foretold happening before our eyes. As to the fear of God, or a sense of justice, or charity, or good works, faith inspires us to none of them. No one gives thought of the fears that the future holds in store: the Day of the Lord and the wrath of God, the punishments that await unbelievers, the eternal torments appointed for the betrayers of their faith, no one gives them a thought. Whatever a believing conscience should fear, our conscience, because it no longer believes, knows not fear. If only it believed, it would take heed; if it took heed, it would escape. (Ibid. 25)

Cyprian, for one, understood where the cure lay.

Our Lord, whose precepts and admonitions we are bound to observe, ordered the high office of the bishop and the system of his Church when he speaks in the Gospels and says to Peter, "Thou art Peter, and upon this rock I shall build my Church . . ." (Matt. 16:18, 19). Therefore age has followed age and bishop has followed bishop in succession, and the office of the episcopate and the system of the Church has been handed down, so that the Church is founded on the bishops and every act of the Church is directed by these same presiding officers. Since this has been established by divine ordinance, I am astonished that certain persons have been rash and bold enough to choose to write to me in such a manner as to send their letter in the Church's name, when the Church consists of the bishop, the clergy and all the faithful. (Cyprian, *Letter* 33:1)

The unity of the Church would be preserved, then, through the authority of the bishops, those faithful transmitters of Jesus' teaching through their succession back through the Apostles. But such was not the case. In Anatolia charismatics called Montanists asserted the autonomous authority of the Holy Spirit in the face of both bishops and "rules of faith." All around the Mediterranean basin some Christians offered their own, more private and progressive understanding of both Scripture and tradition. And in Cyprian's own Africa a local and indigenous Christian tradition struggled against the very idea of "catholicity" that both Ireneus and Cyprian had been espousing as a cure for divisiveness.

3. Constantine Summons a Council of the Whole Church

The bishops attempted to maintain the unity by acting in concert through the instrument of the synod or council, and they legislated to continue the practice in the first of the great councils of the whole Church, held in 325 C.E..

. . . And in order that this inquiry (into abuses and complaints) may be conveniently made, it is decreed that it is proper that synods should be assembled twice every year in every province, that all the bishops of the province being assembled together, such questions may be looked into, so that those who have confessedly offended against the bishop may appear to be excommunicated with reason by all the bishops, until it shall seem fit to their general assembly to pronounce a more lenient sentence upon them. And let these synods be held, the one before Lent, that the pure gift may be offered to God after all bitterness has been put aside, and let the second be held in the autumn. (Council of Nicea, Canon 5)

These earliest synods of bishops were essentially provincial meetings and so had limited jurisdiction. But the spread of what appeared to be nontraditional teaching, and particularly the opinions of the Alexandrian presbyter Arius, across the eastern Mediterranean far outstripped the reach of either his own bishops or all the bishops of Egypt meeting in synod. The conversion of the Roman emperor to the Christian faith in 312 C.E. seemed to offer a fortuitous solution to this epidemic of heresy. No single bishop had authority over the whole Church, but the ruler of the empire might be thought to have such jurisdiction, or at least the same responsibility of preserving the unity of the Church as he did that of the Roman Empire. Constantine, it appeared, had no hesitation in exercising that responsibility, nor did anyone gainsay it to him. Here it is the emperor who speaks.

It must now be clear to everyone that there is nothing more honorable in my sight than the fear of God. And now because it was earlier agreed that the Synod of Bishops should meet at Ancyra [Ankara] of Galatia, it seems good to us for many reasons that another synod assemble at Nicea [that is, the present Iznik], a city of Bithynia, because the bishops of Italy and the rest of Europe will be attending, because of the excellent temperature of the air, and so that I myself might be present as a spectator and participant in those matters that will be treated. And so I give you public notice, my beloved brethren, that all of you promptly assemble at that said city, namely Nicea. Let every one of you, therefore, with an eye to what is best, as I said before, be diligent in attending, promptly and without delay, that all may be present in person. (Acts of Nicea)

4. A Christian Statement of Belief: The Creed

The bishops convened as bidden in the city of Nicea in Anatolia in 325 C.E. What emerged from their deliberations was a statement of belief that was to provide the standard of orthodoxy for all Christians. It was not the first such. There was, for example, the "Apostles' Creed," which, though first cited in this form by Epiphanius ca. 400 C.E., was nonetheless regarded as the rule of faith composed by the Apostles themselves in Jerusalem. It, or something quite like it, was certainly in use in various churches—at Rome, for example—by the fourth century.

> I believe in the Father Almighty,
> And in Jesus Christ, His only Son, our Lord,
> Who was born of the Holy Spirit and the Virgin Mary,
> Who was crucified under Pontius Pilate and was buried,
> And the third day arose from the dead,
> Who ascended into heaven,
> And sits at the right hand of the Father,
> Whence he comes to judge the living and the dead,
> And in the Holy Spirit,
> The Holy Church,
> The remission of sins,
> The resurrection of the flesh,
> The life everlasting.
> (Epiphanius, *Panarion* 72:3)

The creed enunciated at Nicea, which we know in the form approved at the Council of Chalcedon in 451 C.E., seems to have been drawn from the Catechetical Lectures of Cyril of Jerusalem and to reflect the statement of faith professed early on by the Jerusalem church.

We believe in one God, the Father All-sovereign, maker of heaven and earth, and all things visible and invisible.

At this point the preoccupations of the Council of Nicea begin to appear in the formulary.

And in one Lord Jesus Christ, the only-begotten Son of God, Begotten of the Father before all ages, Light of Light, True God of True God, begotten not made, of one substance with the Father, through whom all things were made;

Who for us men and for our salvation came down from the heavens, and was made flesh of the Holy Spirit and the Virgin Mary, and became man, and was crucified for us under Pontius Pilate, and suffered and was buried, and rose again on the third day according to the Scriptures, and ascended into heaven, and sits at the right hand of the Father, and comes again with glory to judge the living and the dead, of whose kingdom there will be no end;

And in the Holy Spirit, the Lord and Life-Giver, that proceeds from the Father, who with the Father and the Son is worshiped together and glorified together, who spoke through the prophets;

In one holy, catholic and apostolic church;

We acknowledge one baptism for the remission of sins. We look for a resurrection of the dead, and the life of the age to come. (Acts of Nicea)

5. How the Council Proceeded

The records of the Council of Nicea are not complete, but we can get some idea of how the bishops proceeded from an account by the church historian Eusebius, bishop of Caesarea in Palestine. His formulation, presented to the synod, included the clause: "And (we believe) in One Lord Jesus Christ, the Word of God, God from God, Light of Light, Life from Life, Only-begotten Son, firstborn of all creation, before all ages begotten by the Father, by whom also all things are made." The statement appeared unexceptionable, save that it did not quite address the issue that had brought them all there, that of the essential relationship—the relationship in substance—between Father and Son. Eusebius' account, which is not a little self-serving, proceeds.

On this (statement of) faith being publicly put forth by us, no room for contradiction appeared; for our Most Pious Emperor testified before anyone else that it was most orthodox. He confessed, moreover, that such were his own sentiments, and he advised all present to agree to it and to subscribe to its articles and assent to them, with the insertion of the single word "consubstantial," which, moreover, he interpreted himself, saying that the Son is consubstantial (with the Father) not according to bodily affects, and that the Son subsisted from the Father neither by division nor severance: for the immaterial and intellectual and incorporeal nature (of the Father) could not be the subject of any bodily affect, but that it became us to conceive of such things in a divine and ineffable manner. And our most wise and religious Emperor reasoned but they [that is, the assembled bishops] drew up the following formulary:

"We believe in one God, the Father All-sovereign, maker of heaven and earth, and all things visible and invisible.

"And in one Lord Jesus Christ, the Son of God, Begotten of the Father, the Only-begotten, that is, from the substance of the Father; God from God, Light from Light, True God of True God, begotten not made, consubstantial with the Father, through whom all things were made, those in heaven and those on earth;

"Who for us men and for our salvation came down and was made flesh, suffered and rose again on the third day, ascended into heaven, and is coming to judge the living and the dead.

"And in the Holy Spirit.

"And those who say 'There was time when he was not,' and 'before his generation he was not,' and 'he came to be from nothing' or those who pretend that the Son of God is 'of other hypostasis or substance,' or 'created' or 'alterable,' the Catholic and Apostolic church anathematizes." (Eusebius in Socrates, *Church History* 1.8)

6. Excommunication from the Church Catholic

The Council, then, proposed in almost juridical fashion its own "rule of faith." There remained, however, the question of how to deal with those who did not subscribe to it. This too was taken up, both at Nicea and at subsequent councils.

Concerning those, whether of the clergy or the laity, who have been excommunicated by the bishops in different provinces, let the sentence of the canon prevail, which pronounces that those persons who have been cast out by one bishop are not to be received again into communion by any others. Inquiry should be made, however, whether they have been excommunicated through petty jealousy or contentiousness or other such-like bitterness of the bishop. And in order that this inquiry may be conveniently made, it is decreed that it is proper that synods should be assembled twice every year in every province, that all the bishops of the province being assembled together, such questions may be looked into, so that those who have confessedly offended against the bishop may appear to be excommunicated with reason by all the bishops, until it shall seem fit to their general assembly to pronounce a more lenient sentence upon them. And let these synods be held, the one before Lent, that the pure gift may be offered to God after all bitterness has been put aside, and let the second be held in the autumn. (Council of Nicea [325 C.E.], Canon 5)

All who enter the Church of God and hear the Holy Scriptures, but do not communicate with the people in prayers, or who turn away, by reason of some disorder, from the holy partaking in the Eucharist, are to be cast out of the Church until, after they have made confession, have brought forth fruits of penance, and have made earnest entreaty, they shall have obtained forgiveness; and it is unlawful to communicate with excommunicated persons, or to assemble in private houses and pray with those who do not pray in the church, or to receive in one church those who do not assemble with another church. And if any one of the bishops, presbyters or deacons, or any one in the canon shall be found communicating with excommunicated persons, let him also be excommunicated, as one who brings confusion on the order of the Church. (Council of Antioch [341 C.E.], Canon 2)

If anyone has been excommunicated by his own bishop, let him not be received by others until he has either been restored by his own bishop, or until, when a synod is held, he shall have appeared and made his defense, and, having convinced the synod, shall have received a different sentence. And let this decree apply to the laity, and to the presbyters and deacons, and all those who are enrolled on the clergy list (of a diocese). (Ibid., Canon 6)

Later in the fourth century heresy was made a criminal offense by imperial decree, and thus excommunication from the Church was ratified and reinforced in the law of the state.

20 August 379 C.E.: All heresies are forbidden by both divine and imperial laws and shall forever cease. If any profane man by his punishable teachings should weaken the concept of God, he shall have the right to know such noxious doctrines only for himself but shall not injure others by revealing such doctrines to them. (Theodosian Code 5.5)

25 July 383 C.E.: All persons whatsoever who are tossed about by the false teachings of diverse heresies, namely, the Eunomians, the Arians, the Macedonians, the Pneumatomachi, the Manicheans, the Encratites,

the Apotactites, the Saccophori, and the Hydroparastatae, shall not assemble in any groups, shall not collect any crowds, shall not attract any people to themselves, shall not give the walls of any private houses the appearances of churches, and shall practice nothing publicly or privately which may be detrimental to the Catholic sanctity. Furthermore, if there should exist any person who transgresses what has been so evidently forbidden, he shall be expelled by the common agreement of all good men, and the opportunity to expel him shall be granted to all who delight in the cult and the beauty of the correct observance of religion. (Ibid. 5.11)

11 May 391 C.E.: If any persons should betray the Holy Faith and should profane holy baptism, they shall be segregated from the community of all men, shall be disqualified from giving testimony, and, as We have previously ordained, they shall not have testamentary capacity; they shall inherit from no person, and by no person shall they be designated as heirs. We should also have ordered them to be expelled and removed at a distance if it had not appeared to be greater punishment to dwell among men and to lack the approval of men. (Ibid. 16.7.4)

The crime of heresy is unlike other civil crimes in one important regard: it may be expiated by simple recantation and repentance.

15 November 407 C.E.: Although it is customary for crimes to be expiated by punishment, it is our will, nevertheless, to correct the depraved desires of men by an admonition to repentance. Therefore, if any heretics, whether they are Donatists or Manicheans or of any other depraved belief and sect who have congregated for profane rites, should embrace, by a simple confession, the Catholic faith and its rites, which we wish to be observed by all men, even though such heretics have nourished a deep-rooted evil of long and continued meditation, to such an extent that they seem to be subject to the punishments of the laws formerly issued, nevertheless, as soon as they have confessed God by a simple expression of belief, we decree that they shall be absolved from all guilt. (Theodosian Code 5.41)

7. The Catholic Church

For the first two centuries of Christianity's existence, it was not always a simple matter to distinguish between orthodoxy and heresy in a Church that was still attempting to define itself. But certainly by the time of Constantine there had

emerged a kind of Christian consensus that was based on the twin pillars of the
Apostolic tradition and the Apostolic succession and that constituted the doctrinal
foundation of what was called the Church Catholic. It was a consensus well enough
defined and widely enough accepted to constitute an "orthodoxy" against which
subsequent opinions, movements, and practices could be measured and judged. This
is how it was defined and understood by Vincent of Lerins, writing in 434 C.E.

In the Catholic Church itself, every care should be taken to hold fast
to what has been believed everywhere, always, and by all. This is truly and
properly "catholic," as indicated by the force and etymology of the name
itself, which comprises everything which is truly universal. This general
rule will be truly applied if we follow the principles of universality, antiquity and consensus. We do so in regard to universality if we confess that
faith alone to be true which the entire Church confesses, all over the
world. We do so in regard to antiquity if we in no way deviate from those
interpretations which our ancestors and fathers have manifestly proclaimed as inviolable. We do so in regard to consensus if, in this very
antiquity, we adopt the definitions and propositions of all, or almost all,
the bishops and doctors.

The matter is not so simple, however, as Vincent himself recognizes.

What, therefore, will the catholic Christian do if some members of
the Church have broken away from the communion of universal faith?
What else but prefer the health of the body universal to the disease of the
corrupt member? What if a new contagion strives to infect not only a
small part but even the whole Church? Then he will endeavor to adhere
to the antiquity which is manifestly beyond the danger of being seduced
by the deceit of some novelty. What if in antiquity itself an error is
detected, on the part of two or three men, or even on the part of a city
or a province? Then he will take care to prefer the decrees of a previous
ecumenical council, if there was one, to the temerity and ignorance of a
small group. Finally, what if such an error arises and nothing like a council can be found? Then he will take the pains to consult and interrogate
the opinions of his predecessors, comparing them with one another only
as regards the opinions of those who, though they lived in various periods, and at different periods and different places, nevertheless remained
in the communion and faith of the One Catholic Church, and who therefore have become reliable authorities. As he will discover, he must also
believe without hesitation whatever not only one or two but all equally
and with one consent, openly, frequently, and persistently have held,
written and taught. (Vincent of Lerins, *Commonitorium* 2–3)

8. The Holy War against Heresy

The presence of that orthodoxy and of Vincent's pragmatic touchstones of quod ubique, quod semper et quod ab omnibus did not preclude or even much inhibit heresy. The Church authorities continued to argue with, denounce, anathematize, and excommunicate those who were judged deviant from the ever better defined Christian doctrine. Roman law contributed its authority to that same end, as we have seen, but generally the distinction of the two jurisdictions left both the conviction and the punishment of heretics in the hands of the Church. The Fourth Lateran Council convoked by Pope Innocent III in 1215 C.E. marked a radical change in tactics, however. The Albigensians, Cathars, and a number of other dualist and Manichean-inspired churches had entrenched themselves in a broad arc from northern Italy across Languedoc and Provence in southern France and into Spain. Unable to extirpate these beliefs by preaching and teaching, and since excommunication was of little avail where the heretics constituted the community, the third canon of Lateran IV turned to more serious measures, which now involved the secular arm of government.

We excommunicate and anathematize every heresy that raises itself against the holy, orthodox and catholic faith which we have above explained, condemning all heretics under whatever names they may be known, for while they have different faces, they are nevertheless bound to each other by their tails, since in all of them vanity is a common element. Those condemned, being handed over to the secular rulers or their bailiffs, let them be abandoned, to be punished with due justice, clerics being first degraded from their orders. As to the property of the condemned, if they are laymen, let it be confiscated; if clerics, let it be applied to the churches from which they received revenues.

Those who are only suspected (of heresy), due consideration being given to the nature of the suspicion and the character of the person, unless they prove their innocence by a proper defense, let them be anathematized by all until they have made suitable satisfaction; but if they have been under excommunication for one year, let them be condemned as heretics.

Secular rulers who refuse to cooperate may be deposed by papal dissolution of their subjects' oath of allegiance and new rulers invited in.

Secular authorities, whatever offices they may hold, shall be admonished and induced and if necessary compelled by ecclesiastical censure, that if they wish to be esteemed and numbered among the faithful, so for the defense of the faith they ought publicly to take an oath that they will

strive in good faith and to the best of their ability to exterminate in the
territories subject to their jurisdiction all heretics pointed out by the
Church, so that whenever anyone shall have assumed authority, whether
spiritual or temporal, let him be bound to confirm this decree by oath.
But if a temporal ruler, after having been requested and admonished by
the Church, should neglect to cleanse his territory of this heretical foul-
ness, let him be excommunicated by the metropolitan and other bishops
of the province. If he refuses to make satisfaction within a year, let the
matter be made known to the Supreme Pontiff, that he may declare the
ruler's vassals absolved of their allegiance and may offer the territory to
be ruled by Catholics.

*Finally, an extraordinary privilege is granted: whoever enrolls in this holy war will
gain the same spiritual blessings enjoyed by those who take the cross against the
Muslims for the liberation of the Holy Land.*

Catholics who have girded themselves with the cross for the exter-
mination of heretics will enjoy the indulgences and privileges granted to
those who go in defense of the Holy Land. (Fourth Lateran Council,
Canon 3)

*Nothing was said in that canon of the death penalty, but it is unhesitatingly
vindicated by Thomas Aquinas (d. 1274 C.E.), a member of the Dominican order
that has been commissioned precisely to do combat with the Albigensians. The
question under discussion is: "Whether Heretics Are To Be Tolerated?"*

As regards heretics, two points ought to be observed: one from the
perspective of the heretics; the other from the point of view of the
Church. On the heretics' side there is the sin, whereby they deserve not
only to be separated from the Church by excommunication, but also to
be severed from the world by death. For it is a much graver matter to
corrupt the faith, which quickens the soul, than to forge money, which
supports temporal life. Wherefore if counterfeiters and other malefactors
are forthwith condemned to death by the secular authority, there is even
greater reason for heretics, as soon as they are convicted of heresy, to be
not only excommunicated but even put to death.

From the perspective of the Church, however, there is a mercy
which looks toward the conversion of those who have strayed, and so she
does not condemn immediately, but "after the second and third admonition," as the Apostle directs (Titus 3:10–11). After that, if he is still
stubborn, the Church, because she no longer hopes for his conversion,
looks rather to the salvation of others, by excommunicating him and
separating him from the Church, and furthermore delivers him to the

secular tribunal to be exterminated thereby from the world to death.
(Aquinas, *Summa Theologica* II/2, ques. 11, art. 3)

9. The Jews and the Church in the Middle Ages

There was very little ambiguity—none in theory and perhaps only a very slight hesitation in practice—in the Church's dealing with heretics. The Jews presented a more complex problem, however. Unlike the heretics, they were overt disbelievers in the basic premise of Christianity, whether that was put forward as a belief in Jesus' divinity or even his Messiahship. Nor were they heathen, since they worshiped the same God the Father and possessed and ratified the very same Scripture out of which the Christians traced their own version of sacred history. The Christians may have claimed those "Hebrews" of the Old Testament for their own progenitors, but they did not, it is clear, venerate contemporary Jews as either spiritual cousins, learned informants, or even cherished fossils of a bygone age. Nor did they attempt to exterminate them or their religious practices. As heirs to a Roman legal tradition whose treatment of the Jews we have already noted, the Christian authorities attempted to maintain the status quo, to protect the Jews from generally hostile local populations and at the same time to confine them to their already limited condition, as in this decree issued in slightly differing forms by Popes Alexander III, Innocent III, and here by Gregory X in 1272 C.E.

. . . Even as it is not allowed to the Jews in their assemblies presumptuously to undertake for themselves more than has been permitted to them by law, even so they ought not to suffer any disadvantage in those practices which have been granted to them. Although they prefer to persist in their stubbornness rather than to recognize the words of their prophets and the mysteries of Scripture, and thus to arrive at a knowledge of the Christian faith and salvation; nevertheless, inasmuch as they have made an appeal for our protection and help, we therefore admit their petition and offer them the shield of our protection through the clemency of Christian piety. In so doing we follow in the footsteps of our predecessors of blessed memory, the Popes of Rome Calixtus, Eugene, Alexander, Clement, Celestine, Innocent and Honorius.

We decree moreover that no Christian shall compel them or any one of their group to baptism unwillingly. . . . For indeed that person who is known to have come to Christian baptism not freely, but unwillingly, is not believed to possess any Christian faith. Moreover, no Christian shall presume to seize, imprison, wound, torment, kill or inflict violence on them; furthermore, no one shall presume, except by judicial action of the authorities of the country, to change the good customs of the land where they live for the purpose of taking their money or their goods from them or from others. In addition, no one shall disturb them in any way during the celebration of their festivals, whether by day or by night, with clubs or stones or anything else. Also no one shall exact compulsory service from them unless it be that they have been accustomed to render it in previous times.

Inasmuch as the Jews are not able to bear witness against the Christians, we decree furthermore that the testimony of Christians against them shall not be valid unless there is among those Christians some Jew who is there for the purpose of offering testimony.

How urgently that protection was needed in some places cries out from what follows in the decree.

Since it sometimes happens that some Christians lose their Christian children, the Jews are accused by their enemies of secretly carrying off and killing these same Christian children and of making sacrifices of the heart and blood of these very children. It also happens that the parents of these children or some other Christian enemies of the Jews secretly hide these same children in order to cause injury to these Jews and to be able to extort from them a certain amount of money by buying themselves out of their difficulties. And most falsely do these Christians claim that the Jews have secretly and furtively carried away these children and killed them, and that the Jews offer sacrifice from the heart and blood of these children, since their law in this matter precisely and expressly forbids Jews to sacrifice, eat or drink the blood, or eat the flesh of animals having claws. This has been demonstrated before our court many times by Jews converted to the Christian faith; but nonetheless a great many Jews are still seized and detained unjustly because of this.

We decree therefore that Christians need not be obeyed against Jews in a case or situation of this type, and we order that Jews seized under such a frivolous pretext be freed from imprisonment, and that they should not be arrested again on such a miserable grounds, unless—which we do not believe—they are caught in the very commission of the crime.

We decree that no Christian should stir up anything new against them, but that they should be maintained in the same status and position which they were in during the time of our predecessors, from antiquity till now. We decree, in order to stop the wickedness and avarice of evil men, that no one shall dare to vandalize or destroy a cemetery of the Jews or dig up human bodies for the sake of getting money.

If anyone, with full knowledge of the contents of this decree, should—which we hope will not happen—be so bold as to act contrary to it, let him suffer punishment in the matter of his rank and position, or let him be punished by the penalty of excommunication, unless he makes amends for his temerity by appropriate compensation. Moreover, we wish that only those Jews who have not attempted to contrive anything toward the destruction of the Christian faith be fortified by the support of such protection. (Gregory X, *Concerning the Jews*)

10. "There Is Only One Holy, Catholic and Apostolic Church"

On 18 November 1302 Pope Boniface VIII issued his bull Unam Sanctam. *Its occasion was another round in the ongoing struggle between the Papacy and the authority of the emperor. But it is also one of the classical medieval statements on the unity and authority of the Church, expressed here from a Western and so Petrine and monarchical point of view. Both the arguments and the scriptural citations, Old Testament and New, are now smooth and supple from long centuries of use.*

We are compelled to believe and to hold that there is only one Holy, Catholic and Apostolic Church. So our faith urges us and so we firmly believe and simply confess; and likewise (we hold) that there is no salvation or remission of sins outside of her—as the bridegroom proclaims in the Song of Songs: "One is my dove, my perfect one is but one; she is the only one of her mother, the chosen of her that bore her" (Song of Songs 6:8), which represents one mystical body whose head is Christ; and of Christ, God is the head. And in it there is "one Lord, one faith, one baptism" (Eph. 4:5). At the time of the Flood there was indeed one ark of Noah, prefiguring one Church; it had been finished in one cubit, had one steersman and commander, namely Noah, and we read that outside it all things existing on earth were destroyed. This Church we venerate, and this alone, as the Lord says through the prophet: "Deliver, O Lord, my soul from the sword, and my only one from the hand of the dog" (Ps. 21:21). He [that is, Jesus] prayed for the soul, that is, for himself—for the head and the body at the same time—which body, namely, he called the one and only Church because of the promised unity of faith, sacraments and charity of the Church. That is the "seamless garment" (John 19:23) of the Lord which was not cut but fell (to one of the soldiers at the crucifixion) by lot. Therefore, in this one and only Church there is one body and one head, not two heads as if it were a monster: namely Christ, and Peter the vicar of Christ, and the successor of Peter; because the Lord said to Peter, "Feed my sheep" (John 21:17). "My sheep," he said, speaking generally and not particularly about these or those sheep; so that it must be understood that he committed to him all his sheep. If therefore the Greeks and others say they were not committed to Peter and his successors, they necessarily confess that they are not the sheep of Christ, for the Lord says in John, "There shall be one flock and one shepherd" (John 10:16).

And, in the concluding sentence in the bull:

Consequently we declare, state, define and pronounce that it is altogether necessary to salvation for every human creature to be subject to the Roman Pontiff. (Boniface VIII, *Unam Sanctam*)

11. The People of the Book

Islam is, on the testimony of the Quran itself, a successor community to those other peoples who had gone before it. They had had their messengers, and they too had been given the benefit of God's Book.

Remember We gave to Moses the Book and sent after him many an apostle; and to Jesus son of Mary We gave clear evidence of the truth, reinforcing him with divine grace. Even so, when a messenger brought to you what did not suit your mood, you turned haughty, and called some impostors and some others you slew.

And they say: "Our hearts are enfolded in covers." In fact, God has cursed them in their unbelief, and only a little do they believe. (Quran 2:87–88)

How many of the followers of the Books having once known the truth desire in their heart to turn you into infidels again, even after the truth has become clear to them! But you forbear and overlook till God fulfills His plan; and God has power over all things.

Fulfill your devotional obligations and pay the alms tithe. And what you send ahead of good you will find with God, for He sees all that you do.

And they say: "None will go to Paradise but the Jews and the Christians," but this is only wishful thinking. Say: "Bring the proof, if you are truthful."

Only he who surrenders to God with all his heart and also does good, will find reward with his Lord and have no regret and fear.

The Jews say, "The Christians are not right," and the Christians say, "The Jews are in the wrong," yet both recite the Scriptures. And this is what the unread had said too. God alone will judge between them in their differences on the Day of Reckoning. (Quran 2:109–113)

12. The Errors of the Jews

The first of those people to have been given Scripture were the Jews.

Men belonged to a single community; and God sent them messengers to give them happy tidings and warnings and sent the Book with them containing the truth to judge between them in matters of dispute; but those who received it disagreed concerning it after receiving clear proofs, on account of waywardness among them. Then God by His dispensation showed those who believed the way to the truth about which they were differing; for God shows whom He pleases the path that is straight. (Quran 2:213)

The Muslim commentators on the Quran were not sure about the duration of the period when "men belonged to a single community." But the Book that was sent down and to whom it was given and why were matters of no dispute.

. . . God means that the Book, that is, the Torah, should decide between the people on matters on which they disagreed. God has assigned the decision to the Book and established it and not the Prophets and the Apostles as the decisive criterion between the people, since whenever one of the Prophets or Apostles had to bring down a judgment, he did it on the basis of the indications which are contained in the Book which is sent down by God. . . .

God's words "disagreed concerning it" mean that they disagreed concerning the Book that God had sent down, that is, the Torah. His words "those who received it" refers to the Jews of the Children of Israel. They are the ones who had been given the Torah and its knowledge. . . . Thus God proclaims that the Jews of the Children of Israel disobeyed the Book, the Torah, and they disagreed concerning it in spite of the knowledge which it contains. In so doing they deliberately disobeyed God since they violated His command and the decision of His Book.

"Then God showed those who believed the way to the truth . . . " means that God granted success to those who are believing, that is, those who support belief in (the one) God and His Apostle, Muhammad, and who put their trust in Him and are convinced that His message, about which the previous recipients of the Book had earlier disagreed, comes from God. The disunity in which God left these people alone, while rightly guiding and helping to the truth those who believe in Muhammad, refers to (Friday as) the "day of gathering" (for worship). Although this day had been enjoined on them [that is, the Jews] as an obligation just as it had been enjoined on us, they deviated from it and changed (their day of worship) to the Sabbath. The Prophet has said: Although we are the last, we surpass (the others in obedience to God's commands), even though the Book was given to them before it was given to us, and so we possessed it after they did. God has rightly guided us even to this day, on matters on which they disagreed. The Jews have taken (as their day of worship) the day following (Friday) and the Christians have taken the day after that.

Concerning the matters about which the people disagreed, Ibn Zayd is reported to have said, according to Yunus ibn Abd A'la, that God's words "then God showed those who believed the way to the truth" mean that He led the believers to Islam. The people disagreed concerning prayer. Some prayed facing toward the East while others faced toward Jerusalem. Then God led us to the right direction of prayer toward Mecca. Also the people disagreed concerning fasting. Some fasted at certain times of the day while others fasted at certain times of the night. Then God led us to the right times for fasting. Also the people disagreed concerning the day of congregational worship. While the Jews chose the Sabbath, the Christians took Sunday; then God led us to the right day [that is, Friday]. Also the people disagreed about Abraham. The Jews considered him a Jew and the Christians considered him a Christian. Then God freed him from such suspicions and demonstrated that he was a *hanif* who was surrendered to God, and that he also was not to be classed among the heathen, as some maintained, who claimed that he had been one of the unbelievers. Finally, the people also disagreed about Jesus. The Jews considered him to be the victim of a lie, while the Christians considered him to be a god. Thereupon God led us to the truth concerning him. (Tabari, *Commentary*, *ad loc.*)

13. The Jews Warned by Their Own Prophets

We sent down the Torah which contains guidance and light; in accordance with which the prophets, who had surrendered themselves [or became *muslims*], gave instructions to [or, judged] the Jews, as well as the masters (of the law) and the rabbis, following the portion of God's Book that had been entrusted to them. (Quran 5:44)

This is one of the central Quranic texts explaining the position of the Jews with respect to God's revelation. As such, it receives full treatment at the hands of the commentators.

". . . [T]he prophets, who had surrendered themselves": Submission [that is, *islam*] is an attribute which is used in praise of the prophets generally and not as a distinguishing characteristic (of the Jewish prophets), just as is the case with attributes one uses in reference to the Eternal One. The use of this attribute (with reference to the biblical prophets) shows that the Jews are far from acknowledging Islam, which is the (true) religion of the prophets in both ancient and modern times, and that Judaism is remote from acknowledging this. God's words, "the prophets, who had surrendered themselves, judged the Jews" emphasizes this in a forceful manner.

"As well as the masters (of the law) and the rabbis": This refers to the ascetics and the learned men among the descendants of Aaron, who remained faithful to the ways of the prophets and have remained aloof from the religion of the Jews.

"Following the portion of God's Book that had been entrusted to them": The portion of God's Book that the prophets had instructed the rabbis and masters (of the Law) to preserve was the Torah. That is, the prophets had ordered them to preserve the Torah from change and distortion. (Zamakhshari, *The Unveiler of the Realities, ad loc.*)

14. The Jewish Falsification of Scripture

Zamakhshari has taken the larger view, but the immediately preceding verses of this same sura were understood by the Islamic tradition to refer to a specific incident with the Jews in the life of the Prophet.

And there are Jews who listen to tell lies, and spy on behalf of others who do not come to you, and who distort the words (of the Torah) out of context, and say: "If you were given (what we say is true), accept it, but if you are not given, beware." . . . Those are the people whose hearts God does not wish to purify. . . . Eavesdropping for the purpose of lying, earning through unlawful means! So if they come to you, judge between them or decline to do so. And if you decline, they can do you no harm; but if you judge, you should do so with justice, for God loves those who are just. But why should they make you a judge when they themselves have the Torah in which is God's Law? Even then they turn away. They are those who will never believe. (Quran 5:41–43)

Ibn Ishaq's Life *sets out the context:*

Ibn Shihab al-Zuhri told me that he heard a learned man of Muzayna telling Sa'id ibn al-Musayyab that Abu Hurayra had told them that Jewish rabbis had gathered in their school when the Messenger (first) came to Medina. A married man had committed adultery with a married woman and they said: "Send them to Muhammad and ask him what the Law about them is and leave the penalty to him. If he prescribes scourging, then follow him, for he is a king and believe in him. If he prescribes stoning, then he is a prophet so beware lest he deprive you of what you hold." . . . The Messenger went out to them and commanded that the two should be stoned and they were stoned at the door of his mosque among the Banu Ghanm ibn Malik ibn al-Najjar. . . .

Salih ibn Kaysan from Nafi', freedman of Abdullah ibn Umar, told me: When the Messenger gave judgment about them he asked for a Torah. A rabbi sat there reading it, having put his hand over the verse of stoning. Abdullah ibn Salam struck the rabbi's hand, saying, "This, O Prophet of God, is the verse of stoning which he refuses to read to you." The Messenger said, "Woe to you Jews! What has induced you to abandon the judgment of God which you hold in your hands?" They answered: "The sentence used to be carried out until a man of royal birth and noble origin committed adultery and the king refused to allow him to be stoned. Later another man committed adultery and the king wanted him to be stoned, but they said, No, not until you stone so-and-so. And then they said that they agreed to arrange the matter by scourging and they did away with all mention of stoning." The Apostle said: "I am the first to revive the order of God and His Book and to practice it." They were duly stoned and Abdullah ibn Umar said, "I was among those that stoned them." (*Life* 393–395) [IBN ISHAQ 1955: 266–267]

Thus the Jews were not merely unfaithful to the Covenant made with God; they had, as this incident testifies, concealed and distorted the revelation that God had given them.

15. The Error of the Christians

The Christians too had been in Muslim eyes unfaithful to God's word.

O People of the Book, do not be fanatical in your faith, and say nothing but the truth about God. The Messiah who is Jesus, son of Mary, was only a Messenger of God, and a word of His which He sent to Mary, as a mercy from Him. So believe in God and His apostles, and do not say "Three." Refrain from this for your own good; for God is only one God, and far from His glory is it to beget a son. (Quran 4:171)

Once again Zamakhshari provides the proper exegetical perspective.

"Do not be fanatical in your faith": The Jews went too far in that they degraded the position of Christ in regarding him as an illegitimate child (of Mary). And the Christians went too far in that they unduly elevated him in considering him a god.

"His word": Jesus is designated as "the word of God" and as "a word of His" (Sura 3:39) because he alone originated through the word and command of God rather than through a father and a sperm. For this reason he is also designated as "the spirit of God" (Sura 66:12) and "a spirit from Him," since Jesus was a spirit-endowed man who originated without any element from a spirit-endowed man, such as the sperm that is discharged from an earthly father. He was created by a new act of creation by God whose power is unlimited.

The word "three" (in this verse) is the predicate of an understood subject. If one accepts the Christian view that God exists in one substance with three divine persons, namely, the Father, the Son and the Holy Spirit, and if one accepts the opinion that the person of the Father represents God's being, the person of the Son represents His knowledge, and the person of the Holy Spirit represents His life, then one must supply the subject (of the clause) as follows: "God is three(fold)." Otherwise, one must supply the subject thus: "The gods are three." According to the evidence of the Quran, the Christians maintain that God, Christ and Mary are three gods, and that Christ is the child of God by Mary, as God says (in the Quran): "O Jesus son of Mary, did you say to men: 'Take me and my mother as gods, apart from God'?" (Sura 5:116) or "The Christians say: 'The Messiah is the Son of God' " (Sura 9:30). Moreover, it is well known that the Christians maintain that in Jesus are (combined) a divine nature derived from his Father and a human nature derived from his mother. God's words (in this verse), "The Messiah who is Jesus, son of Mary, was only a Messenger of God," are also explained on the basis of such an interpretation (of the Christians). These words confirm (the Christian view) that Jesus was a child of Mary, that he had with her the usual relationship between children and their mothers, and that his relationship to God was that he was His Messenger and that he became a living being through God's command and a new act of creation without a father. At the same time these words exclude (the Christian view) that Jesus had with God the usual relationship between sons and their fathers. (Zamakhshari, *The Unveiler of the Realities*, ad loc.)

16. Jews and Christians Compared

In some few instances the Quran weighs Jews and Christians together in the scales of divine justice.

You will find the Jews and the idolaters most excessive in hatred of those who believe; and the closest in love to the faithful are the people who say "We are followers of Christ," because there are priests and monks among them, and they are not arrogant.

For when they listen to what has been revealed to this Apostle, you can see their eyes brim over with tears at the truth which they recognize, and say: "O Lord, we believe, so put us down among those who bear witness." (Quran 5:82–83)

Zamakhshari spells out the nuances of the sacred text.

Here God is portraying the Jews as unyielding and as acknowledging the truth only grudgingly, while the Christians are of gentle disposition, easily guided and with an inclination toward Islam. Because of their violent animosity toward the believers, God places the Jews together with the idolaters; in fact He goes even further and puts them at the head, since He mentions them before the idolaters. Each of them wishes he could be given a life of a thousand years; but the grant of such life would not save him from chastisement—"for God sees well what they do!" (Sura 2:96). The Jews are surely like this, and even worse! A Prophetic tradition says: "If a Muslim is alone with two Jews, they will try to kill him."

God bases the judgment that the Christians are to be treated kindly and held in high esteem by the Muslims on the fact that there are priests and monks among them, that is, men of learning and servants, and that they are modest and humble people who know no arrogance, while the Jews are just the opposite. Here is a clear example showing the struggle for knowledge is exceedingly useful, leading first to good and then to success, even among the (non-Muslim) priests. The same is likewise true of a concern for the Hereafter and discussions about the End, possibly another characteristic of the monk, just like freedom from arrogance, even though it is a question of a Christian here. (Zamakhshari, *The Unveiler of the Realities*, ad loc.)

17. The Muslim Community

For the Muslims then, on the testimony of the Quran, both the Jews and the Christians constituted defined religious communities, corporate bodies of believers in possession of an authentic revelation. As on most other subjects, the Quran offers no systematic or extended treatment of the subject of the new community of Muslims whose birth it was chartering. But the notion of community occurs often there, sometimes in the context of the Muslims' treatment of each other, sometimes in their distancing themselves from those older communities of "Peoples of the Book."

O believers, if you follow what some of the People of the Book say, it will turn you into unbelievers even after you have come to belief.

And how can you disbelieve? To you are being recited the messages of God, and His Prophet is among you. And whosoever holds fast to God shall verily be guided to the path that is straight.

O believers, fear God as He should be feared, and do not die except as those submitting to him. Hold on firmly together to the rope of God, and be not divided among yourselves, and remember the favors God bestowed on you when you were one another's foe and He reconciled your hearts, and you turned into brethren through His grace. You had stood on the edge of the pit of fire and He saved you from it, thus revealing to you His clear signs, that you might perchance find the right way.

So let there be one community among you who may call to the good, enjoin what is esteemed and forbid what is odious. They are those who will be successful.

So be not like those who became disunited and differed among themselves after clear proofs had come to them. For them is great suffering. . . .

These are the commandments of God We recite to you verily; God does not wish injustice to the creatures of the world. For to God belongs all that is in the heavens and the earth, and to God do all things return. Of all the communities raised among men, you are the best, enjoining the good, forbidding the wrong, and believing in God. If the People of the Book had come to believe, it would have been better for them; but only some believe, and transgressors are many. (Quran 3:100–110)

The foolish will now ask and say: "What has made the faithful turn away from the direction toward which they used to pray?" Say, "To God belongs the East and the West. He guides who so wills to the path that is straight." We have made you a middle community that you act as witness over man, and the Prophet as witness over you. (Quran 2:142–143)

The Quranic notion of Islam as a "central" or "middle" community elicited considerable reflection from the medieval commentators.

I regard the word "middle" in this context as signifying the mean between two extremes. God described the Muslims as a people of the middle path because of their middle position in religion. They are neither people of excess like the Christians, who went to extremes in their monastic practices as well as in what they said concerning Jesus, nor are they people of deficiency like the Jews, who altered the Book of God, killed their prophets, gave the lie to their Lord, and rejected faith in Him. Rather they are people of the middle path and of balance in their religion. God characterized them as people of the middle path because the things which God loves most are those of the middle position. (Tabari, *Commentary*, *ad loc.*)

And this from the standard authority, Abdullah ibn Umar a-Baydawi, three centuries after Tabari:

The word "middle" or "in the middle" was originally a designation for a position with equal distances on each side. Then it came to refer to certain praiseworthy attributes of character because these lie (in the middle) between extremes of excess and exaggeration on both sides. Thus, generosity lies between wastefulness and stinginess and boldness between foolhardy recklessness and cowardice. The word is now also applied to a person who possesses such characteristics. . . . From the words of God in this verse one can (also) draw the conclusion that consensus is a valid authority (in questions of faith), since if that on which Muslims are agreed were delusion, then a gap would be created in their integrity (and thus they would not stand in the middle). (Baydawi, *The Lights of Revelation*, *ad loc.*)

18. An Arabic Quran

Islam is a universal community, it is clear from the Quran and Muhammad's own preaching. But it is also true that Muhammad was an Arab sent to preach God's message in the first instance to Arabs. The Arabs were not a "chosen people" the way the Israelites understood themselves to be, but Arabic was in some sense God's "chosen language." A number of verses in the Muslim Scripture lay emphasis on the *fact that this is an Arabic Quran. The language is in fact such an important element in interpreting the Book, and particularly in understanding its legal prescriptions, that the jurist al-Shafi*i (d. 820 C.E.) devoted considerable space to it in his Treatise on the Roots of Jurisprudence. His reflections cast an interesting light on the tension between cultural Arabism and religious Islam.*

Someone said: There are in the Quran Arabic and foreign words.

Shafi*i replied: The Quran indicates that there is no portion of the Book of God that is not in the Arab tongue. He who expressed such an opinion [namely, that there are foreign words in the Quran] . . . perhaps meant that there are certain particular words which are not understood by some Arabs.

Of all tongues that of the Arabs is the richest and most extensive in vocabulary. Do we know any man except a Prophet who apprehended all of it? However, no portion of it escapes everyone, so that there is always someone who knows it. Knowledge of this tongue is to the Arabs what knowledge of the tradition of the Prophet is to the jurists: We know of no one who possesses a knowledge of all the tradition of the Prophet without missing a portion of it. So if the knowledge of all the scholars is gathered together, the entire tradition of the Prophet would be known. However, if the knowledge of each scholar is taken separately, each might be found lacking in some portion of it, yet what each may lack can be found among the others. . . .

In like manner is the (knowledge of the) tongue of the Arabs possessed by the scholars and the public. No part of it will be missed by all of them, nor should it be sought from other people; for no one can learn this tongue save that he has learned it from the Arabs, nor can anyone be as fluent in it as they unless he has followed them in the way they learned it. He who has learned it from them should be regarded as one of the people of that tongue. . . .

Someone may ask: What is the proof that the Book of God was communicated in a pure Arabic tongue, unmixed with others?

Shafi*i replied: The proof is to be found in the Book of God itself, for God said:

"We never sent a Messenger save in the tongue of his people." (Quran 14:4)

But if someone says: Each of the Messengers before Muhammad was sent to his own people, while Muhammad was sent to all mankind. This may mean either that Muhammad was sent with the tongue of his people and that all others must learn his tongue—or whatever they can learn of it—or that Muhammad was sent with the tongues of all mankind. Is there any evidence that he was sent with the tongue of his own people rather than with foreign tongues?

Shafi'i replied: Since tongues vary so much that different people cannot understand one another, some must adopt the language of others. And preference must be given to the tongues that others adopt. The people who are fit to receive such a preference are those whose tongue is their Prophet's tongue. It is not permissible—but God knows best— for the people of the Prophet's tongue to become the followers of peoples whose tongues are other than that of the Prophet even in a single letter; but rather all other people should follow his tongue, and all people of earlier religions should follow his religion. For God has declared this in more than one communication of His Book:

"Truly, it is the revelation of the Lord of the worlds, brought down by the Faithful Spirit, upon your heart, that you may be one of those who warn, in a clear Arabic tongue." (Quran 26:192–195)

And He also said:

"Thus have We sent it down as an Arabic Law." (Quran 13:37)

And He said:

"And so we have revealed to you an Arabic Quran in order that you may warn the Mother of the Towns and the people of its vicinity." (Quran 42:5)

The "Mother of the Towns" is Mecca, the city of the Prophet and of his people. Thus God mentioned them in His Book as a special people and included them among those who were warned as a whole, and decreed that they were to be warned in their native tongue, the tongue of the Prophet's people in particular.

It is obligatory upon every Muslim to learn the Arab tongue to the utmost of his power in order to be able to profess through it that "there is no god but the God and Muhammad is His servant and Apostle," and to recite in it the Book of God.

Shafi'i finally returns to his lawyer's point.

The reason I began to explain why the Quran was communicated in the Arab tongue rather than in another, is that no one who understands clearly the total meanings of the (legal) knowledge of the Book of God would be ignorant of the extent of that tongue and of the various meanings of its words. . . . Doubts that appear to one who is ignorant (of the Arab tongue) will disappear from him who knows it. . . . Calling the attention of the public to the fact that the Quran was communicated in the Arab tongue in particular is advice to all Muslims. This advice is a duty imposed on them which must not be put aside and is the attainment of a supererogatory act of goodness which no one will neglect. (Shafi'i, *Treatise*) [SHAFI'I 1961: 88–94]

19. The Five Pillars of Islam

What then constituted a Muslim? When the Muslim tradition came to define the essentials of Islam, the "pillars of Islam" as they were called, the emphasis clearly lay not upon the modalities of belief—though belief was certainly required—but in the performance of certain ritual and political acts.

It is narrated on the authority of Ibn Abbas that a delegation of (the tribe of) Abd al-Qays come to the Messenger of God, may peace be upon him, and said: Messenger of God, truly ours is a tribe of (the clan) Rabi'a and there stand between you and us the unbelievers of Mudar and we find no freedom to come to you except in the Sacred Month. Direct us to an act which we should ourselves perform and invite those who live beside us (to perform). Upon this the Prophet remarked: I command you four things and prohibit to you four acts. (The prescribed acts are): Faith in God, and then he explained it for them and said: Testifying the fact that there is no god but the God, that Muhammad is the Messenger of God, establishment of prayer, payment of the alms tax, and that you pay one-fifth of the booty fallen to your lot. And I prohibit you to use the round gourd, wine jars, wooden pots or skins for wine. (Muslim, *Sahih* 1.7.22)

The prohibition against gourds, wine jars, wooden pots, and skins for wine may have been directed against a particular penchant of the Abd al-Qays for drinking. What was far more important, at least as the bedouin tribes outside Mecca were concerned, was the alms tax, as this tradition from the era just following upon the death of the Prophet reveals.

It is narrated on the authority of Abu Hurayra that when the Messenger of God, may peace be upon him, breathed his last and Abu Bakr was appointed as his Caliph after him, those among the Arabs who wanted to become apostates apostatized. Umar ibn al-Khattab said to Abu Bakr: Why would you fight against the people when the Messenger of God declared: "I have been directed to fight against people so long as they do not say: There is no god but the God. . . ." Upon this Abu Bakr said: By God, I would definitely fight against him who separated prayer from the alms tax, for it [that is, the alms tax] is the obligation upon the rich. By God, I would even fight against them to secure the hobbling cord which they used to give to the Messenger of God (as alms tax) but now they have withheld it. Umar ibn al-Khattab remarked: By God, I found nothing but the fact that God opened the heart of Abu Bakr for fighting (against those who refused to pay the alms tax) and I fully recognized that (his stand) was right. (Muslim, *Sahih* 1.9.29)

Adherence to Islam, it is clear, was more than a simple profession of faith in God and His prophet. It also required acts: the ritual acts of prayer, fasting, and pilgrimage, and the social and political act of paying the alms tax. Fasting and the pilgrimage do not occur as part of the obligations mentioned in the traditions cited above, but they are certainly prescribed in the Quran. They are also included in this summary tradition setting out the five pillars of Islam.

It is narrated on the authority of Abdullah ibn Umar that the Messenger of God, peace be upon him said: (The superstructure of) Islam is raised on five (pillars): testifying that there is no god but the God, that Muhammad is His servant and Messenger, and the establishment of prayer, payment of the alms tax, pilgrimage to the House (of God at Mecca) and the fast of (the month of Ramadan). (Ibid. 1.6.20)

20. "Catholic" Islam:
Staying Close to the Tradition

In Muhammad's own day membership in the community of Muslims might be understood simply as embracing anyone who acknowledged the unity of God and the Quran as the Word of God and who performed the ritual acts prescribed in the five Pillars. Those grounds had soon to be extended to a detailed affirmation of the teachings of the Quran, as broadened and explained by the various Prophetic traditions attributed to Muhammad himself, as we have already seen in Chapter 3 above. But the process of enlargement did not end there; it soon came to embrace the notion of "consensus," the agreement of Muslims on certain points of belief and practice, even without the authority of a Quranic text or a Prophetic tradition to support them. The validity of "consensus" as an operative element in Islam was argued in what became the classic statement of the position, the Treatise on the Roots of Jurisprudence of the Egyptian lawyer al-Shafi°i (see Chapter 5 above). In this passage an anonymous questioner is willing to concede the binding nature of the Quran and the Prophetic traditions, but he requests further proof on the matter of "consensus."

What is your proof for following what people have agreed upon, where there is no command in a text from God [that is, in the Quran], or related from the Prophet? Would you assert what others have held, that consensus can never occur except on a firm "tradition," even though it may not have been related [that is, even if it has not reached us in the form of a Prophetic tradition]?

I told him [said Shafi'i]: As to what they agreed upon and say that it has (also) been related from the Prophet, let us hope that it is (accepted) as they say. However, as for what is not related [that is, there is no specific Prophetic tradition on the matter], it may be that it was actually said by the Messenger of God, or it may be otherwise. It is not, however, permissible to attribute sayings to him (without grounds), for one is only permitted to relate what one has heard, and it is not permitted to relate anything one fancies, in which there may be things (the Prophet) did not say.

Therefore we hold to what they held to, following them. We know that if these were practices of the Messenger, they would not be remote to the generality of Muslims, even though they are remote to the few; and we know that the generality of Muslims will not agree on what is contradictory to the customary practice of the Messenger of God, or on an error, please God.

If it is asked, is there anything to indicate or prove that? we reply: Sufyan informs us on the authority of Abd al-Malik ibn Umayr from Abd al-Rahman the son of Abdullah ibn Mas'ud, from his father, that the Messenger of God said, "God prospers a servant who listens to what I say, remembers it, pays attention to it, and passes it on. Often one may transmit insight who himself is not perspicacious, and often he transmits it to one with more insight than he. There are three things which cannot be resented by the heart of a Muslim: sincerity of action for God, good advice to the Muslims, and keeping close to the community of the Muslims. . . ."

It was asked, what is the meaning of the Prophet's command to keep close to the community?

I said: There is but one meaning to it. . . . Since the community of the Muslims is scattered in different countries, one could not keep close to the physical community whose members were scattered, and besides, they were found together with Muslims and unbelievers, with pious men and sinners. Thus it could not mean a physical "closeness" since that was not possible, and because physical nearness would in itself effect nothing, so that there is no meaning in "keeping close to the community" except in agreeing with them in what they make lawful and forbidden, and obedience in both these matters. He who maintains what the community of the Muslims maintains is keeping close to the community, and he who deviates from what the community of the Muslims maintains deviates from that community to which he is commanded to remain close. Error arises in separation. In the community there can be no total error concerning the meaning of the Book, of the Prophetic tradition, or of analogical reasoning, please God. (Shafiʿi, *Treatise*) [SHAFIʿI 1961: 285–287].

Much the same point is made in a ninth-century statement of belief from Ahmad ibn Hanbal (d. 855 C.E.). Ibn Hanbal may have differed from the somewhat older Shafiʿi on important points of the law, but he was as convinced as Shafiʿi that the essential truth of the community lay in its adherence to the "tradition." This "creed" begins, then, with what is in effect a conservative's plea for unity, for adherence to "the tradition and the collectivity."

Ahmad ibn Hanbal said: The principles of "the tradition" for us are holding fast to the practice of the Companions of the Messenger of God and seeking guidance from that; and abandoning innovation, for every innovation is an error. Also, abandoning quarrels and not consorting with people who do as they please and leaving off strife and contentiousness in religion. "The tradition" to us means the footsteps of the Messenger of God, may God bless him and give him peace, and "the tradition" explains the meaning of the Quran and is the guide to the Quran. There is no use of logical analogies in "the tradition," nor coining of similitudes nor perception by use of reason or inclination. "Tradition" is nothing more than following, and surrendering up one's own inclinations.

The statement then grows more specific, and we have before us a ninth-century theological agenda: articles of belief that had already been debated to the point of orthodoxy and heresy.

A part of the essential "tradition," such that if one leaves aside any part of it, not accepting and believing it, he cannot be considered as being of the "People of Tradition," is belief in the predestination of good and bad, and the affirmation of the Prophetic traditions about it and belief in them, not saying "Why?" or "How?" but simply affirming them and believing them. If anyone does not know the explanation of these Prophetic traditions or his intelligence does not apprehend them, it is still sufficient, and his sentence is that he shall believe in them and submit to their authority, such as the Prophetic traditions (affirming predestination), and those that the beatific vision is possible, all in their entirety. And even if he turns away from hearing about this, or feels dislike at hearing about it, still he must believe in it, and must not contradict a single letter of it, or any other Prophetic tradition transmitted by dependable narrators. No one should dispute, or speculate about it, or recognize any contention about it, for speaking about predestination and the beatific vision and the (nature of the) Quran and other matters established by the Prophetic traditions is disapproved of and to be avoided. Whoever speaks of them, if he criticizes "the tradition," is not one of the "People of the Tradition" until he abandons contention and submits and believes in "the tradition."

A number of specifics follow in turn: the Quran as the uncreated Word of God, the vision of God on the Day of Resurrection, the reality of the details of the Final Judgment, the coming of the False Messiah and then the return of Jesus, who will "slay him at the Lydda Gate" of Jerusalem. Finally, there is an article on the nature of faith.

Faith is word and act, and increases and decreases, as is stated in the Prophetic traditions. "The most perfect of believers in faith is the best of them in morality." Also, "He who leaves off the ritual prayers has rejected God," and there is no act which, when neglected, occasions infidelity except the ritual prayers. Whoever quits them is an infidel, and God makes killing him lawful. (Ahmad ibn Hanbal, *Creed*)

[WILLIAMS 1971: 28–30]

21. A Shi°ite View of the Community

Shafi°i's view soon became the orthodox one in Islam, particularly among those Muslims like Ahmad ibn Hanbal who identified themselves as "People of the Tradition [sunna] and the Collectivity" and whom we call "Sunnis." But as Ibn Hanbal stated, "The principles of 'the tradition' [sunna] for us are holding fast to the practice of the Companions of the Messenger of God and seeking guidance from that." There were those among the Muslims, notably the "Partisans [shi°a] of Ali," generically called "Shi°ites," who preferred not to go the way of the "Companions of the Messenger of God," particularly since these latter had elected first Abu Bakr and then Umar and Uthman to lead the community instead of Ali ibn abi Talib, on whom the divine and Prophetic choice had obviously fallen. This is the way the case is argued by the Shi°ite scholar Ibn Babuya (d. 991 C.E.), beginning with the Quran itself.

Every verse in the Quran which begins with the expression, "O you who believe" refers necessarily to Ali ibn abi Talib as their leader and prince and the most noble among them. And every verse which directs the way to Paradise applies to the Prophet or to the Imams [that is, Ali and his designated successors], the blessings of God be upon them and all their partisans and followers. . . . These (Imams) are immune from sin and error. . . . They may be likened in this community to the Ark of Noah; he who boards it attains salvation or reaches the Gate of Repentance. (Ibn Babuya, *Creed*)

The Shi'ite was not, then, willing to grant infallibility to the "collectivity" in the manner of al-Shafi'i. The community had in fact already erred, or at least part of it allowed itself to be carried into error on the issue of the Imamate. The issue is stated clearly in a Shi'ite creed of the thirteenth century.

The Imam [that is, the head of the community; the officer called "Caliph" by the Sunni Muslims] cannot be elected by the community. He is the absolute ruler, who imposes his final judgment upon his followers. The principle of "consensus" in accepting certain religious laws and practices is completely false. If one were to accept this principle, he should regard Muhammad as not a real Prophet, because all of the people to whom he first addressed himself, or at least the majority of them, did not at first recognize him as such. . . . Only the Imam, appointed by God, is infallible, but the community obviously cannot be considered as infallible. . . .

The community became split and fell into disagreements after the death of the Prophet, thus taking the way of error. This was chiefly due to their reluctance to follow "the Household" [that is, Ali and his descendants]. Only a small group among the Muslims remained faithful to the commandments and the will of the Prophet, suffering for this reason at the hands of different oppressors. . . .

One who follows the religion of his ancestors by "the tradition," without having ascertained for himself whether it is correct or wrong, is not right. He should know and act in accordance with the Quran and "the tradition" as taught by the Imams of the family of the Apostle. . . .

Religion and faith are to be found only in Shi'ism (along with true) following of the tradition of the Prophet. . . . The Prophet predicted the splitting up of the Islamic community into seventy-three sects after his death; and of these only one brings salvation. It is the one which follows the Prophet and his descendants (through the house of Ali), who are the Ark of Noah, giving religious salvation. (*A Shi'ite Creed*)
[WILLIAMS 1971: 40–41]

22. The Prophet Warns against Heresy

The split between Sunni and Shi'ite was only one of a number of fissures that opened within the Muslim community even in the first century of its existence. Some were, like Shiʿism, the result of differing views on such fundamental political questions as "Who is a Muslim?" or "Who shall rule the community?" Others were more theological in their orientation, though not without political implication, like the questions of free will and determination that troubled the early community. Indeed, heresy and schism seemed so unavoidable that there were current a number of traditions from the Prophet himself predicting these torments for his community.

From the Mother of Believers, Umm Abdullah Aisha, with whom may God be pleased, who said: "the Messenger of God, on whom be God's blessing and peace, said: 'Whosoever introduces into this affair of ours [that is, Islam] something that does not belong to it is a reprobate.' " Both Bukhari and Muslim relate it. According to one line of transmission in Muslim (it reads): "Whosoever works a work which has for it no command of ours is a reprobate." (Nawawi, *The Forty Traditions*, no. 5) [JEFFERY 1962: 146]

From Abu Najih al-Irbad ibn Sariya, with whom may God be pleased, who said: The Messenger of God, may God's blessing and peace be upon him, preached a sermon whereby our hearts were made afraid and our eyes dropped tears, so we said: "O Messenger of God, it is as though this were a farewell sermon, so give us a testamentary exhortation." He said: "My testamentary exhortation to you is that you have a pious fear of God, magnified and exalted be He; that you hearken and obey, even though it should be a slave who is appointed over you. He among you who lives long enough will see great disagreement, so take care to observe my custom and the custom of the Rightly Guided Caliphs [that is, the first four: Abu Bakr, Umar, Uthman, and Ali], holding on to them with your molar teeth. Beware of matters newly introduced, for every innovation is an error." So Abu Dawud relates it, as does al-Tirmidhi, who says, "An excellent, sound Prophetic tradition." (Ibid., no. 28) [JEFFERY 1962: 154]

Ibn Masʿud reported God's Messenger as saying: "There was no Prophet whom God raised up among his people before me who did not have from among his people apostles and companions who held to his Prophetic tradition and followed what he commanded. Then they were succeeded by people who said what they did not practice and did things they were not commanded to do. So he who strives against them with his hand is a believer, he who strives against them with his tongue is a believer, and he who strives against them with his heart is a believer. Beyond that there is not so much faith as a grain of mustard." (Baghawi, *Mishkat al-Masibih* 1.6.1)

Abdullah ibn Amr reported God's Messenger as saying: "My people will experience what the Israelites experienced as closely as one sandal resembles another. . . . The Israelites divided into 72 sects, but my people will divide into 73, all but one of which will go to hell." On being asked which that latter was, he replied, "It is the one to which I and my Companions belong." Tirmidhi transmitted this tradition. A version by Ahmad ibn Hanbal and Abu Dawud from Mu'awiya has: "72 will be in hell and one in Paradise, and that latter is the community." (Ibid. 1.6.2)

23. Wrong Belief and Unbelief

Opinions might differ, but there were differences in substance and importance even among those various opinions. Muslims came to recognize in practice and in theory a juridical distinction between "unbelief," the rejection of one of the basic teachings of Islam and so disqualification as a Muslim, and "heretical innovation," the introduction of some belief or practice unsupported by Islamic teaching or custom and not described in the Prophetic traditions. In matters of doubt an authoritative judicial opinion could be solicited, as Caliph Mustazhir (1094–1118 C.E.) did of the jurist-theologian Ghazali on the subject of certain radical Shi'ite groups. Ghazali carefully builds a legal case for their exclusion from the Muslim community, with all the political consequences of such a judgment.

Their declarations fall into two categories, one of which makes it necessary to declare they are in error, are astray and are guilty of innovation, the other of which makes it necessary to declare that they are unbelievers and (the community) must be cleansed of them.

What constitutes for Ghazali the heretical innovation of the group in question are standard Shi'ite beliefs on the legitimacy and nature of leadership in the Islamic community. Ghazali proceeds with the matter of innovation.

With regard to the first category (of beliefs) which makes it necessary to declare that they are in error, are astray and are guilty of innovation, it is where we encounter those unlearned folk who believe that the leadership (of the community) belongs by right to the immediate family of the Prophet, and that he who should rightly have it in our day is their Pretender [that is, the contemporary descendent of Ali who laid claim to the office]. Their claim is that in the first (Muslim) century the one who should have rightfully had it was Ali [the cousin and son-in-law of Muhammad], may God be pleased with him, but that he was wrongly deprived of it. . . . Nevertheless, they do not believe that it is lawful to shed our blood [that is, the Sunni Muslims who have a different view of the leadership question], nor do they believe that we are in unbelief. What they do believe about us [and, Ghazali might have added, we about them] is that we are iniquitous folk whose minds have erroneously slipped from comprehension of the truth, or that we have turned aside from their leader out of obstinacy and a spirit of contention. It is not permissible to shed the blood of a person in this category or to give judgment that he is in unbelief because he says such things. . . . Judgment should be confined to the declaration that such a one has (merely) gone astray, for he does not express belief in any of the erroneous teachings of their sect . . . concerning certain theological beliefs and matters of resurrection and the Judgment. With regard to all such matters they express no beliefs other than those we express ourselves.

For the Sunnis, the "people of the tradition and the collectivity," the notion of a consensus of the Muslim community was an important one. Does not, then, the Shiʿites' violation of the universal consensus on the question of the early leaders of Islam qualify them as unbelievers?

But someone might ask: But do you not declare them in unbelief because of what they say about the office of community leader in the first years (of Islam), how it belonged by right to Ali and not to Abu Bakr and those who succeeded him, but he was wrongly deprived of it, for in this they go contrary to the consensus of Muslims? Our answer is that we do not deny the dangerous nature of this opposition to the consensus, and for that reason we go beyond charging them with being in undisguised error . . . and charge them with leading others astray, causing heresy and introducing innovation, but we do not go so far as declaring them in unbelief. This is because it is not clear to us that one who goes contrary to the consensus is an unbeliever. Indeed, there is a difference of opinion among Muslims as to whether the proof of a doctrine can rest on consensus alone.

Ghazali pushes the objection a step farther. Some Shiʿites were not content to say merely that Ali had been wrongfully passed over for the leadership on four successive occasions; they went on to denigrate those first four "Successors of the Prophet," men who in the Sunni tradition were called "the Rightly Guided Caliphs."

If someone should ask: Then if someone were to say plainly that Abu Bakr and Umar were in unbelief, ought he to be considered the same as one who calls any other of the Muslim chiefs or judges or leaders who came after them an unbeliever? Yes, we do so teach. To charge Abu Bakr or Umar with unbelief is not different from charging unbelief to any of the leaders or judges of the community, nor, indeed, to any individual who professes Islam, save in two regards. First, it would also be going against and contradicting consensus, though, indeed, one who charges them with unbelief because of some perplexity might not even be contradicting reliable consensus. The second is that there are many traditions from the Prophet passed down concerning the two of them, according to which they were promised Paradise, are eulogized, have judgments expressed as to the soundness of their religion and the steadfastness of their convictions and declaring that they have precedence over the rest of humanity. If these traditions from the Prophet have reached the ears of one who makes the charge (of unbelief against Abu Bakr and Umar), and in spite of it he expresses his belief that they are in unbelief, then he himself is an unbeliever, not because he accused them of unbelief, but because he is giving the lie to the Apostle of God, upon whom be God's blessing and peace, and by general consent anyone who treats any word of his sayings as a lie is an unbeliever.

Ghazali now comes to the rock-bottom issue: Who is a Muslim and who is not? What must one believe to be reckoned a member of the community, secure against all attempts to be read out of the community?

Let us suppose someone asks: What is your teaching with regard to someone who declares a fellow Muslim to be in unbelief, is such a one an unbeliever or not? Our answer is: If such a one is aware that this (fellow Muslim whom he has accused of unbelief) believes in the divine Oneness, had confident trust in the Apostle, upon whom be God's blessing and peace, and held other proper doctrines, then whensoever he declares him an unbeliever with respect to these doctrines, he is himself an unbeliever, since he is expressing an opinion that the true religion is unbelief and is untrue. On the other hand, if he thinks (erroneously) that a fellow Muslim believes that the Apostle was false, or that he denies the Creator, or is a dualist, or some such other that necessarily involves one in unbelief, and so, relying on this opinion, declares him to be in unbelief, then he is in error with respect to his opinion of this person but right in declaring that anyone who so believes is in unbelief.

Ignorance, Ghazali explains, of anything beyond the two propositions in the simple profession of faith does not affect one's position as a Muslim.

It is not a condition of a man's religion that he knows the state of belief of every Muslim or the unbelief of every unbeliever. Indeed, there is no one person who can be imagined who, if we did not know about him, would affect our religious standing. More, if a person believes in God and His Apostle, diligently performs his acts of worship, and yet had not heard of the names of Abu Bakr and Umar, in fact dies before ever hearing of them, he would nevertheless die a Muslim, for belief in what is told about them is not among the pillars of religion, such that any mistake with respect to what must or must not be attributed to them would necessarily strip one of his religion.

What makes this group of Shi'ites infidels, then, is that they have read the Sunni Muslims out of the religion of Islam as unbelievers, despite obvious evidence to the contrary. Ghazali constructs that "obvious evidence" into a small Muslim creed.

They believe that we (Sunnis) are in disbelief, so that it is lawful to plunder our property and shed our blood. This necessarily leads to *their* being declared to be unbelievers. This is unavoidable since they know that we believe that the world has a Maker, Who is One, Powerful, Knowing, Willing, Speaking, Hearing and Seeing; Who has no one like Him; that His Apostle is Muhammad ibn Abdullah, upon whom be God's blessing and peace, who spoke the truth in all that he told about the resurrection and the Judgment, and about Paradise and Hell. These are the doctrines which are pivotal for sound religion. (Ghazali, *On the Disgraceful Doctrines of the Esoteric Sects* 8.1) [JEFFERY 1962: 255–260]

24. The Excommunication and Execution of Unbelievers

Where the Muslims encountered unbelief was not among the "Peoples of the Book," the misguided Jews and Christians who nonetheless possessed the authentic Word of God, but on the part of outright polytheist pagans—the Hindus of India, for example—or among those who had once been, or still claimed to be, Muslims but who nonetheless rejected some basic tenet of Islam—in short, apostates. Apostasy was reckoned a formal crime—the most serious of crimes—and so was subject to the statutory penalties of Islamic law, in this case death, as appears in the law code of Ibn Qudama (d. 1223 C.E.).

Every Muslim, male or female, who apostatizes, should be put to death. The Prophet has said: "When a Muslim denies his religion, kill him."

The apostate should not be executed before he has been three times called upon to make an act of contrition. If he makes an act of contrition, his life should be spared; otherwise he should be decapitated with a sword.

The man who denies the existence of God, or who gives God an associate, a wife, or a son; who calls God a liar or insults Him; who calls a Prophet a liar or insults him; who denies the mission of a Prophet; who denies, in whole or in part, a revealed Book; who rejects one of the Pillars of Islam; or who considers permissible universally recognized prohibitions, such a one is an apostate, or at least does not know the obligations and prohibitions that the law prescribes. In this latter case, he should be instructed; if he refuses to recognize them, he will be considered an apostate.   [IBN QUDAMA 1950: 269–270]

We return to Ghazali and the case of the Shi'ite extremists. He has pronounced them guilty of unbelief; he now proceeds to trace the practical consequences of this judgment.

A concise statement is that they are to be treated in the same manner as apostates [that is, those who were once Muslims but have formally renounced Islam] with regard to blood, property, marriage, slaughtering, execution of judgments and the performing of cult practices. With regard to their spirits, they are not to be treated in the same manner as a born unbeliever, since the Imam (al-Shafi'i) gives a choice, when it is the case of a born unbeliever, between four expedients, to wit, (extending him a period of) grace, (allowing him the chance of) ransom, enslaving him, or putting him to death, but he gives no options in the case of an apostate. . . . The only (treatment for such) is that they be put to death and the face of the earth cleansed of them. This is the judgment on those Esotericists who have been adjudged to be in disbelief. Neither the permissibility nor the necessity of putting them to death is limited by being (confined to when we are) in a state of war with them, but we may take them unawares and shed their blood, so that (all the more) when they are involved in fighting is it permissible to kill them.

Should someone ask: "Would you put their women and children to death?" our answer is: As for the children, no, for a child is not to be blamed, and their judgment will come. As for the women, we ourselves would (favor) putting them to death whenever they plainly state beliefs which are (in the category of) unbelief, in accordance with the decision we have already rendered. For the female apostate is, in our opinion, deserving of death in accordance with the all-inclusive statement of him [Muhammad] upon whom be God's blessing and peace: "Whoever changes religion, put that one to death." It is allowable, however, for the leader of the community to follow in this matter the result of his own deliberations, and if he thinks he should follow the way of (the jurist) Abu Hanifa with regard to them and refrain from putting the women to death, the question is one that belongs to the realm of individual deliberation and decision. . . .

As regards the property (of unbelievers), the regulation concerning it is the same as that with regard to the property of apostates. Whatever is taken in conquest, save the corpses of horses and riders, falls wholly under the category of "apostate spoils," which the leader is to distribute rightfully to those to whom such spoils are due, in accordance with the principles of division given in the words of the Most High: "What God has given as spoil to His Messenger from the towns belongs to God and His Messenger etc." (Quran 59:7). . . . When they die their property cannot be inherited, nor can one of them inherit from another. They cannot inherit from a true believer nor can a true believer inherit their property, even though there should have been a kinship between them, for the inheritance relationship between unbelievers and Muslims is severed. Cohabitation with their women is forbidden, just as marriage with a female apostate is illegal. . . .

Closely connected with the unlawfulness of such marriage contracts, is the unlawfulness of (ritual) slaughtering (by an unbeliever). No act of slaughtering by any of them is legally valid any more than a slaughtering by a Magian [that is, a Zoroastrian] or a Manichean. (Ritual) slaughtering and marriage contracts are very similar (in their juristic aspects) and both are unlawful when associated with any group of unbelievers save Jews and Christians, in whose case there is a relaxing of strictness because they are People of the Book which God sent down to a faithful prophet whose trustworthiness is apparent and whose Book is well known.

As for the execution of legal judgments in connection with them, it is invalid and (such judgments) are not to be carried out. Also their testimony is to be refused, for these are all matters whose validity is conditional on the person concerned being a Muslim, for which reason no one among them who has been judged to be in unbelief can properly have a part in such matters. Furthermore, their cult performances are useless. Neither their fastings nor their prayer services have any value, nor do their pilgrimages or almsgivings count for anything, so that whenever one of them repents and cleanses himself of his (erroneous beliefs), and we are satisfied that his repentance is genuine, then he must make up all the cult performances that have slipped by and were performed while he was in a state of unbelief, just as is incumbent in the case of an apostate (who returns to the faith). This is as much as we wished to draw attention to in connection with their legal position. (Ghazali, *On the Disgraceful Doctrines of the Esoteric Sects* 8.2) [JEFFERY 1962: 264–268]

25. "That Was Gabriel.
He Came To Teach You Your Religion"

"Creeds" and statements of belief embodying the essence of Islam become progressively more elaborate even in the Prophetic traditions. This is one reported from Muhammad on the authority of Umar and eventually included among the forty essential traditions of Islam by al-Nawawi (d. 1278 C.E.), which was described in Chapter 3 above.

While we were one day sitting with the Apostle of God, on whom be God's blessing and peace, there appeared before us a man in a very white garment and with very black hair. No traces of journeying were visible on him, and none of us knew him. He sat down close to the Prophet, upon whom be God's blessing and peace, rested his knees against his, put his palms on his thighs, and said: "O Muhammad, inform me about Islam." Said the Apostle of God, upon whom be God's blessing and peace: "Islam is that you should testify that there is no god save the God and that Muhammad is His Apostle, that you should say the prayers, pay the legal alms, fast during Ramadan, and go on pilgrimage to the House [that is, the Kaʿba at Mecca], if you can find a way to do so." Said he: "You have spoken truly." We were astonished at his thus questioning him and telling him he was right, but he went on to say: "Inform me about faith." Muhammad answered: "It is that you should believe in God and His angels and His Books and His Messengers and in the Last Day, and that you should believe in the decreeing of both good and evil." He said: "You have spoken truly." Then he said: "Inform me about the best behavior." Muhammad answered: "It is that you should serve God and as though you could see Him, for though you cannot see Him, He sees you." He said: "Inform me about the Hour." Muhammad said: "About that the one questioned knows no more than the questioner." So he said: "Well, inform me of the signs thereof [that is, of its coming]." Said Muhammad: "They are that the slave girl will give birth to her mistress, that you will see the bare-footed, the naked, the destitute, the herdsmen of the sheep building arrogantly high houses." Thereupon the man went off. I [that is, Umar] waited a while, and then the Prophet said: "O Umar, do you know who that was?" I replied: "God and His Apostle know better." He said: "That was Gabriel. He came to teach you your religion." (Nawawi, *The Forty Traditions*, no. 2) [JEFFERY 1962: 145]

26. Moral Islam

The following Prophetic traditions are from the same collection by al-Nawawī, though here the emphasis is, as it was for most pious Muslims, moral and social rather than dogmatic.

From Abu Hurayra, with whom may God be pleased, who said: Said the Apostle of God, upon whom be God's blessing and peace: "Do not envy one another; do not vie with one another; do not hate one another; do not be at variance with one another; and do not undercut one another in trading, but be servants of God, brothers. A Muslim is a brother to a Muslim. He does not oppress him, nor does he forsake him, nor deceive him nor despise him. God-fearing piety is here," he said pointing to his breast. "It is enough evil for a man that he should despise his brother Muslim. The blood, property and honor of every Muslim is inviolable to a fellow Muslim." Muslim relates this tradition. (Nawawi, *The Forty Traditions*, no. 35) [JEFFERY 1962: 157]

From Abu Hurayra, with whom may God be pleased, who said: Said the Apostle of God, upon whom be God's blessing and peace: "In truth God, may He be exalted, has said: 'Whoever acts with enmity toward a friend of Mine, against him will I declare war. No servant of Mine draws near to Me with anything I like more than that which I have laid upon him as an incumbent duty, and a true servant of Mine will continue drawing near to Me with supererogatory acts of worship so that I may love him. Then when I am living with him, I am his hearing with which he hears, his seeing with which he sees, his hand with which he takes things, his foot with which he walks. If he asks of Me, I will surely give him, and if he takes refuge with Me, I will surely give him refuge.' " (Ibid., no. 38) [JEFFERY 1962: 158–159]

27. Faith and Good Works in Islam

The early problem of unbelief and its political consequences caused Muslims to look closely at the nature of faith and its relationship to good works. The following reflections are from the so-called Testament of Abu Hanifah. *That Muslim jurist died in 767 C.E., but the* Testament *is likely by some later member of his legal school (Chapter 5 above).*

Faith may neither increase nor decrease, for decrease in it could only be conceived of in terms of unbelief, and increase in it in terms of the decrease of unbelief, but how could a single person be at one and the same time both a believer and an unbeliever? The true believer is in truth a true believer and the infidel is in truth an infidel. Faith is not a matter which admits of doubt, nor is unbelief a matter which admits of doubt, for the Most High has said, "These are in truth true believers" (Quran 8:74), and "these are in truth unbelievers" (Quran 4:151). Even the disobedient ones of the community of Muhammad, upon whom be God's blessing and peace, are all of them true believers, and are not to be classified (despite their disobedience) as unbelievers.

Works are something other than faith, and faith is other than works. This is proved by the fact that there are numerous occasions when a true believer is granted exemption from works, whereas it is not permissible to say that he is ever exempted from faith. Thus a women in menstruation or childbirth is granted exemption by God, praised and exalted is He, from prayers, but it is not permissible to say that God has granted her exemption from faith and bidden her abandon her faith. Also to such the Lawgiver says: "Give up fasting but make it up later," but it could not be that one is told to give up faith and make it up later. . . .

We confess that the predetermining of good and evil is from God, exalted be He, for should anyone claim that the predetermining of good and evil is from other than He, he would be one who disbelieves in God and annuls his own confession of the divine unity.

We confess that works are of three kinds, to wit, obligatory, meritorious, and sinful. The obligatory are by God's command and in accordance with His will, His liking, His judgment, His knowledge, His help and His writing on the "Preserved Tablet" (see Quran 85:21). The sinful are not (such) by God's command but in accordance with His will, not in accordance with His liking but by His decreeing and His predetermining, by His creation but not by His help, in accordance with His abandoning and His knowledge, but not with His recognition, and in accordance with His writing on the "Preserved Tablet." (Abu Hanifah, *Testament*)

[JEFFERY 1962: 342–343]

28. Alms and Charity

One of the pillars of Islam, and so an obligation binding upon every Muslim, was the paying of a statutory alms tithe. The complex subject of tithing—how much, to whom, from whom, and for what purpose—is discussed at length in Muslim law books. But there are two Prophetic traditions in al-Nawawi's summary collec-

tion that look at alms not in their legal aspect but as a function of the virtue of charity.

From Abu Dharr, with whom may God be pleased, who said that some from among the Companions of the Apostle of God, upon whom be God's blessing and peace, said to the Prophet, upon whom be God's blessing and peace: "O Apostle of God, the rich take off all the rewards. They say prayers just as we do, they fast just as we do, but they can give in charity out of the superabundance of their wealth (and so surpass us in storing up merit)." He said: "Has not God appointed for you that you should give in charitable alms? Truly, in every ejaculation 'Glory be to God!' there is such an alms, in every 'God is the greatest!' in every 'Praise be to God!' in every 'Hallelujah!' in every bidding what is right and forbidding the doing of what is wrong; even when one of you has sex with his wife, there is an alms in that." They said: "O Apostle of God, (do you mean to say that) when one of us satisfies his desires (with his wife), there will be a reward for that?" He answered: "What do you think? Had He put it among the things forbidden, it would have been sinful for one, so when He put among the allowable things, there was a reward for it also." Muslim relates this tradition. (Nawawi, *The Forty Traditions*, no. 25)
[JEFFERY 1962: 153]

From Abu Hurayra, with whom may God be pleased, who said: Said the Apostle of God, upon whom be God's blessing and peace: "An alms is due each day that the sun rises from every finger joint of all the people. If you straighten out some trouble between two individuals, that is an alms. If you help a man with his beast, mounting him thereon or hoisting up onto it his luggage, that is an alms. A good work is an alms. In every step you take in walking to prayer there is an alms. Whenever you remove something harmful from the path, that is an alms." Al-Bukhari and Muslim both relate this tradition. (Ibid., no. 26) [JEFFERY 1962: 153]

29. Militant Islam: War in the Sacred Month

The Messenger sent Abdullah ibn Jahsh off in (the month of) Rajab [624 C.E.] on his return from the (first skirmish) at Badr. He sent with him eight "Emigrants," without any of the "Helpers." He wrote for him a letter, and ordered him not to look at it until he had journeyed for two days and then to do what he ordered him, but not to put pressure on any of his companions (to do likewise). . . . When Abdullah had traveled for two days he read the letter and looked into it and this is what it said:

"When you have read this letter of mine proceed until you reach Nakhla between Mecca and al-Taʾif. Lie in wait there for the Quraysh and find out what they are doing. Having read the letter he said, "To hear is to obey." Then he said to his companions, "The Messenger has commanded me to go to Nakhla to lie in wait there for the Quraysh so as to bring him news of them. He has forbidden me to put any pressure on you, so if anyone wishes martyrdom let him go forward, and he who does not, let him go back; as for me, I am going on as the Prophet has ordered." So he went on, as did all his companions, not one of them falling back. . . .

A caravan of Quraysh passed them carrying dry raisins and leather and other merchandise. . . . When the caravan saw them they were afraid because they had camped near them. But Ukkasha, who had shaved his head, looked down at them, and when they saw him they felt safe and said, "They are only pilgrims, you have nothing to fear from them."

The raiders took council among themselves, for this was the last day of Rajab, and they said, "If we leave them alone tonight they will get into the sacred area and be safe from us; and if we kill them, we will kill them in the sacred month." So they were hesitant and feared to attack the Quraysh. Then they encouraged each other and decided to kill as many as they could and take what they had. . . .

When they returned to the Apostle, he said, "I did not order you to fight in the sacred month," and he held the caravan and the two prisoners in suspense and refused to take anything from them. When the Messenger said that, the men were in despair and thought they were doomed. Their Muslim brethren reproached them for what they had done, and the Quraysh said, "Muhammad and his companions have violated the sacred month, shed blood therein, taken booty and captured men." The Muslims in Mecca who opposed them said it actually occurred in (the month of) Shaʿban and the Jews turned this raid into an omen against the Apostle. . . . When there was much talk about it, God sent down to his Messenger (the verse):

"They will ask you about the sacred month, and war in it. Say, war therein is a heinous thing, but keeping people from the way of God and disbelieving in Him and the sacred shrine and driving out His people therefrom is more heinous with God. And persecution is more heinous than slaying." (Quran 2:217)

That is, if you have killed in the sacred month, they have kept you back from the way of God with their disbelief in Him, and from the sacred shrine, and have driven you from it when you were its people. This is a more serious matter with God than the killing of those whom you have slain. "For persecution is worse than killing," that is, they used to persecute the Muslim in his religion until they made him return to disbelief after believing, and that is worse with God than killing. "And they will not cease to fight you until they turn you back from your religion if they can," that is, they are doing more heinous acts than that and with evil intent.

And when the (verse of the) Quran came down about that and God relieved the Muslims of their anxiety in the matter, the Messenger took possession of the caravan and the prisoners. (Ibn Ishaq, *Life* 423–426)
[IBN ISHAQ 1955: 281–282]

The point is clear: it was permitted to fight for God's cause, even in previously banned time, on the principle of a higher good being served. It was a taking of sides, and the test was a profession of faith in the Lord God of all.

It is reported on the authority of Abu Hurayra that the Messenger of God said: I have been commanded to fight against people so long as they do not declare that there is no god but the God, and he who professed it was guaranteed the protection of his property and life on my behalf, and his affairs rest with God. (Muslim, *Sahih* 1.9.30)

So reads an early tradition reported of Muhammad, justifying the militant quality of his calling—"I have been commanded"—and the test that qualifies one for membership in and protection of the community of Muslims. In this version that test has but a single article, belief in the one true God. Immediately after it, however, another tradition adds a second clause.

It is reported on the authority of Abu Hurayra that he heard the Messenger of God say: I have been commanded to fight against people until they testify the fact that there is no god but the God, and believe (in me) that I am the Messenger (from the Lord), and in all that I have brought. And when they do it, their blood and riches are guaranteed protection on my behalf except where it is justified by law, and their affairs rest with God. (Ibid. 1.9.31)

30. The Sixth Pillar: War in the Path of God

Islam was an activist faith, as the Prophet had demonstrated in both his words and deeds, and the theme of "struggling on the path of God" runs throughout the Quran. In some instances the struggle was a personal one against sin or toward perfection; in others the context was social or communal—in short, as part of a "Holy War" in the quite literal sense of armed combat, what came to be called

Jihad. Thus there came into being another candidate for inclusion among the basic prescriptions of Islam, the "struggle in the path of God" commanded to Muhammad and to all Muslims. The following tradition reported after the death of the Prophet appears to reflect some kind of debate in the community on just how widely that obligation extended. In this tradition at least, war in God's name is quite explicitly denied parity with the other pillars of Islam.

It is reported on the authority of Ta'us that a man said to Abdullah ibn Umar: Why don't you carry out a military expedition? Upon which he replied: I heard the Messenger of God, may peace be upon him, say: In truth Islam is founded on five (pillars): testifying that there is no god but the God, establishment of prayer, payment of the alms tax, the fast of Ramadan and pilgrimage to the House. (Muslim, *Sahih* 1.6.21)

Whether or not Jihad was formally one of the "pillars"—and the lawyers continued to debate the question—militancy on behalf of the cause of Islam, or better of God, was a fundamental duty, as the Quran itself leaves no doubt.

Fight those in the way of God who fight you, but do not be aggressive: God does not like aggressors. And fight those wheresoever you find them, and expel them from the place they had turned you out from. Oppression is worse than killing. Do not fight them by the Holy Mosque unless they fight you there. If they do, then slay them: such is the requital for unbelievers. But if they desist, God is forgiving and kind.

Fight them until sedition comes to an end, and the Law of God (prevails). If they desist, then cease to be hostile, except against those who oppress. (Quran 2:190–193)

Enjoined on you is fighting, and this you abhor. You may dislike a thing, yet it may be good for you; or a thing may haply please you but may be bad for you. Only God has knowledge, and you do not know. (Quran 2:216)

Those who barter the life of this world for the next should fight in the way of God. And We shall bestow on who fights in the way of God, whether he is killed or is victorious, a glorious reward.

What has come upon you that you fight not in the cause of God and for the oppressed, men, women and children, who pray, "Get us out of this city, O Lord, whose people are oppressors; so send us a friend by Your will, and send us a helper."

Those who believe fight in the way of God; and those who do not fight only for the powers of evil; so you should fight the allies of Satan. Surely the stratagem of Satan is ineffective. (Quran 4:74–76)

31. The Prophet's Instructions on the Holy War

Some of the traditions attributed to the Prophet are brief and pointed. Others are schematic, as if they had been pronounced by a lawyer, like this one setting out the terms and conditions governing the conduct of a Holy War.

Sulayman ibn Burayda told on his father's authority that when God's Messenger appointed a commander over an army or a detachment he instructed him to fear God and consider the welfare of the Muslims who were with him. Then he said: "Go forth in God's name in God's path and fight with those who disbelieve in God. Go forth and do not be unfaithful regarding booty, or treacherous, or mutilate anyone, or kill a child. When you meet the polytheists who are your enemy, summon them to three things, and accept whichever of them they are willing to accept and then leave them be. First, summon them to Islam, and if they agree accept it from them and leave them be. Then summon them to leave their abodes and join the ranks of the Emigrants, and tell them that if they do so they will have the same rights and responsibilities as the Emigrants; but if they refuse to join, then tell them they will be like the desert Arabs who are Muslims, subject to God's judgment which applies to believers, but they will have no spoils or booty unless they fight with the Muslims. If they refuse, demand the tribute from them, and if they agree, accept it from them and leave them be; but if they refuse, seek God's help and fight against them.

"When you invest a fortified place and its people wish you to grant them the protection of God and His Prophet, grant them neither but rather grant them your protection and that of your companions, for it is less serious to break your guarantee of protection or that of your companions than to break that of God and His Messenger. If you invest a fortified place and its people offer to capitulate and have the matter referred to God's judgment, do not grant this, but let them capitulate and have the matter referred to your judgment, for you do not know whether or not you will hit God's judgment regarding them."

This tradition was transmitted by Muslim. (Baghawi, *Mishkat al-Masabih* 18.4.1)

And as it did in Christianity, the struggle on behalf of Islam had its rewards in the afterlife. These were considerable, since the duty of the Holy War was a "community obligation," that is to say, it could be fulfilled by a few taking up arms, without the rest of the community being blamed (see Chapter 5 above). Thus it shared the additional merit of being a work of supererogation.

Ibn Abbas reported God's Messenger as saying to his companions: "When your brethren were smitten at the battle of Uhud, God put their spirits in the crops of green birds which go down to the rivers of Paradise, eat its fruits and nestle in lamps of gold in the shadow of the Throne (of God). Then when they had experienced the sweetness of their food, drink and rest, they asked who would tell their brethren about them, that they were alive in Paradise, in order that they (the living believers) might not cease to desire Paradise or recoil in war. God Most High said He would tell them about them so He sent down the verses:

'Never think that those who who are killed in the way of God are dead. They are alive, getting succor from their Lord, rejoicing at what God has given them of His grace, and happy for those who are trying to overtake them and have not joined them yet, and who will have no fear or regret. They rejoice at the kindness and mercy of God; and God does not suffer the wages of the faithful to go to waste' (Quran 3:169–171)."

This tradition has been transmitted by Abu Dawud. (Baghawi, *Mishkat al-Masabih* 3.818)

31. Just War and Homicide

There was, however, a difference between this just war in the cause of religion and the crime of homicide. The distinction is drawn with some care in the Quran.

It is not for a believer to take a believer's life except by mistake; and he who kills a believer by mistake should free a slave who is a believer and pay blood money to the victim's family, unless they waive it as an act of charity. If he belonged to a community that was hostile to you but was himself a believer, then a slave who is a believer should be freed. In case he belonged to a people with whom you have a treaty, then give blood money to his family and free a believing slave. For he who has no means (to do so) should fast for a period of two months continuously to have his sins forgiven by God, and God is all-knowing and all-wise.

Anyone who kills a believer intentionally will be cast into Hell to abide there forever, and suffer God's anger and damnation. For him a greater punishment awaits.

O believers, when you go forth (to fight) in the way of God, be discreet and do not say to anyone who greets you in peace: "You are not a believer." You desire the gain of earthly life, but there are prizes in plenty with God. You were also like him (an unbeliever) in the past, but

God has been gracious to you. So be careful and discreet, for God is aware
of what you do.

The faithful who sit idle, save those who are disabled, are not equal
to those who fight in the way of God with their wealth and lives. God has
exalted in rank those who fight for the faith with their wealth and souls
over those who sit idle. Though God's promise of good is for all, He has
granted His favor of the highest reward to those who struggle in preference to those who sit at home. (Quran 4:92–95)

33. "There Is No Compulsion in Religion"

*The Holy War, or Jihad, was fought against unbelievers living in the "Abode of
War," that is, the territories outside the political control of the Muslim community.
Within the "Abode of Islam" itself lived others who did not accept either the Quran
or the Prophet but who were not heathens or polytheists. These were the "Peoples
of the Book," the "Scriptuaries" who practiced Judaism, Christianity, and, it will
appear, Zoroastrianism. They were not required to embrace Islam; the proof-text is
this verse of the Quran.*

There is no compulsion in matters of faith. Distinct now is the way
of guidance from error. He who turns away from the forces of evil and
believes in God, will surely hold fast to a handle that is strong and un-
breakable, for God hears all and knows everything. (Quran 2:256)

*The interpretation of this famous verse was fairly standard, despite a great deal of
uncertainty about the circumstances of its revelation.*

Wahidi [d. 1076 C.E.] relates on the authority of Sa'id ibn Jubayr,
who related on the authority of Ibn Abbas: "When the children of a
woman of the Helpers [that is, early Medinese converts to Islam] all died
in infancy, she vowed that if a child were to live, she would bring it up
as a Jew. Thus when the Jewish tribe of al-Nadir was evicted from Medina, there were among them sons of the Helpers. The Helpers said, 'O
Messenger of God, what will become of our children?' Thus God sent
down this (above-cited) verse." Sa'id ibn Jubayr said: "Therefore whoever wished to join them did so and whoever wished not to join them did
so likewise." According Mujahid, this (same) verse was sent down concerning a man who had a black male servant called Subayh. The man
wished to compel his servant to enter Islam. Al-Suddi said that the verse
was sent down concerning a man of the Helpers known as Abu al-Husayn
who had two sons. One day merchants from Syria came to Medina to sell
oil. The sons of Abu al-Husayn came to the merchants, who converted

them to Christianity. They then went to Syria with the merchants. When Abu al-Husayn knew this, he came to the Prophet and asked: "Shall I pursue them?" God then sent down "There is no compulsion in religion." The Messenger of God said: "May God banish them! They are the first two who rejected faith." Mujahid said: "This was before the Messenger of God was commanded to fight against the People of the Book. God's saying 'There is no compulsion in religion' was abrogated and he was commanded to fight against the People of the Book in the Sura 'Repentance' (9:29)." . . .

According to other traditions, the verse was revealed in reference to the People of the Book, who should not be compelled to enter Islam so long as they pay the tribute. The verse is, therefore, not abrogated (by 9:29). Tabari [d. 923 C.E.] relates on the authority of Qatada: "Arab society was compelled to enter Islam because they were an unlettered community, having no book which they knew. Thus nothing other than Islam was accepted from them. The People of the Book are not to be compelled to enter Islam if they submit to paying the (tribute of the) poll tax or the land tax." . . .

Razi [d. 1209 C.E.] . . . comments: "This (verse) means that God did not rest the matter of faith on compulsion or coercion but rather based it on free will and the ability to choose. . . . This is what is intended here when God made clear the proofs of the Divine Unity. He said that there is no longer any excuse for a rejecter of faith to persist in his rejection. That he should be forced to accept faith is not lawful in this world, which is a world of trial. For coercion and compulsion in the matter of faith is the annulment of the meaning of trial and test." [AYOUB 1984: 252–254]

34. The People of the Book: War and Tribute

Whatever recognition was granted to their beliefs and cult, the People of the Book were required to pay tribute in acknowledgment of the Muslims' political sovereignty.

Fight those People of the Book who do not believe in God and the Last Day, who do not prohibit what God and His Apostle have forbidden, or accept divine law, until all of them pay protective tribute in submission. (Quran 9:29)

The standard exegesis explains.

According to this verse, tribute is restricted to the People of the Book. This is confirmed by the fact that Umar [Caliph, 634–644 C.E.]

accepted no tribute from the Zoroastrians until Abd al-Rahman ibn Awf
testified that the Prophet had collected tribute from the Zoroastrians of
Hajar (in southern Bahrayn) and had said: "Establish for them the same
custom as for the People of the Book, for they have a similar Book." Thus
they are regarded as possessing the Book. But on our view tribute may
not be collected from other unbelievers. According to Abu Hanifa, however, it should be collected from them, from all except the pagan Arabs,
for al-Zuhri relates that the Prophet concluded peace treaties with the
idolaters who were not Arabs. Finally, according to Malik ibn Anas, tribute should be collected from all unbelievers except apostates.

The minimum tribute is one (gold) dinar per year, with the rich and
poor treated equally. Abu Hanifa, however, says that it is forty-eight
(silver) dirhams for the rich, half that amount for those who are moderately capable of earning a living, and nothing at all for the poor who are
not capable of earning a living. (Baydawi, *The Lights of Revelation, ad loc.*)

35. Guidelines for Christian Behavior under Islam

*The following is a very late version of a widely circulated and cited covenant of
submission (dhimma) said to have been originally drawn for the second Caliph,
Umar (634–644 C.E.), by the Christians of Syria.*

We heard from Abd al-Rahman ibn Ghanam [d. 697 C.E.] as follows:
When Umar ibn al-Khattab, may God be pleased with him, accorded a
peace to the Christians of Syria, we wrote to him as follows:

"In the name of God, the Compassionate, the Merciful.

This is a letter to the servant of God Umar (ibn al-Khattab), Commander of the Faithful, from the Christians of such-and-such a city.
When you came against us, we asked you for safe conduct for ourselves,
our descendants, our property, and the people of our community, and we
undertook the following obligations toward you:

We shall not build, in our cities or their neighborhood, new monas-
teries, churches, convents, or monks' cells, nor shall we repair, by day or
by night, such of them as fall in ruins or are situated in the quarters of the
Muslims.

We shall keep our gates open for passersby and travelers. We shall
give board and lodging to all Muslims who pass our way for three days.

We shall not give shelter in our churches or in our dwellings to any
spy, nor hide him from the Muslims.

We shall not teach the Quran to our children.

We shall not manifest our religion publicly or convert anyone to it. We shall not prevent any of our kin from entering Islam if they wish it.

We shall show respect toward the Muslims, and we shall rise from our seats when they wish to sit.

We shall not seek to resemble the Muslims by imitating any of their garments, the *qalansuwa*, the turban, footwear or the parting of hair. We shall not speak as they do, nor shall we adopt their names.

We shall not mount on saddles, nor shall we gird on swords or bear any kind of arms or carry them on our persons.

We shall engrave Arabic inscriptions on our seals.

We shall not sell fermented drinks.

We shall not clip the fronts of our heads.

We shall always dress in the same way wherever we may be, and we shall bind the special cincture about our waists.

We shall not display our crosses or our books on the public ways or the markets of the Muslims. We shall use clappers in our churches only very softly. We shall not raise our voices in our church services or in the presence of Muslims, nor shall we raise our voices when following our dead. We shall not show lights on any of the roads of the Muslims or in their markets. We shall not bury our dead near the Muslims.

We shall not take slaves who have be allotted to the Muslims.

We shall not build houses overtopping the houses of the Muslims. . . .

We accept these conditions for ourselves and for the people of our community, and in return we receive a pledge of safe conduct.

If in any way we violate these undertakings, for which we ourselves stand surety, we forfeit our covenant (*dhimma*) and we become liable to the penalties for contumacy and sedition."

Umar ibn al-Khattab replied: Sign what they ask, but add two clauses and impose them in addition to what they have written. They are: "They shall not buy anyone made prisoner by the Muslims," and "Who ever strikes a Muslim with deliberate intent shall forfeit the protection of this pact." (Tartushi, *Siraj al-Muluk* 229–230) [LEWIS 1974: 2:217–219]

35. A Christian Dress Code for the Other Peoples of the Book

Similar restrictions were in force on the Jews living under Islam, restrictions that were in reality now more severe, now considerably more lenient than they appear on the lawyers' books. Christians too had restrictive codes for the Jews living under their sovereignty, codes that were extended to Muslims as parts of the "Abode of Islam," in Spain for example, began to fall back under Christian control.

In some provinces a difference in dress distinguishes the Jews and Saracens from the Christians, but in others confusion has developed to such a degree that no difference is discernible. Whence it happens sometimes through error that Christians mingle with the women of the Jews and Saracens, and, on the other hand, Jews and Saracens mingle with those of the Christians. Therefore, that such ruinous commingling through error of this kind may not serve as a refuge for further excuse for excesses, we decree that such people of both sexes [that is, Jews and Saracens] in every Christian province and at all times be distinguished in public from other people by a difference of dress, since this was also enjoined on them by Moses. On the days of Lamentations and on Passion Sunday they may not appear in public, because some of them, as we understand, on those days are not ashamed to show themselves more ornately attired and do not fear to amuse themselves at the expense of the Christians, who in memory of the Sacred Passion go about attired in robes of mourning. That we must strictly forbid, lest they should presume in some measure to burst forth suddenly in contempt of the Redeemer. And since we ought not to be ashamed of him who blotted out our offenses, we command that the secular princes restrain presumptuous persons of this kind with condign punishment, lest they presume to blaspheme in some degree the one crucified for us. (Fourth Lateran Council [1215 C.E.], Canon 68)

Short Titles

ABOTH RABBI NATHAN 1955. *The Fathers According to Rabbi Nathan.* Translated by Judah Goldin. New Haven: Yale University Press.

ALEXANDER 1984. P. S. Alexander, *Textual Sources for the Study of Judaism.* New York: Barnes and Noble.

ANAWATI & GARDET 1961. G. C. Anawati and Louis Gardet, *Mystique musulmane.* Paris: Librairie philosophique J. Vrin.

AQUINAS 1945. *Basic Writings of Thomas Aquinas.* Edited and annotated by Anton Pegis. 2 vols. New York: Random House.

ARBERRY 1950. A. J. Arberry, *Sufism: An Account of the Mystics of Islam.* London: George Allen & Unwin, Ltd., 1950; rpt. New York: Harper & Row, 1970.

ARBERRY 1964. A. J. Arberry, *Aspects of Islamic Civilization, as Depicted in the Original Texts.* London: George Allen & Unwin, Ltd., 1964; pbk. Ann Arbor: University of Michigan Press, 1976.

ARNOLD 1928. T. Arnold, *Painting in Islam.* Oxford: Oxford University Press, 1928; rpt. New York: Dover Books, 1965.

ASHʿARI 1953. Richard J. McCarthy, S.J., *The Theology of al-Ashʿari.* Beirut: Imprimerie Catholique.

ATTAR 1966. *Muslim Saints and Mystics. Episodes from the Tadhkirat al-Awliya ("Memorials of the Saints") by Farid al-Din Attar.* Translated by A. J. Arberry. Chicago: University of Chicago Press.

ATTAR 1984. Farid ud-Din Attar, *The Conference of the Birds.* Translated by Afkham Darbandi and Dick Davis. Harmondsworth: Penguin.

AUGUSTINE 1947. *Writings of Saint Augustine,* vol. 4: *Christian Instruction.* Translated by J. J. Gavigan. New York: Cima Publishing Company.

AUGUSTINE 1948. *Basic Writings of Saint Augustine.* Edited by Whitney J. Oates. 2 vols. New York: Random House.

AVERROES 1954. *Averroes' Tahafut al-Tahafut (The Incoherence of the Incoherence).* Translated by Simon van den Bergh. 2 vols. London: Luzac & Company.

AVERROES 1961. *Averroes on the Harmony of Religion and Philosophy.* Translated by G. F. Hourani. London: Luzac & Company.

AVICENNA 1951. A. J. Arberry, *Avicenna on Theology.* London: John Murray.

AYOUB 1984. M. Ayoub, *The Qurʾan and Its Interpreters.* Vol. 1. Albany: State University of New York Press.

BAYNES 1955. N. H. Baynes, "Idolatry and the Early Church." In N. H. Baynes, *Byzantine Studies and Other Essays,* pp. 116–143. London: Athlone Press.

BIRUNI 1879. Al-Biruni, *The Chronology of Ancient Nations....* Translated and edited by C. E. Sachau. London: 1879; rpt. Frankfurt: Minerva, 1969.

BOKSER 1981. Ben Zion Bokser, *The Jewish Mystical Tradition*. New York: Pilgrim Press.

BURTON 1977. John Burton, *The Collection of the Qur'an*, Cambridge: Cambridge University Press.

(PSEUDO)-DIONYSIUS 1987. *Pseudo-Dionysius: The Complete Works*. Translated by Colm Luibheid with Paul Rorem. New York: Paulist Press.

FARABI 1961. Al-Farabi, *Fusul al-Madani: Aphorisms of the Statesman*. Edited and translated by D. M. Dunlop. Cambridge: Cambridge University Press.

GHAZALI 1953. W. Montgomery Watt, *The Faith and Practice of al-Ghazali*. London: George Allen & Unwin, Ltd.

GUILLAUME 1924. Alfred Guillaume, *The Traditions of Islam: An Introduction to the Study of the Hadith Literature*. Oxford: Clarendon Press, 1924; rpt. Lahore: Universal Books, 1977.

HALEVI 1905. Judah Halevi, *The Kuzari: An Argument for the Faith of Israel*. Translated by H. Hirschfeld. 1905; rpt. New York: Schocken Books, 1964.

HALPERIN 1984. D. J. Halperin, "A New Edition of the Hekhalot Literature." *Journal of the American Oriental Society* 104 (1984), 543–552.

HAUSHERR 1927. I. Hausherr, *Le méthode d'oraison hésychaste*. Rome: Orientalia Christiana.

HUJWIRI 1911. *The "Kashf al-Mahjub," the Oldest Persian Treatise on Sufism by al-Hujwiri*. Translated by Reynold A. Nicholson. London: Luzac & Company, 1911; rpt. London: Luzac, 1959.

IBN AL-ARABI 1980. Ibn al-Arabi, *The Bezels of Wisdom*. Translated and edited by R.W.J. Austin. New York: Paulist Press.

IBN BATTUTA 1959–1962. *The Travels of Ibn Battuta, A.D. 1325–1354*. Translated and edited by H.A.R. Gibb. 2 vols. Cambridge: Cambridge University Press.

IBN ISHAQ 1955. *The Life of Muhammad: A Translation of Ishaq's Sirat Rasul Allah*. Translated and edited by A. Guillaume. London: Oxford University Press.

IBN KHALDUN 1967. Ibn Khaldun, *The Muqaddimah: An Introduction to History*. Translated by Franz Rosenthal. 3 vols. 2nd corrected ed. Princeton: Princeton University Press.

IBN QUDAMA 1950. H. Laoust, *Le Précis de droit d'Ibn Qudama*. Beirut: Institut Français de Damas.

JEFFERY 1962. A. Jeffery, *A Reader on Islam: Passages from Standard Arabic Writings Illustrative of the Beliefs and Practices of Muslims*. 's-Gravenhage: Mouton and Company.

JOHN CLIMACUS 1982. *John Climacus, The Ladder of Divine Ascent*. Translated by Colm Luibheid and Norman Russell. New York: Paulist Press.

JUNAYD 1962. Ali Hassan Abdel-Kader, *The Life, Personality and Writings of al-Junayd*. London: Luzac & Company.

JUWAYNI 1968. M. Allard, *Textes apolégetiques de Juwaini*. Beirut: Dar al-Machreq.

LANE 1836. Edward Lane, *Manners and Customs of the Modern Egyptians* (1836). 5th ed. rpt. New York: Dover Publications.

LAURENT 1873. J.C.M. Laurent, *Peregrinatores Medii Aevi Quattuor*. 2nd ed. Leipzig: J. C. Hinrichs.

LE GOFF 1984. Jacques Le Goff, *The Birth of Purgatory*. Chicago: University of Chicago Press.

LERNER & MAHDI 1972. R. Lerner and M. Mahdi (eds.), *Medieval Political Philosophy: A Sourcebook*. Glencoe, Ill.: Free Press, 1963; pbk. Ithaca: Cornell University Press, 1972.

LEWIS 1974. Bernard Lewis, *Islam from the Prophet Muhammad to the Capture of Constantinople*. 2 vols. New York: Harper & Row.

LEWIS 1976. Bernard Lewis, "On That Day: A Jewish Apocalyptic Poem on the Arab Conquests." In *Mélanges d'Islamologie . . . de Armand Abel*, pp. 197–200. Leiden: E. J. Brill, 1974. Reprinted in Bernard Lewis, *Studies in Classical and Ottoman Islam (7th–16th Centuries)*. London: Variorum Reprints, 1976.

MCNEILL & GAMER 1938. J. T. McNeill and H. M. Gamer, *Medieval Handbooks of Penance*. New York: Columbia University Press.

MAIMONIDES 1963. Moses Maimonides, *The Guide of the Perplexed*. Translated and edited by Shlomo Pines. Chicago: University of Chicago Press.

MAIMONIDES 1965. *The Code of Maimonides: Book XIV*. New Haven: Yale University Press.

MAIMONIDES 1968. *The Commentary to Mishneh Aboth*. Translated by Arthur David. New York: Bloch Publishing Company.

MANGO 1972. Cyril Mango, *The Art of the Byzantine Empire, 312–1453: Sources and Documents*. Englewood Cliffs, N.J.: Prentice-Hall.

MASSIGNON 1968. Louis Massignon, *Essai sur les origines du lexique technique de la mystique musulmane*. Paris: J. Vrin.

MASSIGNON 1982. Louis Massignon, *The Passion of al-Hallaj: Mystic and Martyr of Islam*. Translated by Herbert Mason. 4 vols. Princeton: Princeton University Press.

MIDRASH RABBAH 1977. *The Midrash Rabbah*. Translated by H. Freedman et al. 5 vols. London, Jerusalem, New York: Soncino Press.

NACHMANIDES 1971. Ramban (Nachmanides), *Commentary on the Torah: Genesis*. Translated by C. B. Chavel. New York: Shilo Publishing House.

NEMOY 1952. *Karaite Anthology: Excerpts from the Early Literature*. Translated by Leon Nemoy. New Haven: Yale University Press.

NICHOLSON 1921. Reynald A. Nicholson, *Studies in Islamic Mysticism*. Cambridge: Cambridge University Press.

PALAMAS 1983. Gregory Palamas, *The Triads*. Edited by John Meyendorff, translation by Nicholas Gendle. New York: Paulist Press.

PESIKTA RABBATI 1968. *Pesikta Rabbati*. Translated by William G. Braude. 2 vols. New Haven and London: Yale University Press.

PETER LOMBARD 1917. E. F. Rogers, "Peter Lombard and the Sacramental System." Ph.D. diss., Columbia University.

PHILO 1945. Philo, *Selections*. Edited and translated by H. Lewy. In *Three Jewish Philosophers*. Philadelphia: Jewish Publication Society, 1945; rpt. New York: Meridian Books, 1960.

PHILO 1981. Philo of Alexandria, *The Contemplative Life, The Giants, and Selections*. Translated by David Winston. New York: Paulist Press.

PINES 1971. S. Pines, *An Arabic Version of the Testimonium Flavianum and Its Implications*. Jerusalem: Israel Academy of Sciences and Humanities.

RAHMAN 1958. F. Rahman, *Prophecy in Islam: Philosophy and Orthodoxy*. London: George Allen & Unwin, Ltd.

RUMI 1925–1940. Jalal al-Din Rumi, *Mathnawi*. Edited, translated, and annotated by R. A. Nicholson. 8 vols. London: Luzac & Company.

SAADYA 1945. Saadya Gaon, *Book of Doctrines and Beliefs*. Abridged translation by A. Altman. In *Three Jewish Philosophers*. Philadelphia: Jewish Publication Society, 1945; rpt. New York: Meridian Books, 1960.

SAADYA 1948. Saadya Gaon, *The Book of Beliefs and Opinions*. Translated by S. Rosenblatt. New Haven: Yale University Press.

SACHEDINA 1981. A. Sachedina, *Islamic Messianism: The Idea of the Mahdi in Twelver Shi'ism*. Albany: State University of New York Press.

SAHAS 1972. D. J. Sahas, *John of Damascus on Islam: The "Heresy of the Ishmaelites."* Leiden: E. J. Brill.

SCHAEFER 1982. P. Schaefer, *Synopse zur Hekhalot-Literatur*. Tübingen: J.C.B. Mohr.

SHAFI'I 1961. *Islamic Jurisprudence: Shafi'i's Risala*. Translated by Majid Khadduri. Baltimore: Johns Hopkins University Press.

SMITH 1931. Margaret Smith, *Studies in Early Mysticism in the Near and Middle East*. London: Sheldon Press, 1931; rpt. Amsterdam: Philo Press, 1973.

SMITH 1950. Margaret Smith, *Readings in the Mystics of Islam*. London: Luzac & Company.

SOKOLOW 1981. M. Sokolow, "The Denial of Muslim Sovereignty over Eretz-Israel in Two 10th Century Karaite Bible Commentaries." In J. Hacker (ed.), *Shalem*, 3: 309–318. Jerusalem: Yad Izhak Ben-Zvi Institute.

STANIFORTH 1968. *Early Christian Writings: The Apostolic Fathers*. Translated by Maxwell Staniforth. Harmondsworth: Penguin.

SYMEON NEOTHEOLOGUS 1980. *Symeon the New Theologian: The Discourses*. Translated by C. J. Catanzaro. New York: Paulist Press.

TRIMINGHAM 1971. J. Spencer Trimingham, *The Sufi Orders in Islam*. London: Oxford University Press.

TWERSKY 1980. I. Twersky, *Introduction to the Code of Maimonides (Mishneh Torah)*. New Haven and London: Yale University Press.

VAN BERCHEM 1922. Max Van Berchem, *Corpus inscriptionum arabicarum. Syrie du Sud*, vol. 2: *Jerusalem, "Ville."* Cairo: Institut français d'archéologie orientale.

VERMES 1968. Geza Vermes, *The Dead Sea Scrolls in English*. Harmondsworth: Penguin

WENSINCK 1932. A. J. Wensinck, *The Muslim Creed: Its Genesis and Historical Development*. Cambridge: Cambridge University Press.

WILLIAMS 1971. J. A. Williams, *Themes of Islamic Civilization*. Berkeley: University of California Press.

WRIGHT 1848. T. Wright, *Early Travels in Palestine*. London: H. G. Bohn.

ZENKOVSKY 1963. Serge A. Zenkovsky, *Mediaeval Russia's Epics, Chronicles and Tales*. New York: E. P. Dutton.

ZERNOV 1945. N. Zernov, *The Russians and Their Church*. London and New York: Macmillan.

Index